Guide to Digital Video
PC Magazine®

Guide to Digital Video
PC Magazine®

Jan Ozer

Wiley Publishing, Inc.

PC Magazine® Guide to Digital Video

Published by
Wiley Publishing, Inc.
10475 Crosspoint Boulevard
Indianapolis, IN 46256
www.wiley.com

Copyright © 2004 by Wiley Publishing, Inc., Indianapolis, Indiana

Published simultaneously in Canada

ISBN: 0-7645-4360-1

Manufactured in the United States of America

10 9 8 7 6 5 4 3 2 1

1Q/RS/RR/QT/IN

Credits

EXECUTIVE EDITOR
Chris Webb

DEVELOPMENT EDITOR
Mark Enochs

PRODUCTION EDITOR
Angela Smith

COPY EDITOR
Kim Cofer

EDITORIAL MANAGER
Mary Beth Wakefield

VICE PRESIDENT & EXECUTIVE GROUP PUBLISHER
Richard Swadley

VICE PRESIDENT AND EXECUTIVE PUBLISHER
Bob Ipsen

VICE PRESIDENT AND PUBLISHER
Joseph B. Wikert

EXECUTIVE EDITORIAL DIRECTOR
Mary Bednarek

PROJECT COORDINATOR
April Farling

GRAPHICS AND PRODUCTION SPECIALISTS
Joyce Haughey, LeAndra Hosier,
Stephanie D. Jumper

QUALITY CONTROL TECHNICIAN
Carl William Pierce
Brian H. Walls

PERMISSIONS EDITOR
Laura Moss

MEDIA DEVELOPMENT SPECIALIST
Kit Malone

INDEXING
TECHBOOKS Production Services

PROOFREADING
Christine Sabooni

About the Author

Jan Ozer has worked with digital video since 1990, originally as VP of Marketing for Iterated Systems, a video compression developer, and thereafter as contributing editor to *PC Magazine* and *E-Media*. Since then, Jan has written three books on digital video and has instructed two- and three-day video compression seminars, most recently for the University of Wisconsin.

For the girlies who make life worth videotaping, Barb, Whatley, and Rose.

Acknowledgments

I'm grateful for many industry experts who freely contributed to this effort, including Will Fastie, Ralph LaBarge, Don Labriola, Stephen Nathans, Rich Popko, Ken Santucci, Jeff Sauer, Pat Tracey, and Jim Taylor. Thanks for sharing. I owe you one.

This book would have been impossible without great support for the video hardware, software, and camera community, especially the endless patience of product managers and the like who answered my many frantic queries in a timely and friendly manner. I would especially like to mention ADS Technologies, Microsoft, Muvee, Matrox, Pinnacle Systems, Pioneer Electronics, SCM Microsystems, SmartSound, Sony, Sonic Solutions, Sunland International, Ulead, and Verbatim. Special thanks to the many PR professionals who worked feverishly to get me what I needed when I needed it.

I've written for *PC Magazine* now for ten years and have been fortunate to have worked with some great product testers, particularly Rich Fisco, Jeff Mace, Jonathan Roubini, Nick Stam, and Glenn Menin, and some wonderful editors, including Sarah Anderson, Jamie Bsales, Jenn DeFeo, Ben Gottesman, Matthew Graven, Bill Howard, Vicki Jacobson, Jeremy A. Kaplan, Konstantinos Karagiannis, Carol Levin, Carol Mangis, Laarnie Ragazza, Sharen Terdeman, Lance Ulanoff, and, of course, the man who keeps the lid on, Michael Miller.

Thanks to the Wiley team for pulling this book together in Internet time, with special thanks to my infinitely patient editor Mark Enochs, executive editor Chris Webb, Laura Moss, who convinced all the companies to contribute to the CD-ROM, the eagle-eyed copy editor, Kim Cofer, and production editor Angela Smith.

I owe my little girlies and their mom big time for serving as my most frequent subjects and audience, and for hanging out patiently while daddy worked overtime in his cave. Most of all, I owe them for kindling a small creative flame into a raging urge to create watchable video. Thanks to the grandparents for smiling and laughing at all the right places.

Perhaps most of all, dear reader, I owe my thanks to you. All books, best-seller or laggard, require monumental efforts in time and emotion, in weekends and nights and family vacations spent home alone working. Yet each book, good or bad, by whatever metric you care to apply, is a unique opportunity to create a body of work that imparts some useful, relevant knowledge to a group of readers, to commune, to share and perhaps even delight. Without readers, we wouldn't write. Thanks for the opportunity to come into your life and assist your video creation efforts.

Contents at a Glance

Contents

Introduction

Thanks for buying this book or at least checking it out in a bookstore or online.

Let me tell you a little bit about me, and what I hoped to accomplish with this book.

In my day job, I test products ranging from camcorders to video editors to DVD authoring programs, basically the products described in this book, and I write about them. I've been doing this for about ten years now and have tested hundreds of products during this time.

In my night job, as husband, parent, and self-appointed chronicler of the growth of my two daughters, I wrestle with many of the same issues that you may be facing. What type of equipment should I buy, and what should I bring with me when I shoot? How do I shoot what's most relevant in a way that will look good after editing?

Most of all, how do I shoot and edit videos worth watching. For some videos — namely peripheral events — how do I do this most efficiently, like in 30 minutes or less? For others — the more significant events in our lives — when I choose to invest more time, how do I create a video that will amuse and delight the viewers? How do I produce a video worthy of the event?

As you may have already learned, succeeding at these diverse goals isn't about the technology. Rather, it's about understanding what it takes to create a watchable video, identifying the tools at your disposal, and using them to their best effect. It doesn't take a degree in movie making or even a particularly creative bent, just a focused eye on the target.

This is the core focus of the book. I zero in on what makes a video worth watching, identify the tools at your disposal, and teach you how to use them efficiently and effectively.

How to Read This Book

This book was not intended to be read from start to finish. Part I describes how to purchase the tools of the trade, from camcorder to DVD recorder to computer, so skip these sections if you already own the tools.

Part II is a great section to read before a big event you intend to videotape. You'll learn basics of shot composition and story telling, when and how to use tools like zoom and auto-focus, and optimal shooting techniques for delivering on DVD or via streaming media.

Part III is the production stage. Most readers will find the chapters on capture (Chapter 10) and especially editing (Chapter 11) helpful, with Chapter 16, on project rendering, a practical necessity. From there, you can pick and choose based on the topic of the chapter, with chapters devoted to still-image slideshows, background audio, and automatic movie generation.

Part IV describes DVD production, which is where you assemble your videos, create your menus, and build the DVD. Chapter 19 details how to build a DVD using three of the most popular authoring tools available, while Chapter 18 provides a focused look on how to quickly and efficiently convert videotapes to DVD.

Icon boxes appear in the text throughout the book to indicate important or especially helpful items. Here's a list of the icon boxes and their functions:

NOTE

This icon box provides additional or critical information and technical data on the current topic.

TIP

This icon box provides helpful hints, shortcuts, or things to keep in mind as you create your own video productions.

CROSS-REFERENCE

This handy icon box points you to a place where you can find more information about a particular topic.

ON THE CD-ROM

This icon box refers you to products or files on the CD accompanying this book.

Additional Resource

The author has a listing of current articles and other digital-video-related matters of interest at www.docco.com.

Guide to Digital Video
PC Magazine®

Part I

Buying Your Equipment

Chapter 1

Choosing a DV Camcorder

There are many fine analog camcorders out there that deliver lovely quality video that translates to high-quality streaming video or DVD output.

On the other hand, if you're buying a DV camcorder, it's easy to get confused by the multiple formats that are available today and the rich feature sets of the individual camcorders. To help you sort through all the options, this chapter starts by identifying the digital video formats available today and their strengths and weaknesses.

Then, looking primarily at DV camcorders, I'll identify the basic components and features of a camcorder, describing which are important and which aren't. Then we'll look at the current crop of Sony camcorders to identify the types of features that boost the price from $699 to $1,499 and when it's worth spending the extra dollars.

The chapter concludes with a look at the types of features that higher-end camcorders deliver as well as a short section on how to test-drive a camcorder before buying.

Reviewing the Digital Formats

A digital camcorder is any camcorder that stores video in digital rather than analog format. Life was simple about five years ago, because camcorders using DV as the storage format were the only digital camcorders, so if it was digital, it was DV. Now the field has expanded into a number of siblings and kissing cousins that are related to DV but different. Starting with DV, let's review the most relevant members of the digital camcorder family.

Why I Love the DV Format

DV cameras store video in digital rather than analog format. They first appeared around 1996, promising and delivering exceptional quality and ease of use. I switched over from Hi8 to DV in 1998 and never looked back. If you're working in analog format and considering DV, here are the top seven reasons digital is better than analog:

- Tapes are more robust. Hi8 tapes are very fragile.

- The ability to control the camera from software simplifies all camera and computer interactions.

- Capture is much simpler with DV. There are no brightness or color adjustments and no volume controls; just a simple file transfer.

- Time codes in the DV tape allow software video editors to scan the tape and identify scenes, saving hours of scanning time.

- Captured video is free from the ragged edges pervasive in analog video, which usually appear on the top or bottom of your captured video.

- Video quality is outstanding.

- Grabbing still frames is much simpler, and frames are higher quality.

DV Format

The first and most widely used format for digital camcorders is DV, an interlaced format with a resolution of 720x480 pixels and a combined audio/video data rate of approximately 3.6MB per second. Resolution and interlacing are discussed in more detail later in the chapter.

DV uses JPEG compression on each frame to achieve roughly a 5:1 compression ratio, which is generally unnoticeable on most video. DV uses two kinds of tapes: full-size and Mini-DV tapes, the latter being about the size of a small matchbox. Virtually all camcorders under $5,000 use Mini-DV tapes, and I'll talk exclusively of Mini-DV cameras from here on out.

DV has several professional offshoots, including DVCPRO, DVCAM, and DVCPro-50 that use heavier-duty tapes and slightly different encoding schemes. None of these formats appear in consumer camcorders, so I won't mention them again.

DV camcorders use a serial port transfer mechanism called IEEE 1394 to send video back and forth to computers. This transfer mechanism also includes "machine control," which allows software on the computer to control the camera's playback mechanism, for playback, fast-forwarding, and rewinding operations.

IEEE 1394 was invented by Apple as FireWire, dubbed iLink by Sony and other names by various vendors. As Billy Joel might say, "It's all 1394 to me," and these devices by any name are almost universally interoperable.

Digital8

Digital8 camcorders use the DV format but store video on Hi8 rather than DV tapes. This was important back in the early years of DV when DV tapes cost $25 or more, which was prohibitive for many consumers. Most, but not all, Digital8 camcorders also can play Hi8 tapes, allowing backwards compatibility for those with significant libraries in this format. In addition to sharing the DV format, Digital8 camcorders also use 1394 to communicate with computers.

Overall, Digital8 camcorders are wonderfully inexpensive mechanisms to enter the world of digital video with. On the other hand, one of the key benefits of the DV format is the robustness of the tapes, and in my experience, solely using Hi8 to capture analog video, are fragile as flowers. Now that prices of entry-level DV camcorders and DV tapes have dropped so significantly, I would probably spend the extra money and go DV.

MicroMV

MicroMV camcorders encode their video in MPEG-2 format, which is more highly compressed than DV, allowing tapes and camcorders to be smaller. The only characteristic they share with DV is the transport mechanism to the computer, FireWire. Sony does enough things differently with MicroMV, however, that few video editors support the format, and those that do, like Pinnacle Studio, had significant startup issues. This, and the inherently lower quality of MPEG-2, makes DV a better choice for those who want to edit digitally on their computers and produce top-quality video.

What You Need to Know about MPEG-2

MPEG-2 is the format used in MicroMV and DVD camcorders as well as in DVD videos. Briefly, MPEG-2 is a compression technology, or codec, that typically outputs between 1MB per second (DVD videos) and 1.375MB per second (MicroMV). It's a scalable format that also can encode at much higher or lower rates.

DV is also a codec and uses intra-frame-only techniques, which means it encodes each frame without reference to other frames. In contrast, MPEG-2 uses intra-frame and inter-frame compression, which eliminates redundancy between frames. This inter-frame compression allows MPEG-2 to produce very good quality at much lower rates than DV, but it also complicates editing on the computer, since the computer is constantly having to re-create frames encoded with inter-frame compression.

MPEG-2 quality depends upon the encoding tool used. Hollywood producers use expensive, high-end equipment that can take hours or days to produce a movie. MicroMV and DVD camcorders use inexpensive chips that must store the video in real time. For this reason, don't expect MPEG-2-based camcorders to output the same quality as Hollywood DVDs.

In my view, MPEG-2 is a great *delivery* codec — or a compression technology optimized for delivering content. In contrast, DV is a great *capture and editing* codec, delivering much higher quality and better responsiveness during editing.

Certainly MicroMV and DVD camcorders are great for simple shooting and playback, but if editing quality is your major goal, stick to DV.

DVD Camcorders

DVD camcorders store captured video in MPEG-2 format on either DVD-RAM or DVD-R disks. The former is ideal for rewriting and instantly accessing individual scenes without the usual capture process; DVD-R disks are targeted for immediate playback of the videos on a DVD player. The MPEG-2 compression used in these cameras is scalable and peaks at 1.125MB per second for DVD-RAM and 750K per second for DVD-R.

These camcorders are fairly new and share many of the same issues as MicroMV, including reduced quality and little compatibility with video-editing programs. For these reasons, unless you have a compelling need to capture directly to DVD, you're probably better off with a DV-based camcorder.

Table 1-1 summarizes the similarities and differences between the four formats discussed so far.

Table 1-1   Characteristics of DV, Digital8, MicroMV, and DVD Camcorders

	DV	*Digital8*	*MicroMV*	*DVD Camcorder*
Storage format	DV	DV	MPEG-2	MPEG-2
Recording medium	DV tape	Hi8 tape	MicroMV tape	DVD-RAM/DVD-R disk
Outputs	Analog (composite, S-Video and stereo audio)	Analog (composite, S-Video and stereo audio)	Analog (composite, S-Video and stereo audio)	Analog (composite, S-Video and stereo audio)
Transfer to computer via: method	1394	1394	1394	USB or disk

Camcorder Basics

Now that we've reviewed the camcorder formats, let's focus our attention on the camcorders themselves, starting with the major components and then working our way down to individual features.

Charge Coupled Devices

Charge Coupled Devices (CCDs) are the electronic chips that sense the image coming from the lens. When comparing camcorders, we care primarily about the number of CCDs employed by the camcorder, their physical size, and the number of pixels each chip can resolve.

THE NUMBER OF CCDS

Briefly, CCDs use light-sensitive regions that create electrical charges based upon the intensity of the light hitting the CCD, distinguishing between bright and dark regions by measuring the electrical charge at each pixel. To discern colors, camcorders with three CCDs split the incoming light with a prism, sending red, green, and blue streams to the respective CCDs and then merging the three signals electronically.

In contrast, single-CCD camcorders use an array of colored filters over the CCD to separate the colors, which is less effective. For this reason, three-CCD camcorders almost always produce video with superior clarity and color accuracy.

As you might expect, most consumer camcorders use one CCD while all prosumer and professional camcorders use three CCDs. In the past, most three-CCD camcorders started at around $2,000, but Panasonic announced a three-CCD camcorder for under $1,000 in mid-2003, and I'm sure other vendors will follow suit.

Probably the most significant determinant of quality and price between camcorders is the number of CCDs used in the camera. Whenever comparing camcorders, be sure to identify this first.

CCD SIZE

CCDs typically range in size between ⅙ and ½ inch. Though some experts claim that CCD size doesn't directly relate to quality, higher-end camcorders typically use larger chips than consumer models.

Still, this is a fairly esoteric metric; in several tests at *PC Magazine,* camcorders with smaller CCDs outperformed those with larger. For this reason, I wouldn't pick one camcorder over another because it has larger CCDs.

CCD RESOLUTION

On the other hand, CCD resolution, or the number of pixels captured by the CCD, is a very key metric, especially if you plan to use the camcorder for capturing still images as well as video. Interestingly, if the camcorders' primary focus is DV video, which has a resolution of 720x480 pixels, the ability to capture about 340,000 pixels is sufficient, and more is a waste. That's why CCDs for prosumer camcorders, like Sony's DCR-VX2000, have fewer pixels than many consumer camcorders.

In contrast, more pixels are better on camcorders designed to capture high-quality stills, and most vendors offer models with 1.5-or 2-megapixel CCDs for still-image capture. When comparing camcorders, be sure to identify both the CCD resolution and maximum picture resolution, typically represented as 640x480, 1600x1200, or similar numbers.

If the number of pixels in the largest image exceeds the number of pixels in the CCD, the camcorder is zooming the image digitally, which delivers less quality than a pixel-for-pixel image capture. For example, the JVC DV3000U camcorder has a 1.33-megapixel CCD with 1,330,000 pixels yet outputs images as large as 1600x1200, which really requires 1.92 megapixels, derived by multiplying 1,600 times 1,200.

In contrast, the Sony DCR-TRV80 shares the same maximum image size of 1600x1200 but creates the picture with a true 2.1-megapixel CCD. All other things being equal, the larger CCD will deliver a higher-quality image.

In short, as with still image digital cameras, if the picture output in pixels is larger than the actual pixels on the CCD, the camera is zooming the image digitally, which you could do in your image editor. Obviously, however, this doesn't add any quality. Accordingly, when assessing a DV camera's still-image capabilities, compare pixels on the CCD, not output size, which can be arbitrary.

SCAN CAPABILITIES (INTERLACED VERSUS PROGRESSIVE)

Scan capabilities refers to the technique used to store the incoming frames. There are two methods, interlaced and progressive.

Televisions in the United States operate under the NTSC (National Television Standards Committee) standard. NTSC video consists of 29.97 frames per second, with each frame made up of two fields, essentially two half frames, the first containing odd lines (1, 3, 5, 7) and the second even lines (2, 4, 6, 8). When shooting NTSC video, the camcorder actually shoots about 60 times a second. The first shot becomes field one and contains the odd lines in the first frame. The second shot becomes field two and contains the even lines in the first frame. Because the two fields are combined to make a frame, this video is considered interlaced.

Interlaced video works well at 60 fields per second but causes problems when shooting for still-image capture, especially if there's high motion in the video. That's because a surprising amount of motion can occur during the $\frac{1}{60}$ of a second between the two fields, resulting in two pictures of slightly different things. This is shown on the left in Figure 1-1, where the two fields don't combine into a matched frame.

In contrast, progressive scan CCDs store images from top to bottom (lines 1, 2, 3, 4, and so on), just like digital still-image cameras. When shooting in progressive scan mode, DV camcorders shoot only 30 times a second, capturing a complete frame from top to bottom, then dividing each frame into the two fields required for NTSC compatibility, one with even lines and one with odd lines. Similarly, when capturing still images only, the progressive scan camcorder shoots only once, just like a digital still-image camera. As you can see on the right in Figure 1-1, a progressive image of the same motion is very sharp, because the two fields precisely match.

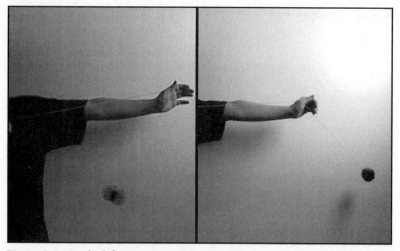

Figure 1-1: On the left is an image shot in interlaced mode, showing the dual images from the two fields that comprise the frame. On the right is an image from a progressive scan camcorder, which shows no such artifacts, or visual anomalies within the frame.

In practice, the image on the left in Figure 1-1 is an extreme example, because camcorders use de-interlacing techniques to minimize the artifacts, and we disabled this for our tests. Still, a camcorder shooting a still image in interlaced mode must combine two disparate fields to create a single frame, generally resulting in a slightly blurry image like that shown in Figure 1-2. Clearly, if you're shooting

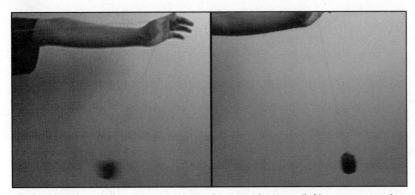

Figure 1-2: Most camcorders use de-interlacing techniques (left) to minimize the artifacts, which produces fuzzy images. As the image on the right shows, you get a much clearer image with progressive scan capture.

for still-image capture, the progressive scan technique provides better quality than interlaced, even after de-interlacing.

Interestingly, progressive scan capabilities first appeared to produce video that could easily be converted to film, which consists of 24 discrete frames per second. That's why newer DV camcorders like Panasonic's DVX100 can capture 24 frames per second in progressive scan mode. Progressive scan capture is also useful, but not essential, when converting to frame-based digital formats like MPEG-1 or streaming formats like Real, QuickTime, or Windows Media Technologies.

As I'll discuss in more detail below, if you already have a high-resolution still-image camera and just want to capture video for video's sake, progressive scan probably isn't a feature worth paying extra for. If you're looking for a high-resolution CCD to capture high-quality still images and video, you should verify that the camcorder captures in progressive scan mode, but virtually all camcorders with high-resolution CCDs do.

If you're looking to produce a movie that ultimately will be displayed on film, as in a theater, progressive scan is essential. Be sure to identify the number of progressive frames per second (fps) the camcorder outputs, however, because some, like the VX2000, produce only 15 fps, which is inadequate for film. Most DV camcorders produce 30 fps, which can be converted to 24 fps for film, though native 24 fps, or the ability to capture directly at 24 fps, is preferable. (Check out Table 1-2 for a comparison of CCD types.)

Table 1-2   Comparing CCDs

	Consumer	*Mid-Range*	*Prosumer*
Number of CCDs	1	1	3
Size	⅙ inch	⅓ inch	⅓ inch
Pixel resolution	340,000	1–2 MP	340,000
Scan capabilities	Interlaced	Interlaced and progressive	Interlaced and progressive

Analyzing Lens Capabilities

Most major camcorder vendors source their lenses from other vendors, with Sony buying from legendary vendor, Carl Zeiss, for many cameras, while Panasonic and Canon employ DICOMAR lenses from equally legendary vendor, Leica. Both brands have their advocates, some quite vocal, and they're both excellent companies, which complicates a brand-based buying decision.

Instead, when I compare camcorders, I focus on comparative performance, particularly how they perform in low-light conditions. Figures 1-3 and 1-4 show why. Though low-light performance is a function of CCDs and camcorder electronics as well as lenses, I'll discuss it here.

Briefly, I took these videos using Sony's three-CCD DCR-VX2000 on the left and a one-CCD consumer camcorder on the right. (I won't name the camcorder because it's simply not a fair comparison; no consumer camcorder can compete with the VX2000.) I placed both camcorders in fully automatic mode and then shot the videos, shutting lights and shades during the shoot to darken the scene.

On the CD-ROM

An MPEG-1 file containing side-by-side shots of the videos is on the CD-ROM, titled Figure 1-3.MPG.

In Figure 1-3, the scene is generally well lit, and the consumer camcorder holds its own. If you were seeing the image in color, you would probably notice that Rosie's sweater (she's on the left) isn't quite the right color and that the contrast and detail overall isn't quite as good. Still, you probably wouldn't pay $1,500 extra for the camcorder on the left based upon this image.

VX2000   One-CCD

Figure 1-3: The one-CCD camcorder on the right does fairly well when lighting conditions are good.

However, in Figure 1-4, when lighting conditions are poor, the VX2000 still produces a usable image while the one-CCD camcorder is pretty much worthless. Now the moral of the story isn't that you need to buy a three-CCD camcorder to produce good video in low light. Rather, if you likely will shoot in low-light conditions (and believe me, you will), there are a number of features to look for to improve your chances of shooting good quality.

VX2000   One-CCD

Figure 1-4: Under low-light conditions, however, the consumer one-CCD camcorder falls apart completely.

ASSESSING LOW-LIGHT CAPABILITIES — LUX

The best measure of a camcorder's low-light capabilities is its lux rating. Briefly, one lux is the light of one candle one yard away from the subject. The VX2000, which performed so well in Figure 1-4, has a lux rating of 2, which translates to good quality even under low-light conditions. The other camcorder has a lux rating of 7, which is pretty standard among consumer camcorders. Essentially, less is more when it comes to lux, because it indicates that the camera can capture a usable image in less than perfect lighting conditions.

Note that some vendors don't publish their lux rating, or they publish them as zero using "NightShot" and similar features that claim to capture images in zero light. These work, but the images are usually white or faintly green, almost other worldly. Alternatively, camcorders slow the shutter speed (defined below) so severely that any motion creates severe blurriness.

Figure 1-5 compares the VX2000 with the other camcorder using its NightShot equivalent, while Figure 1-6 shows the VX2000 and the other camcorder's normal shooting mode. Figure 1-5.mpg on the CD-ROM is the video from which these frames were captured and provides much better detail than the black and white picture on the page.

Obviously, with the low-end camcorder, NightShot mode is better than normal mode, but isn't a panacea. The best solution is a camcorder with a great low lux rating, so be sure to ascertain the camcorder's lux rating without NightShot or similar mode before making your purchase decision.

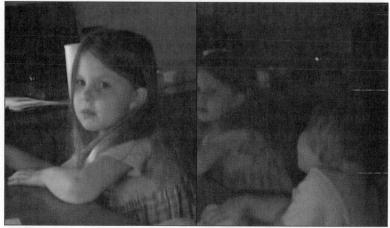

VX2000   One-CCD

Figure 1-5: The low-lux VX2000 (on the left) does a great job capturing the image, while NightShot (on the right) has the greenish tinge of infrared light.

VX2000   One-CCD

Figure 1-6: Without NightShot mode, however, the image falls apart completely with a one-CCD camcorder.

LINES OF RESOLUTION

The DV format is capable of more than 550 lines of resolution, compared to 220 or so for VHS and 400 for S-Video. This doesn't relate to the number of pixels in the frame, of course, which is always 480 for all DV camcorders, but the number of distinct lines the camcorder can resolve.

To test this, we shoot an image of a test chart at the specified range, capture the image to disk, and then use markings in the test chart to assess the detail preserved by the lens. Figure 1-7 is an example

Best NightShot

Speaking of NightShot, here's my favorite DV camcorder story.

When Sony introduced the DCR-TRV9 camcorder in 1998, it debuted infrared-only NightShot, which some enterprising videographers soon discovered could see through sheer synthetic fabrics like bathing suits in direct sunlight and certain other conditions.

Rumors started circulating, and mention of this appeared in several prominent news magazines, belying that old adage that "any PR is good PR." The camcorder immediately became a best seller until Sony pulled it off the market.

Sony continued the NightShot feature on future versions, but according to a company official, they changed the camcorder mechanics "to eliminate this unintended function."

of a resolution test chart. This is a fairly common test performed during formal product reviews and is occasionally included on camcorder specification sheets, especially for higher-end camcorders.

The VX2000 generally achieves around 530 lines in tests, with some consumer camcorders producing as low as 350. The general rule here is that more lines of resolution are better.

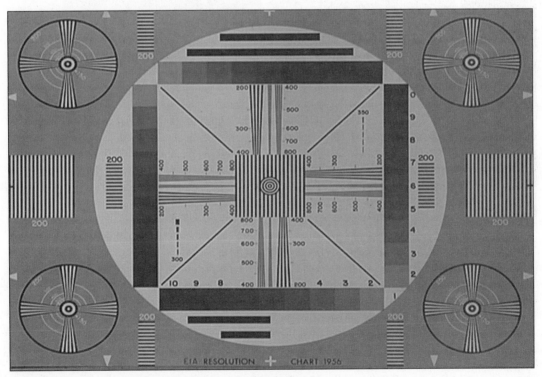

Figure 1-7: A test chart used to determine camcorder resolution.

DIGITAL VERSUS OPTICAL ZOOM

A camcorder's zoom is a measure of its ability to magnify an image. At 1X, the camcorder sees approximately what the human eye sees from the same distance. At 10X, the camcorder can zoom the image ten times larger than normal.

There are two different techniques used to achieve zoom: optical and digital. Optical zoom is produced by the optics in the lens and is generally distortion-free. Digital zoom is magnification produced by camcorder electronics, much like you can zoom a still image in an image-editing program. Though filtering and interpolation techniques can reduce pixilation to some degree, at high-magnification levels, distortion is inevitable.

Figure 1-8 shows an image zoomed at 1X, 20X, and 120X. As you can see on the right, the image is visibly distorted with pixilation showing around the wheel rim. However, the 20X image is reasonably clear, and some camcorders, like Canon's GL2, produce pretty clear video up to 40X zoom.

Figure 1-8: A wheel is a wheel is a wheel at 1X (upper left), 20X (lower left), and 120X (on the right). Note the lack of clarity in the highly zoomed image.

Nonetheless, some video purists recommend disabling the digital zoom, which generally is the course I follow. However this isn't always possible. In the past, all the camcorders I owned were all or nothing; either digital zoom was enabled or disabled—there was no in between. While this prevents you from creating zoom distortion unnoticeable on a 2.5-inch LCD screen while shooting, it also prevents you from accessing lower levels of distortion-free zooming.

I've seen two great compromises to look for when buying. First, several newer camcorders eschew the all-or-nothing approach and let you choose between no digital zoom, the maximum zoom, and some in-between figure ranging from 20X to 40X, which should be reasonably distortion-free. The other approach is a visual indicator in the viewfinder that reveals the magnification level and is especially useful when you've left optical and moved into digital zoom territory.

Needless to say, however, you should assume that any zoom capabilities over 40X to 50X are useless and ignore them when comparing camcorders.

FOCAL LENGTH

Focal length is a measure of zoom ratio that's widely used in the 35mm world. The easy answer here is to ignore focal length in favor of zoom ratio, but let's press on, if only for 35mm analog camcorder jockeys making the conversion to DV.

As with zoom, the focal length is a measure of lens power or magnification. In the 35mm camcorder world, a focal length of 50mm is the standard. Shorter focal lengths, like 24 to 35, are considered wide-angle lenses, while larger numbers are zoom lenses that increase magnification levels proportionately. For example, a lens with a 100mm focal length delivers an image that is twice the normal size, while a 300mm focal length delivers 6X magnification.

If you're coming over from the analog camcorder world, recognize that because digital camcorders and DV camcorders use much smaller CCDs than film cameras, the focal lengths are much smaller, often in the 4 to 40 range. For example, where a typical consumer DV camcorder has a CCD that's ¼ inch in size, the Canon EOS-1D, or the equivalent of the Canon EOS film camera, has a CCD over 1 inch in size.

You can translate the focal length of DV camcorders to 35mm camcorders by multiplying the value by the "focal length multiplier," but this value changes for each camcorder depending upon the size of the CCD. To help clear the confusion, some vendors list what's called a "35mm conversion" to help those used to 35mm cameras understand the camcorder's capabilities. For example, the true focal length for Sony's VX2000 is 6.0mm to 72.0mm, while the 35mm conversion is 43.2 to 518.4.

Cross-Reference

See www.lonestardigital.com/multipler.htm for an excellent explanation of the math underlying the focal length multiplier and its relation to the size of a CCD.

Interestingly, the difference in CCD size is why DV camcorders can deliver stunning optical zoom ratios with relatively small lenses. That is, the larger the CCD, the larger the lens has to be to deliver data to the CCD.

Since DV camcorders only need to resolve 340,000 pixels to create video, a small CCD can do the trick, which allows a lens the size of a lipstick container to deliver 10X zoom. In contrast, delivering the same magnification level to a data-hungry 35mm camcorder requires a lens costing thousands of dollars that's the size of a 64-ounce bottle of soda.

Now that we've analyzed the camcorder lens, let's move on to other features.

ELECTRONIC VERSUS OPTICAL IMAGE STABILIZATION

Most DV camcorders offer image stabilization, a technique that attempts to reduce or eliminate minor shakes that occur during shooting. High-end camcorders typically use optical image stabilization, which actually moves the lens system in the camcorder to compensate for the motion. This is generally considered superior to electronic image stabilization, though many professionals simply disable all image stabilization and shoot from a tripod.

In contrast, electronic image stabilization (EIS) shifts the captured image around after it's through the lens and CCD system and digitized by the camcorder. Since it involves chips rather than mechanical components, EIS is cheaper than optical.

When originally introduced, EIS worked by zooming the video frame slightly to provide margins for shifting the captured image around, which degraded quality to some degree. However, most consumer camcorders now use larger-resolution CCDs to capture enough margin to shift the image without zooming. For this reason, though optical image stabilization is still preferred, the qualitative difference between the two has narrowed significantly.

Viewfinder and LCD Panel

Most DV camcorders offer two mechanisms for viewing while shooting and displaying your video post-shoot: a viewfinder and an LCD panel. When comparing camcorders, be sure to note the following characteristics of both.

For viewfinders, look for the following:

- **Color or black and white.** Most consumers prefer color, while many professionals prefer black and white because it focuses their attention on exposure, which they can control more effectively than color.

- **Number of pixels.** More is better, because it translates to a crisper image, with inexpensive camcorders usually offering around 115,000 pixels, while higher-end models provide at least 180,000 pixels.

- **Fixed or movable.** Many small camcorders have an unmovable viewfinder, which complicates shooting from a tripod or other fixed positions. Most other camcorders allow you to shift the viewfinder up and down for more flexibility.

- **Focus diopter.** Virtually all camcorders have a mechanical wheel diopter for focusing the viewfinder, which is absolutely critical, especially for those who wear glasses.

- **Rubber eyepiece.** The primary reason most people use the viewfinder (rather than the more convenient LCD) is because direct sunlight fades the image of most LCD displays. Better camcorders have a rounded eyepiece that shades the eyes from sunlight.

For LCDs, look for the following:

- **LCD size.** This is expressed in inches, which are measured diagonally. Larger is better, but often LCD size drops proportionately with the size of the camcorder. On standard camcorder-sized models, look for 2.5 inches or larger.

- **Number of pixels.** As with the viewfinder, the number of pixels translates directly to image crispness, which is especially important for larger LCD sizes. For example, Sony's

DCR-TRV80 has a 3.5-inch LCD panel with 184,000 pixels, while the JVC GR-DVL820 has a 3.5-inch LCD panel with only 110,000 pixels. The image on the Sony LCD is noticeably crisper, providing better feedback during shooting and better quality during playback.

- **Brightness controls.** Not all low-end camcorders have brightness controls, which come in handy when shooting outdoors.

- **Range of motion.** Most LCD panels can rotate 180 degrees for use in "vanity" mode when you're shooting yourself. Be sure that the LCD can rotate to this degree and that the image will shift 180 degrees so that you're not upside down when shooting.

Camcorder Input/Output

Figure 1-9 shows the compact input/output panel similar to that found on the Sony DCR-TRV80. We'll take a closer look at most of these connectors in Chapter 11, when we capture video. In this chapter, we'll simply discuss what these connections do and what you should look for when buying a camcorder.

Most connections are fairly standard and don't help you differentiate between camcorders. I'll start by describing those that do.

KEY DIFFERENTIATING INPUT/OUTPUT

Pay attention to the availability of these ports and their capabilities when making a buying decision:

- **Microphone port (plug-in power).** If you plan on doing any serious shooting at all, a microphone port is essential, and it's not standard on lower-end models.

- **Note also that there are two types of microphone ports.** Those with plug-in power, like that shown in Figure 1-9, work with microphones without separate power, allowing you to use very inexpensive computer microphones. Most low-end consumer camcorders do *not* supply plug-in power, which means you'll have to purchase a more expensive powered microphone. Virtually all microphone connectors are simple stereo microphones; you'll have to go into the $3,000-plus range to see professional XLR connectors.

- **USB port.** Universal Serial Bus ports serve multiple purposes including transferring still images from camcorder to computer, and USB streaming, where the camcorder can replace a Web cam for Internet videoconferencing. There are other ways to get still images to your computer, like transferring the physical storage medium or using Bluetooth (discussed later in this chapter), but USB is often the most convenient. Note that USB is never used to transfer DV video to your computer, though some DVD camcorders use USB for this purpose, as do camcorders that support MPEG-1 encoding.

STANDARD I/O PORTS

These items are included in or with most DV camcorders, so they probably won't help you differentiate between two camcorders that you're considering.

- **FireWire (IEEE1394).** This DV port (shown in Figure 1-9) is used to connect the camcorder to your computer or another FireWire device. Virtually all consumer DV camcorders come with FireWire connectors.

- **S-Video port.** Most consumer DV camcorders also support S-Video output, an analog format that is higher quality than composite output. This is true even with the tiniest of tiny MicroMV camcorders, though sometimes the S-Video port is placed on a separate connecting chassis. You'll use the S-Video port to copy DV video to an S-VHS camcorder or player, to view it on a television set, and for camcorders that support analog input (discussed in the next section), to input analog video into the DV camcorder.

- **Stereo audio/composite video port.** Virtually all DV camcorders have a single port for outputting composite video, the lowest-quality analog output, and stereo audio, using a three-headed, color-coded cable with yellow (composite video) and red-and-white stereo audio connectors.

- **Headphone port.** Most camcorders have a port that lets you plug in headphones for previewing the audio while shooting and listening in while playing. Note that few consumer camcorders actually allow you to adjust incoming volume, so your only option to get better sound may be to move closer to or farther away from the subject.

- **LANC.** This is a camcorder control protocol used before the advent of FireWire. Like your appendix, it's vestigial, since FireWire is both more commonly supported on the computer and more accurate than LANC.

Analog Input

Unless your DV camcorder is your first camcorder, you likely have substantial quantities of analog tapes. Analog input is a feature that makes it easy to convert these tapes to DV format; you simply connect the audio video cables from your analog camcorder or VCR to your DV camcorder, and use menu controls in the DV camcorder so the camcorder looks for input through its ports rather than the lens.

During the conversion, the DV camcorder digitizes and compresses the analog footage to DV format, just like it does with input through the lens. Once copied over, you treat the analog footage exactly like DV footage originally shot by the camcorder.

Since DV capture systems are so inexpensive, this is a great way to edit analog videos on your DV system. For example, I've used analog input many times to copy yoga and Tai Kwon Do tapes from VHS to DV to edit and burn them to DVD.

Cross-Reference

On the other hand, using the analog input on a camcorder to convert analog footage to digital is not your only alternative. Chapter 11 discusses devices that can capture your analog footage in DV and MPEG-2 formats, saving the time and tape cost associated with this analog input feature.

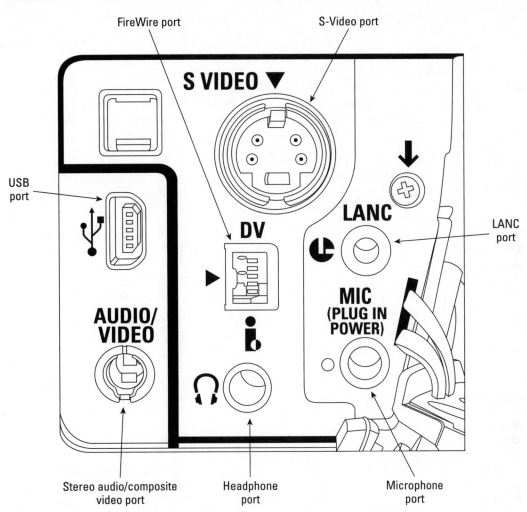

FireWire port   S-Video port

USB port

LANC

LANC port

S VIDEO ▼

DV

AUDIO/ VIDEO

MIC (PLUG IN POWER)

Stereo audio/composite video port

Headphone port

Microphone port

Figure 1-9: The connections panel from a camera similar to the Sony DCR-TRV80.

Microphone

All DV camcorders incorporate stereo microphones, almost universally omnidirectional microphones that capture sound equally from all directions. You'll get the best audio quality with microphones attached to the camcorder's handle, like the camera shown in the center of Figure 1-10 (very similar to Sony's VX2000). Next best are microphones on the front of the camcorder body, like on the camera on the right (similar to my ancient but still-working TRV9), while microphones mounted on top of the camcorder typically produce the worst results, primarily because they pick up noise from the camcorder user, which both other locations minimize. This is where Sony placed the microphone on the PC7 camcorder (represented by the camera on the left).

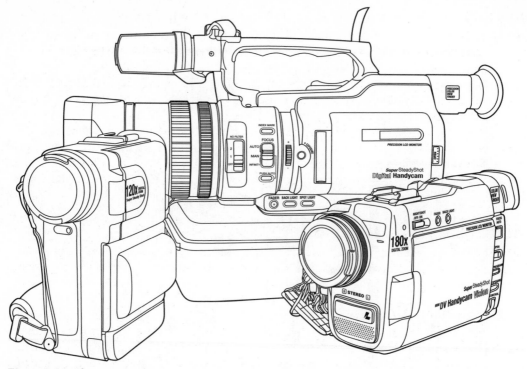

Figure 1-10: These camcorders represent Sony DV camcorders I have known and loved. Note microphone location: on the boom for the center camcorder, which delivers the best audio quality; on the front for the one on the right, which is next best; and on top for the one on the left, which is generally noisier than the other two.

These microphone locations generally represent the typical microphone placement for each camcorder body type. That is, larger camcorders with handles place the microphone on the handle, while traditional camcorder bodies place them on the front. Smaller camcorders almost always have the microphone on top, accounting for generally lagging performance in audio quality.

When comparing camcorders, you might also consider the cost of a unidirectional, shotgun microphone to help improve audio quality, especially the capture of speech in a noisy environment. For example, Sony offers an optional microphone for its consumer camcorders for $99; the lowest-cost Canon option in $199.

Accessory Shoe

Accessory shoes are slots that sit atop most DV camcorders. There are two types: intelligent and non-intelligent shoes. An "intelligent" accessory shoe provides power and operational commands to a range of supported accessories like microphones and lights, and a non-intelligent accessory shoe simply functions as a bracket to attach accessories to that have separate power and manual controls.

Intelligent shoes obviously give you greater flexibility; if you plan on purchasing a microphone and/or additional lighting in the future, this is definitely the way to go.

Batteries

Most camcorders now ship with Lithium Ion batteries, which offer good performance and high-energy density, which translates to lots of power in a small package. If the battery isn't Lithium Ion, it's a significant red flag.

When comparing camcorders, be sure to identify the life and recharging time of the battery actually *included* with the camcorder. Some vendors cite long operation times, but you have to buy an optional battery pack to actually achieve it.

Battery charging is also an issue. While some vendors provide a separate charger, allowing you to charge a battery while you're off shooting, others don't, forcing you to charge the battery in the camcorder or purchase a separate charger. Since chargers can cost well over $100, you should factor this into your price comparisons—unless your use will be so infrequent that this doesn't matter that much.

Automatic and Manual Settings

A number of factors, including exposure or gain control, aperture, shutter speed, white balance, and focus, impact the ultimate quality of your video. Let's define each element in turn and then discuss how much control over these variables different camcorders provide.

EXPOSURE AND GAIN CONTROL

Whether analog or digital, still or video, taking a picture involves admitting light through a lens to expose the light-sensitive film or CCD. Two factors control the amount of light that gets through: the aperture, which is the size of the lens opening, and the shutter speed, which is the length of time the shutter stays open. All DV camcorders have an auto-exposure function that measures the amount of available light and adjusts aperture and shutter speed accordingly.

Sometimes, however, even the widest aperture and slowest shutter speed doesn't let in enough light. In this instance, DV camcorders cheat, so to speak, and digitally boost the "gain" in the picture, much like you can boost the brightness of a picture in an image editor. This is called automatic gain control, and it's a feature in virtually all DV camcorders.

Many camcorders also enable manual gain adjustment, usually calling it exposure adjustment. This gives you creative control over lighting and is definitely a desirable feature.

APERTURE

Some high-end camcorders also let you adjust aperture, providing control over depth of field (the portions of your image that are in focus). This is shown in Figure 1-11.

Using the VX2000's aperture priority mode, I set the aperture to an F-Stop of 2 on the left, which is wide open. While the subject's hair is clearly focused, the picture in the background is quite blurry. This technique is used for artistic effect but also for producing streaming media, because an image with a blurry background has less detail, making it easier to compress.

On the right in Figure 1-11, the F-Stop is set to 11, a much smaller opening that brings the background picture into focus. This would be useful in shots where all detail, foreground and background, need to be in focus.

Few consumer-level camcorders enable manual control over the aperture, so you'll likely have to upgrade to a prosumer camcorder to take advantage of this function.

Figure 1-11: Focusing on the model on the right, the left image was taken with the aperture wide open (F.2), blurring the background considerably. On the right, the aperture is relatively closed (F.11), bringing much more of the picture into focus.

SHUTTER SPEED

If you're into sports and other fast-action photography, control over shutter speed can be very useful. For example, if you're shooting a sporting event, you'd want to be able to select a fast shutter speed, say ¼₀₀₀ of a second. Though all camcorders support multiple shutter speeds, they are implemented automatically or in Program AE modes (see the next section); few allow you to select shutter speed directly.

PROGRAMMED AE MODES

In addition to fully automatic and fully manual modes, some camcorders offer a series of "Program AE" (Auto-Exposure) settings for common shooting scenarios like sports, sunlight, moonlight, spotlight, dusk, and others. When you select the program, the camcorder uses the gain, shutter, and aperture settings that deliver the best results under those conditions.

For example, in sports mode, the camcorder would force a fast shutter speed to avoid blurriness during high motion, adjusting the aperture and perhaps the gain to ensure sufficient light hits the CCDs. Most camcorders also have controls on the camcorder body to adjust for backlighting or spotlight effects, which are also helpful.

Advanced users will benefit from shutter and aperture priority modes that allow you to select values for either of these options to achieve the desired effect, with the camcorder automatically selecting all other values. This is how we shot the videos shown in Figure 1-11.

WHITE BALANCE

White balance is something you pay little attention to until you shoot for an entire day and then notice that your video is tinged with blue or yellow and pretty much unusable. Then you smack yourself on the forehead, find the camcorder manual, and learn how to white balance.

Simply speaking, white balance is the process of telling your camcorder what is white in the scene, which allows the camcorder to adjust the other colors accordingly. While we think white is white, it looks slightly different in the sun, in the shade, and under different types of lights.

It Pays to Shop Around

You probably know this already, but it pays to shop around when buying a camcorder and accessories. I'm not sure why there is such a disparity, but there it is. Here are a couple of examples:

DV cable (camera to computer):
$8 at www.adaptec.com
$75 at www.sony.com

Canon GL2 camcorder:
$2,800 at www.ritzcamcorder.com
$1,693 at www.newworldvideodirect.com
$1,025 (lowest price for new product, but not yet sold) at www.ebay.com

All DV camcorders offer automatic white balancing, which generally works by assuming that the lightest object in the scene is white. This can be a problem if the object is actually light yellow or pink.

While most consumer camcorders allow you to adjust for common lighting situations, like fluorescent or incandescent light, few allow you to manually white balance. To address this, it's generally good practice to start each shoot by zooming into a white object until it fills the screen, and then shooting for about ten seconds. Do this again each time you change lighting conditions dramatically, such as moving from sunlight to shade and especially from indoors to outdoors or vice versa.

FOCUS

Focus, of course, is the process of adjusting lens position to achieve the sharpest possible image. All consumer-level camcorders offer auto-focus — where the camcorder does this work for you — and manual focus as well.

Note, however, that camcorders differ in how they implement manual focus. The best and most common approach, at least for my taste, is a focus ring on the end of the camcorder, just like 35mm camcorders. Note however, that many low-end camcorders use completely digital controls on the camera body for manual focus, which isn't quite as intuitive.

Features to Disregard

Here are some features that sound great and are often trumpeted by the manufacturers. However, they aren't truly useful if you plan on editing on a computer and should be ignored when buying a DV camcorder.

- **Digital effects.** Some camcorders can fade in and fade out for you, or even convert the video to black–and white or sepia. Since you're reading this book, I'll assume you want to edit on your computer, and if so, any video editor — even free ones like Microsoft's Movie Maker 2 — can perform a much greater range of special effects than your camcorder. Plus, if you change your mind, you're not stuck with the results, like you are with your camcorder.

- **Titling capabilities.** Same deal here. You'll get better results with any video editor on the computer.

■ **Assemble editing.** Several consumer-level camcorders offer assemble editing, which lets you identify discrete segments in the video and then write them in sequence to another analog deck. These simple cut-and-paste functions work well, but again, they don't offer the flexibility or ease of use available on your computer.

■ **16:9 mode.** As you may know, most Hollywood films are shot with a wider aspect ratio than NTSC video, usually 16:9 rather than NTSC's 4:3. Widescreen Hi-Definition Television (HDTV) sets can display movies and specially prepared television shows in their widescreen glory, and 16:9 mode in a DV camcorder harkens up images of HDTV.

Unfortunately, this isn't the case. DV is a fixed format of 720x480 pixels, and when shooting in 16:9 mode, the camcorder simply lops off the top and bottom of the screen, creating an effective resolution of 720x405. This is shown in Figure 1-12. On the left is chez Ozer, here in Galax, Virginia, shot in normal mode, while on the right is 16:9. Note that the video is no wider on the right; it's simply stubbier, with large strips shorn off the top and bottom. Though it may be tough to see in the screenshot, the quality of the 16:9 shot is also degraded.

With all this as background, let's look at some features and factors to consider when buying a one-CCD camcorder.

Figure 1-12: 16:9 video on a DV camcorder (on the right) isn't really widescreen as much as stubby screen. As you can see by comparing it to the full resolution DV on the left, the camcorder simply cuts strips from the top and bottom of the video.

Buying an Inexpensive Camcorder

Most readers will purchase a one-CCD DV camera priced between $500 and $1,500 street, so I'll focus my discussion on this segment, ignoring MicroMV, Digital8, and DVD camcorders. To illustrate the types of features that drive camcorder prices from bargain basement to pricey, I'll use the 2003 Sony line of camcorders, shown in Table 1-3. Similar features differentiate camcorders in the Canon, JVC, and Panasonic lines, which are not quite as extensive. Prices are all list; I'm sure you can do much better at any number of online or discount retailers.

When buying a consumer camcorder, your first key decision relates to the form factor, or size and shape of the camera. Simply stated, tiny camcorders, whether DV or MicroMV, are easier to pack, fun to use, and sexy, but they are more expensive and typically trail other camcorders in both audio and video quality. For example, Sony's DCRPC120 is a very small mini-DV camcorder that costs $1,799, only $200 less than the TRV950, a standard-sized, three-CCD camcorder.

I haven't tested either camcorder, but experience tells me that the TRV950 will produce vastly superior audio and video. For example, in *PC Magazine*'s 2002 DV Camcorder roundup, the three worst performers were the three smallest camcorders, including the Canon Elura 10 and JVC GR-DVP3, both slightly larger than a pack of cigarettes. Both scored two out of five in video and audio quality. Unless you're a spy or need a tiny camcorder for some other reason, I would go with a more traditional camcorder design.

After choosing a form factor, your next decision relates to how you intend to use the camcorder and the features you find necessary. For that, let's jump to Table 1-3. Note that the bolded items in the table represent features upgraded from the previous model, essentially highlighting the justification for the higher price.

Table 1-3   Feature Summary for Sony Consumer Camcorder Line

Camcorder	*TRV19*	*TRV22*	*TRV33*	*TRV38*	*TRV39*	*TRV70*	*TRV80*
Price	$599	$699	$799	$899	$999	$1,299	$1,499
Camcorder features							
Lines of resolution	500	500	**520**	520	520	**530**	530
Viewfinder (pixels)	Black & White (113K)	**Color (113K)**	Color (113K)	Color (113K)	**Color (180K)**	Color (180K)	Color (180K)
Color LCD (pixels)	2.5" (123K)	2.5" (123K)	2.5" (123K)	**3.5" (184K)**	3.5" (184K)	2.5" (211 K)	**3.5" (184K)**
Lux	5	5	**7**	7	7	7	7
Analog input	No	**Yes**	Yes	Yes	Yes	Yes	Yes
Manual focus ring	No	No	No	**Yes**	Yes	Yes	Yes
USB Network capable	No	No	No	No	**Yes**	Yes	Yes
Bluetooth	No	No	No	No	No	No	**Yes**
MPEG video	No	**Yes**	Yes	Yes	Yes	Yes	Yes
Still image							
Maximum still-image size	640x480	640x480	**1152x864**	1152x864	1152x864	**1600x1200**	1600x1200
Progressive scan	No	**Yes**	Yes	Yes	Yes	Yes	Yes
Flash	No	No	No	No	No	**Yes**	Yes
Memory Stick®	N/A	**8MB**	8MB	8MB	8MB	8MB	8MB
Standard features							
USB streaming	Yes	Yes	Yes	Yes	Yes	Yes	Yes
Zoom (optical/digital)	10/120X	10/120X	10/120X	10/120X	10/120X	10/120X	10/120X

Continued

Table 1-3   Feature Summary for Sony Consumer Camcorder Line *(continued)*

Standard features

Intelligent accessory shoe	Yes	Yes	Yes	Yes	Yes	Yes	Yes
NightShot	Yes	Yes	Yes	Yes	Yes	Yes	Yes
Manual focus	Yes	Yes	Yes	Yes	Yes	Yes	Yes
Manual white presets	Yes	Yes	Yes	Yes	Yes	Yes	Yes
Program AE	Yes	Yes	Yes	Yes	Yes	Yes	Yes
Gain control	Yes	Yes	Yes	Yes	Yes	Yes	Yes
Manual aperture	No	No	No	No	No	No	No
Manual shutter	No	No	No	No	No	No	No
Image stabilization	Yes	Yes	Yes	Yes	Yes	Yes	Yes

As you can see from the standard feature list, Sony has raised the bar for entry-level camcorders. USB streaming is a nice feature that lets you use your camcorder as a Web cam or for videoconferencing, and an intelligent accessory shoe helps you make use of available accessories. Even the base-level camcorder has image stabilization, manual focus, and several program AE and white-balance selections (but no manual white balance on any camcorder). On the other hand, there are no manual aperture or shutter controls, though these are adjusted automatically in the various program AE modes.

If I were choosing between the TRV19 and TRV22, paying $100 extra for the latter is a bit of a no-brainer, since you get a color viewfinder and analog input capabilities. Progressive scanning of still images and the Memory Stick to store it on are nice throw-ins, though you really can't do much with 640x480 images these days.

Similarly, MPEG video is the ability to encode and store MPEG-1 files on the supplied Memory Stick. It's a nice way to shoot and transmit video quickly, though quality is lacking in most tests that I've performed. Ditto for camcorders that output MPEG-4, a video format that offers greater compression than MPEG-1 but much lower quality. Unless you have a specific need for this capability, I wouldn't pay extra for it.

Best Reviews of Consumer Camcorders

- www.pcmag.com
- www.CNET.com
- www.camcorderinfo.com
- www.dvspot.com

Key Accessories to Purchase with Your Camcorder

OK, in a few pages, I'm going to tell you to dig deep and spend as much as you can for your camcorder. Dig a bit deeper and buy these accessories with the camera:

- Clear lens filter to protect the camcorder lens ($15–$25)

- A spare battery ($50–$150, depending upon recording time)

- A battery charger if not included ($60–$150)

Consider these accessories once you've paid off the initial credit card charges:

- Gun or boom microphone ($60+)

- Video light ($100+)

The TRV3 series is an interesting sell, primarily because 1152x864 still images, while over the magic megapixel mark, are still too small for printing larger than 4x6-inch pictures. If you're going to print your pictures or have them printed by a service, you'll probably still need a digital still-image camera with a higher resolution. In addition, there's no flash, so you'll either pay extra to buy a flash or forgo indoor shots.

On the other hand, the TRV39 introduces the networking concept into the Sony line, providing a modem connector that allows you to dial into an ISP for sending images and MPEG movies and even view and send e-mail messages. This could be very helpful in specialized vertical market applications like journalism or insurance or simply for sending pictures back home from the road. However, unless this capability or the 3.5-inch color LCD is particularly alluring to you, most budget-conscious buyers will probably stick to the TRV22.

At 1600x1200, the TRV70 and TRV80 offer twice the resolution of the TRV3 series and a flash, allowing serious use as a still-image camera. Lines of resolution are highest of all listed cameras though the lux rating of 7 is actually higher than the TRV19 and TRV22, which means that images captured in low light won't look as good as the lower-cost models, which is worse. The TRV80's Bluetooth capabilities are clearly the wave of the future, allowing wireless transmission of images or MPEG-1 video from camcorder to printers or compatible computers and handheld devices.

If shooting video is your primary concern, however, the TRV80 doesn't offer that much more than the TRV22. If I were contemplating spending these kind of dollars for a DV camcorder, I'd be comparing this unit more to the three-CCD Sony TRV950, which will deliver much better quality.

The takeaway from this exercise should be these key points:

- Decide form factor first. Recognize that if you purchase a tiny camcorder, part of the price you'll be paying for convenience is reduced audio and visual quality.

- Before buying, decide whether still-image capabilities are important. Large progressive-scan CCDs and flash capabilities bump the price significantly, but they don't improve video quality significantly, if at all. Don't pay for them if you don't plan to use them.

- If you want a camcorder for video and still images, make sure the still images are at least 2 megapixels in size and that the camcorder has an embedded flash. Make sure that all the controls you care about, like exposure, F-Stops, and timer are as accessible in the video camcorder as they are on a digital still camera. Finally, make sure that the price premium you're paying for the still-image capabilities doesn't exceed the cost of a good standalone digital still-image camera. You may still decide to combine the two functions into one camera, but at least you'll know what it's costing you.

- Understand that camcorder vendors change their lines frequently, so the camera you read about in a review may not be available when you decide to buy. It's frustrating but an unfortunate reality.

- Before buying, decide whether you'll actually use enhanced features like MPEG-1 videos, USB streaming, or Internet connectivity via USB or Bluetooth. If not, don't spend extra money on camcorders with these features.

The Prosumer Line

Say you want to step up to the next level and purchase a three-CCD prosumer camcorder. Using the VX2000 as an example, let's look at the types of features you can expect.

The VX2000 has three ⅓-inch CCDs and a lux rating of 2 that produces high-quality video under dismal lighting conditions. At 13 inches long, it's much bulkier than the average consumer camcorder and sports only a 2.5-inch LCD—though with 200,000 pixels, the image is very sharp.

In addition to manual focus on the lens, the VX2000 offers a manual zoom ring on the lens that's much less twitchy than the electric controls on most consumer camcorders, facilitating precise adjustments. The camcorder has a handle for below-the-waist shooting with a separate start and stop control easily accessible from the handle.

Several features help ensure optimal quality. First is a zebra pattern, which displays a black-and-white pattern over regions in the video that are overexposed. Second is an internal two-step neutral density (ND) filter that reduces incoming light without changing colors, which is very useful in direct sunlight and other bright conditions. Even better for beginners, the VX2000 displays a blinking status indicator in the LCD panel telling you when to turn the filter on and off.

Best Sites for User Feedback and Forums

- www.pcmag.com
- www.epinions.com
- www.cnet.com
- www.camcorderinfo.com
- www.dvinfo.com
- www.dvdoctor.net
- www.amazon.com

Best Reviews of Prosumer Camcorders

- www.pcmag.com
- www.videomaker.com
- www.dv.com
- www.cnet.com
- www.zdnet.com
- www.videouniversity.com
- www.emediapro.net
- www.camcorderinfo.com

You have full control over shutter speed and exposure, all available on the camcorder body where you can easily access them while shooting. That said, automatic modes work exceptionally well, so novices can achieve nearly as good quality as advanced users.

The camcorder's microphone input port can handle both microphone and line input with manual gain control and an audio meter for precise adjustments. Necessary options are surprisingly affordable with a 3-watt flash costing around $100, and a gun/zoom microphone (explained in Chapter 8) around $60.

Beyond this tech-speak gobbledygook is the simple fact that this camcorder shoots video so striking that my technology-iconoclast wife sat up and took notice, a first in my memory. In double-blind jury tests, *PC Magazine* test subjects have been equally impressed, awarding the VX2000 five out of five stars for video and still image quality, though with a 640x480 maximum still image resolution, it's inadequate for most still image functions.

Overall, here's the pitch for a high-end camcorder. Video is the ultimate garbage-in/garbage-out medium, so if the source footage is poor, there's little you can do to fix it. You can get away with inexpensive equipment the rest of the way through the production cycle, capture with a $15 FireWire card, edit with a free editor, and produce a DVD with a $49 program, and your output quality will match that of systems costing thousands of dollars.

But if you skimp on the camcorder, you've limited production quality from the start. Long story short, I'm not going to tell you to buy a new computer, a hot new capture card, and the most expensive editor available, but I will tell you to spend as much dough as possible on a great DV camcorder. I guarantee you'll be happy you did.

Test Drive

Let's face it; a department store or camcorder shop is no place to test-drive a camcorder, but if that's all you've got, here are about ten minutes of tests you can use to avoid buying a lemon. Test two camcorders side by side to help see the difference or one after the other if the store has a monitor you can connect to the camcorder during testing.

For low-light performance, look for the following:

■ Make sure the camcorder is in fully automatic mode. Aim the camcorder at a dark region in the store, say behind or under the counter, and see how well the camcorder reproduces the scene. Look for graininess or snow that indicate noise from electronic gain.

■ Try to find brightly colored objects in less-than-optimal lighting conditions. Compare the real images with their reproductions in the LCD and assess their brightness.

For performance under normal lighting, look for the following:

■ Focus on a face (hopefully someone you know). Determine whether the camcorder preserves the contrast in the face or whether it converts it to one blob of largely uniformed color. Have the subject stand directly under a bright light and see if the camcorder handles it well or if there's a bright white glare on the forehead.

■ Focus on some brightly colored objects and observe how close the color in the LCD or viewfinder matches the real objects.

For focus performance, look for the following:

■ Make sure that digital zoom is off and auto-focus on. Aim the camcorder toward an aisle or other area where people are walking into view. Zoom in so that each individual takes up about ¼ of the screen. Hold the camcorder steady, and as individuals walk into view, observe how long it takes for the camcorder to come into focus. A few milliseconds or two is OK, but two or three seconds is far too long.

■ Zoom into a scene with high contrast, like text on a wall, and see if the focus stays firm or if it seeks back and forth attempting to focus in. Try this in normal light and low light. If the focus doesn't stay constant, this may be a recurring problem during operation.

■ Zoom into the same high contrast scene, wait for the camcorder to get focused, and then slowly zoom away. The camcorder should maintain focus throughout.

■ Engage manual focus in the camcorder. Find the manual zoom controls and use them to focus in on a nearby object. Are these twitchy or smooth?

■ Close the LCD panel and focus through the viewfinder. If you wear glasses, take them off. Use the mechanical focus diopter to bring the viewfinder into focus. If you can't, the camcorder will be tough to use in bright sunlight and other conditions where the LCD isn't viewable.

For zoom controls, look for the following:

■ Zoom noise. Hold the camcorder close to your head and zoom in and out a few times. If you can hear the zoom noise, usually you'll hear it on your tapes.

- Zoom feel. Try to zoom slowly into or away from an object and gauge how firm the controls are. Many consumer camcorders are twitchy and over-responsive, making it tough to smoothly control camcorder motion.

- Zoom controls. This may sound petty, but I like horizontal controls that you push to zoom in and pull to zoom out. Vertical controls always confuse me. Decide which type works best for you.

For audio quality, look for the following:

- If it won't make you feel totally geeked out, bring a set of stereo headphones with a standard stereo computer jack to the store. Go to a quiet place, plug in the headphones, place the camera in shooting mode, and observe how much ambient noise the camcorder picks up. If there's lots of noise, that bodes poorly for capturing high-quality speech from talking-head subjects in your videos. On the other hand, if there's no noise, the camcorder may be insensitive. Move to the next test.

- Have the sales rep or someone else speak to you from about five feet away. The voice should be clear and free of distortion.

- If you have the headphones, perform the zoom test described above, zooming the camcorder in and out to see if you can hear the zoom noise. Once again, if you can hear the noise, it's likely the onboard microphone will pick it up as well.

Look for the following general mechanical issues:

- Check to see if there are threads on the lens, either for a clear filter to protect the lens from scratches or for a wide-angle or telephoto lens.

- Does the camcorder feel like it's made of plastic, or is it clearly magnesium or other high-grade metal? Plastic camcorders simply don't last as long.

- Check the access to the cassette mechanism. If it's on the bottom, you may not be able to change tapes while on a tripod.

- Open all access panels to analog, DV, electrical, microphone, and headphone jacks. Are the panels well secured and sturdy, or are they flimsy?

- Open the LCD panel and swivel it around. It should feel firm and sturdy, not loose and flimsy.

- Hold the camcorder in shooting position. Are all relevant controls for zooming and other operations accessible?

Summary

OK, you've evaluated all the features discussed above and identified the best model for your needs. You're ready to buy, and the money is burning a hole in your pocket. Whoa, Nelly, take these steps first:

- Go to www.pcmag.com, and check for reviews and user comments. Check for the best available price.

- Go to www.cnet.com and www.amazon.com for user comments.

- Check www.epinions.com, read reader comments, and check for the best available price.

- Go to the manufacturer's Web site and make sure the camcorder is still currently available.

Chapter 2

Getting Video to Your Computer

T his chapter reviews the universe of products that capture analog footage (analog-capture cards or devices), transfer DV video from a camera to a computer (DV-capture cards or devices), or capture both analog and DV video (combination of capture cards or devices). I'll start by identifying buying considerations and then apply these considerations to each product category to spot the strengths, weaknesses, and optimal target users. Though I may occasionally stray over the line, I focus primarily on products that cost under $500.

Note that unless otherwise stated, all prices quoted in this chapter are either official retail prices or the direct price available on the manufacturer's Web site. In many instances you can find a lower price at a brick and mortar or online retail location, or at my favorite spot for pricing video-related products: www.videoguys.com.

Video-capture products range in price from free FireWire ports embedded into your computer to board/software combinations that cost over several thousand dollars. Like most product reviewers, I have free access to most of these products, yet the most common capture hardware I use is a bargain-basement FireWire board or the FireWire port on my Dell laptop (see Figure 2-1). As I said in the last chapter, one of the lovely characteristics of FireWire is that you don't have to spend a bundle to get great results.

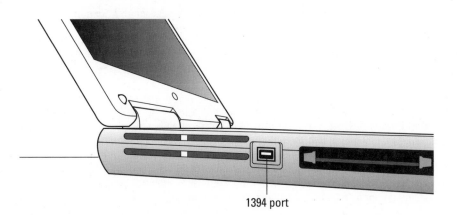

1394 port

Figure 2-1: My favorite capture device is the 1394 port on my Dell laptop. I still haven't figured out a way to capture on the handheld PocketPC device in the back, but I have produced video to play on it!

That said, I only work with DV cameras, so the answer would change if I needed to capture analog video. The answer would also change if I was cranking out three projects a week, or typically used multiple layers of special effects that would stretch production time immeasurably without hardware acceleration. I might consider a different product altogether if my primary goal was to convert my analog tapes to DVD. In this manner, capture devices have gotten increasingly application-specific.

Most sections in this chapter include a table that lists products in that category and relevant features and specifications. These tables are meant to be representative, not comprehensive, and I've primarily listed products that I've reviewed for *PC Magazine* or that I'm otherwise familiar with.

Analog Signal Primer

There are three common analog signals and storage formats: component, S-Video, and composite, listed from best to worst quality. I say storage format because analog video must be stored on tape in one of these formats. I say signal because the cables you connect between camera and capture device will be either composite, S-Video, or component.

Let's define them quickly and then discuss what you need to know about them.

- **Component video.** Video is stored in three separate channels, usually one channel for red, green, and blue, though there are variations. Most important is that each signal has its own channel, which lessens noise and promotes clarity, much like a three-CCD camera produces better quality than a one-CCD camera.

- **S-Video.** This includes one channel for luminance and one for color information. With two signals and two channels, S-Video is noisier than component, but superior to composite.

- **Composite video.** All color and brightness information is stored in one channel. This is the noisiest signal and the one used for NTSC color and black-and-white television. Thus, when you plug analog cable into your television set, it's only one cable.

You should care about two things when it comes to analog formats. First is how the video is stored by the format, which largely determines format quality. Next is how you transfer video from camcorder to computer.

Briefly, VHS and 8mm cameras store video in composite format, which is the primary reason quality is so poor. These devices typically offer composite-only output, which is universally accepted, since outputting in a higher-quality signal can't improve the quality already stored to disk.

In contrast, Hi8 and SVHS cameras store video in S-Video, producing better quality. In addition, they offer both composite and S-Video outputs, the latter providing better quality when viewing on television or capturing to your computer.

High-end analog formats like BetaSP store in component format, and typically output composite, S-Video, and component signals. When viewing or capturing from these devices, you should always use the highest-quality signal supported by your capture device or television monitor.

I'll look at S-Video and composite cables in the following sections; the general rule for video capture is to always connect at the highest signal quality supported by both analog source and video capture device. For VHS and 8mm, that's composite; for SVHS and Hi8, it's S-Video.

Buying Considerations

Video-capture products offer an array of features and functionality. The following sections discuss the factors to consider when making a buying decision.

Format Support

The first question, of course, is whether the device can actually connect to your camera. That is, if you have a DV camera, you need a FireWire port, and if you have an analog camera, you need analog connectors.

You may also want a product with both analog and DV video, perhaps because you're working in analog now but may soon buy a DV camcorder, or because you still edit in both formats. Whatever the case, when buying analog-capture devices, favor products that do the following:

- Capture the higher-quality S-Video as well as composite video.

- Capture audio as well as video on board, sending a synchronized stream to the computer. In contrast, other products that don't capture audio "on board" capture audio with the system soundcard and synchronize audio and video inside the computer, which occasionally leads to synchronization problems.

- Convert the analog footage to DV format, as opposed to MPEG-2 or other formats, unless your primary goal is to simply convert your analog tapes to DVD.

- Have "analog output" capabilities, so you can write your project back to tape if desired.

Your Technical Capabilities

Before choosing a capture solution, take an honest look at your technical capabilities for both installation and everyday usage. Though capture-card installation has become simpler over the years, some users still don't like to crack open their computers and install a card. For this reason, many vendors have introduced external products that connect via USB or FireWire connectors, simplifying installation and the ability to share among multiple desktop computers and laptops.

Your DVD Camcorder — An Analog-Capture Device?

One quick note for folks with both DV and analog footage. Remember that many DV camcorders have an analog input feature that allows you to convert analog footage to DV in the camera. Then you can capture the video using a DV-capture device.

If your use of analog footage is casual (like mine), this may suffice. Otherwise, if you'll be editing with both analog and DV video for some time to come, get a combination capture device that supports both analog and DV input.

Regarding day-to-day usage, most capture cards, whether analog or DV, include video-capture and video-editing software, each targeting varying levels of user sophistication. For example, while Pinnacle Studio or Ulead VideoWave are well within the reach of even non-technical users, products like Adobe Premiere will stymie most video-editing novices. For this reason, you need to match the software bundle with your technical capabilities, both present and future.

Note that the next chapter will provide a complete discussion of video-editing programs; here I'll focus primarily on the input/output capabilities of each solution and comment only briefly on the software capabilities.

Intended Use

As the consumer video production market became more mainstream, it also became more stratified, with many products targeting slightly different segments. For example, Pinnacle Studio MovieBox USB, an external product that connects via a 2.0 USB port, provides a rich development environment for both video editing and DVD production. However, there's no simple way to convert VHS tapes to DVD.

In contrast, Adaptec's VideOh! DVD, which also connects via USB, ships with Sonic's MyDVD!, which enables one-step conversion of VHS tapes to DVD. You can also edit video and produce more creative DVDs, but the environment isn't as flexible or cohesive as Pinnacle Studio.

If your primary focus is converting analog tapes to DVD, Adaptec is the better buy. On the other hand, if you plan to meticulously edit and author your productions, Studio provides a better environment. In this manner, your primary production goals should definitely drive your purchase decision.

Required Performance

Performance is also an important consideration for some users. If you're producing multiple, complex projects in a production-like environment, paying extra for real-time performance may be worthwhile. On the other hand, if you're a casual user, you can save hundreds of dollars by choosing a product that delivers largely the same result, only slower.

Your Current Computer

For the most part, any Pentium III or Pentium 4 computer is more than capable of effectively running these generally entry-level products. If you're working with an older computer, be sure to check the minimum system requirements for processor, RAM, operating system, and hard disk space before buying.

For external USB products, ascertain whether they're USB 1.0 or the much faster 2.0. While USB 2.0 products will still run on older computers, they are nowhere near as efficient. To get the most out of these products, you'll either need a computer with a USB 2.0 port or an add-in card that provides USB 2.0 capabilities, which are sold by several companies, including Adaptec.

With these considerations as prologue, let's jump in and start looking at some products.

DV-Only Products

This section targets readers who don't need to capture analog video on their computer, perhaps because they have no analog footage, or perhaps because they can use the analog input capabilities on their camcorders for whatever analog footage they need to capture.

If you're working with DV only, you have four basic options:

- If you're running Windows XP, you can use your current FireWire port (or buy a plain-Jane DV-capture card) and download Microsoft's free Movie Maker 2 software.

- You can buy an inexpensive DV-capture card with a consumer-editing bundle.

- You can buy an inexpensive DV-capture card with a professional bundle.

- You can buy a real-time capture card with a professional bundle (and gain analog input capabilities in the bargain, since virtually all real-time capture cards include analog capabilities).

I'll address the strengths and weaknesses of each approach next.

Movie Maker 2

The homegrown approach with Movie Maker 2 is a great way to jump in at low cost. Note that Microsoft invested significantly in Movie Maker 2, which is vastly superior to the original version. If your XP computer is currently running the original version of Movie Maker, you can upgrade at www.microsoft.com/windowsxp/moviemaker/downloads/moviemaker2.asp.

Many newer computers and laptops ship with a DV port. If your computer doesn't have one, you should be able to find a generic DV-capture card for around $30. For the most part, all recently released products are compatible with Open Host Controller Interface (OHCI) specifications 1.0 and 1.1, ensuring compatibility with Movie Maker 2 and other video-editing programs. All new products should also support Windows XP, but check to be sure.

Note

Many DV-card-only solutions *do not* ship with a DV cable. Since most cameras don't ship with a cable either, you need to find a DV-card product with a cable or buy one separately. Since DV cables can cost anywhere from around $8 to $75, be sure to factor this into your price comparisons.

Once you get the card installed, you'll be fully able to transfer video from camcorder to computer; edit your video with transitions, titles, and special effects; and output back to the camera or in a range of other formats. Movie Maker 2 is also a great way to experiment with AutoMovie, a feature that builds videos for you and synchronizes them to background music.

Cross-Reference
For more on Movie Maker 2, turn to Chapters 3 and 15.

On the other hand, while Movie Maker 2 is reasonably easy to use and functional, it's not my top choice for consumer video editors, for reasons discussed fully in Chapter 3. Briefly, it can't output into MPEG-2 and doesn't have DVD-authoring capabilities, a staple on most consumer editors. So I wouldn't upgrade to Windows XP just to run Movie Maker 2, or purchase an el-cheapo 1394 card if my computer didn't have a FireWire port.

Rather, I'd spend a few extra dollars and get one of the products described in the next category. That way, you'll be getting a superior editing environment and, if you are running Windows XP, a capture device that's compatible with Movie Maker 2 to boot.

Inexpensive DV-Capture Cards with Consumer-Editing Bundles

These products range in price from around $49 to $129 and include a 1394 card and software providing both video-editing and DVD-authoring capabilities. As you can see in Table 2-1, sometimes you get both editing and authoring in the same program, sometimes in two separate programs.

Table 2-1   DV-Capture Cards with Consumer Editors

Company	Adaptec	ADS Technologies	Dazzle	Pinnacle
Product	FireConnect Plus	Pyro 1394 DV	DV Editor	Studio DV
Price	$69.99	$79	$69.99	$129.99
Editing software	MyDVD!	Ulead VideoStudio 6.0 SE	MovieStar 5	Pinnacle Studio
Authoring software	ArcSoft Showbiz	Ulead DVD MovieFactory	Dazzle DVD Plug-in	Pinnacle Studio Complete
Ports on board	Three	Three	Three	Three
Cable included	Yes	Yes	Yes	Yes
Web site	www.adaptec.com	www.adstech.com	www.dazzle.com	www.pinnaclesys.com

As a category, these products are well within the capabilities of even beginning users, and you won't need the hottest new computer for reasonable editing responsiveness, though as with all video-editing products, more disk space is always better. From a hardware perspective, all four FireWire cards include a cable and three ports, so you can use the board with other peripherals like hard disk drives and CD/DVD recorders.

What to Look for in an Inexpensive DV-Capture Card

- It must be Open Host Controller Interface (OHCI) compatible (version 1.0 and 1.1).

- It should have at least three IEEE1394 ports, preferably on the bracket.

- It should be Windows XP compatible.

- It should include a DV cable.

- It shouldn't cost more than $40.

Of the four products, Adaptec's FireConnect Plus is the most DVD-authoring-centric, as MyDVD! is a great consumer DVD-authoring tool while the bundled ShowBiz offers only modest editing capabilities. MyDVD! is great for converting analog tapes to DVD, but Showbiz isn't the best choice for pushing the creative envelope on the editing side. If video editing is your primary interest, choose one of the other bundles.

If you skip ahead to Chapter 3, you'll see that Pinnacle Studio is a perennial *PC Magazine* Editor's Choice, and it's the product I use most extensively for simple capture and editing tasks. From my perspective, the Pinnacle Studio DV bundle (software shown in Figure 2-2) is also attractive because you're getting both hardware and software from the same vendor, which ensures one phone number to call when things go wrong and eliminates finger pointing between the hardware and software vendor.

Figure 2-2: Pinnacle complements their excellent software with a range of hardware input options, including Studio DV.

When Buying a DV-Capture Card with a Consumer Bundle

- Choose the best software bundle for your intended application.

- Make sure you're getting the most current version of software.

- Don't go bargain basement — stick to recognized software programs.

- When possible, buy products featuring hardware and software from the same vendor.

- Don't pay more than $130.

While the same is true with the Dazzle bundle, you have to learn two separate products to edit and author, while Studio does both. Dazzle's software, while functional, has never quite risen to the top tier of consumer video editors, which in my view is owned by Pinnacle Studio, Ulead's VideoStudio, and Roxio's VideoWave Movie Creator.

Inexpensive DV-Capture Cards with Prosumer Editing Bundles

Products in this category are simple, non-accelerated DV-capture cards with a more advanced editing and authoring bundle affording a significantly increased range of creative flexibility (see Table 2-2 for a comparison). Not only do they afford greater precision and flexibility than consumer editors with features like transitions and titles, they also enable a range of capabilities not found in consumer editors, like video overlay, motion paths, and 3D effects.

The price you pay, however, is program complexity, since the hardware is the same, but the software is much more complicated, which translates to a much longer learning curve when you start using the program. If you have the time, these bundles work extremely well for experienced users with far-reaching creative goals.

Cross-Reference

Chapter 3 details the relative strengths and weaknesses of MediaStudio Pro and Premiere.

Table 2-2   DV-Capture Cards with Prosumer Editors

Company	ADS Technologies	ADS Technologies
Product	Pyro ProDVD	Pyro PlatinumDV
Price	$329	$329
Editing software	Ulead MediaStudio Pro (Directors' Cut)	Adobe Premiere
Authoring software	Ulead DVD Workshop SE	Ulead DVD Workshop SE
Ports on board	Three	Three
Cable included	Yes	Yes
Web site	www.adstech.com	www.adstech.com

In general, MediaStudio Pro (see Figure 2-3) is targeted at enthusiasts, as opposed to professionals, and is a bit more accessible and responsive. In contrast, Premiere focuses on the creative professional using other Adobe products like PhotoShop and After Effects. While highly functional by itself, much of Premiere's allure to this class of buyer relates to common interface elements and the flexibility of working with native formats like PhotoShop's PSD format.

Figure 2-3: Ulead's MediaStudio Pro.

Understand that when buying products in this category, you may not be getting full versions of the bundled software, especially if you see initials like SE (special edition) or LE (limited edition), or another term like "Directors Cut" indicating a special version. In the case of MediaStudio Pro Director's Cut, this means you won't be getting two modules shipped with the full version, Video Paint or CG Infinity (a titling utility), a significant limitation for those seeking to access the advanced effects these modules provide.

Similarly, DVD Workshop SE limits slideshows to 20 images, chapter points within a video to 20, and motion menus to five seconds, essentially making the feature unusable, because motion menus that repeat every five seconds have the creative appeal of a skipping record (for readers who remember such things).

Cross-Reference

Chapters 4, 17, and 19 discuss DVD authoring in general, including slideshows, chapter points, and motion menus.

When Buying a DV-Capture Card with a Prosumer Bundle

- Choose the best software bundle for your intended project.

- Make sure you're getting the most current version of software.

- Learn whether you're getting full or "special" versions of the software.

- If it's a special version, determine which features are limited and how much they are limited.

- Ascertain the upgrade price to the full version (if applicable).

Since both ADS products in Table 2-2 include DVD Workshop SE, this doesn't help you differentiate between the two as much as set your expectations. That is, if you're excited about buying Workshop so you can develop DVDs with motion menus, you're likely to be disappointed with the special version. Accordingly, when buying products in this category, discover whether limitations exist, what they are, and how much it costs to upgrade to the full version.

Real-Time DV-Capture Cards

Products in this category combine professional quality software with hardware enabling a range of real-time effects, speeding up production. Two of the three products listed in Table 2-3 can handle both analog and DV input and output, and all products include a DVD-authoring program, providing a comprehensive video production system.

On the whole, however, though these products are relatively affordable, they're more appropriate for professionals than consumers for three primary reasons. First, the benefit of real-time effects typically kicks in only with highly complex projects that include multiple tracks and effects like chromakeying and picture-in-picture, which most consumers don't have a need for. If your projects tend to be simple, you won't notice the difference.

Cross-Reference

Chapter 14 discusses high-end editing techniques like chromakeying and picture-in-picture.

Second, these hardware/software combinations are highly temperamental and typically work best on dedicated workstations. On your day-to-day computer, loading and unloading other programs, especially multimedia programs and 3D games, may corrupt operation, forcing a time-consuming uninstall and reinstall.

Finally, none of the bundled programs are truly consumer-oriented programs and won't be intuitive to novice users.

Table 2-3   Real-Time DV-Capture Cards

Company	Canopus	Matrox	Pinnacle
Product	DVRaptor RT2	RT.X10 Xtra	Edition Pro
Price	$499	$599	$949.99
Editing software	Canopus EZEdit	Adobe Premiere (full version)	Pinnacle Edition
Bundled software	Canopus DV Capture, Xplode Basics, SoftMPEG Encoder	Matrox MediaTools and MediaExport, Ligos GoMotion, Pixelan Video Spice Rack lite, Sonic Desktop SmartSound Quicktracks	Pinnacle Hollywood FX, TitleDeko RT
Authoring software	DVD Workshop SE	Sonic DVDit! SE	Integrated into Edition
Analog and DVD I/O	Optional	Yes	Yes
Minimum processor	Pentium III 700 MHz	Pentium III 1 GHz	Pentium 4
Operating system	Windows XP or Windows 2000	Windows XP	Windows 2000, XP
Disk	AV-rated (10 MB/second)	Separate hard drive	10 MB/second transfer rate
Cable included	Yes	Yes	Yes
Web site	www.canopus.com	www.matrox.com	www.pinnaclesys.com

Choosing the ideal product in this category is complicated. First, make sure the product runs on your intended editing station. For example, Windows 98 is out for all products, and some don't even work on Windows 2000. Second, check the required processor and hard drive configurations, and make sure you meet the minimum.

Next, looking at the editing software, Canopus EZ Edit is generally easier to learn than Adobe Premiere or Pinnacle Edition, but EZ Edit can't do as much. If you're in this category to push the creative envelope, pick a board with Premiere or Edition. If you're looking for accessible real-time performance, Canopus is a great choice but not really oriented toward novice users, so expect a longer learning curve than with most typical consumer video editors.

Cross-Reference

Chapter 3 details the relative strengths and weaknesses of consumer and prosumer editors.

When Buying a DV-Capture Card with a Prosumer Bundle

- Verify machine requirements (processor and operating system).

- Identify which features are real time (preview, render DV, MPEG-2 encoding, and so on).

- Determine whether you're getting full or "special" versions of the software.

- If it's a special version, determine which features are limited and how.

- Ascertain the upgrade price to the full version (if applicable).

Also consider the extras bundled with the program. For example, Pinnacle's TitleDeko is a great utility for creating titles, and Hollywood FX is a wonderful source of creative transitions. Matrox counters this with Pixelan Video Spice Rack lite, a strong source of additional special effects, and Sonic SmartSound, which creates custom-length background audio tracks.

Next, look at DVD authoring, which is used to build your DVD projects. With this version of Edition, Pinnacle incorporated authoring into the editing program, which means you don't have to learn a separate program to create a DVD. Matrox offers Sonic DVDit! for authoring, a capable stand-alone product, while Canopus offers DVD Workshop SE, a feature-limited version of Ulead's excellent authoring program. I'd give a slight advantage here to Edition because its authoring features are most comprehensive.

Before buying any of these products, however, look for the latest review in *PC Magazine*, *DV Magazine*, or *E-Media Professional*. This is a fast-moving category, and products change very quickly.

Analog-Capture Devices

Analog-capture devices run the gamut from simple, inexpensive USB products that capture low-resolution files to sophisticated boxes that capture in MPEG-2 for simple conversion to DVD. The following sections discuss the strengths and weaknesses of each category, some representative products, and suggestions on how to choose between them.

USB Analog-Capture Devices (MPEG-1)

The inexpensive products shown in Table 2-4 connect to your USB port and capture in either MPEG-1 or a proprietary format that limits capture resolution to 320x240 or smaller. This makes them easy to install and acceptable for streaming video or CD-ROM production, but inadequate for DVD production, which requires higher-resolution files. Accordingly, while these products are adequate "starter" products, most ambitious producers will quickly outgrow this category.

Table 2-4   USB Analog-Capture Devices (MPEG-1)

Company	Dazzle	Pinnacle Systems
Product	Digital Video Creator	LINX USB Plus
Price	$69.99	$69.99
Inputs	S-Video, Composite, Stereo audio	S-Video, Composite, Stereo audio
Capture format	MPEG-1	Proprietary codec
Audio on board	Yes	Yes
Editing software	MovieStar	Pinnacle Studio LE
Authoring software	Dazzle DVD Authoring	Pinnacle Studio LE
Maximum capture resolution	352x240	320x240
Analog output	Yes	No
Web site	www.dazzle.com	www.pinnaclesys.com

Both products capture audio on board and save in a quarter-screen format, so there's no real differentiation there. However, Pinnacle LINX USB doesn't offer analog output, while Dazzle's Digital Video Creator (Figure 2-4 shows a representation of this company's products) does, making it the only choice for producers distributing on tape.

Figure 2-4: Dazzle's Digital Video Creator features analog output, so you can write back to your analog camcorder, an operation that Pinnacle's LINX USB can't perform.

Cross-Reference

Chapter 16 discusses rendering out to tape and other project-rendering alternatives.

Conversely, I'd give the nod to Pinnacle LINX if output to tape wasn't a required feature, simply because Studio is a more polished and capable program. Note, however, that the "LE" after Studio in Table 2-4 means "Limited Edition," so before buying, you should identify the limitations and upgrade price to the full version.

Internal Analog-Capture Cards

Products in this category (refer to Table 2-5) are internal PCI cards that are physically installed in your computer — an operation that Plug and Play has simplified to a great degree. Once installed, I prefer internal solutions over external because it's one less device I have to power with my chronically overcrowded power strips and there's less clutter. But if the thought of installing a PCI card makes you nervous, don't sweat! I'll cover external alternatives in the next section.

Table 2-5   Internal Analog-Capture Cards

Company	Canopus	InterVideo	Pinnacle Systems	Pinnacle Systems
Product	ADVC-1394	WinDVD Creator Plus AVDV	Studio AV version 8	Studio Deluxe
Price	$249 — Vegas Video LE $399 — Premiere	$129	$129.99	$299.99
Inputs	DV, S-Video, Composite, Stereo audio	DV, S-Video, Composite, Stereo audio	S-Video, Composite	DV, S-Video, Composite, Stereo audio
Audio on board	Yes	Yes	No	Yes
Editing software	Vegas/ Premiere	WinDVD Creator Plus AVDV	Studio 8	Studio 8
Authoring software	WinProducer	WinDVD Creator Plus AVDV	Studio 8	Studio 8
Other software	None	None	None	Hollywood FX
Maximum capture resolution	720x480	720x480	608x464	720x480
Capture format	DV	DV	Motion JPEG	DV
Analog output	Yes	Yes	Yes	Yes
Web site	www. canopus.com	www. intervideo.com	www. pinnaclesys.com	www. pinnaclesys.com

When Buying a USB Analog-Capture Device (MPEG-1)

- Identify the maximum capture resolution.

- Determine whether audio is captured on board.

- Determine whether the product has analog output capabilities.

- Determine whether you're getting full or "special" versions of the software.

- If it's a special version, determine which features are limited and how much they're limited.

- Ascertain the upgrade price to the full version (if applicable).

Note that Studio AV uses the system soundcard for audio capture, raising the specter of sound-synch issues. I've used the card a bunch without problems, but it's definitely a red flag, especially if you're operating on slower computers.

In addition, though the product supports analog output, it captures at 608x464 resolution, which is less than optimal for tape-based output as well as DVD production. Finally, there's no upgrade path if you subsequently purchase a DV camcorder, since there's no DV connector, so you'll have to purchase an entirely new product. If you're sold on an internal solution, I'd only go this route if a short-term budget was my most important consideration.

In contrast, Studio Deluxe captures audio and video on board and converts it directly into DV, a full-resolution format that's ideal for output to tape or DVD production. Using DV as the lingua franca from both analog and DV footage makes it easy to mix and match clips from the two different sources. Pinnacle also throws in Hollywood FX, supplementing Studio with about 100 additional transitions.

Of course, as a video editor, Studio lacks much of the flexibility and power offered by Adobe Premiere or Sonic's Vegas Video, so those seeking to push the creative envelope might prefer either of the Canopus ADVC-1394 solutions.

Of course, at $399, the Premiere version of the Canopus ADVC-1394 is priced close to some of the Premiere-based real-time capture cards described earlier that input both DV and analog video and perform many operations in real time. So I would definitely consider a real-time board before buying the ADVC-1394.

Finally, the InterVideo product looks like a total winner but was announced late in the cycle so I couldn't review it before finishing the book. Throttling my enthusiasm to a great degree, however, is the fact that my previous experience with InterVideo editing software was dismal, though their DVD player is great. Definitely check out product reviews before jumping on this one.

USB Analog-Capture Devices (MPEG-2)

Devices in this category (refer to Table 2-6) connect to your USB port and capture MPEG-2 video to disk in real time, making them ideal for converting analog tapes to DVD. Most also supply editing software enabling a full range of editing and output options.

On the other hand, just like MPEG-2 isn't the optimal capture format for a digital camcorder (see Chapter 1), it's also not my top choice for capture and editing on the computer for two reasons.

When Buying an Internal Analog-Capture Card

- Determine whether audio is captured on board.

- Identify the maximum capture resolution.

- Determine whether the product has analog output capabilities.

- Determine whether DV support is an important consideration.

- Match the software bundle to your own technical experience and creative goals.

MPEG-2 offers lower quality than DV and the inherent inter-frame compression makes working with MPEG-2 more computationally intense, which often manifests as sluggishness within the editing program.

Table 2-6   USB Analog-Capture Devices (MPEG-2)

Company	Adaptec	ADS Technologies	Dazzle	Pinnacle Systems
Product	VideOh! DVD	USB Instant DVD	DVD Creation Station 2000	MovieBox USB
Price	$179	$229	$229	$249
USB standard	2.0	1.0	1.1	2.0
Inputs	S-Video and Composite video, Stereo audio	S-Video and Composite video, Stereo audio	S-Video and Composite video, Stereo audio	S-Video and Composite video, Stereo audio
Audio on board	Yes	Yes	Yes	Yes
Capture format	MPEG-2	MPEG-2	MPEG-2	MPEG-2
Editing software	ArcSoft Showbiz	VideoStudio 6 DVD	MovieStar 5	Studio
Authoring software	MyDVD! 4.0	MyDVD! 3.5	DVD Complete	Studio
One-step analog to DVD	Yes	No	No	No
Analog output	No	No	Yes	Yes
Web site	www.adaptec.com	www.adstech.com	www.dazzle.com	www.pinnaclesys.com

Working through Table 2-6, our first consideration is the USB standard supported by the product. USB 1.0 and 1.1 transfer information at 12 Mbps, while USB 2.0 transfers at 480 Mbps, 40 times faster. Though USB 2.0 devices won't deliver 40 times the video quality, they will support higher capture rates more efficiently, reducing dropped frames during capture or while writing back to tape.

Note that you don't need a computer with USB 2.0 ports to operate these devices, since USB 2.0 devices are backwards-compatible with computers with 1.1 and 1.0 USB ports. However, if you have an older computer, several vendors, including Adaptec, sell inexpensive PCI cards with USB 2.0 ports. Even if you decide not to upgrade your current computer, buying a USB 2.0 device today ensures top performance when you purchase your next computer, making USB 2.0 a desirable feature.

All products listed in Table 2-6 capture audio on board (as opposed to using the system sound-card), the preferred approach, and store captured audio/video into MPEG-2 format, so there's no differentiation there. As I stated up top, software is a huge differentiator, with Adaptec (see Figure 2-5) providing the only one-step conversion from analog to DVD, ideal for those simply converting analog assets to DVD. Surprisingly, VideOh! doesn't offer analog output, so it's useless for producers distributing their edited productions on videotape.

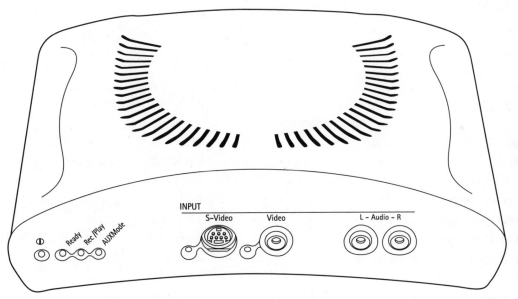

Figure 2-5: Adaptec's VideOh! DVD is great for quickly converting analog assets to DVDs, but it lacks analog output capabilities and can't be used for writing to tape.

In contrast, with stronger video-editing programs and analog output capabilities, Pinnacle and ADS Tech present a stronger environment for editing and authoring. Note that ADS Tech includes MyDVD! 3.5, compared to 4.0 for Adaptec, highlighting the need to identify the software version included in the bundle before buying.

When Buying a USB Analog-Capture Device (MPEG-2)

- Match it to the USB standard supported on your capture station, either USB 1 or USB 2.

- Determine whether audio is captured on board.

- Identify the capture format and resolution.

- Determine whether the product has analog output capabilities.

- Make sure you have the most current version of software.

FireWire Analog-Capture Devices

These devices (refer to Table 2-7) connect to your FireWire port and capture both DV and analog video. Rather than using MPEG-2 as the capture format, like the USB products, all products in this category convert analog video to DV for storage, preserving quality and editing responsiveness. Unless your overarching goal is one-step conversion of analog assets to DVD, these products are superior to USB products for editing analog and DV video, even if you have to purchase a FireWire port to get it installed.

Table 2-7   FireWire Analog-Capture Devices

Company	Dazzle	Pinnacle Systems
Product	Hollywood DV-Bridge	MovieBox DV
Price	$299	$299
Inputs	DV, S-Video and Composite video, Stereo audio	DV, S-Video and Composite video, Stereo audio
Audio on board	Yes	Yes
Capture format	DV	DV
Editing software	MovieStar 5	Studio
Authoring software	DVD Complete	Studio
One-step analog to DVD	No	No
Analog output	Yes	Yes
Web site	www.dazzle.com	www.pinnaclesys.com

Basically, these products are identical from a hardware perspective, leaving software as the key differentiator. I'd pick Studio, which comes with MovieBox DV (see Figure 2-6), over Hollywood DV-Bridge's MovieStar.

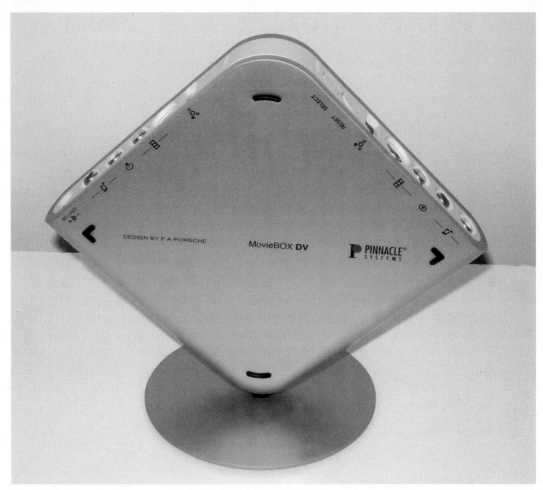

Figure 2-6: MovieBox DV is the best solution for producers seeking analog and DV compatibility without having to open their computers.

Summary

Here's a suggested checklist to work through before buying. Some duplicate those shown in the individual sections.

1. Is this the product that I want?

   - Will it connect to my current and future camera(s) (analog and DV)?

   - Does it provide the performance (real-time or non-real-time) that I want?

- Does it provide the capabilities that I need?

  Software — editing, authoring, and so on?

  Hardware — full-resolution capture and output to tape?

  How does it handle audio (on board or through the system soundcard)?

- Are these the best programs for me?

  Read Chapters 3 and 4 for editing and authoring.

  Read the latest reviews in *PC Magazine*.

  Also check the CNET and Epinions Web sites.

- Am I getting the latest versions of the program (go to software vendor's site and determine the latest version)?

- Am I getting a special version with limited features? If so, identify which features aren't available and how much it costs to upgrade (if applicable).

2. Will it work on my computer?

   - Check the minimum system requirements to make sure the product will run on your current computer, considering primarily the operating system, processor speed, and connectors (for example, USB 2.0 or FireWire).

   - Check that the product provides all necessary cables (or buy them separately).

3. Verify that you're getting the best price. Check at:

   - www.pcmag.com

   - www.videoguys.com

   - www.epinions.com

   - www.cnet.com

   - Vendor Web site

Chapter 3

Choosing Your Video Editor

In general, my theory about buying a video editor is to buy the least expensive editor that will get the job done for you. Less is definitely more, given the price and learning curve of more expensive systems.

If your needs are modest — capture, cut, paste, and post — Microsoft's Movie Maker 2 should do just fine. As your editing goals grow, you'll need to move on, first into consumer editors like Pinnacle Studio and Ulead VideoStudio, then to prosumer products like Adobe Premiere Pro, Pinnacle Edition, Sonic Foundry Vegas, or Ulead MediaStudio Pro.

In this chapter, I start by taking a quick look at the basic capabilities of video editors in general. Then I examine each of these products, starting with Movie Maker 2, identifying their strengths and weaknesses and discussing when you need to move on to a different editor. I also take a good, hard look at when you need to make the jump from consumer to prosumer.

Given that many of these products cost under $100, even if you already have a video editor not listed here (perhaps bundled with your camcorder or DVD recorder), you should read through this chapter to get a feel for how your product stacks up. There are a number of fine choices out there; at these prices it's both frustrating and unnecessary to lock yourself into a product just because you got it for free.

Editing 101

Let's briefly touch on the basics of video editing, which I discuss in detail in Chapter 11.

The first step in all video productions is video capture or inserting previously captured clips into the editor. All listed products can both capture and import video, audio, and digital images, from a scanner, digital camera, or otherwise.

After capture, you build your production. In terms of interface, most video editors have four main windows, as shown in Figure 3-1 (Microsoft Movie Maker 2). On the upper right is the preview window, which allows you to see the output before you actually render. Most editors have "libraries" or "collections" containing the content you've captured or inserted, as well as the special effects included with the program. Figure 3-1 shows the library containing captured clips, while Figure 3-2 shows the library containing special effects.

Video library

Preview window

Tools

Storyboard

Figure 3-1: Microsoft Movie Maker 2 in storyboard mode.

All video editors have storyboards (see Figure 3-1), timelines (see Figure 3-2) or both, which is where you actually assemble the pieces of your video puzzle. Storyboards show each asset individually, and usually little else, and are great for sequencing your assets in the project.

Cross-Reference

For more on storyboards, turn to Chapter 7.

In contrast, the timeline is a longitudinal, time-based representation of your project with separate tracks for each content type. For example, the timeline in Figure 3-2 has five tracks as follows:

■ **Video track** — This track contains the captured video and can also contain still images.

■ **Transition track** — This track contains transitions or effects inserted *between* clips placed in the project.

■ **Original audio track** — This track contains the audio captured with the video file above it.

■ **Additional audio track** — This is another audio track that can be used for narration, background music, or sound effects.

■ **Title track** — This track contains text titles inserted into the project.

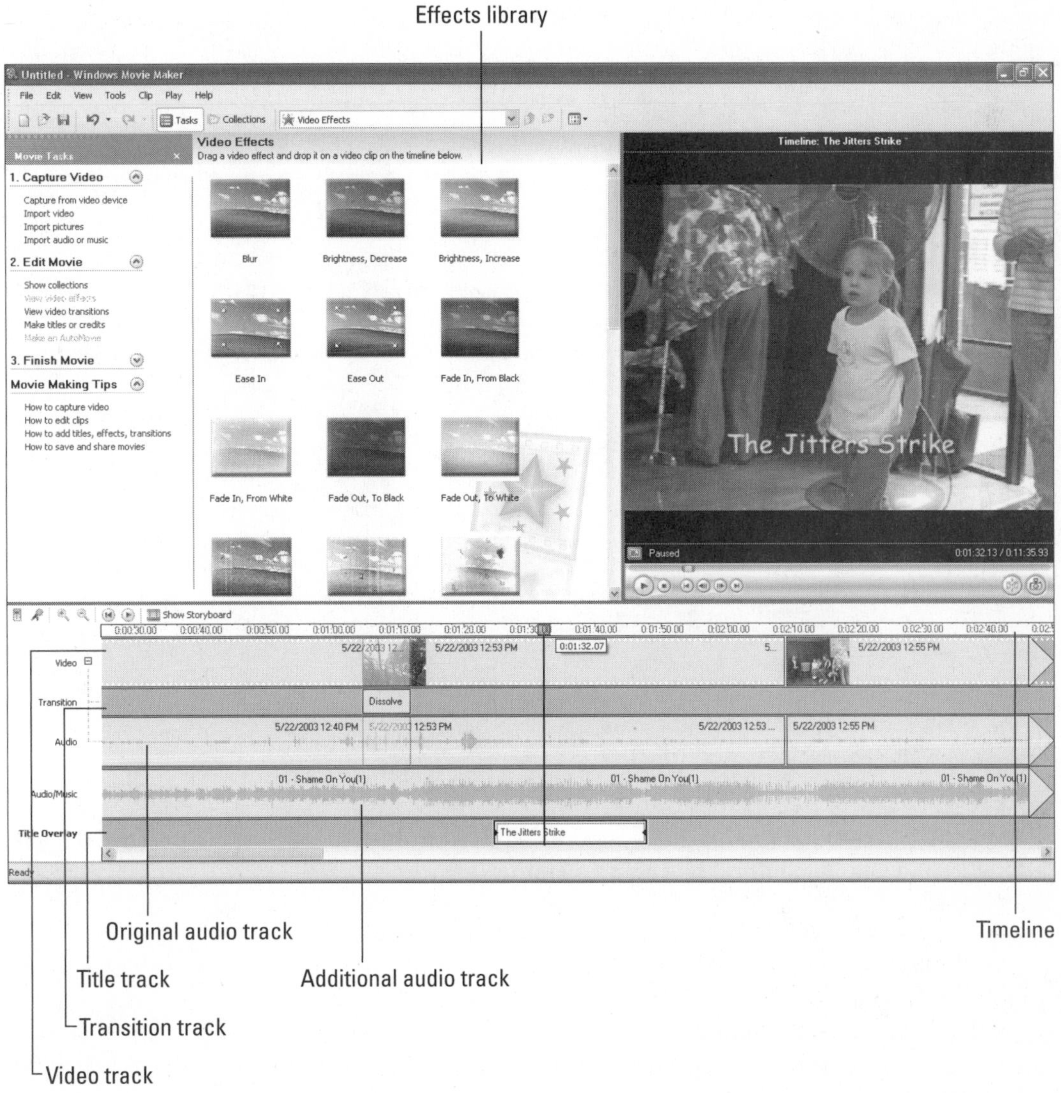

Figure 3-2: Movie Maker 2 in timeline mode.

Timelines allow you to precisely sequence your assets and to see how they interrelate. They're invaluable for visualizing effects that impact more than one video file, like a long title or background audio tracks. All listed entry-level products offer both timeline and storyboard views.

The bulk of your editing involves trimming or deleting unwanted frames at the start and end of the video. Then, you sequence your audio/video assets and add titles, transitions, and other special effects that can change the appearance of your video in various ways. For example, with Movie Maker 2, you can fade to black at the end of a clip, change your color footage to black and white, and insert film grain into the video so it looks like 16mm film. Generally, when applying these transitions, titles, and effects, you check your production in the preview window to ensure you're achieving the desired result.

After applying these effects, video editors "render" (or produce) the files required for the desired distribution medium. If you're working with DV video and writing the video back to tape, the editor will render a DV file. If you're producing a DVD, most video editors can produce the required file in MPEG-2 format, and most can also create streaming media files for posting to a Web site or sending via e-mail.

With this as background, let's look at consumer-oriented video editors.

Movie Maker 2

Movie Maker 2 is a basic get-the-job-done program with two primary strengths and several weaknesses. Its most compelling feature, of course, is that it's free. Beyond this is the AutoMovie feature, discussed in detail in Chapter 15, which automatically converts your video footage into MTV-like music videos, with theme-based effects packages that allow you to select style and pace (see Figure 3-3). While not appropriate for all productions, it's a great tool to have in your arsenal.

Select an AutoMovie Editing Style
Click 'Done' to automatically edit the movie.

Name	Description
Flip and Slide	Flip, slide, reveal, and page curl video transitions are applied bet...
Highlights Movie	Clean and simple editing with cuts, fades, a title, and credits
Music Video	Quick edits for fast beats, and longer edits for slow beats
Old Movie	Film age video effects applied to clips to make an older-looking m...
Sports Highlights	Video clips with fast pans and zooms are selected to capture the ...

Figure 3-3: Microsoft's AutoMovie tool is Movie Maker 2's most intriguing feature.

Movie Maker 2's weaknesses include very limited trimming tools, which slows production, and a general lack of configurability. For example, you can't set levels on filters like blur, pixelate, and other special effects, which is standard on virtually all other editors. You can apply the filter twice to double the value, but if the levels are already too high in the base setting, you're out of luck.

Though Microsoft includes a great range of text motion effects for rolling credits and similar animations, there are no canned text styles to aid the design-challenged. You can't adjust audio volume at specific locations, only for the entire track, which complicates the use of background audio. There's no way to delete the original audio track (though you can mute it), which complicates sophisticated techniques like insert editing.

Cross-Reference

Insert editing is discussed in greater detail in Chapter 11.

The program has no DVD-authoring capabilities and can't output an MPEG-2 file, though it can output DV files compatible with virtually all third-party authoring programs. The only real deal breaker is the inability to place a graphic over the video, so if you want to add a logo or watermark, you're out of luck. Otherwise, Movie Maker 2 can get the job done, though it may take longer and be a less compelling video than that offered by the other programs discussed here.

VideoStudio 7

VideoStudio is a mature, capable video editor, though more muscular than artistic. Compared to its closest rival, Pinnacle Studio, VideoStudio offers more video-editing features but fewer creative options, and trails Studio significantly in DVD-authoring capabilities.

VideoStudio's interface is dominated by a large preview window that can be enlarged even further by clicking the arrow button on the bottom right. You can work in either timeline or storyboard mode (timeline mode is shown in Figure 3-4). The program directs workflow via the menu tabs on top, opening the proper libraries and tools as you select each tab. This structured workflow makes it simple for beginners to quickly get up and running.

VideoStudio is the only consumer editor that can batch capture clips based on time codes (a time-saving feature discussed in Chapter 10), and it's the only consumer editor with multi-cut editing, a mechanism for scanning through a captured file, marking in and out points of desired segments, and eliminating unwanted scenes. This is very efficient when you're capturing analog files without the scene detection provided by DV video.

The retail version of VideoStudio ships with a special edition of Cool 3D, a great tool for quickly and easily creating 3D titles, animated logos, and other effects. Though not as capable as the $49 retail version of Cool 3D, it's a great value that complements VideoStudio's overlay track, which can insert both still images and videos over the background video. That's how I inserted the Doceo Publishing Logo in the bottom right corner of the preview window shown in Figure 3-4.

In addition, VideoStudio provides great control over special effects, including the ability to set key frames, which allow you to customize effect values over the duration of the video, another professional feature (see Figure 3-5, Screen a).

Cross-Reference

Key frames and how to use them are discussed in Chapter 14.

However, Ulead lacks finesse in several key areas. First, its titling tool has crude positioning controls and lacks style presets (see Figure 3-5, Screen b). Like Movie Maker 2, you can only adjust the audio volume for each track as a whole; you can't adjust segments, which complicates the use of background audio (see Figure 3-5, Screen c). Finally, as discussed in the next chapter, VideoStudio offers very limited navigational flexibility when it comes to DVD design.

Tools   Preview window   Libraries

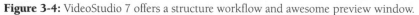

Background music track   Narration track   Title track

Overlay track

Video track

Figure 3-4: VideoStudio 7 offers a structure workflow and awesome preview window.

Pinnacle Studio 8

Studio 8 is my favorite consumer video editor, primarily because it helps me quickly and easily create high-quality productions and has truly awesome DVD-authoring capabilities. Weaknesses include a microscopic preview window, very limited special effects, and a slightly complicated interface.

Like VideoStudio and Movie Maker 2, Studio can operate in both storyboard and timeline mode, with timeline shown in Figure 3-6. All windows are fixed, and the library window converts to the tool window for trimming and accessing most other controls.

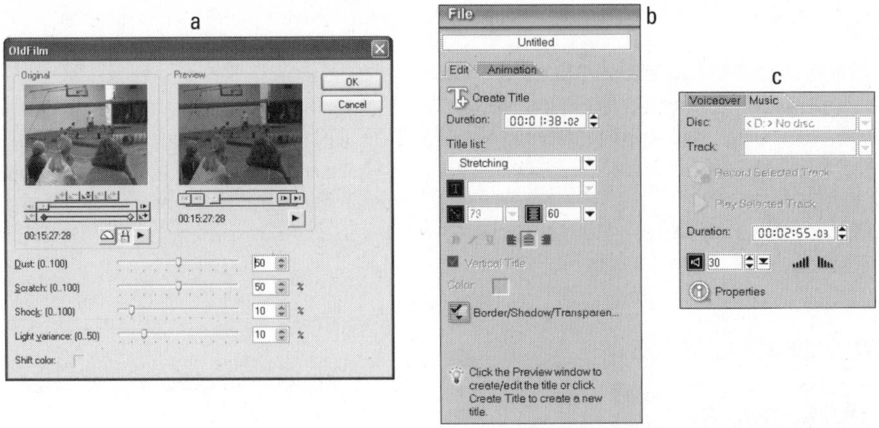

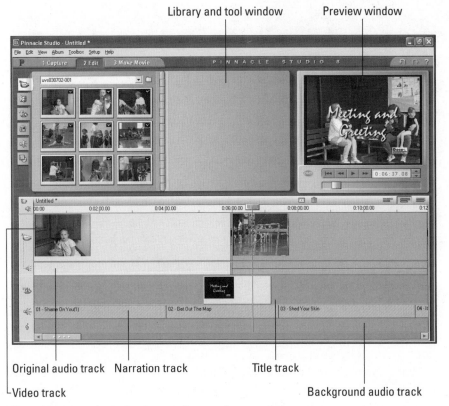

Figure 3-5: Among VideoStudio's special effects, (a) key frame support is great, but (b) titling tools and (c) audio volume adjustments are crude.

Library and tool window   Preview window

Original audio track   Narration track   Title track

Video track   Background audio track

Figure 3-6: Pinnacle Studio 8 in timeline mode.

Pinnacle has done a great job trickling down tools from its professional video-editing programs. For example, as I'll discuss in Chapter 11, its Hollywood FX transitions are exceptional for adding content-sensitive transitions that can make or break a video.

In addition, the title creation and text presets found in Title Deko — Studio's integrated title (and DVD menu) creator — are awesome, especially for those, like myself, who are font-challenged (see Figure 3-7, Screen a). As you can see with the Doceo Publishing logo in Figure 3-7, Studio also supports image overlay. As I'll discuss in more detail in the next chapter, Studio offers a highly functional DVD-authoring environment that far exceeds any other program in the consumer class as well as a great selection of transitions.

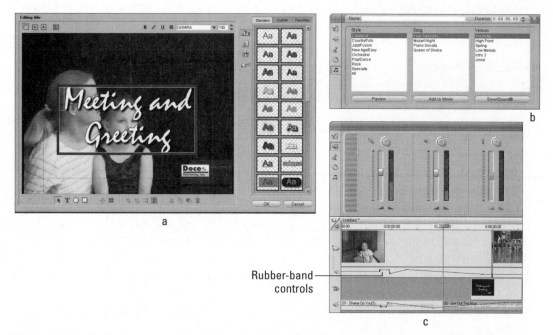

Figure 3-7: Studio high points include (a) a great titling utility, (b) integrated SmartSound (for custom-length, theme-based background audio creation), and (c) a real-time audio mixer with rubber-band controls on the timeline enabling further customization.

On the audio front, Studio is the only consumer editor to include SmartSound, a utility for creating custom soundtracks discussed in Chapter 12 (shown in Figure 3-7, Screen b). It's the only consumer program with a real-time audio mixer, so you can play your production and adjust the volume in all three tracks in real time. Studio is also the only editor with rubber-band controls on the timeline so you can customize volume even further (as shown in Figure 3-7, Screen c). To me, these last three features make background audio truly usable within Studio.

On the other hand, Studio hides many features in panels that aren't obvious to new users and doesn't really provide the workflow guidance VideoStudio offers, or the batch capture or multi-cut tool. Special effects are very limited, which isn't a big deal for me, since I'm pretty conservative, but this is a major issue for many other editors. Overall, however, for both consumer and many business users, Studio is all the video editor they'll ever need.

Why Only Three?

There are a number of consumer video-editing programs available, so why am I only describing three and ignoring the rest?

I take a pretty cavalier attitude about video editors. Specifically, unless they're from bona fide companies that are and have been in the video business, I tend to ignore them, at least until version three or four. Here's why.

Companies like Pinnacle and Ulead are in the video business because that's what they do. Their products are mature and honed by feedback from literally millions of users. Their products follow recognized user interface paradigms which themselves have been market proven. As long as either company is in business, they will be in the video business, so they care about their reputation for quality and support.

Most new companies that enter the video market do so to complete their product portfolio or perhaps extend into new markets. In two or three years, when growth slows in the video market, these newcomers will either be gone exploring other growth markets or just plain gone.

Invariably, products developed by market entrants without significant video experience violate established user interface paradigms. They almost have to, since if they don't, there's no compelling reason to buy them or no unique selling proposition. Unfortunately, in most instances, different isn't better. It's just different.

In addition, video has a unique set of hurdles you don't see until you try to jump them. When creating a new video-editing product, the developers may test with three or four DV cameras or DVD recorders, declare themselves compatible, and ship the product. However, variables in the general market are much broader, and problems invariably develop and usually only get ironed out after the third or fourth version.

At the same time, it's not like the established developers are sitting still. Studio is on version 8, with version 9 coming in early 2004, while VideoStudio is up to version 7. In the DVD-authoring market, Sonic's MyDVD is up to version 5. So these products have evolved quite nicely and offer a very competitive feature set at a price that's only slightly more expensive.

So do yourself a favor. When buying video-related products, stick to video companies, at least until other products entering the market are up to version 4.

Moving On Up to the Prosumer Level

The next level up from consumer video editors is prosumer editors, including Adobe Premiere Pro ($699), Pinnacle Edition ($699), Sonic Foundry Vegas ($399), and Ulead MediaStudio Pro ($495). Not only are these tools much more expensive than the consumer tools, they're also more complicated to learn. Unless you edit frequently, you'll find yourself learning how to use these programs each time you attempt to edit video, which is frustrating.

Still, some users will find themselves bumping into limitations of the consumer video editors. Consider moving on up if you need these additional capabilities:

- **More video tracks.** Most consumer editors offer only four or five tracks, while prosumer products offer up to 99 tracks. These additional tracks can be used for video overlay or picture-in-picture effects, both discussed later in this chapter, or simply multiple titles.

- **Chroma key/blue-screen effects.** These effects allow two videos to be combined with specified areas of one video superimposed on the other.

- **Picture-in-picture effects.** This is where one or more videos play in a small window within the larger video window.

- **Superior color correction.** While most consumer editors offer some color correction capabilities, it's generally crude and often doesn't work well with problem footage. Prosumer editors offer more advanced controls and interfaces that are much more effective.

- **Motion controls.** These allow developers to zoom into a region in the video or pan across a video or still image.

- **Multiple sequences.** For longer projects, rather than edit the video as one long component, often it's convenient to edit sequence by sequence and later merge the various sequences into the final production.

Cross-Reference

For more on these additional capabilities provided by the prosumer editors, turn to Chapter 14.

These are the high points in the prosumer category; as you'll see in the following discussion, each product presents its own unique strengths and weaknesses.

What's Past Is Past

A touch of history assists our understanding of the current state of the market, circa December 2003. For years, if you looked in Webster's dictionary under "prosumer video editor," you would have seen a screenshot from Adobe Premiere. Well, not really, but you get the point.

Ulead's MediaStudio Pro was always there but was generally regarded by most as far behind in features, usability, or both. However, Adobe was slow to respond to changing market conditions like DV cameras, DVD authoring, streaming, or even the availability of processors with hyper-threaded technology.

Though Adobe added some useful capabilities like a new title maker and SmartSound audio in version 6.5, the interface changed very little overall, and Premiere's editing and special effects capabilities, once the best in the industry, were definitely slipping. This left both a features gap and a technology gap for other companies to march through.

Having reached the magical fourth version, Sonic Foundry's Vegas struck first in early 2003, with excellent color correction and chroma key tools and outstanding audio production capabilities, including the ability to create Dolby 5.1 surround-sound audio tracks. Then Ulead MediaStudio Pro shipped with real-time MPEG-2 capture and outstanding real-time preview capabilities. Most impressive is Pinnacle Edition 5, with an elegant, if somewhat cryptic interface, excellent chroma key, color adjustment and motion path tools, as well as a brilliant architecture for leveraging the benefits of hyper-threaded processors.

Then, just when it felt safe to discount Adobe's long-term survival in the prosumer market, Premiere Pro shipped, a complete rewrite that seemingly answered all these challenges and more. I'll discuss the strengths and weaknesses of all these programs by reviewing them component by component.

By the time you read this book, of course, the aspects of each program we're discussing will likely have changed, and new products will have been launched by other vendors. Hopefully, the descriptions here will help you understand each feature in more depth so you can judge the effectiveness of the upgraded feature set or new product entries.

Interface

Few things in life are more subjective than assessing the effectiveness of a program's user interface. All of the programs discussed are at least up to version 4, with two (MediaStudio Pro and Premiere) up to version 7. All have raving fans that would argue long into the night that their chosen program is miles ahead of the other in editing effectiveness. Clearly, all of their interfaces have been refined to a great degree by user feedback and are highly usable.

Let's take a look at the respective interfaces, while I identify their strengths and weaknesses, and you can draw your own conclusions. Just for fun, I'll rank all the programs on a scale from three to zero in this and future comparisons. Then I'll add up all the points at the end and see who wins.

SONY VEGAS

Vegas (shown in Figure 3-8) was developed by Sonic Foundry, the developer of Sound Forge, my all-time favorite audio editor, and the fourth generation editor has many compelling features. First, it avoids clutter by allowing you to anchor or snap control windows into defined locations, something Premiere and MediaStudio don't enable. I adore the large preview window, especially in split-screen view. You may not be able to see it, but in color it shows the area on the left with a heinous blue tinge, with color correction very evident and effective on the right.

However, to a degree, Vegas' roots in audio editing puts it at a slight disadvantage against products with a more video-intensive heritage, because many of the interface metaphors feel audio-related, not video-related, and are foreign to me. For example, in most editors, like Premiere, if I want to adjust audio volume at a particular point in the video, I touch the audio track to create a contact point and drag it down. With Vegas, I have to create an "envelope," which is a foreign concept.

I'm also a big stickler for being able to set duration, in part because I run tests on multiple programs and need to create the exact same scenario, and in part because I'm a precision freak. Vegas doesn't let you directly set the duration of an asset on the timeline; you have to grab and pull it to the desired location. Generally, this means you need to zoom deeply into the timeline, which also slows things down, and Vegas provides no duration feedback when you're dragging an asset, something most other programs provide.

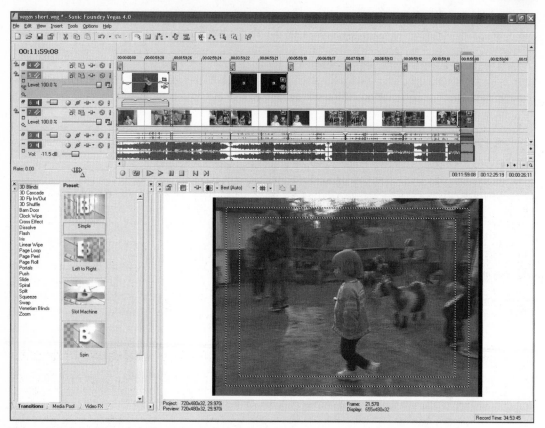

Figure 3-8: Sony Vegas; love that split-screen preview window.

If you're a "feel" editor, who doesn't really care about fixed durations, but instead goes with what feels good and looks right, you probably don't care about this. Some Vegas users have told me they didn't know you couldn't set duration before I told them, which obviously means it's not important to them. Still, for me, this deficit makes it tough to be precise, which slows me down significantly.

Equally important to some publishers is that Vegas is the only editor that can't open multiple projects simultaneously, a problem if you're working with large products. In addition, I don't find Vegas' timeline intuitive in use, which means that many controls are seldom where I expect them to be or work the way I expect them to work. As you'll see, Vegas makes some top-notch tools, but in my view, the timeline interface is a bit more difficult to use than several others.

Finally — and call me shallow — I like exciting interfaces with good colors and modern-looking tools, just like I'd prefer driving an expensive European sedan over a Yugo. Vegas is a drab, khaki brown that doesn't inspire me the way that Edition or Premiere Pro do, or even Final Cut Pro on the Mac side. If I'm going to spend five hours editing a video, I prefer a classy environment, while Vegas tends more toward the functional.

MEDIASTUDIO PRO (MSP)

MSP is a quietly functional product that's kind of old school, with the basic four-window interface (source, preview, tools, and timeline) with very video-centric controls, which makes it easy for users graduating from consumer programs to pick up (see Figure 3-9). Though the interface can get cluttered as you move windows around, Ulead includes a project template that snaps it back into place, a feature shared by Premiere.

Figure 3-9: MediaStudio Pro, a quietly compelling product that's capable but a bit dowdy.

Unlike Vegas, which is almost entirely menu-driven, Ulead calls many tools via icons, which is a touch more intuitive, once you learn what each icon does. However, also unlike Vegas and all other editors, MSP still uses the A|B roll-editing interface, an editing paradigm that assumes that there are two primary tracks, the A and B roll, and only enables transitions to be inserted between these two tracks. This complicates organization and takes the very potent transitions tool out of your hands above the first two tracks.

In terms of large project handling, Studio can import one project into another project, essentially combining them, which is a nice step up from Vegas, but unlike Edition and Premiere, you can't simultaneously manage multiple project separately. Aesthetically, however, MediaStudio is more functional than compelling, a consideration if the appearance of your editing environment is important.

PINNACLE EDITION

If Pinnacle Edition were a girl, she'd be a dark-haired Italian, gorgeous, mysterious, and petulant. You could spend years getting to know her and still find deep hidden spots of brilliance. Oh yes, and she would be quite difficult at times, and you'd definitely have to learn Italian to get along.

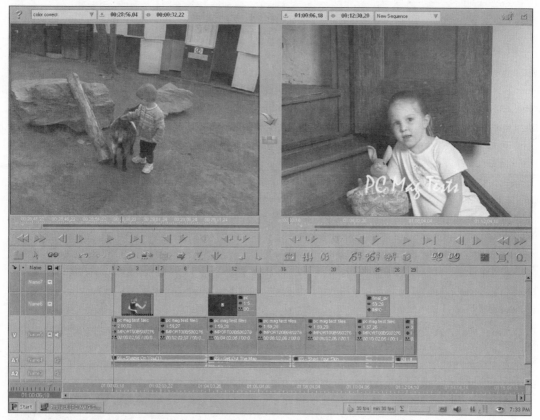

Figure 3-10: Pinnacle Edition: definitely the best looking, but perhaps not the most likely to succeed.

Probably the most descriptive comment I've heard about Edition is from a friend who sat down and said, "I thought I would have to learn to read hieroglyphics to use the program." If you look at Figure 3-10, you'll see why, with icons driving almost the complete editing experience.

This and the other features discussed here make Edition extremely difficult to learn. However, icon selection and placement are entirely customizable, so you can create your own optimal editing environment. Once you're up and running, it feels like you're working with all of your key tools within quick reach, which turbo-charges your efforts.

Edition handles multiple open sequences with aplomb, simplifying large project production. It resists clutter stubbornly with totally nested windows but provides one-button access to most critical tools via hot keys. The interface is a tasteful muted green (yes, there is such a thing) and is easy on the eyes and soul, the kind of place you don't mind spending hours and hours working. Edition also saves your edits after every edit decision, so after spending those hours working, you can quickly recover from a random crash or power outage.

Edition also has an integrated DVD-authoring interface, which saves dollars and learning time over the two-program solutions offered by other vendors. Though I don't like it as much as Studio, it certainly is functional, and overall, Edition sets a very high bar for other editors in the class.

ADOBE PREMIERE PRO

Then came Premiere Pro (see Figure 3-11). I generally pull for the underdog, rather than the favorite, and was quite prepared to dislike Premiere Pro, but there's really not much to dislike. Adobe did its job, finding the best aspects of other programs and designing them in, while coming up with a few great touches itself, mostly in the tools arena.

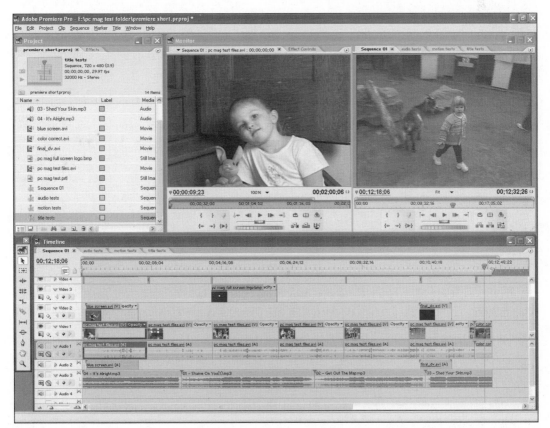

Figure 3-11: Adobe Premiere Pro. Despite all the hoopla about radical changes, it still looks pretty familiar, which is a good thing.

Best of all if you're considering upgrading to Premiere Pro, the basic interface is pretty much unchanged, so you'll be able to run the program with a minimal learning curve. This and Premiere's overall general usability make the program pretty easy to learn, even for complete beginners.

Adobe added multiple project support via tabbed windows on the timeline — more elegant than Edition's approach — and consolidated many windows, which should help reduce clutter. As with the previous version, you can snap the interface back into customizable workspace configurations, a one-click mechanism for restoring order to your workspace.

Gone is the A|B roll-editing metaphor, so you can use transitions on any track. Adobe moved its toolbar into a separate window, which is a touch more convenient than before but still less accessible than Edition's. Other than this, most of the radical function upgrades are under the hood, in the tools section like color correction and motion controls discussed next. Table 3-1 lists how these four products added up in the interface category.

Table 3-1   Interface Scores

	Sony Vegas	*MediaStudio Pro*	*Pinnacle Edition*	*Adobe Premiere Pro*
Ease of use	1	2	0	3
Editing speed	2	2	3	2
Precision	1	2	2	3
Handling big projects	0	1	2	3
Clutter	2	1	3	1
Overall interface	1.2	1.6	2	2.4

Color Correction

The importance of color correction really hit home after a day at the Atlanta Zoo, working with an incorrectly white-balanced camera. As a result, the video was tinted blue and was unusable, but I had some very relevant test footage for color correction trials. Let's see how the prosumer editors stack up (see Figure 3-12).

Vegas' tool offers several great features (see Figure 3-12, Screen a). First, the three levels of correction are for low, mid-, and high tones, providing the precision necessary to fine-tune your settings. You adjust colors by moving the little white dot around within each of the circles, which is the technique I use most often, or by using the eyedropper controls to choose either the complementary or adjustment colors, a technique that never really sunk in. I'd get nasty messages from Mac fanatics if I didn't point out that three-wheel color correction controls first appeared on Final Cut Pro, a Mac-only program, so consider it so pointed out.

The second way cool feature is the split-screen preview, which you can view on-screen or out on an analog monitor, which makes it very easy to see the fruits of your adjustments. Overall it's an excellent tool for advanced users, though a bit tough for beginners.

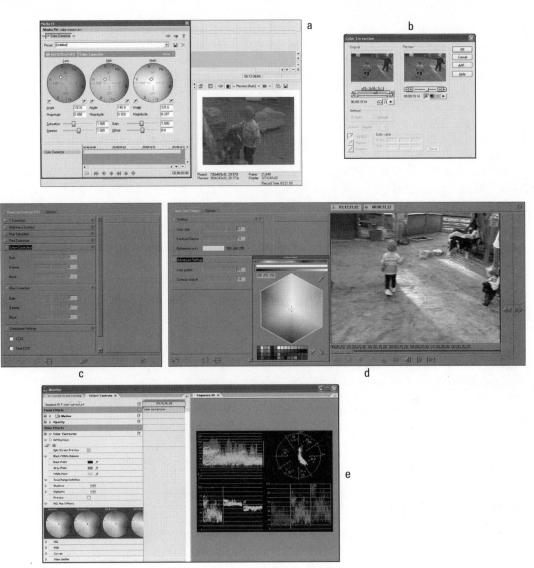

Figure 3-12: The many shades of color correction. (a) Vegas color wheels, (b) Ulead's limited functionality, (c) and (d) Pinnacle Edition's alternative controls, and (e) Adobe Premiere's kitchen sink approach.

As you can see from Figure 3-12, Screen b, Ulead didn't invest a lot here, and in truth, the adjustment isn't that much better than those available with consumer programs. Though it's probably tough to see, MediaStudio Pro offers two modes, auto mode, which works pretty well, and manual, which simply doesn't have the breadth of controls offered by any of the other tools. Definitely not a program strength.

Figure 3-12, Screens c and d, showcases Edition's unique strength of multiple controls for most tasks. Screen c shows their serious control for advanced users, which allows you to adjust virtually every color parameter you can think of. With this tool, I was able to adjust blue tones directly, which worked well.

Screen d shows Edition's relatively new Auto Color adjustment, which is much less complicated. Here, you click the whitish box next to reference color, which opens the color selection screen that you see. Use the eyedropper to choose a color that's supposed to be white, and Edition makes it white and automatically adjusts all other colors. Then you can play with the other controls to fine-tune the results. This approach worked the best for me among all tools that I've tested, though I still long for a split-screen preview like Vegas.

As shown in Figure 3-12, Screen e, Premiere came out with a kitchen sink control that includes color wheels, histograms, and vector scopes — or funky graphical representations of color in the video Between you, me, and the wall, the latter two are eye candy that play to the 1 to 2 percent of Premiere users who actually worked in an analog production studio. They look nice, but most users get little benefit.

Fortunately, Adobe also put in some simpler tools, like the Black, Gray, and White Point adjustments that work very much like Edition's auto-correction tool — you touch an area that should be black, gray, or white, and Premiere makes it so, magically adjusting all other colors. Of course, you can use all the other tools to fine-tune the results.

In use, Adobe's control was much more "twitchy" and tended to produce bizarre, almost psyche-delic results if you selected an area on-screen that it didn't like. This was easy enough to correct (just choose an adjacent area) but a touch disconcerting nonetheless.

Just before press time, Pinnacle sent us beta color-correction capabilities that will start shipping with Edition version 5.5. Pinched from Edition's big sister product, Liquid Purple, the new capabilities include advanced vector scopes, secondary color correction that enables producers to match video shot on the same location with different cameras, and other tools.

Obviously, Adobe struck very close to the mark, and Pinnacle felt the need to boost these suddenly high-profile color-correction capabilities. Though Premiere's capabilities were impressive, the new modules boost Edition to the top point-getter in all categories, as shown in Table 3-2.

Table 3-2   Color-Correction Tools

	Sony Vegas	MediaStudio Pro	Pinnacle Edition	Adobe Premiere Pro
Ease of use	2	2	3	2
Range of tools	2	1	3	2
Effectiveness	2	1	3	2
Overall color correction	2	1.33	3	2

Motion Controls

Video editors use motion controls for a variety of purposes, including zooming into or around a video, moving a title or logo or panning around a still image. To be truly useful, both precision and a visual working environment are critical.

As you can see in Figure 3-13, Vegas (shown in Screen a) presents the biggest canvas, a great working environment for visualizing your motion in and around the image. Numeric controls on the upper left complement the manual positioning tools to a great degree, with full key frame control available on the bottom.

MediaStudio (shown in Figure 3-13, Screen b) presents the same basic toolset, but the canvas is much smaller, making it much more difficult to use. However, MediaStudio does offer some 3D tools for manipulating the video on the X, Y, and Z planes.

Edition is even more robust in this regard (see Figure 3-13, Screen c), with controls for manipulating camera and motion, and inserting effects like shadows and frames, along with a much better visual environment than MSP, though not quite up to Vegas' standards. Buried in one of Edition's classic editors, however, is the still-image motion creation environment shown in Figure 3-14, which is almost up to the standards set by Canopus Imaginate, discussed in Chapter 13. While Vegas' tool comes close, MSP and Premiere are clearly behind for still image work.

Premiere (see Figure 3-13, Screen d) offers only 2D motion controls and some interesting camera view filters that provide limited 3D capabilities, though most 3D effects come from vendors who bundle capture cards and their own software with Premiere, like Matrox and Canopus. Adobe's design palette is great if you know exactly what you're trying to accomplish, but it's inferior to Vegas if you're designing an effect from scratch.

Adobe's unique contribution to the mix is the ability to set key frames by editing parameter, which makes it much easier to create complex effects. For example, if you're adjusting size, motion, and opacity for a clip in Premiere, each parameter gets its own key frames, which are easy to set and monitor. With other editors, you have to set all three parameters for each key frame. Oftentimes, when you adjust size, you may affect position in some way, which can't happen with Premiere. Table 3-3 summarizes how these four products match up in the motion control arena.

Table 3-3　Motion Controls

	Sony Vegas	MediaStudio Pro	Pinnacle Edition	Adobe Premiere Pro
Visual design	3	0	2	2
Precision	2	2	3	3
3D motion	0	2	3	0
Still image	2	1	3	2
Overall motion	1.75	1.25	2.75	1.75

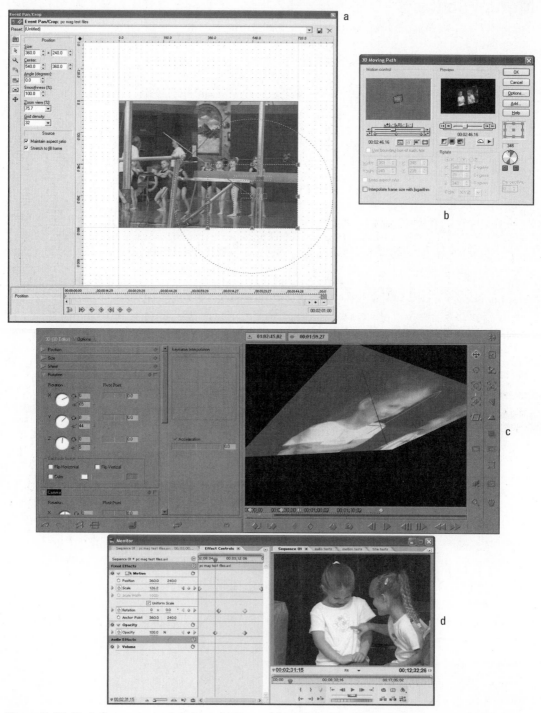

Figure 3-13: Tools for moving and shaking: (a) Vegas, (b) MediaStudio, (c) Pinnacle Edition, and (d) Adobe Premiere.

Figure 3-14: Edition's excellent image-panning tool almost rivals Canopus Imaginate in functionality.

Transitions

Transitions are effects that help move viewers from one clip to another. As you'll see in Chapter 11, I'm not big on the aggressive use of transitions, or most special effects for that matter, but the number and configurability of transitions has become a big battleground for prosumer editors.

All video editors will have a number of basic transitions that preview in real time and some advanced transitions that may require rendering to view. All can preview on-screen or out to an analog monitor, which makes preview capabilities a wash between the programs.

Cross-Reference

For a complete discussion of transitions and how to include them in your video projects, go to Chapter 11.

Accordingly, when I look at a program's transition offering, I analyze four basic factors: the number of 2D and 3D effects, their configurability, the nature and extent of "motivated" transitions, and the effects that relate to the content of the video. More on this in a moment when I discuss Pinnacle Edition. Figure 3-15 contains screens from all four programs.

Vegas has a good range of 2D and 3D effects that are highly configurable and key-frameable, but there are no motivated transitions (see Figure 3-15, Screen a). MediaStudio (see Figure 3-15, Screen b) has fewer 3D transitions, fewer configuration options, and again makes you work in a very cramped workspace.

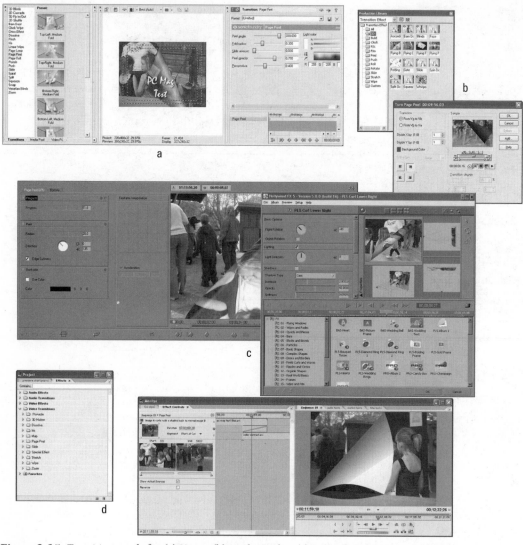

Figure 3-15: Transitions tools for (a) Vegas, (b) MediaStudio, (c) Pinnacle Edition, and (d) Adobe Premiere.

Pinnacle Edition is the star of this show (see Figure 3-15, Screen c), with an extensive range of highly configurable 2D and 3D effects, and best of all, it has Hollywood FX, which is an integrated transition package that provides an additional range of even more highly configurable and motivated transitions. Here's the skinny on motivated transitions and why I like them so much.

When I'm producing a wedding video, I want to stick to the theme as much as possible. This means using wedding bells, rings, photo albums, and hearts as transitions whenever possible. For example, as you'll see in Chapter 11, when transitioning from the ceremony to the reception, I might use a photo album transition that shows the video being placed in a photo album and then the album slowly closes (see Figure 11-36 in Chapter 11).

This kind of transition makes people smile, while a double zig-zag Venetian blind transition makes them wonder "why the heck did he use that one?" That's the power of the motivated transition, and only Pinnacle offers it, as well as outstanding configurability and selection. If you're a transition freak, Edition is your only choice.

Premiere is only average in this regard (see Figure 3-15, Screen d), which translates to a decent range of transitions and a good range of configuration options for most transitions other than page peel. There's not a motivated transition to be found, however.

Table 3-4 shows how these products stack up against each other with transition controls.

Table 3-4   Transition Controls

	Sony Vegas	MediaStudio Pro	Pinnacle Edition	Adobe Premiere Pro
2D effects	2	2	3	2
3D effects	2	1	3	2
Motivated effects	0	0	3	0
Configurability	2	1	3	2
Overall transitions	1.5	1	3	1.5

2D and 3D Effects

Two dimensional and 3D effects comprise the largest body of effects included with most video editors. In my view, the most important special effects are color correction and video overlay, which are covered separately, and picture-in-picture and speed adjustments, which I'll address here.

All editors otherwise support a fairly common range of similar effects, like blur, pixelate, mosaic, speed change, mirror, clip, crop, and many others. Beyond these common features, each editor tends to go its own way as categorized in Table 3-5. Note that this table presents what I consider to be the highlights and is not intended to be comprehensive.

Vegas, for example, incorporates multiple film effects, allowing producers to make their video look like a variety of old films. Sony throws in a sprinkling of "true" special effects, like light rays, newsprint, and wave effects. You can apply 3D page peel transitions to move objects on and off the timeline, and supplement both 3D effects and 3D picture-in-picture effects with a third-party plug-in called the Plugin Pac, available at www.debugmode.com.

In contrast, MediaStudio goes heavy on true special effects like wind, lightning, clouds, and spotlight, while also including some video painting effects. Again, 3D and picture-in-picture effects are fairly limited.

Edition ignores film and paint effects almost entirely but goes all out on true special effects, 3D effects, and especially picture-in-picture effects, with Hollywood FX again supplementing the program's base offering. Since most advanced Premiere users will create special effects in Adobe After Effects, Premiere's offering is somewhat limited.

Table 3-5   Types of Effects by Program

	Sony Vegas	MediaStudio Pro	Pinnacle Edition	Adobe Premiere Pro
Film effects	Five film effects, two grain effects	Limited	Limited	Limited
Painting effects	No	Charcoal, watercolor, oil painting, and texture mapping	No	No
True special effects	Black and white, lens flare, light rays, newsprint, sepia, wave, and shatter (with plug-in)	Black and white, bubbles, lens flare, noise, wind shear, lightning, animation, spotlight, clouds	Accordion, black and white, curtain, explosion, lens flare, page peel, stained glass, and waterwave	Black and white, lightning, lens flare, wind, and strobe
3D effects	Limited	Motion only	Very extensive, including Hollywood FX	Limited
Picture-in-picture	2D/3D via plug-in	2D/3D, limited configurability	Dedicated picture-in-picture with multiple controls, including 3D	2D/3D limited configurability

SLOW MOTION

All programs can change the base playback speed of your video. From a technology standpoint, this is very easy when speeding the video up, since the editor can simply drop frames out.

However, it's much more complicated when slowing the video down, since the editor must create a number of additional frames. For example, when accelerating playback by four times, the editor simply drops three frames out of every four. However, slowing playback to 25 percent of the original forces the editor to create three additional frames for every one.

Editors use two basic techniques to create these additional frames: frame duplication and frame interpolation. As the name suggests, frame duplication merely duplicates the frame as many times as necessary, which is precise but somewhat choppy in appearance.

During frame interpolation, the editor looks at the actual video frames and creates intermediate frames that attempt to predict where the objects in motion should be for those particular frames. Figure 3-16 shows the difference between the two approaches.

As you can see, MediaStudio Pro and Edition are frame duplicators, as evidenced by the crisp image shown in Figure 3-16. If you page through the file frame by frame, you'll notice that every other frame is identical, creating a slightly staggered appearance during real-time playback.

Vegas

MediaStudio Pro

Edition

Premiere

Figure 3-16: MediaStudio Pro and Edition duplicate frames, while Vegas and Premiere interpolate.

In contrast, Vegas and Premiere actually create new frames, which is why we see shadows of the golf club in the upper left-hand corner. If you page through these files frame by frame, every frame is different, though frames with motion are definitely less crisp.

Note that this video is probably worst-case footage for the interpolators, since the sharp detail in the golf club highlights any aberrations. It's difficult to say which approach is best, and it's probably more important to understand the difference and how to spot it when looking at your footage.

There's one more point relating to the ability to transition into a speed change effect. For example, suppose you were filming your child at bat during a Little League game and want to slow the video down just before the pitch she hits for the game-winning home run. However, you don't want to quickly cut from full speed to slow motion; you want to transition into it slowly.

Two editors, Vegas and Edition, handle this with specific features. Vegas' is called a "velocity enve-lope" (see Figure 3-17), which allows you to smoothly segue from full speed into slow motion. Edition uses a "dynamic time warp" to accomplish the same result.

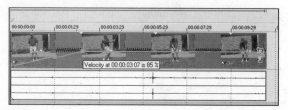

Figure 3-17: Vegas' velocity envelope transitions smoothly from normal to fast or slow motion.

With Premiere, you can moderate speed from one key frame to another to a moderate degree, but not with as much precision as Vegas or Edition. With MediaStudio you're forced to cut between the two clips using different playback speeds, abruptly shifting the viewer from full speed to slow motion.

PICTURE-IN-PICTURE

Picture-in-picture (P-i-P) is another effect I frequently use, and the respective program's capabilities are shown in Figure 3-18. With the aforementioned plug-in pack, Vegas (see Figure 3-18, Screen a) becomes quite functional with both 2D and 3D picture-in-picture, and you can use the program's own border effect to create a border around the P-i-P, but no shadow effects. MediaStudio (see Figure 3-18, Screen b) can create both 2D and 3D P-i-P effects, but we were unable to find a way to create either borders or shadows.

P-i-P is another Edition strong point (see Figure 3-18, Screen c), with extensive dedicated 2D and 3D P-i-P controls complete with borders, shadows, and transparency controls. In addition, Hollywood FX incorporates some pretty nifty transitions involving P-i-P effects, another advantage. Finally, though Premiere (see Figure 3-18, Screen d) can get the job done, creating both 2D and 3D P-i-P effects with borders (but no shadows), you have to incorporate multiple filters to get there.

Taking all these factors into account, Table 3-6 shows the total ratings for 2D and 3D effects.

Table 3-6   2D and 3D Effects

	Sony Vegas	MediaStudio Pro	Pinnacle Edition	Adobe Premiere Pro
2D effects	2	2	2	2
3D effects	2	1	3	1
True special effects	2	3	2	1
Speed change	3	2	3	2
Picture-in-picture	2	1	3	2
Overall special effects	2.2	1.8	2.6	1.6

Figure 3-18: Pretty as a picture-in-picture effect. Picture-in-picture controls for (a) Vegas, (b) MediaStudio, (c) Edition, and (d) Premiere.

Titling Utility

Virtually all productions have titles, and the titling utilities should make it simple for designers to create and implement attractive titles. This involves several components.

First, the titling utility should allow designers to create titles over the background video, with precise free-form placement, as opposed to using the carriage return and space bar to place the title.

Second, the titling utility should have text styles that include font, color, shadow, edge, and background that users can easily drag and drop into the production and save for later use. You definitely should not have to design from scratch.

In addition, the utility should allow the designer to kern text and alter the leading of the text as well as create objects like squares, circles, and rectangles to sit behind the text. Beyond these minimums, titling utilities get extra credit for components like title styles and animated effects beyond those enabled via motion controls. With this as background, let's see how each editor stacks up, using Figure 3-19 as a reference.

Vegas (see Figure 3-19, Screen a) has an acceptable titling utility but nothing more. You design in one window and preview in another, which is awkward, though free-form placement tools are nice. Vegas offers both kerning and leading controls, but it lacks text styles and the ability to create objects. Deformation, or the ability to warp or bend letters, is the only extra capability.

MediaStudio (see Figure 3-19, Screen b) is actually a step down from Vegas, since you don't design directly over the background video, and there is no free-form text placement. MediaStudio shares the same lack of objects and text styles, but it adds text-specific motion and special effects.

Figure 3-19: Comparing title editors: (a) Vegas, (b) MediaStudio, (c) Edition, and (d) Premiere.

Edition (see Figure 3-19, Screen c) is frustrating because it uses the same title designer that Studio used several versions ago, not Studio's latest, which is actually top-notch. This means that Pinnacle's $99 product has a better titling utility than its $699 product, which definitely shouldn't be.

You design over the video, which is nice, and Edition offers multiple styles, though not as many as Studio. You can create objects, kern and lead your text, and save your presets, all very nice features.

What's frustrating is that Edition retains archaic text-editing capabilities that seem to treat every letter in a title as a separate entity. If you insert a carriage return to split a title into two lines, Edition treats it as two entities, complicating alignment issues immensely. As with the DVD-authoring module, Pinnacle needs to get its design teams together and share the best components between the products.

Then there's Premiere (see Figure 3-19, Screen d), which did it right in version 6.5 and wisely saw no reason to change a thing with Premiere Pro. Premiere is the complete titling package, with exquisite precision, text styles, object creation, kerning, leading, and free-form text placement over the background video. Premiere even ships with "motivated" title styles, which, like Edition's Hollywood FX transitions, are event-specific.

That is, if you're creating a golfing video, you have several golf-related titles to choose from, including that shown in Figure 3-19. There are also templates for business, weddings, music, nature, birth ceremonies, and many other events, rounding out clearly the best titling utility available on a prosumer package. Table 3-7 sums up how the editors compare in titling.

Table 3-7   Titling Tools

	Sony Vegas	*MediaStudio Pro*	*Pinnacle Edition*	*Adobe Premiere Pro*
Visual design	1	1	2	3
Text styles	0	0	2	3
Object creation	0	0	2	3
Precision	1	0	1	3
Overall titling	0.5	0.25	1.75	3

Overlay

Overlay effects allow videographers to combine two videos into one by "keying out" certain portions of video. The most common application of video overlay is the weatherperson on the nightly news, who actually stands in front of a green wall in the television studio staring at a television monitor off to the side that's showing the video weather map. Back in the production room, the real-time video-editing equipment "keys out" the green, "overlaying" the weather person over the weather map video and sending it out over the airwaves.

Most video overlay is shot over bright blue or green backgrounds because it's easy for weatherpersons and other subjects to avoid wearing clothing containing these colors, which obviously would get keyed out along with the background. To get good results, you need very even, shadow-free lighting and high-quality input; VHS and 8mm need not apply.

Once the video is captured and input into the editor, you use the overlay tool to identify the color to eliminate, usually by clicking on the background with an eyedropper, and the editor does the rest.

In the good old days, there were basically two tools you had to worry about: similarity and edge smoothness.

Similarity tells the editor how far to stray from the original color chosen, since even the most evenly lighted background has a range of colors, rather than just one. Typically, you raise the similarity control until the background color is eliminated, but no further, since if the similarity is increased too far, you may start to eliminate clothing, hair, or other elements that are supposed to remain. The other very common tool was edge smoothness, which filtered the line between the keyed and the background video, smoothing out jagged edges (also called *jaggies*) that often appear in diagonal lines.

Today, programs have eschewed these simple and obvious names for a host of other names like "threshold" or "cutoff" that accomplish similar functions. Sometimes you see a control for smoothness, sometimes not, but basically you just go in and wiggle the controls until you find one that makes the background color go away and another to smooth the edges between the foreground and background video.

Cross-Reference

I cover video overlay in detail in Chapter 14.

When comparing video editors, ease of use and clarity of controls is nice, but like color correction, the proof of the pudding is in the actual performance. As shown in Figure 3-20, this is an area where Vegas really excelled, with a very smooth transition between the dancing girl and my daughter Whatley in the background, and excellent color. As you'll see in a minute, however, this quality comes at pretty stiff price, as Vegas was the slowest editor in the bunch by a significant margin.

In contrast, MediaStudio Pro was a poor performer, primarily because the smoothness controls created a blue halo effect that rendered the video unusable. No smoothing translates to extreme jaggies, which is what you see in Figure 3-20.

Edition produced the second best quality, with only faint jaggies showing through in the video, while Premiere was a bit behind Edition. Note that we ran all tests for Vegas, Edition, and Premiere with smoothness set to the maximum setting. Table 3-8 ranks the program's respective video overlay performance.

Table 3-8   Video Overlay Performance

	Sony Vegas	MediaStudio Pro	Pinnacle Edition	Adobe Premiere Pro
Chroma key	3	0	2	1

Audio Controls

Audio is becoming increasingly important to many projects. Traditionally, audio editors produced the audio, while video editors produced the video, and the two streams met for final production just before rendering. Since Vegas entered the market with extensive audio capabilities, video editors

Vegas

MediaStudio Pro

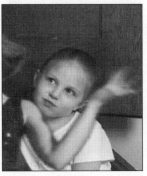

Edition

Premiere

Figure 3-20: Overlay is all about jagged-free edges, and Vegas excels here. Here we're overlaying a dancing girl over my daughter, who looks like she's giving her the evil eye.

have taken an increasing share of the audio-editing load. Table 3-9 identifies the key features of the four prosumer editors.

Table 3-9   Audio Feature Set and Score Card

	Sony Vegas	MediaStudio Pro	Pinnacle Edition	Adobe Premiere Pro
Audio editor	No	Yes	No	No
Real-time audio mixer	No	Yes	Yes	Yes
Noise-removal filter	No	No	No	Yes
Surround sound	Yes	No	No	No (third party, $299)
AC-3 encoding	Stereo	Stereo	No	No (third party, $299)
Third-party audio filters	Direct X	Direct X	No	VST Filters
Overall audio rating	3	2	1	3

Briefly, an audio editor is a separate tool for performing simple edits on the audio component of your video, which often is convenient. MediaStudio provides one, while Adobe, Pinnacle, and Sony, which sell separate audio editors, don't.

A real-time audio mixer allows you to play your video and adjust the volume of the respective tracks in real time, which you can later fine-tune. This is a great feature that really speeds multi-track audio production.

Noise removal gives you the ability to remove background noises from your video, but as discussed in Chapter 12, it's not a panacea. For example, if there's an air conditioner running in the background or your camera simply generates a consistent hum while shooting, noise removal can often limit or remove these noises. However, it doesn't always work well, and it's better to shoot good quality audio rather than allowing in background noises and assuming you can edit them out later. Still, it's a real convenience if the video editor includes them, but if not, you can generally purchase third-party products to accomplish the same purpose.

Surround-sound mixing gives you the ability to assign audio tracks to a specific location in the surround-sound spectrum. For example, in Figure 3-21, you see the five-speaker setup in the surround panner. The small diamond shown in front of the front center speaker in the large surround panner window is the assigned speaker location. Smaller diamonds in the smaller panner windows next to each track show their assigned locations. While very cool, this feature is primarily important only to those creating surround-sound productions, whether for DVD or distribution via Windows Media format.

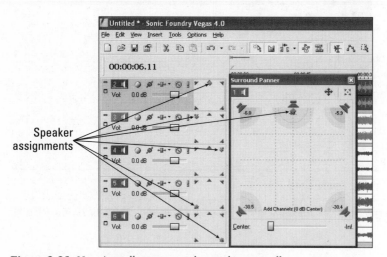

Figure 3-21: Vegas' excellent surround-sound panner allows you to assign each audio track to a speaker.

As you'll see in Chapter 17, AC-3 encoding helps ensure compatibility of DVDs in the U.S. market, which is clearly a good thing. Finally, the ability to use third-party audio filters is a huge feature that allows videographers to access extensive editing functionality like noise reduction within the video editor. Absent this feature, you essentially have to do all audio processing in a separate audio editor, which is time-consuming and can lead to synchronization and other production problems.

With this as background, let's see how the editors stack up. Early releases of Vegas debuted a number of features, like the ability to implement third-party audio filters directly within the video editor, essentially making it unnecessary to use a separate audio editor. Then, as surround-sound mixing became important for DVD authors, Vegas gained this capability, as well as encoding to AC-3 format.

Vegas lacks a real-time audio mixer, which comes standard on all other video editors, so you have to adjust volume track by track in non-real time, which can get tedious. While you can access the excellent noise-removal feature demonstrated in Chapter 12 from Vegas, you have to purchase it from Sony separately.

MediaStudio offers a good mix of audio functionality, with a separate audio editor, real-time audio mixer, stereo AC-3 encoding, and the ability to use third-party DirectX filters. Missing is surround sound and a noise-removal filter.

Other than a real-time audio mixer and minimal audio filters, Edition doesn't do much on the audio front, though the recent acquisition of Steinberg should bolster Edition's capabilities in future versions. Especially onerous for mass-market DVD publishers is the inability to produce or even handle AC-3 audio files.

Note

Pinnacle Edition does have an X-send feature that can send audio to a designated audio editor for processing and automated return.

Armed with their own acquisition of Syntrillium Software, the developer of Cool Edit Pro, Premiere Pro has a very competent audio offering, though not quite up to Vegas standards, especially for DVD authors. Specifically, though Premiere offers surround-sound mixing, it's via a $299 third-party plug-in you have to purchase after three surround-sound encodes, a little detail somehow missing from all marketing materials. Unless you license the third-party program, you no longer can produce AC-3 files, though Encore (Adobe's DVD-authoring program) can. So as long as you're authoring in the Adobe environment, you're covered.

Otherwise, I prefer DirectX filters over the VST filters Premiere supports because I've worked with them on Sound Forge, but can't cite a major quality difference. Premiere's awesome key framing capabilities extend to audio, so you can key frame filter parameters separately, a killer feature for complex projects. The real-time audio mixer is another advantage over Vegas, as is the noise-removal feature.

Rendering

For the most part, the obvious qualitative differences produced by these products relate to special effects like color correction and video overlay, not simple encoding, which is generally pretty similar between the products. For this reason, your focus during rendering will primarily be speed.

I look at three characteristics relating to rendering speed. First is how long it takes to produce the initial output file. Second, since I seldom get things right the first time and usually end up rendering several times, I consider how long it takes to render a second time. Finally, I'm also interested in how I can accelerate the process by throwing a hyper-threaded processor or multi-processor computer at the problem. The first and third issues are ferreted out in Table 3-10.

Table 3-10   Rendering Performance *(hrs:mins:secs)*

	P4 2.4 GHz HT disabled	P4 2.4 GHz HT enabled	Single 3.06 GHz Xeon	Dual 3.06 GHz Xeon
Adobe Premiere (render and encode 12.5-minute project)	64:25	47:59	47:06	24:12
Pinnacle Edition (render and encode 12.5-minute project)	41:13	35:53	30:06	28:56
Sony Vegas (render and encode 12.5-minute project)	1:37:20	1:32:59	1:18:59	1:15:28
Ulead MediaStudio Pro (render and encode 12.5-minute project)	40:31	34:30	25:41	21:25

Here I tested on two computers, an HP xw4100 running a 2.4-GHz Pentium 4 with HT (hyper-threaded) technology and a Dell Precision 650 workstation running dual 3.06-GHz Xeon processors. Note that you can disable HT technology on the 4100 and disable one of the two processors on the Precision. By comparing encoding times with and without these features, you can measure the benefits of the additional processing power.

In terms of pure encoding speed, MediaStudio was the champ, edging out Edition on the HP computer and beating it soundly on the dual-processor Dell. As shown in Table 3-10, Vegas was the slowest program but produced the best quality in my overlay tests. In talking to Sony engineers, they stated that they performed a processor-intensive Gaussian blur to achieve the edge smoothness that gained them the top ranking. My test included two overlay sections, which is probably why Sony ranked so far behind.

A Quick Processor Primer

HT technology stands for hyper-threaded, which means a chip that can handle two logical operations simultaneously, though only one execution operation. Imagine a coal-burning locomotive with one door for feeding coal to the engine. The door is the logical operation, while the burner itself is the execution operation.

If the locomotive is slowed because it can't get enough coal, you create a second door to feed the beast so it's operating at full speed all the time. That's hyper-threading. In contrast, dual-processor (DP) computers have multiple processors, each of which may or may not be hyper-threaded.

Note that programs need to be modified to take advantage of HT or DP computers, and that the efficiency of this support varies by program. A program that's not optimized for these technologies may actually run slower, because both technologies create additional overhead for the operating system to manage. This is why all HT and DP computers allow you to disable these features during startup.

Interestingly, Vegas also produced the least incremental benefit from moving to HT-enabled or dual-processor machines. This is because when multiple processor threads are available, Sony splits them between the audio and video processing. Since my tests were primarily video-related, the additional processor threads allocated to audio pretty much went to waste. If your projects are equally weighted between audio and video processing, you should expect to see significant benefits from HT and dual-processor computers with Vegas.

Otherwise, Premiere proved extremely efficient at leveraging the benefits of the dual-processor computer in particular. Since each Xeon processor itself featured HT technology, this meant that four threads were available, and Premiere certainly made the most of them. If Premiere is your editor, a dual-processor computer will likely pay for itself in a matter of weeks, if not days.

How I Tested

For those of you who care about such things, I tested these products with a 12:30 project comprised of the following:

1. Six 2-minute segments and one 35-second sequence.

2. Insert a 1-second cross dissolve between the clips.

3. Over clip one, insert a 20-second blue-screen video, slowed to one-fourth of normal speed (1:40 total).

4. Zoom clip two from 100% to 200%.

5. Insert a logo that spins one revolution over clip three.

6. Blur clip four moderately (control values differ by product).

7. Zoom into the upper-right corner of clip five at 200% level. Pan to bottom-right corner over the duration of the clip.

8. Insert a 1-minute picture-in-picture in the middle of clip six at 50% size.

9. Color correct the 35-second sequence.

10. Insert seven 10-second titles over the start of each clip (60-point Casmira, "PC Mag Tests" centered on the bottom third).

11. Insert four background audio tracks, and reduce volume to approximately 30%.

12. Print to tape, time how long it takes to render, change the first transition to a wipe, re-render, and time again.

13. Delete all temporary files rendered during the first test, then render to MPEG-2, one pass VBR, 6 mbps average, 7 mbps max, MPEG stereo audio, 224 kbps at 44 kHz. Change transition to a wipe, and re-render.

Since the Vegas results were anomalous, I sent the project file to Sony for its engineers to review. They made several suggestions, which I followed, and my results are similar to those achieved by Sony in its labs.

Other tests revealed that all programs were relatively efficient in second renderings to DV, as would occur if you decided to tweak a title or change a transition between your first and second render. Basically, each program renders a small temporary file to effectuate the change, and then the program is ready to again write to tape.

However, MediaStudio is the only program that accomplishes the same result when making modest changes to MPEG-2 files via a process Ulead calls Smart Rendering. Change a transition or title with MediaStudio, and re-rendering to MPEG-2 takes only a minute or so. With all other programs, you're pretty much starting from scratch, and the second rendering takes approximately the same time as the first. See Table 3-11.

Table 3-11   Rendering Ratings

	Sony Vegas	MediaStudio Pro	Pinnacle Edition	Adobe Premiere Pro
First render	2	3	2	2
Ability to accelerate via HT or DP computers	2	2	1	3
Second render — DV	3	3	3	3
Second render — MPEG-2	0	3	0	0
Overall rendering performance	1.75	2.75	1.5	2

Prosumer Summary

As you can see from Table 3-12, Edition is our winner, edging out Vegas and barely beating Premiere. Of course, this overall score may be totally irrelevant depending upon your production needs. For example, Edition offers minimal editing functionality, which may push commercial DVD producers or those producing audio-intensive projects toward Vegas.

Similarly, Premiere offers very little 2D and 3D special effects. If you don't want to purchase and learn After Effects, the overall score is relatively meaningless to aggressive users of special effects.

That said, most people currently using Premiere should probably upgrade to Premiere Pro, while those drawn to Vegas for its extensive audio capabilities will likely be happy to stay as well. At $499 with loads of other programs, MediaStudio leads the value section, and its performance is incredible.

One last caveat about Edition: It really, really is a frustrating program at first, but once you climb the learning curve, you'll likely be happy that you did.

Table 3-12   Summary Findings

	Sony Vegas	MediaStudio Pro	Pinnacle Edition	Adobe Premiere Pro
Overall score	16.9	11.98	19.6	18.25

Summary

Here's a summary of the key points of this chapter:

1. Generally, less is more with video editors, and you should buy the least expensive editor that gets the job done for you.

2. Microsoft's Movie Maker 2 gets the job done, but offers minimum configurability. Ulead's VideoStudio offers great production tools but is light on the artistic side. Pinnacle Studio, in addition to offering great DVD-authoring capabilities, has great tools for motivated transitions, audio track creation and mixing, and title creation.

3. The best video tools come from video companies. Avoid early versions of tools from general-purpose companies like ArcSoft and Broderbund.

4. Consider moving to a prosumer editor when you need more tracks or advanced features like video overlay, color correction, motion controls, and picture-in-picture.

5. Prosumer tools are difficult to learn and best used by those who use them regularly, rather than periodically.

Chapter 4

Choosing a DVD-Authoring Package

The first DVD-authoring program I ever reviewed back in 1997 cost about $50,000 and was the most complicated program I had ever worked with at that point. I needed to learn an arcane DVD-production-specific language (program chains and first titles?) and accessed most features via scripting, which is only slightly less complicated than programming in Visual Basic or some other programming language. Serious stuff.

Needless to say, however, given the price of the software and the cost of the only available DVD-R burner ($17,000), the software was not targeted toward consumers. Hollywood and other movie distributors were the key customers, and studios had plenty of technicians around to master the software.

Even back then, however, it was easy to see that DVDs were relatively simple animals comprised of two basic elements: menus and videos. You build your menus, and you link your videos.

Since you could build menus and link to videos in Microsoft PowerPoint then and now, it was only a question of time before software developers responded with software that added the last critical element, the ability to write the resulting production to a recordable DVD. Similarly, since CD recorders had dropped from $6,000 to under $200, it was also obvious that DVD recorders would experience a similar drop to consumer-friendly prices.

Today, it's hard to turn around without bumping into DVD-authoring capabilities that have shown up as both standalone products and components of video-editing and CD-mastering products.

At a high level, the market has broken into four basic categories:

- **Tape converters** — These products automate the conversion of analog or DV tapes into DVDs. Products include Pinnacle Expression, MyDVD, and Ulead MovieFactory 2.

- **Consumer editing/authoring programs** — These products are capable of both video editing and authoring. Products include Ulead's VideoStudio, which incorporates authoring as a separate step after editing, and Pinnacle Studio, which integrates editing and authoring into the same interface.

- **Prosumer authoring programs** — Designed for use with a separate video editor, these products provide primarily authoring with more corporate-level DVD-specific features than either of the previous two categories. Products include Adobe Encore DVD, Sonic Solutions DVDit!, and Ulead DVD Workshop.

■ **Professional authoring** — These products are designed for professional/commercial DVD titles and expose the entire DVD feature set, like multiple-angle videos, the ability to create director's cuts, and similar high-end functionality, usually in a highly complex interface. Products here include Sonic Scenarist and DVD Producer.

This taxonomy isn't perfect, but most readers will find themselves choosing a product from one or more of the first three categories. After describing DVD-authoring technology in general, I'll discuss each of the first three categories in greater detail, identifying when to buy a product in each category and how to differentiate the various market entrants.

The fourth category is beyond the scope of this book. Readers seeking truly high-end authoring programs should check www.sonic.com, since Sonic is the predominant player at the high end.

DVD Basics

Let's start at the beginning, as in what is a DVD? Quite simply, a DVD is an optical disc containing content, which can be video, slideshows, or audio, and menus for navigating through the content. At a high level, DVD production has three steps: content creation, menu creation, and then linking menus to content and other menus. After that, it's previewing to make sure everything works as planned, then compressing the video files to MPEG-2 format and rendering and burning the disc.

Technically, a DVD contains 4.7GB of information on one layer on one side. DVDs mastered in professional facilities can contain two layers of data on the same side (*dual layer*) and can be dual-sided, pushing capacity up to 18.8GB of data. Virtually all Hollywood DVDs are single-sided, dual-layer discs. Commercial DVD players and DVD-ROMs on computers can read one layer from start to finish, then start the next layer seamlessly, which is why you don't have to flip the disc over to access the second layer, and you don't notice an interruption when the second side starts playing.

In contrast, DVD recorders can write one layer of data but can't produce dual-layer discs. There are *dual-sided* DVD-R media where each side can store 4.7GB of data for a total of 9.4GB, but you have to flip the media manually to access both sides.

Audio/Video Content

DVDs can contain video, audio, text, and still images. Virtually all DVD video is in MPEG-2 format, though technically, DVDs can also handle MPEG-1. All authoring programs can import video produced by a separate video editor, while many can also capture video as well.

Most consumer DVD-authoring programs can output audio in either Linear Pulse Code Modulated (LPCM) format (a bulky, uncompressed format) or the more efficient MPEG format. Note that while most DVD players sold in the U.S. support MPEG audio, not all of the older ones do. For this reason, if you have the space on your disc, LPCM is a safer choice in that all DVD players in the U.S. support Dolby AC-3 audio, which is why many prosumer and virtually all professional authoring programs can either create or import AC-3 audio files.

SlideShows

Virtually all consumer DVD-authoring programs enable the production of slideshows comprised of digital images, either scanned or transferred from a digital camera. Most offer the ability to add background music to the slides, which is invaluable, while some also offer the ability to synchronize slide duration to the background music, an absolutely killer feature that can save loads of development time.

Higher-level features include the ability to rotate images, which also saves time when you take both portrait and landscape shots with your digital camera. Also helpful is cropping and the ability to separately archive digital images in a data section of the DVD, so grandma can download and edit them if she likes. Otherwise, the images are encoded into impregnable DVD files, and she can't access the individual photographs.

Menus

The typical DVD menu has a background image and linkable foreground elements called buttons, which generally can be either text or graphic images. During development, you create the buttons and links, which the viewers will use to navigate through the menus and access the content.

Virtually all authoring programs supply libraries of menu templates that you can customize by changing the background images and the font and font size of any text. Most also provide libraries of other menu components like buttons to assist your menu development or customization efforts.

One key advantage of DVD over tape-based formats like VHS or Hi8 is interactivity, or the viewer's ability to click to specific spots in the video. If your DVD is comprised of multiple, separate videos, like separate segments from a summer's worth of videotaping, you may create separate files for each segment, one for the trip to the beach, another for the Fourth of July, and so on. When creating your DVD, you could import the separate files and then create a link to the start of each video.

However, your DVD may be one long video like a videotape of a play or lecture, where you want access to individual points within the video. To accomplish this, most DVD-authoring programs allow you to create *chapter points* in the long video file, either manually or by using scene change detection based upon DV time codes or some other technique.

For example, in Figure 4-1, I'm creating chapter points using time-based intervals in Ulead's DVD MovieFactory, primarily because the video (of my daughter performing her gymnastics routine) was captured as MPEG-2, so time-code-based scene change was not available. Accordingly, you can typically link to the start of any video (or other asset like a slideshow) or any chapter point you create in the asset.

In addition to enabling the creation of chapter points, some authoring programs allow producers to designate the First Play videos, or those that play before the initial menu appears. As you probably recall, on Hollywood DVDs, these are typically the FBI copyright warnings.

NAVIGATION

Navigation refers to your ability to control how your viewer accesses your content, and different authoring programs provide varying levels of navigational flexibility. It's easiest to understand by looking at the two extremes.

Figure 4-1: Chapter points (shown on the right side of the screen) are linkable spots within a file that you can either create manually, via scene detection, or through some other technique. Here we're creating chapter points in Ulead's MovieFactory 2. Look at that extension!

On one hand are wizard-based programs that insert all content in page templates that link sequentially from one menu to another. Choose a menu page with three video buttons, representing three videos per page, insert 38 scenes (the number of scenes in the gymnastics video), and the program automatically creates the required 13 menus (see Figure 4-2).

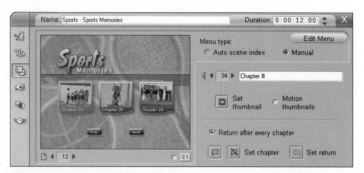

Figure 4-2: Pinnacle Studio's automatic menu creation capabilities. With three videos per page and 38 scenes, the program will create the required 13 menus and all required links.

However, in these template-based schemes, all navigation is sequential, from page to page to page. If I want to show my grandma the awards ceremony at the conclusion of the gymnastics presentation, I have to page through 13 menus to get there. The program takes care of all linking and menu creation, so this approach is simple, but the results are inelegant from a content presentation perspective.

At the other end of the spectrum are custom menu tools that are flexible but complex. You typically start with a blank slate into which you insert all background images, buttons, and links. You're free to create any navigational structure between the menu pages, and you can link to the initial frame of the video or chapter points.

Buzzwords to look for with these products are the ability to create "branched" or "nested" menus. Obviously, this flexibility enables much greater navigational creativity, but it comes with some additional development burdens, as well.

For example, you're in charge of ensuring the integrity of the navigational structure, which complicates testing and quality control. You must manually ensure that all pages are properly linked, forwards and backwards, so the viewer can get back to the main menu if desired. You also have to ensure that all videos are linked into the project, and that all links are actually linked to the desired content.

Between these two extremes are customizable templates, an approach that allows you to change the text and background image of supplied templates, as well as build your own templates from scratch. These enhance your creative options but not your navigational capabilities since the pages must still link sequentially.

MENU ENHANCEMENTS

Many authoring programs enable menu enhancements like *video menus* (menus with videos played behind them), *video buttons* (buttons with frames that play a scaled-down version of the video they're linked to), and *audio menus* (menus that play an audio file while the menu displays).

Video menus and video buttons increase DVD-rendering time significantly, since the authoring program has to produce a separate MPEG-2 file for the video menu, scale the videos presented in the video buttons down to size, and then encode these files.

Tip

Though generally very easy to implement, in my experience, video menus and video buttons tend to increase the risk that the authoring program will crash during rendering, which is why I typically avoid them. Audio menus, on the other hand, are fairly easy to implement and don't seem to increase the risk of crashing.

PRE- AND POST-PLAY OPTIONS

Pre-play options define what occurs if the title is launched and no buttons are selected. Higher-end programs, used to create DVDs for kiosks and other unattended playback applications, allow DVD authors to designate what happens if no button is selected within a certain time period. That way, if video playback was interrupted by a power outage, it would automatically recycle and resume playback once power was restored.

Post-play options describe the ability to direct where the viewer goes after a particular video finishes playing. The two most frequent options are to play the next video in the menu or to return back to the menu that links to the video. More advanced options include jumping to another menu in the DVD or repeating playback automatically until interrupted.

Advanced DVD Features

All DVD-authoring programs offer some mix of content and menu creation. Here are some advanced features cropping up in both consumer and prosumer products.

Editable DVDs

Even with today's cheaper, larger hard disk drives, most producers delete the original files from a DVD project at some point after completion. As it turns out, usually this is just before you realize you'd like to make a change to the project. Until recently, this pretty much left you stranded, since during the encoding and rendering process, all authoring programs convert the content into files that you can't reinsert and re-edit.

In 2002, Sonic Solutions introduced its OpenDVD specification. Discs produced by Sonic's MyDVD, and products that support OpenDVD, store the project file on the DVD. If desired, you can reload the project file back into MyDVD, which will then pull the required assets out of the recorded DVD content and restore the project to its final, pre-burn configuration.

From there, you can edit as desired and even burn the changes to the original disc, assuming that it's a rewritable DVD. If not, MyDVD will recover all required content from the previously recorded DVD, copy it to your hard drive, and allow you to burn that content to another recordable DVD. Either way, since OpenDVD is completely transparent to the DVD player, it doesn't increase the risk of player-disc incompatibility.

Ulead and several other vendors have introduced editable DVD capabilities based upon the DVD+RW and DVD+VR specifications, the latter a somewhat new and exotic specification that isn't widely supported yet. However, these can only be used on rewritable discs, which, as pointed out by Ulead on its Web site, are typically slightly less compatible with older DVD players.

A new feature on programs like Ulead's DVD MovieFactory is the ability to import video directly from a finished DVD and utilize the videos in a project you can burn to any DVD format. This feature is definitely a long time coming; since all authoring programs know how to create the video object files (VOB) files utilized on DVDs, it's no surprise they can now pull video data back out of these files. Look for this to be a key feature on all authoring programs going forward.

Just to be clear, obviously you need a rewritable disc to actually edit the original recorded DVD. If it's not recordable, the authoring program pulls all required assets from the recorded DVD, stores them to hard disk, and allows you to insert them in a project and later burn them to another disc.

VideoCD/Super VideoCD

VideoCD (VCD) and Super VideoCD (SVCD) are two CD-recordable-based formats that play on computers and also some DVD players. These formats were very popular in the past because most consumers couldn't afford a DVD recorder and/or many target viewers didn't have a DVD player. Though waning in popularity as DVD recorder and player prices drop, VCD and SVCD continue to be supported by virtually all consumer and prosumer DVD-authoring programs.

Briefly, VCD was designed to squeeze between 70 and 80 minutes of video onto a 650MB CD-ROM, and uses very low bit rate MPEG-1 video. SVCD uses a format called "half-height MPEG-2" with a resolution of 480x480 pixels, and can store about 40 minutes of video onto a CD-ROM.

In contrast, recordable DVDs can store 4.7GB of data and typically use MPEG-2 encoded at 720x480 resolution. This means that the video quality delivered on a DVD is much, much higher than either alternative format. In addition, note that DVD offers much more interactivity than either VCD or SVCD, which typically can handle only simple menus. Though many DVD players are supposed to be compatible with VCD and SVCD titles, in my experience, compatibility is spotty. In addition, though VideoCD titles should play on virtually any computer, SVCD only plays if an MPEG-2 encoder is installed.

Don't get me wrong, a lot of producers swear by these formats. However, now that DVD players are ubiquitous and DVD recorders relatively inexpensive, DVD production is a much more attractive prospect.

HIGH-END DVD-AUTHORING FEATURES

Here are some other DVD features available primarily in prosumer and professional authoring programs that I'll touch on in a minute:

- **Multiple text and audio tracks** — This DVD specification enables up to eight digital audio and 32 subtitle tracks typically used by Hollywood for producing DVDs (see Figure 4-3). These features are primarily desirable for multinational corporations producing marketing or training DVDs for worldwide distribution. As you would expect, these are not priorities for consumer programs, but they do appear on some prosumer programs and virtually all professional DVD-authoring programs.

- **Multiple angles** — The DVD specification also allows multiple video tracks, usually representing multiple angles of the same subject, to be encoded into the same video stream. In use, this might allow the viewer of a football game to watch from the 50-yard line, the end zone, or to zoom in on the quarterback. This again is a high-end feature typically found only on professional authoring programs.

- **Link checking** — This feature adds an automated layer of quality control over the manual previewing most producers perform. Though the specific capabilities differ from program to program, most check to make sure that all buttons are linked to content, that buttons don't overlap, and that all project menus are linked and accessible (see Figure 4-4).

■ **Copy protection** — Most Hollywood studios attempt to produce their DVD titles with the Content Scrambling System (CSS), a form of copy protection. Only prosumer and professional authoring programs offer this feature.

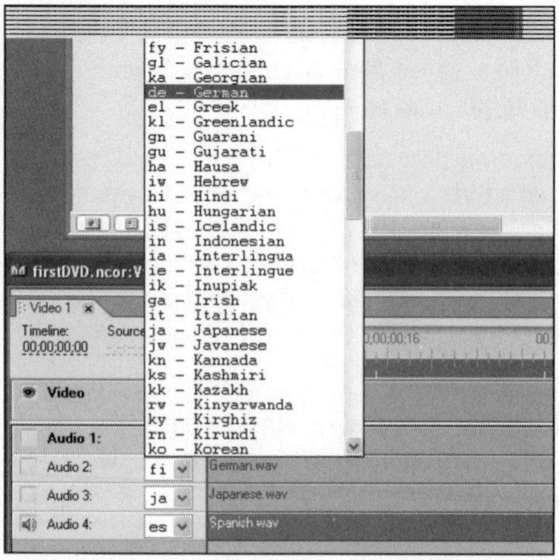

Figure 4-3: Creating multiple audio tracks is easy in Adobe Encore. Just drag the tracks down, and designate which country they should play in.

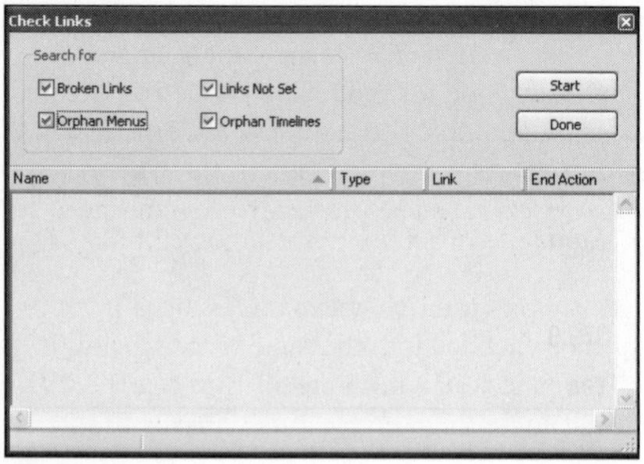

Figure 4-4: Link checking in Adobe Encore is a great quality control feature.

Converting Tapes to DVD

Buy a product in this category if your primary goal is to simply convert your analog or DV tapes to DVD. Your goal isn't necessarily to create a masterpiece, just to produce a simple DVD, perhaps with menus and chapter points, as quickly and efficiently as possible.

Recognize, of course, that you'll need hardware to capture the video, either a FireWire port or an analog-capture device for your VHS and other analog formats.

Cross-Reference

FireWire ports and analog-capture devices are discussed in detail in Chapter 2.

All authoring programs, and most video editors for that matter, can capture video and produce a DVD. The programs in this category do it quickly and efficiently and also make it simple to create slideshows from your digital camera. They all capture the video directly, allow you to trim unwanted segments, create chapter points, and send the result to DVD, VideoCD, and often Super VideoCD.

Conversely, the video editing performed is currently very modest. Sonic's MyDVD added the ability to add transitions and titles in version 5, and it's a great convenience. However, if you're looking for full-featured video editing, look outside of this category.

These products are inexpensive and easy to learn and use. As such, even if you have a much more capable product like Pinnacle Studio or Adobe Premiere Pro and Encore, they may be worth buying simply for this conversion task.

The three best products in the category are Pinnacle Expression, Sonic MyDVD 5, and Ulead MovieFactory 2. All features and prices listed in Table 4-1 are current as of August 2003.

Note that features don't tell the entire tale, as usability, a characteristic that doesn't lend itself to feature table presentation, is also important. The bottom line is that a current product review in *PC Magazine* or some other credible source is always better than a simple feature comparison, especially as newer products enter the market. Features are easy to duplicate, but usability is an art that's often lacking in first generation programs.

Table 4-1   Comparing Tape Conversion Programs

	Pinnacle Expression	*Sonic MyDVD 5*	*Ulead MovieFactory 2*
Price	$49.99 (direct)	$79.99	$34.95 (direct)
Real-time conversion and storage to DVD	No — saves as DV, then encodes and burns	Yes	Yes

Continued

Table 4-1   Comparing Tape Conversion Programs *(continued)*

	Pinnacle Expression	Sonic MyDVD 5	Ulead MovieFactory 2
Captures from DV and other sources	Yes	Yes	Yes
Creates chapters from time-code-based scene changes	Yes	Yes	Yes
Dedicated slideshow function	Yes	Yes	Yes
Transitions between slides	Yes	Yes	No
Matches slide duration to background audio	Yes	Yes	No
Rotates images (landscape to portrait)	Yes	Yes	Yes
Crops and other edits	Yes	No	No
Customizable menu navigation	No	One level	No
Number of supplied menu templates	61	37	44
Audio menus	Yes	Yes	Yes
Video menus	Yes	Yes	Yes
Video buttons	Yes	Yes	Yes
Editable DVDs	No	Yes (OpenDVD)	Yes (DVD+RW and DVD import)
Creates VideoCDs, SVCDs, and DVDs	Yes/Yes/Yes	Yes/No/Yes	Yes/Yes/Yes

Consumer Authoring and Editing Programs

Products here are full-featured video editors and also DVD-authoring programs. They're most appropriate when your goal is to edit your production extensively and then output on DVD. Editing performance and the depth of DVD-authoring capabilities are your primary concerns.

Regarding DVD authoring, these capabilities are either integrated into the editing process or bolted on, either as a post-process that occurs after editing is complete, or as a totally separate program. As discussed in Chapter 3, Pinnacle Studio is the poster child for the integrated approach, while VideoStudio essentially bolts on wizards from MovieFactory to create the DVD once editing is completed.

Both approaches have their strong points. Studio's is both more elegant and flexible, enabling complete custom menu creation and the ability to customize navigation entirely. You can also utilize simple templates and create a fast, simple project.

As a post-process, Ulead's approach is simpler; you finish your editing, start your authoring, follow the simple wizard, and you're done. This will appeal to many users, but VideoStudio offers neither the menu creation nor navigational flexibility available in Studio (see Table 4-2 for a side-by-side comparison of these two products).

If I were choosing an editing/authoring program for myself at home, I would buy the best video editor and work with the authoring capabilities provided. In the corporate setting, I would also buy the best video editor, but if the authoring capabilities were inadequate, I would consider one of the prosumer authoring programs shown in Table 4-3.

Table 4-2   Comparing Consumer Editing/Authoring Programs

	Pinnacle Studio	*Ulead VideoStudio*
Price	$99	$99.95
Video-editing capabilities	Full	Full
Capture from DV and other sources	Yes	Yes
Create chapters from time-code-based scene changes	Yes	Yes
Customizable menu navigation	Yes	No
Audio menus	Yes	Yes
Video menus	Yes	Yes
Video buttons	Yes	Yes
Editable DVDs	No	No
Creates VideoCDs, SVCDs, and DVDs	Yes/Yes/Yes	Yes/Yes/Yes

Prosumer Authoring Programs

The prosumer arena covers a range of users, from corporate marketing and training types, to event videographers to precocious consumers seeking to expand the range of their authoring capabilities. Buy a product in this category if you like your video editor but you need greater flexibility in menu creation, the increased compatibility offered by AC-3 audio, or to distribute titles in multiple languages.

Until mid-2003, this category was the sleepy province of Sonic's DVDit! and Ulead's DVD Workshop. Then came Adobe Encore DVD. Not only does Encore provide great integration with Adobe tools like Premiere and PhotoShop, but it also adds features previously unavailable in the category, like multiple text and audio tracks and a range of professional output functions like dual layering and support for CSS copy protection.

On the other hand, if you're not producing multilingual titles that are professionally mastered or creating the bulk of your content in Adobe applications, Encore has little new to offer. In addition, programs like Workshop and DVDit! have their own niceties, like the ability to capture and trim video directly in the program, wizard-based menu creation, and, in the case of DVD Workshop, a dedicated slideshow function.

Encore will definitely do well among those using Adobe tools and professional title developers. However, for many corporate developers, Workshop and DVDit! are easier to use, cheaper, and provide all relevant features. Refer to Table 4-3 for a comparison of these three products.

Table 4-3   Comparing Prosumer Authoring Programs

	Adobe Encore	*Sonic DVDit!*	*Ulead DVD Workshop*
Price	$549	$299 Standard Edition/$399 Professional Edition	$299/$495 with AC-3
Multiple audio and text tracks	Yes	No	No (coming by late 2004)
AC-3 import/encoding	Yes/Yes	Yes/Yes (PE only)	Yes/Yes (AC-3 version only)
Dedicated slideshow function	No	No	Yes
Transitions between slides	No	No	Yes
Matches slide duration to background audio	No	No	Yes
Customizable menu navigation	Yes	Yes	Yes
Menu templates	Yes	No	Yes
Audio menus	Yes	Yes	Yes
Video menus	Yes	No	Yes
Video buttons	Yes	Yes	Yes
Photoshop file import (PSD)	Yes	Yes	Yes
Adobe integration	Full	None	None
Link checking	Yes		
DLT output	Yes	Yes (PE only)	No (coming by late 2004)
Dual layer/region coding/CSS	Yes/Yes/Yes	No/No/No	No/No/No

Summary

Here's a summary of the high points from this chapter:

1. The DVD-authoring market breaks down into four general markets:

   ■ **Tape converters** automate converting analog or DV tapes into DVDs.

   ■ **Consumer editing/authoring programs** can handle both video editing and authoring.

- **Prosumer authoring programs** provide authoring services aimed at corporate customers.

- **Professional authoring programs** are designed for professional, commercial DVD production.

When buying an authoring product, identify the category most relevant to your production needs and then the most suitable product in that category.

2. DVD content can be video (which is almost always MPEG-2), still images, and audio. While most DVD players in the United States can play MPEG-2 files, they're required to support both LPCM and AC-3 audio, which is why most prosumer programs support AC-3 audio encoding, the only universally supported compressed format in the United States.

3. Slideshow functionality on consumer tape-converting programs is extensive and represents a great format for exhibiting images from digital cameras.

4. The ability to customize menu navigation is the most important feature of prosumer editors, because other than Pinnacle Studio, all tape converters and consumer editors use canned templates with fixed menu flow.

5. Editable DVDs refers to the ability to recover content from a previously burned DVD, essentially allowing a DVD to serve as both a distribution and archival medium. Though relatively nascent, it will become a critical feature on consumer and prosumer products very soon.

6. Multiple language support is an important feature for multinational corporations and other companies that must support multiple languages. Once nonexistent in the prosumer market, it's a key advantage of Adobe Encore DVD and probably will appear soon in other products in the category.

Chapter 5

Choosing a DVD Recorder

Depending upon when you read this chapter, I'll be a visionary, a master of the obvious, or just plain wrong. Hey, nobody ever said writing a book was easy. We'll define all our terms and standards below, but let's set the stage with some history first.

Here's the deal. The personal computer market goes through standards battles periodically, which produce lots of noise and confusion and generally slow the market acceptance of the very products everyone involved is trying to sell. Then, resolution is reached, and it's as if the whole conflict, vitriol, misinformation, and all never happened.

As I sit here in mid-2003, it appears that the DVD-recordable market is about to reach such a resolution. The DVD-R/RW standard versus DVD+R/+RW standard war should be completely resolved by early to mid-2004, at the latest. In a lovely turnaround, both sides fought to a draw, leaving the consumer a clear winner.

Rather than forcing consumers to choose between drives using competing standards, virtually all competitive recorders will support both standards, providing the optimum blend of burning speed, media reliability, and playback compatibility. As I sit here today, Sony has shipped "Dual RW" drives, and Pioneer has announced that their newest drive, the A06, will support both standards.

Though the multiple media types the war spawned will live on, the compatibility issues that plagued the market early on will disappear, since virtually all media will be compatible with all new recorders.

Flowers will grow, birds will sing, and engineers and marketers from the two camps will meet at trade shows and recount past conflicts over pints of amber ale. Trade press like myself will move on to other battles, helping to fan new flames.

Most importantly, however, consumers will be free to ignore standards and simply buy a drive based on traditional factors like price, performance, and software bundle. This, plus price points under $200 by 2004, should truly spawn incredible demand for DVD recorders.

However, then is then, and now is now. Since you may be confronted with single format drives for at least the short term, I'll start with the history behind the standards war and discuss the strengths and weaknesses of the respective camps. If you take one thing away from this chapter, however, it should be that DVD recordable media isn't interchangeable, and unless you have a universal drive, as described below, you have to buy media that's compatible with your DVD recorder.

What's Past Is Prolog

The quality and ubiquity of DVD players makes DVD recorders essential equipment for any budding videographer eager to distribute his or her wares. However, buying a DVD recorder, and stocking it with the proper discs, is truly one of the most confusing tasks in computing. (Optical discs are spelled with a "c"; magnetic disks are spelled with a "k.")

Consider this. There are three recordable standards (which allow a one-time only recording to disc) and three rewritable standards (which allow a disc to be repeatedly recorded to after the initial burn). The standards include DVD-R for General, DVD-R for Authoring, DVD+R, DVD-RAM, DVD-RW, DVD+RW; each standard has its own unique recording media that you actually burn during the recording or rewriting process.

There are additional variations like small, lower-capacity discs for DVD-R and DVD-RAM, especially for camcorders. We're starting to see double-sided DVD-R discs with a 9.4GB capacity, which double-sided DVD-RAM discs have long provided.

You have two distinct camps, the DVD-Forum and the DVD+RW Alliance, each with conflicting marketing messages about compatibility and performance. Looking back, it's as if a diabolical James Bond–esque villain, dedicated to ensuring the failure of the writable DVD market, had ripped control from cooler, more logical heads, way back in the late 1990s. Yes, it's that bad.

Why the conflict and confusion? Well, as they say in the old detective novels, follow the money. Pioneer struck first in the DVD-R market in 1997, creating a write-once disc standard compatible with consumer DVD-Video Players, which would have opened a huge market except that the device cost $17,000.

With the future plain to see, competitors like Hewlett-Packard and Sony were faced with a chilling decision: adopt Pioneer's technology and pay them royalties for each DVD recorder sold, or create their own standard. Heeding the First Commandment of guerilla computer warfare as handed down by William C. Gates; to wit, Thou Shalt Not Pay Royalties, the competitors chose the latter.

Then, after announcing DVD+RW in 1997, these companies followed the Second Commandment: When you have no product, spread fear, uncertainty, and doubt (FUD) about the competitor's products. Certainly Pioneer's reluctance to reduce the price of their drives to consumer levels left the door open.

In any event, by 2002, the market had evolved into two clear camps, the DVD-R/RW camp and the DVD+RW/+R camp. Both offered products that could burn discs compatible with DVD-Video Players with similar recording times and media costs.

So, how do you choose between the two, assuming you still have to, of course? Well, we'll get there in a bit. First let's make sure we're all on the same page when it comes to terms and terminology.

Defining Our Terms

The reason we're talking about DVD recorders in this book is to create video discs that play on DVD players, and when I say *DVD player*, I'm referring to these consumer electronic devices that you can attach to your television set and watch DVDs with.

We also want both data and video discs to play on *DVD-ROM drives*, the Read Only Memory devices that connect to your computers for video and data retrieval.

Note that the recordable/rewritable paradigm you saw with CD-Recordable also exists with DVD-Recordable. Specifically, some discs you can write to only once; others you can rewrite to multiple times. When I say "recordable" or "writable," I'm referring to a DVD or CD disc that can be recorded to once, and that's all. When I say "rewritable" or "re-recordable," I'm referring to a disc that can be written to over and over again, copying new material over previously recorded material.

Briefly, a CD-ROM can hold up to 700MB of data, whereas a DVD-ROM can hold up to 4.7GB. Those readers familiar with CD-ROM technology may know that a 1X CD-ROM drive reads at 150K per second. This means that a 24X drive reads at 3.6MB per second and that an 8X CD-R device records at 1.2MB per second.

When DVD drives first shipped, they could read at approximately 1,350KB per second or 1.35MB per second. Rather than calling this 9X CD-ROM, vendors started calling this 1X DVD. Similarly, a 2X DVD recorder writes at 2,700K per second (2.7MB per second), while 4X recorders write at 5,400K per second (5.4MB per second). Speed is good when it comes to optical media like CD-ROM and DVD-ROM, because it allows the computer or DVD player to retrieve a higher-quality video stream.

At the same time, most DVD recorders still read and write CD-ROM discs and vendors publish their performance numbers rated at these tasks. When referring to these CD-related capabilities, X refers back to CD-ROM speeds.

So, when Pioneer says their DVR-A05 DVD-RW/CD-RW Drive performs as follows, 4.7GB 4X/2X/12X DVD, 16X/8X/32X CD Write/ReWrite/Read internal /DVD-RW/CD-RW drive for PCs, it translates to the performance numbers shown in Table 5-1. Note that in the description the DVD metrics are given first followed by the CD metrics, and that speeds for both DVD and CD come in the following order: write, rewrite, and then read.

Table 5-1   Defining the "X" in DVD-Recordable Drives

DVD Metrics	Actual Speed
4X write	5,400,000K/5.4MB per second
2X rewrite	2,700,000K/2.7MB per second
12X read	16,200,000K/16.2MB per second
CD Metrics	
16X write	2,400,000K/2.4MB per second
8X rewrite	1,200,000K/1.2MB per second
32X read	4,800,000K/4.8MB per second

The Contenders

There are four major DVD-recordable/rewritable specifications floating around, though only two, DVD-R/RW and DVD+RW/+R, are contending for mass-market nirvana. However, I'll cover DVD-RAM/-R and DVD Multi for comprehensiveness.

DVD-R/RW

DVD-R was the first DVD-recordable format, and it uses a technology similar to CD-R for compatibility with most DVD drives and players. For readers who care about such things, DVD-R is, was, and should be pronounced "DVD dash R."

In a diabolical marketing ploy, the DVD+RW camp (pronounced "DVD plus RW") has started referring to -R/RW formats as "minus R/RW," since, of course, plus is always better than minus (unless you're trying to lose weight, of course). Anyway, if you want to annoy people from the -R camp, call their products "minus-R" to their faces.

DVD-R, DVD-RW, and DVD-RAM are all formats championed by the DVD Forum, which includes Pioneer, Sony, Toshiba, Panasonic, Hitachi, and many other companies spanning the consumer-electronics, computer, media, and content industries. However, the DVD Forum is an industry group, not a standards-setting body, so unlike true standards bodies like the IEEE (Institute of Electrical and Electronics Engineers) or ANSI (American National Standards Institute), their specifications are significant but not really enforceable.

In 2000, the DVD Forum divided DVD-R into two formats: "DVD-R for General" and "DVD-R for Authoring." The primary difference is that Authoring media contained a new feature called the Cutting Master Format that allowed DVD-R media to replace Digital Linear Tape (DLT) as the medium for submitting DVD titles for mass production. Though there was some initial confusion as the market sorted it out, today, all consumer-oriented DVD-R or DVD-R/RW recorders are General, as is competitively priced DVD-R media. If it's affordable, it's General, so don't worry about confusing the two. Unless you're running a commercial DVD-authoring facility or making DVDs for Disney and burning DVD-R "check discs" before you send your title out to be replicated for mass distribution, you'll never use Authoring media.

Around 1999, Pioneer introduced DVD-RW (ReWritable), a phase-change erasable format also compatible with many DVD players. In 2001, Pioneer launched the first DVD-R/RW drives in the United States, the DVR-103 and DVR-A03, which also could read and write CD-R and CD-RW.

The 103 was the so-called Super Drive shipped by Apple with some high-end Macintosh computers, and it was also bundled on several Compaq computers. Subsequent drives like the A04 and A05 were simply faster DVD-R/RW drives, but with the A06, Pioneer went dual mode, supporting both DVD-R/RW and DVD+R/+RW (see Figure 5-1 for a similar drive). More on this in a little bit.

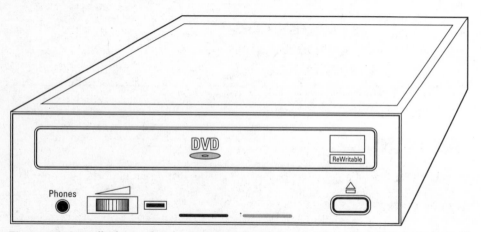

Figure 5-1: Basically this is what the Pioneer DVR-A06, Pioneer's first "Dual RW" drive, looks like.

Both DVD-R and DVD-RW support disc-at-once and incremental recording, so you can use the discs for multiple, incremental data backup sessions. That said, it's important to recognize that the goal of DVD-R/RW was primarily video-related, specifically to create video discs that play on set-top DVD players. This is why DVD-R/RW drives record and write using the Constant Linear Velocity (CLV) method, which changes drive speed to maintain consistent read and write rates.

Most hard disk drives and storage-optimized optical formats like DVD-RAM use the Zoned Constant Linear Velocity (Z-CLV) method or variations thereof, which maintains a fixed RPM rate and varies read and write speed depending upon where the data is stored on the disc. That is, since the disc spins fastest on the outside, read/write rates will be faster there than on the inside of the disc.

Drives using Z-CLV enjoy rapid random read/write access, with more than sufficient speed for the long reads and writes required by video applications. Note that while the DVD+RW specification incorporates Constant Angular Velocity (CAV), which is functionally similar to Z-CLV as well as CLV, no +RW drive supporting CAV writing has ever shipped, and many experts feel one never will.

DVD+R/+RW

DVD+RW (for ReWritable, pronounced "DVD plus RW") was originally announced in the late 1990s, primarily as a data-storage-driven technology that competed more with DVD-RAM and other forms of optical storage than DVD-R. Drives conforming to the original 1.0 DVD+RW specification never shipped, primarily because the data storage capabilities (about 2.8GB) were uncompetitive and obviously incompatible with DVD players.

When DVD+RW drives first shipped in 2001, their focus was still primarily data-oriented, and the drives couldn't reliably produce digital video discs that played on DVD players or DVD-ROMs. With the digital video market burgeoning and DVD players taking off, the companies behind the DVD+RW Alliance, which included Dell, Hewlett-Packard, Philips, and Sony, expanded the specification to include +R discs, which are more compatible with DVD players and DVD-ROMs than +RW discs.

DVD+R/+RW drives first started appearing in 2002. Like DVD-R/RW, they are capable of recording to CD-R/RW as well as DVD+R/+RW. One very popular drive is HP's dvd300i (see Figure 5-2 for a representative drawing).

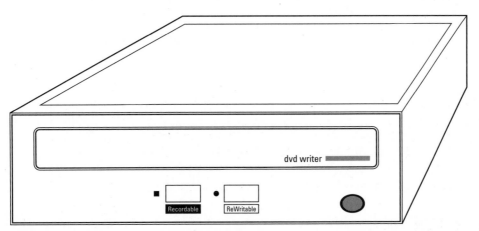

Figure 5-2: And in this corner, a drive similar to the HP dvd300i, a highly capable DVD+R/+RW drive.

Note that DVD+RW was originally focused on storage, not DVD video, which drove its developers to incorporate many key features not then available on DVD-R/RW drives.

Most important is *lossless linking,* which lets DVD+R/RW recorders pause and restart recording at any time and allows +RW recorders to replace 32-bit blocks of data with precision. These, in turn, enabled packet-writing support for incremental data storage, and efficient support for DVD+VR (Video Recording), which allows DVD producers to make minor changes without rewriting the entire disc.

Initially, DVD-R was a poor choice for incremental data storage, with long disc-formatting times and minimum writes of 1GB. However, advances to the format like Multi-Border, Quick Format, and Quick Finalizing have eliminated these limitations and made DVD-R/RW competitive in this arena.

The most enduring DVD+R advantage is hardware support for defect management, which allows the drives to detect and write around physical errors in the optical media, using a technique that's transparent to DVD players and DVD-ROMs. DVD-R/RW drives must use software drivers to accomplish the same task.

Note that due to DVD+RW's superior data-handling capabilities, Microsoft originally planned only to support DVD+R/+RW and DVD-RAM in Longhorn, the next major operating system release, using a specification called Mt. Rainier. However, Microsoft later recanted this position and will now support all writable drives under Longhorn, using defect management in the hardware when available and supplementing this with software defect management for other devices.

DVD-RAM and DV Multi

Where the DVD Forum pointed DVD-R/RW at video-related applications, DVD-RAM (Random Access Memory) was developed for the decidedly un-glorious task of optical data storage. As the name suggests, DVD-RAM can randomly access data stored on the discs, and unlike DVD-RW, the specification includes a robust defect management capability.

Older versions of DVD-RAM media are contained in a cartridge to enhance longevity, though removable versions are now available. Few DVD-ROM drives or DVD players can read DVD-RAM discs, a problem that has hindered the format's acceptance outside storage-oriented applications. Interestingly, the robustness of the format, which can withstand up to 100,000 rewrites (compared to 1,000 for both DVD+RW and DVD-RW), has made it a favorite for digital camcorders, though Sony has several models based on small-format DVD-RW.

In 2002, several vendors started shipping DVD-RAM/-R drives that could produce write-once video discs readable by DVD-ROM drives and DVD players. While this undoubtedly made these drives more attractive to organizations already using the DVD-RAM format, it did little to convert new buyers to DVD-RAM.

Seemingly the last chance for DVD-RAM lies in the DVD Multi specification defining drives that can read and write all DVD Forum standards, including DVD-R, DVD-RW, and DVD-RAM. DVD Multi drives first started shipping in mid-2003, and while compatibility is great, performance in most non-DVD-RAM functions is slower than either DVD+R/+RW or DVD-R/RW drives. This will certainly hinder the success of these drives, but DVD-RAM should remain a vibrant standard if only for the storage element.

See Table 5-2 for a breakdown of all the formats discussed in this section.

Table 5-2   The DVD Formats

Format	Media	In Brief	Discs Play On	Capacity
DVD-ROM	Double-sided/ Double-layered	Mass-replicated discs designed only for computer usage, will not play on DVD players. Primarily for data storage or games.	Computer DVD-ROM Drives Only	4.7–17 billion bytes
DVD-Video	Double-sided/ Double-layered	Mass-replicated discs designed for audio/video content that play on DVD players.	Set-top DVD-Video Players and Computer DVD-ROM Drives	4.7–9.5 billion bytes
DVD-R for Authoring a.k.a. DVD-R(A)	Single-sided/ Single-layered	Write-once recordable disc used to produce DVDs that can be mass-produced. Not widely used at this point.	Set-top DVD-Video Players and Computer DVD-ROM Drives	4.7 billion bytes
DVD-R for General a.k.a. DVD-R(G) or simply DVD-R	Single- or double-sided/ Single-layered	The recordable disc standard for general usage, but not intended to be used to create master discs for mass replication. Can create discs that play on DVD players. Defined by the DVD Forum.	Set-top DVD-Video Players and Computer DVD-ROM Drives	4.7 billion bytes
DVD-RW	Single-sided/ Single-layered	Rewritable disc standard defined by the DVD Forum. Can be rewritten up to 1,000 times.	Set-top DVD-Video Players and Computer DVD-ROM Drives	4.7 billion bytes

Continued

Table 5-2   The DVD Formats *(continued)*

Format	Media	In Brief	Discs Play On	Capacity
DVD-RAM	Double-sided/ Single-layered	Rewritable disc standard defined by the DVD Forum. Can be rewritten up to 100,000 times.	DVD-RAM Drives Only	4.7–9.5 billion bytes
DVD Multi (not technically a format, but a statement of read/write compatibility to work with DVD-RAM/DVD-R/DVD-RW formats)	Single-sided/ Single-layered	Disc drive that can read/write DVD-R/RW and DVD-RAM.	Depends upon disc format used, RAM will only play on RAM and DVD-Multi Drives, all others will play on DVD Players and Computer DVD-ROM Drives.	4.7–9.5 billion bytes
DVD+R	Single-sided/ Single-layered	Recordable disc standard championed by the DVD+RW Alliance.	DVD Players and Computer DVD-ROM Drives	4.7 billion bytes
DVD+RW	Single-sided/ Single-layered	Rewritable disc standard championed by the DVD+RW Alliance. Can be rewritten up to 1,000 times.	DVD Players and Computer DVD-ROM Drives	4.7 billion bytes
The DVD+RW Real Time Video Format, (also +VR or DVD+VR)	Single- or double-sided	DVD+RW Alliance format primarily designed for real-time recording in camcorders.	DVD Players and Computer DVD-ROM Drives	4.7–9.5 billion bytes
Dual RW (not technically a format but a statement of read/write compatibility with DVD-R/RW and DVD+R/+RW formats)	Single- or double-sided	A disc drive capable of recording and playing DVD-R/RW and DVD +R/+RW discs.	DVD Players and Computer DVD-ROM Drives	4.7–9.5 billion bytes

Comparing the Formats

Now that you've got the background, let's compare the two primary contenders: -R/RW and +R/+RW, as shown in Table 5-3.

Table 5-3   Comparing the Formats

	DVD-R/RW	*DVD+R/+RW*
Capacity per side	4.7GB	4.7GB
Double-sided discs (9.4GB total)	DVD-R	No
Rewrites	1,000	1,000
Recordable (10-pack Memorex)	$24.75	$24.75
Rewritable (10-pack Memorex)	$34.35	$34.36
Maximum recordable (write once) speed	4X	4X
Maximum rewritable speed	2X	2.4X (4X by mid-2003)

All prices per www.cdw.com.

In terms of capacity, it's all even; both standards support 4.7GB on a single side. Several manufacturers are shipping dual-sided DVD-R discs with a total capacity of 9.4GB, but you have to turn the disc over to burn both sides, and they typically cost nearly twice as much as single-sided. It's also very difficult to write or otherwise label a double-sided disc, so this capability provides no real advantage.

Both drives are equally robust, with each sector on the disc capable of 1,000 rewrites. In terms of cost, DVD-R/RW was first and once enjoyed a significant price advantage over DVD+R/+RW, but at the time of this writing, format costs were identical from many manufacturers.

The Burning Question

Though both +R and -R drives write at 4X maximum speeds, most tests to date, including those performed by *PC Magazine* and sister publication *ExtremeTech,* show DVD-R drives to write approximately 25 percent faster than +R drives. These results have been confirmed by other publications, including *ZDNet,* though recent +R drives from TEAC and other vendors are coming much closer to -R recording speed.

At the time of this writing, DVD+RW has a 20 percent speed advantage over DVD-RW. Both DVD-RW and DVD+RW should be up to 4X rewritable speed by mid-2004. The race should only continue as both Pioneer and Philips are promising 8X write-once speeds in 2004.

Compatibility

The next stop in our comparison tour is media compatibility, or more specifically, the percentage of DVD players that will be able to read your recorded media. The obvious first point to realize is that no matter which recorder you purchase, the discs you record won't play back on every available player.

This is because most older players and DVD-ROM drives were shipped before recordable DVD became prevalent, and though both -R/RW and +R/+RW camps did what they could to achieve compatibility, perfection was simply not possible. Fortunately, the problem is worse on older players and should ultimately disappear, since most new players are tested on DVD-R, DVD-RW, DVD+R, and DVD+RW to ensure compatibility.

The seminal work on the subject was an article written by Ralph LaBarge published in *DV Magazine* in July 2002, entitled "DVD Compatibility Test." Unfortunately, written before the availability of +R recorders, Ralph tested the compatibility of discs recorded under five different standards with discs from multiple vendors (see `www.dv.com/features/features_item.jhtml?LookupId=/xml/feature/2002/labarge0702` for the report).

As shown in Table 5-4, the results were startling all around. Ignoring the results for DVD-R for Authoring, which have little relevance to casual producers, those using DVD-R for General recorders learned that depending upon the media used, compatibility could be less than 50%. Though -RW drives were slightly more compatible than +RW, both were significantly less compatible than DVD-R for General using Maxell, Sony, or TDK media. (Note that I reformatted Ralph's results to list media vendor by compatibility percentage, rather than alphabetically.)

Table 5-4   Disc Compatibility by Format and Media Supplier

DVD-R for Authoring (3.95GB)	DVD-R for Authoring (4.7GB)	DVD-R for General (4.7GB)	DVD-RW (4.7GB)	DVD+RW (4.7GB)
Mitsui (98%)	Maxell (76%)	Maxell (80%)	Pioneer (61%)	HP (57%)
Pioneer (98%)	Ritek (71%)	Sony (76%)	Sony (61%)	Memorex (57%)
Ridata (98%)	Mitsui (69%)	TDK (76%)	TDK (61%)	Sony (57%)
TDK (96%)	Ridata (69%)	Apple (73%)	Verbatim (61%)	Verbatim (55%)
Verbatim (90%)	TDK (67%)	Imation (71%)	JVC (59%)	
	Pioneer (65%)	Mitsui (73%)	Ritek (59%)	
	Taiyo Yuden (63%)	Panasonic (69%)	Memorex (55%)	
	Verbatim (59%)	Ridata (69%)	Ridata (55%)	
		Verbatim (69%)		
		Vivastar (63%)		
		Memorex (59%)		
		Pioneer (58%)		
		Ritek (51%)		
		CD-Recordable. com (45%)		

Ralph also came up with a great list of suggestions for improving compatibility, which I'll discuss in Chapter 20. The most obvious, of course, is don't use cheap media.

However, since Ralph didn't test +R media, the open question relates to the compatibility of +R discs. Two later tests reported in *PC Magazine* ("DVD Compatibility: It's as Ugly as Ever," October 29, 2002) shed some light on the issue. In a Pioneer-funded study, DVD-R and +R compatibility was about even, with -RW trailing +RW slightly, while a study by Intellikey found DVD+R much more compatible than -R. The results are presented in Table 5-5. (Note that the percentages represent the number of sample discs successfully read by test DVD players.)

Table 5-5   DVD Compatibility

	Pioneer-funded Study	*Intellikey Study*
DVD-R	78%	77%
DVD+R	78%	90%
DVD-RW	58%	66%
DVD+RW	63%	72%

To many long-time DVD-R users, these results, especially the Intellikey study, seem counterintuitive. One study, reported by CDR-Info, tested DVD-R and DVD+R discs on 13 drives, with DVD-R working perfectly on all drives and DVD+R failing on four. While perhaps not statistically significant, this is very representative of the grass-roots opinion of the DVD-authoring community. For example, I work primarily with a trusty old Pioneer A03 drive and have never experienced any incompatibilities until I burned my first DVD+R disc. The fact that this occurred when I was teaching a seminar at the University of Wisconsin did little to strengthen my ardor for the +R standard.

Many industry professionals feel that the general availability of cheap media for -R drives has driven down overall format compatibility. Once these same bargain-basement suppliers ship +R media, compatibility statistics for this format will drop as well.

These perceptions aside, however, the only objective lessons we have learned is that rewritable media is generally less compatible than writable and that DVD+R is at least as compatible as -R media.

Overall Summary

Basically, there are four uses for these drives: creating write-once and rewritable video discs, and writable and rewritable data-storage discs. Keeping in mind that both price and format robustness (for rewriting) are similar, here's my choice for each use:

- **Write-once video applications.** In these applications, when you're authoring and burning a DVD, DVD-R is faster (for now, anyway) and, in my view, more compatible.

- **Write-once data-storage applications.** There is a slight advantage to DVD+R due to hardware defect management.

■ **Rewritable video applications.** +RW has a slight edge due to greater compatibility. That said, unless you absolutely know that the +RW disc will play in the target drive, it's probably safer to use the more compatible +R discs anyway.

■ **Rewritable data applications.** +RW has the edge, but if you're really serious about data, DVD-RAM is your best choice, even though performance will be slower. It's simply the safest, most reliable format.

From this analysis, the optimal drive would be one that supports DVD-R for write-once video applications and +R/+RW for data and video files you'd like to rewrite many times. Someone at Sony must have believed this as well, because in mid-2002, Sony introduced two "Dual RW" drives that could write both DVD-R/RW and DVD+R/RW, the external DRX500ULX ($429) and internal DRU500AX ($349).

These drives offers some compelling advantages. Not only do you have your choice of media, you double your chances of compatibility. If grandma's old DVD player can't read a +R disc, send her a -R. The Sony drive worked wonders for me in my environment, primarily because none of my Pioneer drives, albeit somewhat long in the tooth, would read +R media. So, I burned -R, and they played.

The only knock against the Sony drive is that it's not quite as fast as, say, the Pioneer A05 drive in many DVD-R burning functions, and it commands an $80 price premium over the cheapest drives on the market. Given the compatibility differences we saw with cheap media, buying the cheapest drive isn't a good strategy anyway.

Overall, however, the mere existence of the Sony drive makes it difficult to recommend single standard drives from either camp. Clearly, consumers liked the drive, because by all accounts it sold very well.

So well, in fact, that in May 2003, Pioneer announced that their A06 would be a "Dual RW" drive, a huge turnaround for the primary promoter of the -R format.

As reported in *EMedia, the Digital Studio Magazine,* Andy Parsons, Pioneer's Senior VP explained it like this:

"I know it seems like a big departure, but it's really just a reflection of what the market is doing now. We're now outside of the relatively comfy professional/prosumer environment where users are well-informed about format issues and the various intricacies of how it all works. Now we've got consumers that have absolutely no clue that there is a format war. Some people pick up a given drive — perhaps based on the brand — grab some blank media (whatever is cheapest and closest), and run home with it all. Then they try to get it working, find out the disc is rejected by the drive, and return the whole thing back to the store as defective. Not a good scenario for the user or the retailer."

Since Pioneer makes many of the drives sold by other -R/RW vendors, it's likely the entire -R/RW camp will go Dual RW fairly quickly. Note that the A06 won't write to +RW at 4X speed, leaving room for +R/RW drives to outperform it in this metric, at least temporarily. Just a week before Pioneer's announcement, Verbatim introduced a multi-format drive manufactured by NEC. In addition, +R/RW stalwarts like HP, Ricoh, and Philips have not announced their intent to implement -R in their drives.

So it remains to be seen if all drives will ever become Dual RW. However, it seems likely that consumers will vote with their wallets to avoid the media confusion associated with a single format drive. When this occurs, the +R/RW holdouts can either compete on price, which few top manufacturers like to do, or start producing Dual RW drives. I'm predicting the latter.

Either way, standards issues notwithstanding, choosing a drive will come down to the four typical considerations: price, performance, input/output, and bundled software.

Buying a DVD Recorder

Here are the key considerations to evaluate when buying a DVD recorder.

Internal versus External

Until very recently, this was very much a non-decision, since the fastest external ports included on most computers were the parallel port and USB 1.0 port, both far too slow to handle the maximum read/write throughput of today's DVDs. Now, drives like the external Sony support FireWire (400 megabits/50MB per second) and USB 2.0 (480Mb/60MB per second), both more than fast enough for the fastest DVD operations.

I typically prefer internal drives because they're cheaper than external drives, there's less clutter, and one less AC power outlet to worry about. The only downside is that you can't share the drive that easily among your computers and that you have to crack open your computer to install the drive.

Installation isn't all that complicated, however, though you have to be careful to ensure that the drive is not slowing hard disk performance. Specifically, most internal DVD recorders connect via an IDE cable, the same kind of cable that connects to hard drives. Most computer motherboards have two IDE channels, each capable of handling two devices, called the master and the slave. When you have two devices installed on a single channel, it operates at the speed of the slower of the two.

Pair a comparatively slow DVD recorder with your fast capture and edit drive, and drive performance drops to that of the recorder. For this reason, in systems with two disk drives, it's typically better to place the recorder on the same channel as your boot drive, where performance isn't critical, rather than pairing it with your capture drive. Note that most newer motherboards implementing Serial ATA, a new, faster connection to your hard disk that works independently of IDE, don't have this limitation.

You can avoid all these issues with external drives, which are obviously easier to install and share, especially those with both FireWire and USB connectors. However, they're typically $50 to $80 more than the equivalent internal drive. See Table 5-6 for a look at how internal and external drives compare.

Table 5-6	Internal versus External Recorders	
	Internal Drives	**External Drives**
Pros	Less expensive	Easier to share
	Less clutter	Easier to install
Cons	More difficult to share	More expensive
	More difficult to install	More clutter
	Can slow hard drive speeds if not installed correctly	

Speed Metrics

Each drive has rated performance numbers that often differ quite dramatically from actual test results, a dynamic that keeps product reviewers like me in business. Here we'll look at the theoretical numbers to ascertain, and later we'll identify some good sources of actual performance numbers to augment those you can find in *PC Magazine*.

At this point, I'm recommending that you buy a Dual Mode drive, and it certainly looks like single mode DVD-R/RW drives will soon disappear. So let's compare the two most high-profile Dual Mode drives, the Pioneer A06 and the Sony DRX-500 ULX, primarily to learn what the metrics mean and how to compare them (see Table 5-7).

Table 5-7 Comparing DVD Recorders

	Pioneer A06	*Sony DRX-500 ULX*
DVD-R speed	4X	4X
DVD-RW speed	2X	2X
DVD+R speed	4X	4X
DVD+RW speed	2.4X	2.4X
DVD read speed	12X	8X
CD-R speed	16X	24X
CD-RW speed	10X	10X
CD read speed	32X	32X
Average random access (CD-ROM)	130 ms	160 ms
Average random access (DVD-ROM)	140 ms	200 ms

As I've mentioned throughout this chapter, DVD recorders perform many discrete read/write activities, forcing thorough buyers to compare lots of numbers before choosing a drive. Most current DVD recorders support the same maximum write and rewrite speeds shown in Table 5-7, but each time there's a sea change, like there will be when -RW and +RW speeds go to 4X later in 2003, you need to make sure that the drive you select offers top performance.

DVD read speed is important primarily for users who plan to copy a large number of discs, and as you'll see, Pioneer lives up to its stellar ratings there. If you're a heavy CD-Audio user, CD read and write speeds are important here as well, though the two-minute burn time difference between 16X and 24X will prove significant only to the highest-volume producer.

Of course, rated numbers are nice, but mileage definitely varies in the test lab. The Pioneer drive's startlingly high read speed was recently born out in a recent *PC Magazine* review, where the older A05 drive copied a 4.28GB disc to the test bed hard drive in 6:15, almost a full four minutes faster than the Sony DRX-500ULX.

On the other hand, in a CD-R recording test, the Sony burned a 64-minute disc in 4:18 compared to Pioneer's 4:48, which is far from the 33% performance difference suggested by the comparative specifications. The obvious lesson is that you have to check reviews to make sure the specs bear out.

Bundled Software

After identifying the best hardware alternatives, it's time to look at the software side. As Table 5-8 shows, most commercial bundles include programs in five different classes of software: video editing, DVD authoring, CD/DVD data recording, programs that enable drag-and-drop recording on the drive (drive letter access, or DLA), and a software "player" that allows you to play DVD-Video discs from the drive.

Table 5-8   Bundled Software

	Pioneer A06	Sony
Video editing	ArcSoft ShowBiz	ArcSoft ShowBiz
DVD authoring	MyDVD 4.0 Video Suite	MyDVD 4.0 Video Suite
CD/DVD recording	Roxio Easy CD Creator	Veritas RecordNow/Veritas Simple Backup
Drive letter access (DLA) software	Pinnacle InstantWrite	Veritas DLA
DVD player	Sonic CinePlayer	CyberLink PowerDVD
Other software	N/A	Music Match Jukebox

Check Chapters 3 and 4 for how the bundled editing and authoring programs stack up against each other. Unfortunately, you're on your own regarding the other three categories, which are beyond the scope of the book.

Summary

In addition to *PC Magazine* (which reviewed the Sony and Pioneer drives in May 2003), the best sources of thorough reviews include www.emedialive.com, www.cnet.com, www.pcworld.com (which has a very helpful comparison matrix), and www.cdrinfo.com.

General Information Resources

If you're looking for general information about the standards, the best place to start is at www.dvddemystified.com, which maintains the famous DVD FAQ. I also found www.cdrfaq.org to be helpful.

You can find the DVD-Forum at www.dvdforum.com. The DVD+RW Alliance is located at www.dvdrw.com, with the unofficial site at www.dvdplusrw.com.

Jim Taylor's book, *DVD Demystified*, is the acknowledged standard on DVD technology, while Ralph LaBarge's book, *DVD Authoring and Production*, provides great insight into its namesake activities. Both are widely distributed and available at www.amazon.com.

Pricing Resources

Check prices at www.pcmag.com and www.epinions.com, which has a surprising dearth of customer reviews, making it less useful than normal in this arena.

Chapter 6

Upgrading and Preparing Your Computer

T he lovely thing about computer testing is that you never really know beforehand how the results will turn out. You have your theories and expectations, but every once in a while, you get thrown for a total loop.

For this chapter, and an associated *PC Magazine* article, I developed this wonderful test script designed to measure to the exact percentage point the benefit that components like additional RAM, faster disks, and the latest processor would bring.

As my darling daughter Whatley likes to say, there was "just one problem." Nothing mattered but the processor, and only then with certain programs.

Now that's a touch of an overstatement. I did see 5 to 10 percent increments from other changes that I made, but if you want to make a quantum leap in performance, you have to have a fast processor, preferably one with HT technology (hyper-threading) or even two processors.

If you want to leave now, having heard that critical nugget of information, I'll understand, but then you'll miss my eight simple steps for achieving digital nirvana with your capture station (and probably would never forgive yourself).

1. "Recommended" Is the Minimum

All video editors, capture devices, DVD-authoring programs, and similar products have published minimum system requirements specified by the manufacturer/developer as the minimum configuration that can run the program or hardware. You can generally find them on the company's Web site. Generally, these are fairly low common denominator requirements so as not to exclude potential users with slow underpowered computers. It sounds silly, since most of those users will be unhappy anyway, but that's how it's done.

Most publishers also list "recommended" configuration options. For example, here are the minimum and recommended parameters for Pinnacle Studio:

- CPU: Intel Pentium or AMD Athlon 500 MHz (1 GHz or higher recommended)
- Memory: 128MB RAM (256MB recommended)
- Operating System: Windows 98SE, "Millennium," 2000, XP (XP recommended)
- Graphics Card: Direct X compatible (ATI Radeon or NVIDIA GeForce recommended)
- Sound Card: Direct X compatible
- Hard Disk Space: 300MB of disk space to install software 4GB for every 20 minutes of video captured
- Other: 1394/FireWire port, Mouse, CD-ROM drive
- Optional: CD burner for creating Video CDs or Super Video CDs
- DVD burner drive for creating DVDs

Here they are for Adobe Premiere Pro:

- Intel Pentium III 800-MHz processor (Pentium 4 3.06 GHz recommended)
- Microsoft Windows XP Professional or Home Edition with Service Pack 1
- 256MB of RAM installed (1GB or more recommended)
- 800MB of available hard disk space for installation
- CD-ROM drive
- Compatible DVD recorder (DVD-R/RW+R/RW) required for Export to DVD
- 1,024x768 32-bit color video display adapter (1,280x1,024 or dual monitors recommended)
- For DV: OHCI-compatible IEEE 1394 interface and dedicated large-capacity 7200RPM UDMA 66 IDE or SCSI hard disk or disk array
- For third-party capture cards: Adobe Premiere Pro certified capture card
- Optional: ASIO audio hardware device; surround speaker system for 5.1 audio playback

Generally, you should pick your capture hardware and software programs first, and then ignore the *minimum* settings and make sure your computer meets the *recommended* settings. At the very least, your program will run faster. In my experience, products that run on too little RAM are more likely to crash, so you'll probably get more stable operation as well. I'll discuss how to fine-tune these choices as I go along.

2. Buy, Don't Build

. . . that is, unless you're absolutely sure you know what you're doing.

I've built several computers in my life, and they've all worked well about 99 percent of the time. But they tended to be a bit more fragile than other computers that I've purchased. It's also more of a hassle than it looks, since there's always some funky driver you have no idea you're missing until your performance turns out to be way below what you expected. Then there're power and heat problems with the case (which really wasn't designed for a hot burning Pentium 4 chip), making sure the memory is right for the motherboard (566 MHz? 800 MHz? DIMMs? SIMMs?), ensuring that hard drives match the on board connector (IDE? Serial ATA? SCSI?), and finally simply building the thing with instructions designed for experts, not beginners.

I just finished reviewing workstations from Dell and Hewlett Packard. Starting price for both models is under $1,000, and they come with quiet, well-ventilated cases that feature totally tool-less installation of drives and graphics cards. Technical support is wonderful, with one-day on-site maintenance, and both systems cost about what I would have paid for the components.

So, unless you're really sure you know what you're doing, buy, don't build.

3. Get Current on the Operating System

Forget Windows 98, even the Second Edition. Just let it go. Don't even talk to me if you're still running Windows 95, it's way past time for a change.

To me, Windows 2000 Professional was the best operating system ever made, but just this year, Microsoft won me over to Windows XP, which is more stable than Windows 2000 and has more available current drivers. If you're using anything older than Windows 2000, you're setting yourself up for big, big hassles down the road.

So, before installing your capture, editing, and authoring solutions, think hard about upgrading to Windows XP Pro.

4. Processor — Spend Money Here

If you're buying a new computer, mortgage the home, give up Starbucks for a month, take mass transit, drink American wines, do whatever it takes to buy the absolutely fastest system you can afford. My tests show that the processor has more impact on rendering performance than any other option you buy. In fact, it's probably more than any other options combined. However, at least in the short term, it is extremely program-dependent.

Understand that hyper-threaded (HT) processors just became available in mid-2003, while dual-processor (DP) computers became affordable in late 2003. (See the sidebar, "A Quick Processor Primer," in Chapter 3 for a description of HT and DP technologies and how they work.) This means that programs developed and released in 2002, like Pinnacle Studio and Sony MovieBlast, had no real incentive to support HT or DP computers. This is pretty obvious from the minimal difference seen in rendering speeds in Table 6-1.

Table 6-1   Rendering Speeds for Consumer and Prosumer Video Editors (given in hrs.:mins.:secs.)

	P4 2.4 GHz HT disabled	P4 2.4 GHz HT enabled	Single 3.06 GHz Xeon	Dual 3.06 GHz Xeon
Pinnacle Studio (to render and encode a 7-minute project to MPEG-2)	18:55	18:01	DNT	DNT
Ulead VideoStudio (to render and encode a 7-minute project to MPEG-2)	13:36	9:08	DNT	DNT
Adobe Premiere (to render and encode a 12.5-minute project to MPEG-2)	1:04:25	47:59	47:06	24:12
Pinnacle Edition (to render and encode a 12.5-minute project to MPEG-2)	41:13	35:53	30:06	28:56
Sony Vegas (to render and encode a 12.5-minute project to MPEG-2)	1:37:20	1:32:59	1:18:59	1:15:28
Ulead MediaStudio Pro (to render and encode a 12.5-minute project to MPEG-2)	40:31	34:30	25:41	21:25

*DNT means did not test.

However, now that the technologies are here, developers that fail to eke out the last bit of rendering speed from HT and DP computers will suffer a severe competitive advantage. In other words, it's acceptable to be slow, so long as the quality is there, but failing to leverage additional resources and get faster on HT/DP computers is totally wasteful. You get a glimpse of that from Adobe Premiere; the first editor shipped after HT/DP became prevalent, which proved a very efficient consumer of HT and especially dual processor power.

As I explained in Chapter 3, Vegas showed little difference in rendering speed because when multiple processor threads are available, Sony splits them between the audio and video processing. Since my tests were primarily video related, the additional processor threads allocated to audio pretty much went to waste. If your projects are equally weighted between audio and video processing, you should expect to see significant benefits from HT and dual processor computers with Vegas.

So, even if products like Studio don't necessarily benefit significantly from HT or DP technologies today, they certainly will tomorrow, and the faster clock speeds of DP- and HT-enabled chips are a rising tide that raises all boats in the harbor, so all applications run faster, even Studio.

For example, Studio's rendering time dropped from 18:01 on a 2.4-GHz Pentium 4 system to 13:06 on a 3.2-GHz Pentium 4 system, a speed boost of 25%, which is far more than you'll gain by installing the most RAM you can or the fastest disk drive available. So if you're going to spend the money, spend it on processing speed.

5. RAM — Get Enough but No More

All programs require random access memory (RAM) to operate, much like you need space on your desk to work. If programs run out of RAM, they can use hard drive space to store the needed information, similar to how you might put excess paper in your desk drawers. However, saving to and retrieving from disk is much slower than working solely from RAM, much like you're more efficient when you don't have to reach beneath your desk to store and retrieve paperwork.

Table 6-2 shows two projects tested on a Pentium 4 2.4-GHz computer at *PC Magazine* at the various levels of RAM shown. The Pinnacle Studio project totaled 14 minutes of video, while the MediaStudio project was 12:30 minutes long. Test scores are the time it took to render both projects to MPEG-2.

Pinnacle Studio is an elegant program, but it consumes RAM in voracious amounts. For this reason, I was absolutely certain that upgrading from 128MB to 256MB would produce a significant amount of time saved. However, as you can see, moving from 128MB to 256MB shaved only 24 seconds from the rendering time, while upgrading from 256MB to 512MB saved 48 seconds—not much to write home about, but twice as much as the jump from 128MB to 256MB.

Table 6-2   Performance at Different RAM Configurations

	Pinnacle Studio		Ulead MediaStudio Pro	
	Time	*% Reduction*	*Time*	*% Reduction*
128MB	42:09		39:29	
256MB	41:44	− 0.99%	40:23	+ 2.28%
512MB	40:56	− 2.89%	38:44	− 1.90%
1GB	40:50	− 3.12%	38:40	− 2.07%

Interestingly, a quick check of the Windows XP Performance Monitor revealed that Studio was consuming 303MB of RAM while encoding. At 512MB of RAM, Studio no longer had to store data to disk during rendering, which made it more efficient. Note that the upgrade from 512MB to 1GB shaved only 4 additional seconds off the rendering time, simply because it introduced no new efficiencies into the equation. Hence, after you achieve a level that's beyond what your programs need to operate without storing to disk, additional RAM brings little benefit.

The same is true with MediaStudio Pro, which required about 280MB of operating space to render to MPEG-2 format. The upgrade from 128MB to 256MB actually increased rendering time, an unexplained anomaly, which was recouped when upgrading to 512MB. Beyond that, upgrading from

512MB to 1GB saved a scant 4 seconds. Either way, the total speed improvement was under 3 percent in both cases, which certainly won't get you in the Bang for the Buck Hall of Fame.

Note

For the test described above, I had a relatively fast system and fresh, defragmented disks, so there was plenty of open space to write to when paging back and forth to disk. If you've got an older system or cluttered, slow, and nearly full drives, you can expect that additional RAM would produce incremental performance benefits. In fact, in one test, defragging the system disk (I discuss defragging below) reduced rendering time by over 4 percent.

However, even on the oldest, slowest system, with creaky drives, adding RAM won't produce a night and day difference. Rendering is a processor-intensive operation where the processor is the main bottleneck. Easing the associated storage and retrieval tasks, while helpful, simply doesn't produce incremental performance benefits.

A good general rule to follow is to purchase enough RAM to run your primary design programs without paging back and forth to disk. To find out how much RAM you need, load your primary programs and get them involved in the most RAM-intensive activity, usually rendering. Then press Ctrl+Alt+Del to bring up the Windows Task Manager and click on the Performance tab (see Figure 6-1).

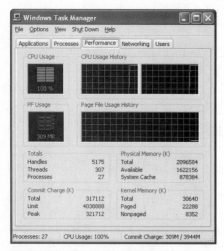

Figure 6-1: The Performance tab lets you know how much RAM is being used by your applications at any given moment. Press Ctrl+Alt+Del to get here.

As you can see in Figure 6-1, I'm currently using only 309MB of RAM, despite rendering in two programs, Ulead's MediaStudio and DVD Workshop, simultaneously. The 100 percent CPU usage tells me my processor is running full out, but I've got plenty of RAM to spare on this 2GB system. Bottom line is that for these applications, anything beyond 512MB would probably be a waste.

On the other hand, I ran a quick test on the system running Adobe Premiere and learned that if I'm encoding in Premiere and load PhotoShop and After Effects, total RAM requirements jump to over 700MB. Anything lower than 1GB would make me nervous if I planned to run the Adobe digital content creation suite.

6. Hard Disk — Buy Capacity, Not Speed

This is another area where I felt that an investment would yield big benefits, but it didn't pan out, at least for day-to-day rendering activities. To test this, I created a 36-minute project in Ulead MediaStudio and rendered it under three different scenarios, outlined in Table 6-3.

Table 6-3   Performance at Different Hard-Disk Capacities

	Configuration	*Rendering Time*
Scenario 1	One drive system (Serial ATA drive)	55:42:42
Scenario 2	Install 15,000-RPM Seagate SCSI drive. Place all project files on new SCSI, with temp, preview, and output files rendered to SCSI.	55:46:22
Scenario 3	Install RPM Seagate SCSI drive. Place all project files on new SCSI, with temp, preview, and output files rendered to original Serial ATA drive.	50:27.32

Note that in Scenario 2, rendering time actually increased slightly, even though the Seagate SCSI drive was much faster than the Serial ATA. However, when I wrote the files to the Serial ATA drive, so that I wasn't reading and writing to the same disk, rendering time dropped approximately 9 percent.

The open question, of course, is whether you need a top-notch 15,000-RPM SCSI drive to gain this 9 percent or whether any second drive will do the trick. To answer this question, I rendered twice on another computer equipped with two older IDE drives. The first time, all project, temporary, and rendered files were on the same drive, similar to Scenarios 1 and 2. The second time all project files were on one drive with temporary and rendered files directe toward the other. This produced a 4 percent speed advantage.

The lesson to take away from this is that since rendering is a non-real-time event that's largely processor driven, and therefore limited by processor speed as opposed to the speed of the peripherals around it, the impact of disk speed is minimal. While you can produce some gain from multiple, fast disks, it's incremental, not exponential as it is with processors. Clearly it also pays to use your capture drive primarily for capture while writing temporary and other project files to another disk, but the difference isn't life changing.

High-Performance Applications

Another open question is whether there are any real-time applications where disk speed does pay off. To answer this, I set up multiple picture-in-picture effects in Pinnacle Edition.

Briefly, a picture-in-picture effect is where one video stream is placed in a small window set into another video or fixed background, kind of like the opening sequence of *The Brady Bunch* show, where they're all happily staring at one another. Each window is a separate 3.6MB/second stream the hard drive has to deliver in real time to the video editor, so multiple streams tax disk performance quickly.

Basically, the test consisted of adding streams until frames started dropping, indicating that performance was no longer in real time. I used Edition because it has a handy-dandy frame rate meter that glows red when frames start dropping, making it easy to see exactly what's going on and where.

I put the source files on the Serial ATA drive and managed to successfully pull four streams without dropping frames, but the system slowed with the fifth stream. In contrast, using the Seagate SCSI, Edition played six streams without dropping frames, an increase of 50 percent (see Figure 6-2).

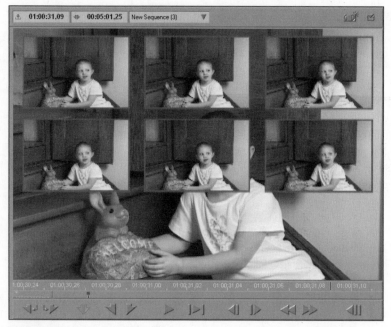

Figure 6-2: If you're developing projects like this, a fast SCSI disk can definitely help.

The lesson here is that if you're doing lots of multiple layer effects and need real-time preview, or you're working with a hardware system that can output in real time, fast SCSI disks can make a huge difference. Otherwise, for the more prosaic, day-to-day projects most of us produce, you're better off buying a large, slow disk that meets your capacity needs than a fast SCSI drive in the hopes of chasing down incremental performance.

7. Graphics — Let Your Video Editor Decide

Unlike architecture and design programs, most video editors require very little in terms of graphics-processing power. The only exception is Pinnacle Edition, which does access the 3D-graphics-processing capabilities of some graphics cards, when available, to render certain effects.

Once you've picked your video editor, check the minimum system requirements for graphics. As you can see from the minimum system requirements posted at the start of the chapter, both Studio and Premiere are pretty basic, but Edition requires "64MB graphics card and SVGA monitor capable of 1024 x 768 @ 32-bit resolution." Dig a bit deeper on the Pinnacle Web site, and you'll find a "Compatibility List" that shows all tested graphics cards. The obvious lesson is to check the minimum system requirements and then the vendor Web site for some recommendations.

If you're buying any Ulead editor or Premiere Pro, you might also consider the Parhelia card from Matrox (www.matrox.com). These cards feature analog output on the card, which you can connect to a TV set or analog monitor to preview your video, a great alternative to routing it through your DV camcorder and out to a monitor.

The only problem with this card is that its 3D-processing capabilities are minimal, so it doesn't work well with Pinnacle Edition. However, I've gotten great results with both Ulead products and Premiere 6.5.

8. Steps Before Installing

There are a number of steps you should take before installing your video editor, especially when installing into an older computer. These will probably take you only an hour or so, especially if you plan well and defrag overnight, but they will probably save you hours in potential frustration down the road.

1. If you're installing into a current system, as opposed to a new system, perform all upgrades before installing your new video-related products. This means upgrading the operating system, adding additional RAM, and installing new hard disks or a new graphics card. Get all this installed and working and then install the video products.

2. Clean house. If you're not going to upgrade to a new operating system, uninstall all programs you're not using, especially games and other multimedia programs. Then run Disk Cleanup — from the Start menu, select Programs → Accessories → System Tools → Disk Cleanup — to delete all temporary and other unnecessary files, and then go on a witch hunt yourself and delete all other files you don't need any more. Your goal is to clear as much disk space as possible before loading the new products.

3. Defragment all disk drives. From the Start menu, select Programs → Accessories → System Tools → Disk Defragmenter to consolidate all files on the hard disk and make the drives as efficient as possible.

4. Get the latest drivers for all retained peripherals, including your graphics card, soundcard, and video-capture card.

5. Get a startup manager like *PC Magazine*'s Startup Cop (www.pcmag.com/article2/0, 4149,2173,00.asp). This will help you control programs that start automatically when you boot your machine, even if you don't know they are there. For example, QuickTime, RealOne, Quicken, Microsoft Office, Adobe Acrobat, and many other programs install memory resident components that take up RAM and can interrupt or slow operations like capture and rendering. Though probably well intentioned, you and your computer can live without most of these, and a startup manager helps you clean them out. One big clue that you've got problems is if the right side of your Windows task bar is laden with small icons, each representing a resident program.

When hunting these out, I'm pretty relentless; if I recognize the program and know what it does (as is the case with Roxio Audio Central as shown in Figure 6-3), I shut it down. If I don't, I note the name, shut it down, reboot and make sure everything is working normally, which occurs 99 percent of the time. If not, it's easy enough to reverse your actions within Startup Cop and even create different startup profiles for different activities.

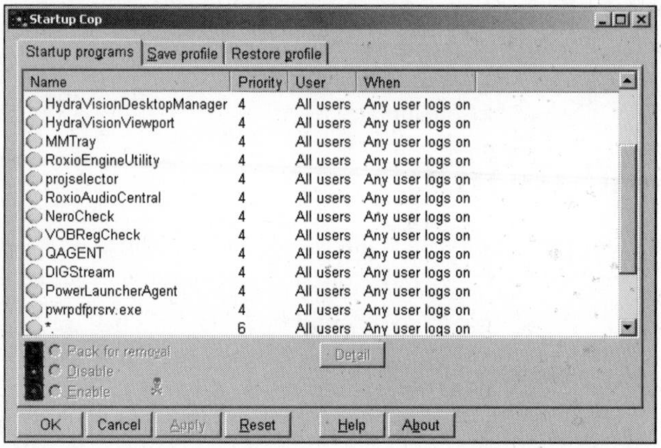

Figure 6-3: *PC Magazine*'s Startup Cop allows you to police and shut down performance-slowing programs that load when you boot your computer.

6. If you're running Windows XP, once you have your system tuned and optimized, create a restore point with the System Restore utility (shown in Figure 6-4). Briefly, if your installation is a total bust and you wish you had never even tried to edit video, this utility allows you to restore your system to its condition on the selected restore point. From the Start menu, select Programs → Accessories → System Tools → System Restore.

7. After loading your video-related products, immediately check for updates on the vendors' Web sites. Many programs will check for updates for you, but some don't, and the last thing you want to experience is a bug that's been fixed in the latest release.

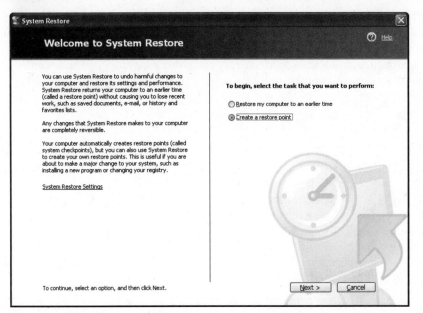

Figure 6-4: Get familiar with Windows XP's System Restore function, which can restore your computer to its original pristine condition.

Rules to Live By

Here are some random last thoughts before you go on your merry way:

- A dedicated video-capture and editing station is a happy capture and editing station. If you use it for this task and this task only, chances are it will work well each and every time you call upon it. If you frequently load children's games and other funky programs on the computer, chances are some day you'll try to run the editor and it won't work.

- Not all editing programs work on all computers, it's a simple fact of life. So buy from a reputable vendor that will allow you to return the product with no questions asked. Then start with modest projects before pushing the creative envelope. That way, you'll learn what the program can do before you learn what it can't. Don't get invested in making any video-related product work. If it crashes repeatedly early in your production efforts, it's probably some impossible-to-diagnose issue like a conflict with another program. Cut your losses fast, return the product, and try another.

- Where there's a will, there's a way, but a positive attitude is key. Video editing is a lot like raising a child, or perhaps like golf. It's perplexing, difficult, time-consuming, at times very frustrating, but ultimately deeply satisfying. OK, so maybe it's not like golf.

If you approach video editing under the assumption that you can breeze in, produce *It's a Wonderful Life* or *Field of Dreams* in a couple of hours, and then walk out, you're going to be sorely disappointed. If you assume that video editing provides a mere palette for creativity that must be developed, honed, and perfected, you'll have a great time and be rewarded with good videos that many around you will enjoy.

If you expect problems, you'll deal with them as they come and move on. If you expect a friction-free editing experience, you're in for a rough time.

Summary

Here's a summary of the key conclusions from this chapter:

1. When purchasing new programs or upgrading your system, check the minimum system requirements for your chosen video editor and capture device, and then go with the recommended — not the minimum — settings.

2. Life is too short, and video editing is tough enough without the added hassle of not having a stable platform. Unless you really, really know what you're doing, don't roll your own.

3. Get the most up-to-date operating system available. Upgrading to Windows XP Professional is probably the best step toward a stable editing experience.

4. Blow your budget on the processor for the biggest bang for your buck.

5. Purchase enough RAM to run your primary design programs without paging back and forth to disk. Usually that's no more than 1GB.

6. Unless you're into mucho real-time effects, a really fast disk subsystem will produce only minimal performance benefits. So always spend your cash on hard disk capacity instead of speed.

7. Generally, video editors require very little in terms of graphics-processing power. Don't spend a lot of money here unless you have to in order to meet the minimum requirements of your chosen video editor.

8. There are a number of steps you can take to ensure a smooth installation and lift off. Save yourself some headaches and take them.

Part II

Shooting Your Video

Chapter 7

The Basics of Shooting

This is the chapter on shooting video. We start by defining three modes of shooting, recording, story telling, and movie making, and then explore the rules for improving your videos in all three modes. Along the way, we cover critical issues like how to compose your shots, how best to handle camera motion and shot composition, and what a cutaway shot is and why you need them.

We conclude with a storyboard, or list of recommended shots, for shooting a birthday party, and a checklist for shooting interviews.

Introduction

Anyone who wields a camcorder is a shooter, and shooters have three basic modes: recording, story telling, and movie making.

When recording, a shooter goes with the flow and shoots whatever looks interesting. There is no plan, simply a desire to capture the experience as it unfolds, whether it's a day at the beach, a wedding, or a Disney World vacation. Instead of shooting to edit your video, you're recording just to watch it from start to finish and relive the experience.

However casual, when working in recording mode, you can make your videos much more watchable by composing your picture properly, using different camera shots, like close-ups and wide shots, to your advantage, and learning when and how to use motion like zooming and panning.

Story telling takes this one step further; you're not there simply to record the action, but to tell a story. Your goal is to edit the video into a cohesive movie with common story elements like a beginning, middle, and end. So, you need to plan for these shots and start shooting to edit rather than for sequential playback, so you can piece the story together in your video editor.

Movie making takes story telling to the furthest extreme. Here you're thinking, "What would Spielberg do if he was here?" How would he tell the story and the stories behind the story? Where would he place the cameras? Which motion would he follow? What mood would he try to create, and how would he use the camera to do it?"

Since you probably only have one camera and certainly only one you, you must get creative. You need to scope out camera placement, consider a whole range of additional shots, and visualize how you'll piece them together back at your editing station to fool the audience into thinking you had four cameras with full crews.

Obviously, these shooting modes are points on a continuum that build upon the skill sets of the previous mode. You need to be skilled in the basics of recording to become a good story teller, and a good story teller to build an intriguing movie. Equally obvious is that different events call for different shooting modes.

For example, recently, at a cousin's wedding, someone thrust a camcorder in my hands at the last minute and said, "Shoot the ceremony." All I could do was frame the shot, hold the camcorder as steady as possible, and shoot the ceremony.

This spring, however, my family attended a high school rodeo in Galax, Virginia, a major event for a small town. My wife was there, so I was free to shed the daddy role, walk around, and shoot different locations, angles, and sights.

I shot close-ups of tense riders seconds before their events and their exultation after tying the "piggy string" round the legs of the calf. I shot strutting 12 year olds with more testosterone than a pro quarterback and giggling school girls who thought nothing of galloping 35 miles per hour around barrels in the ring and turning on a dime.

I shot the loquacious announcers who provided the countrified background audio track, catching a wink from the pretty grandmother with the hennaed hair (pray, don't tell my wife). I shot restless horses, braying calves and the edgy bulls, and blue jeans, spurs, saddles, and lariats. I shot a lone watchful rider against the darkening sky and the silent ambulance, underscoring the ever-present danger of the event.

Ultimately, I'll probably edit the 40 minutes of source video down to 5 minutes or less, just one stop along the "Summer in Galax Video." Stops along the way include the tractor pull, pro rodeo, an upcoming gymnastics recital, the world-famous Galax Fiddler's convention, and a guitar festival or two. Hey, we do it right out here in the country.

But even if I don't edit the video, I had more fun and saw more slices and subtleties than I would have had I simply filmed from my seat or not brought the camcorder at all. Sometimes, the only place the movie plays is in your own mind, and strangely, that doesn't diminish the experience at all. Sometimes I shoot simply because that's how I choose to experience that event.

But, I digress. Or egress. Or something. In any event, you've probably already guessed that I'll follow the modes in sequence, first covering the basics of shooting, then the elements of story telling, and finally the multiple angles of coverage necessary to make a movie.

Working in Recording Mode Shot

Sometimes learning involves unlearning, and I'm afraid that's the case with many of the shooting basics. For example, since we got our first Instamatic, we've been dutifully centering our images and clicking away, which is bad form for still images (check the Kodak Web site, and you'll see they don't recommend centering images for still pictures) and even worse for video. Many shooters feel like a 10X zoom gives license for extreme close-ups that reveal every mole and blemish, ignoring the fact that close-ups seldom tell a story, which is the primary goal.

Finally, when MTV and shows like *Homicide* appeared, not to mention *The Blair Witch Project*, many shooters became enamored with motion, as in more is better, ignoring the great majority of TV shows and movies that use a static camera on a tripod. Motion is a tool that can enhance the story but is not the story itself. Motion is best used when it can be used well, which involves steadicams, dollies, and people to operate them, as well as rehearsals and multiple takes to get it right. For your purposes, moving the camera around a lot will only result in video that most people will find hard or impossible to watch.

So, I'll give it to you straight. To shoot better, more interesting and watchable videos, don't center the camera, don't overuse close-ups, and use camera motion as sparingly as possible.

Framing the Shot — The Rule of Thirds

Simply stated, the rule of thirds says that in framing your shot, divide your image into thirds like a tick-tack-toe board, and place the center of the shot on one of the two vertical lines. This is shown in Figure 7-1. In the words of my friend and veteran shooter Ken Santucci, "action dictates the space." That is, the open two-thirds should be in the direction that the main character is facing and ready to move into. Though the horse is facing off to the left, the rider is intensely focused on the right, where the calf is about to break from the gate.

What to Keep in Your Camera Bag

- Extra tapes

- A pen or marker to label tapes

- Extra batteries

- A lens-cleaning cloth

- Headphones

- An external microphone (with batteries and charger if not powered by the camera)

- An external light (with batteries and charger if not powered by the camera)

- An NTSC video cable (to view on a television) and a FireWire cable (to transfer to PC)

- AC power (preferably with a cigarette lighter attachment)

- White towel to cushion and clean camera, as well as for white balancing

- Various lens filters

Figure 7-1: The rule of thirds says to divide the frame into thirds like a tick-tack-toe board, and place the main subject on one of the vertical lines, with the open space in the direction the actor is facing.

When framing the shot, consider two other zones you might encounter during editing. This is shown in Figure 7-2, which is a video of our cowboy inside Premiere's titling utility.

Notice the two boxes at the edges of the video. The outside box is Safe Action and anything outside this box probably won't be viewable on your television. The obvious lesson is don't frame too closely to the subject's head, or it may get cut off during playback.

Note

Over-scan is an analog-only occurrence, so this isn't a concern for video shot exclusively for display on computers.

The second box, or Safe Title, is even a more restricted zone that shows where title text and graphics can safely be placed during editing and generally isn't a concern during shooting.

Figure 7-2: Mind the Action Safe zone while shooting, because it likely won't be visible on television sets.

Police Your Shoot

Policing your shoot doesn't mean providing security; it means looking through the viewfinder and hunting out any possible disruptions. The list is potentially endless, but the following are some important considerations.

BACKGROUND

Background is important because if not policed correctly, it can detract from the shot.

- The background should enhance, not detract from the video. When I was in Egypt, I could have framed the Sphinx two ways. From one side I could show the edge of Cairo, including fast food stores less than 200 yards away. The other side showed only sand and sky in the background, which, since I wasn't doing a documentary on urban sprawl, was the background I used. When you have a choice, opt for the least distracting background.

- There are certain backgrounds that simply don't work well, creating noise or a patterned moiré effect. Backgrounds to avoid include complex wallpaper, book shelves lined with books, and Venetian blinds. Any background that is really complex (even sometimes leaves and trees) can produce visual artifacts, which are obvious defects in the video, especially when encoded.

LIGHTING

Lighting is important because poor lighting can ruin your shot.

- Here, as you would with still images, make sure you're shooting with the sun to your back whenever you can.

- Remember your camera has programmed AE modes for sunlight, sports, spotlight, and similar environments. Experiment with these before the big shoot to determine their effectiveness.

- Avoid shooting subjects that are backlit, whether by streaming light coming in through windows or other bright lights coming from behind the subject. If unavoidable, check for a backlight button or AE mode on your camera that can compensate for this condition.

- If this is the first shoot of the day or you've just changed to a dramatically different lighting condition, like moving outside from inside, or vice versa, white balance your camera or switch to a different white balance mode if supported by the camera. An alternative is to point the camera at a totally white object for ten seconds and let it adjust itself.

SOUND

Yup, you're the sound crew too. I cover sound in more depth in Chapter 8, but here are some preliminary thoughts to consider.

- Turn off any background noise you don't need. In an office, this can include computers, printers, loud routers or hubs, and white noise.

- In the home, background music is nice, but the television can be distracting. When editing hospital videos of my first daughter's birth, I had to contend with John Madden in the background announcing the AFC Championship game. That's OK, football adds color to any video, especially those tender first moments between mother and daughter in the hospital room (the wife won this one; Madden got cut), but SpongeBob Squarepants or the Wiggles in the background will make everyone involved cringe during subsequent viewings.

- Needless to say, if you're capturing special moments, you should turn off dishwashers, washing machines, dryers, lawn mowers, vacuum cleaners, loud air conditioners, and fans.

- For serious shoots, get your headphones on to better gauge sound quality, and at the very least you should use a directional microphone. As you'll see in Chapter 8, these cost under $100 and make a world of difference.

Calling the Shots

If you're a professional shooter, you need highly defined terms for all shots to direct and plan appropriately, but for our purposes, the following list of terms should suffice.

- A wide shot, also called the establishing shot or extra long shot, shows the subject in its entirety and usually includes background images such as landscapes or buildings.

- A medium long shot shows the subject from head to toe.

- A medium shot shows the subject from waist to head.

- A medium close-up shows the subject from chest to head.

- A regular close-up shows the subject's head and shoulders.

- A big close-up (BCU) is a shot where the subject's face fills the screen.

Things You Should Know How to Do Without Looking at the Manual

Before taking your camera out for a serious shoot, you should spend some quality time getting to know its best features. That way, you won't be scrambling when you need them. Figure 7-3 shows where a bunch of these features are located on the Sony DCR-VX2000. In short, you should know the following:

- How to disable auto-focus and focus manually.

- How to white balance your camera.

- How to disable auto-exposure and boost gain manually.

- How to select a programmed auto-exposure mode.

- How to connect headphones to listen to the audio while shooting.

- The location of special modes like backlighting or spotlight available on the camera body.

- How to use End Search or a similar function (see the "Taking Care of Time Code" sidebar later in this chapter). Use this after playing back some video to move to the end of your last shot.

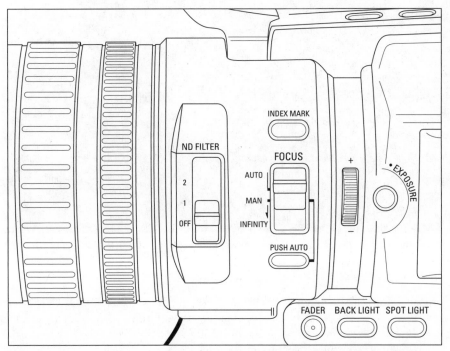

Figure 7-3: My camera has more buttons than your camera! Get to know these controls before you start to shoot, because they're awful tough to figure out in the heat of the moment.

Most casual users can get away with three classifications, defined in terms of the degree to which the primary subject fills the screen. I'll start with the wide shot.

WIDE (ESTABLISHING) SHOTS

Going back to the rodeo shoot from the beginning of the chapter, the first shot I knew I would need was a wide shot (also called the extra long shot or establishing shot) of the rodeo ring, and that I'd need to shoot it from the top of the stands (see Figure 7-4). Wide shots like this provide the visual context for the audience to understand the action to come. They also provide a big picture view of the action unfolding but obviously lack the detail to tell the entire story.

Figure 7-4: Wide shots show the audience where the action will take place, providing valuable context. This is one area where a wide-angle lens really provides benefits.

Most people probably don't take enough wide shots, unless, of course, you're just back from the Alps or Niagara Falls, where a wide shot is the only way to capture the subject. For most other shoots, whether wedding videos, school plays, company outings, or family reunions, try to provide the big picture before starting in on the action.

The only caveat here is that extra long and medium long shots typically only work well on a big screen venue. If you're shooting for the Web, or even quarter-screen video, the scaled-down video won't show enough detail to provide the perspective you're seeking. In these instances, you're better off providing context with a title like "Galax HS Rodeo 2003" than with an indiscernible wide screen shot. Another trick is to shoot the program cover or the entrance sign of whatever event you're attending. It still doesn't provide the big picture view, but it does let the viewer instantly understand what's going on.

Note

If you're shooting with manual focus and want to ensure that you're well focused on a particular subject, zoom in tight, set your focus, and then zoom back out. Zoom has no effect on focus, so once you set the focus, it will be maintained even during the wide shots.

MEDIUM SHOTS

Where wide shots provide context, medium shots show the action and tell the story. For this reason, most movies and television shows are pieced together primarily from medium shots.

As you might expect, the precise framing of medium shots varies by content. In general, if your goal is to show the action, make the frame as large as necessary to show that action with a bit of extra room on all four sides so that none of your subject will fall out of the frame as your subject moves. In an interview situation, you want to include the movement of the head, arms, and body. A good ballpark area to keep in mind is to shoot from the waist up to the head. Anything closer and the arms will move in and out of the screen, which is distracting.

On the other hand, when filming activities like a calf-roping event, you have to frame a bit more loosely, a bit wider around the subject, to catch all the jumping, pulling, and twisting going on (see Figure 7-5). Figure 7-1, also a medium shot, is also framed more loosely to keep the cowboy and horse in the frame as the horse dances nervously before the event.

Medium shots are most overused in static situations like interviews, training, testimonials, and other people-oriented shots where the camera lingers too long in one place, which gets boring and tends to lull viewers to sleep. Next time you're watching the evening news, note the longest period that the anchor sits there reading with nothing else going on. It's seldom longer than 10 to 15 seconds, and most all news channels have incorporated news tickers beneath the screen to keep the reader's attention.

In a one-camera shoot, it takes some planning to shoot the cutaways and reaction shots necessary to intersperse with the actual interview, but these are essential to maintain the viewer's interest. There will be more on these kinds of shots in the "Movie Making" section later in this chapter.

CLOSE-UPS

Where wide shots provide context and medium shots show the primary action of a story, close-ups are shots where the primary subject — whether it be a person's face or hands, or a computer screen — fill almost the entire screen. Close-ups are great for showing reactions and emotions, but they don't tell the story — they show the reaction to the story. Figure 7-6 is a close-up of a rodeo participant seconds before the event, showing the pent-up fury, the raw emotion, and will to win. (Actually, it's a shot of what appears to be a bored bull, but at least my editors let me slide on the permission's letter.)

Most shooters shoot too many close-ups and shoot them closer and longer than necessary. George Clooney and Julia Roberts get $20 million a picture because people like looking at their faces on screen. They're also highly trained professionals who can tell a story with a slight grimace or faint smile.

Figure 7-5: This is probably a medium long shot by Hollywood standards but framed so it includes all motion in the static shot.

Most other faces, including those of our children, significant other, or favorite pet, aren't nearly as expressive or photogenic, at least to those outside of the family. So, don't zoom in any closer than shoulder level unless you have a reason (Little Sally had a nose job? Billie got his braces off?), and don't dawdle on the shot forever.

Overall, don't try to build your story with facial close-ups. They're not the story; they're the garnish.

VARYING CAMERA HEIGHT

One of the lovely benefits of the LCD panels on virtually all camcorders is that you can shoot from many different heights and yet still be able to clearly see what you're shooting. You can turn the LCD down and shoot from above your head, easily shoot from your waist, and even shoot at floor level. With my old Hi8 camera, which only had a viewfinder, this was almost impossible.

Understand that changing camera height can vary the perspective of the video or alter the mood. For example, if you're shooting a video from your child's point of view, the camera should be at child-eye level, staring upward at the teachers and other adults. Filming someone upward from a low angle makes him seem more heroic and dominating, though it can also highlight double chins and other below-the-neck uglies, so be careful.

Figure 7-6: A close-up is close up, and that's no bull. You get the point; close-ups show enough detail to convey a reaction or emotion or provide a detail that you can't capture with the medium shot.

Shooting from above has the reverse effect, making the subject submissive or weak. It also tends to portray a "heavenly view," which is why many movies end with a slow reverse zoom from above, as if to say, "It's the Lord's work!"

Finally, shooting at the subject's eye level is neutral, showing neither domination nor submission. This is why many child photographers like to shoot at eye level and why most interviews are shot at eye level.

The Art of Motion

There are two types of motion in video: unintended motion, often resulting from a shaky camera, and intended motion, using zooms and pans (see the "Glossary of Camera Motion" sidebar later in this chapter). When done poorly, both can absolutely kill your video. This section will give you some ideas for damage control.

Keeping the Camera Steady

Though all camera vendors loudly tout their image stabilization capabilities, none truly mask the motion from an unsteady hand. The only way to keep a camera truly steady is with a tripod or some other fixed resting place.

Note

Tripods intended for still-image cameras are not designed to help move the camera smoothly through motions like pans and tilts. For this, you'll need a fluid head tripod, which costs more. However, this type of tripod is easier to pan and tilt smoothly and therefore worth the investment for more serious shooters.

If you don't use a tripod, try these techniques for keeping the camera stable:

- If you can shoot from chest level, wrap the camera's neck strap around your neck and drop the camera down until the camera's weight is resting on the strap (see Figure 7-7).

- Hold the camera with both hands, keeping your elbows in and resting against your chest. Keep your knees slightly bent and legs about shoulder length apart.

- If you'll be shooting for several minutes or longer, use the eyepiece rather than the LCD and rest this against your face.

- Find a level place to park your camcorder. I've used the top of a car, filing cabinets, the floor, desks, and even fire hydrants in my quest for a stable picture.

- Sit if you can, and if not, lean back against another stable object.

- Limit the use of telephoto lenses when you can, since zoom exacerbates the problems of motion.

Motion Effects

Next time you're watching TV, note the number of times the camera physically moves or pans or zooms through the scene and also the extent of the motion. In most network television shows, you'll see very little of this. Virtually all shots are taken with a tripod, and motion is limited because it's difficult to move a camera smoothly and effectively without rehearsals and multiple takes. Most shows use small, slow, very controlled pans and zooms if any motion at all.

In fact, you'll see that most shows switch back and forth between several statically positioned cameras with different views of the actors. When recording, this it the look that you're seeking to emulate whenever possible.

Where network shows tend to minimize motion, movies tend to push the motion envelope, which is one of the reasons movies cost millions to produce. Needless to say, movie cinematographers don't attempt these effects using $800 camcorders without a tripod. They have real dollies, real cranes, fluid head tripods that enhance motion smoothness, programmable zoom controls, and professionals to run the equipment, not to mention the ability to practice and the benefit of multiple takes.

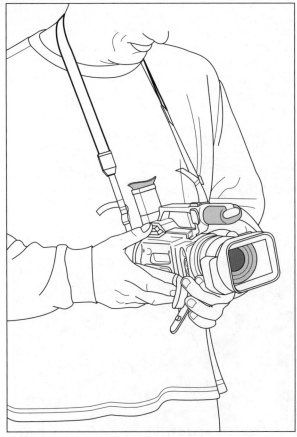

Figure 7-7: Letting the camera rest against the shoulder strap is a great way to stabilize the camera.

Glossary of Camera Motion

- **Pan** — The camera is on a fixed tripod and rotates from one side to the other.

- **Tilt** — The camera is on a fixed tripod and swivels upward or downward.

- **Zoom** — The camera is on a fixed tripod and zooms closer to or further from the subject using zoom controls.

- **Dolly** — The camera is on a dolly (a movable cart of some kind) and moves closer to or further from subject.

- **Truck** — The camera is on a dolly and moves alongside the main subject, oftentimes on some track or other apparatus that keeps the camera moving in a straight line.

- **Crane** — The camera is on a boom arm that can raise and lower the camera height.

The Rules of Motion

When I was a Boy Scout, I remember our scoutmaster teaching us about knife safety. He explained that rule number one was "Never throw a knife." Then he asked "So, if you have to throw a knife, how do you do it safely?" The correct answer, of course, was "Never throw a knife."

There's a little of that feeling going on as I write this section. First I'm going to tell you never to use motion, and then I'm going to tell you how to use it most effectively when you do. I just hope my scoutmaster doesn't catch me.

RULE NUMBER 1: DON'T USE MOTION TO MOVE FROM SHOT TO SHOT

Rule number one is: Don't use camera motion simply as a vehicle to get from shot to shot. For example, Figure 7-8 shows a shot from the Atlanta Zoo. On the left is an over-the-shoulder shot (defined later in the chapter), of the giraffes and an ostrich hanging out eating tall things. On the right is a much closer view of the ostrich.

Figure 7-8: Don't use camera motion to switch between medium long shots like this over-the-shoulder shot and closer views. If you don't plan on editing out the motion, stop the camera, reset the framing, and then restart shooting.

If you were watching this on Discovery Channel, odds are that the video would jump directly from over-the-shoulder view to the close-up. If the shooter chose to zoom in, it would likely be slow and very steady. In contrast, most novices would pan over and zoom into the ostrich, unavoidably introducing shaky motion into the video.

Remember — what you want the viewer to see is the over-the-shoulder shot, which provides perspective for the closer shot, and then the closer shot of Mr. Ostrich. You really don't care (and the viewers certainly don't care) if they see how your camera got there.

So, if you're in recording mode and don't intend to edit the video, stop shooting after the over-the-shoulder shot, zoom in and reframe the picture, and then start shooting again. If you're shooting to edit (see "Shoot to Edit," later in this chapter), keep the camera rolling, just zoom in and reframe the shot as quickly as possible, and plan on editing out the motion.

Taking Care of Time Code

DV tapes store two bits of information besides the audio and video on the tape. First is the data code, or date and time you shot the video, along with shutter speed, exposure, and other settings-related information. This is shown in the lower left on Figure 7-9, typically displayed when you press the Data Code button.

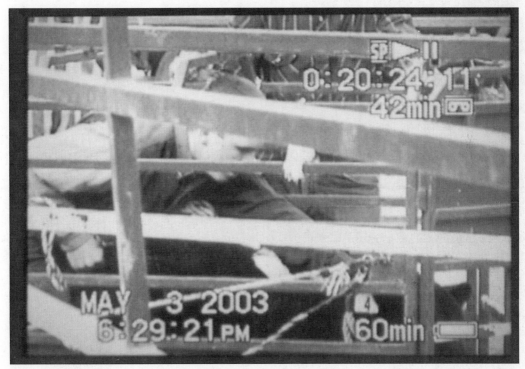

Figure 7-9: Camcorders store two bits of helpful data with the video, the time and date code (lower left) and time code (upper right).

During capture, most video editors break the DV video into scenes by detecting temporal breaks in the data code, a lovely feature that simplifies your work immensely.

The other bit of data is called time code. Time code has nothing to do with real time, as in "what time is it"; it's all about position on the tape. Time code doesn't exist on a blank tape; it's laid down by the camcorder while you're shooting.

Time code is shown in the upper-right corner of Figure 7-9 and reads 0:20:24:11. In time-code speak, this means that frame is zero hours, 20 minutes, 24 seconds, and 11 frames from where you started recording.

Continued

Taking Care of Time Code *(Continued)*

Time code gives capture and video-editing programs the ability to find any frame on the tape, unless, of course, you have duplicate time codes. That happens when you shoot, go into VCR mode and play your video, overshoot the last time code recorded by the camcorder, and then start recording again without closing the gap. Since the camcorder doesn't know any better, it starts time code over at 0:00:00:01, producing duplicate time codes.

It's pretty easy to understand how duplicate time codes would confuse a video editor, so they're always a bad idea. The easy way to prevent duplicate time codes is to record each new tape from start to finish in your camcorder, preferably with the lens cap on. Then, rewind the video. When you actually shoot video, the camera will insert new audio and video and update the data code, but it will use the old time code from start to finish. In the parlance of old-time shooters, this also "exercises the tape," making sure it's ready for shooting.

Otherwise, each time you shoot and replay your video, you have to be sure not to overshoot the end of the last shot, or you'll create a gap. Many camcorders have an "End Search" feature that helps you find the end of the last recorded section. They all work differently, so check your manual for details.

Another example might be shooting a large church or other building. You might start with a wide shot showing the entire structure, and then would want to show individual highlights, perhaps arches, gables, or courtyards. Don't stand far away and pan and zoom over to the individual locations. Stop the camera after the wide shot, walk up to the gable, reframe the picture, and start shooting. Remember, your viewers don't care how you got there; they just want to see the gable.

Tip

Breaks in the time code caused by stopping and starting your camera create individual scenes that your video editor can easily detect during capture. To save time you might want to start and restart the camera even when shooting to edit so your video editor can find these scene changes for you.

RULE NUMBER 2: FIND AN ALTERNATIVE WITHOUT MOTION

I can almost hear it now. You'll be out there shooting, and you'll be telling yourself, "No, I must follow the action," or "I must zoom in slowly," or "I must tilt slowly up to the top of the building to show its true height." There are definitely times where camera motion can enhance the video you're creating.

However, most of the time, there are alternatives that involve no camera motion. For example, you can follow the action without moving the camera using a longer shot. You can avoid the zoom by stopping the shot, walking closer to the subject, and resuming shooting. You can shoot the building from multiple angles that reveal its dominating height.

Unless you can use motion effectively, you're almost always better off with a slightly less creatively appealing option that involves little motion. A series of well-shot scenes with little motion is always better than one scene with jerky motion.

RULE NUMBER 3: IF YOU MUST USE MOTION, HERE'S HOW

Here's the part my scoutmaster would have loved. If you find that you have to use motion, here's how to use it most effectively.

All Motion Effects

Here are some simple rules to follow when shooting with camera motion:

- Rehearse the motion beforehand whenever possible, hunting for obstacles that don't appear in the initial frame but may soon crop in (see Figure 7-10).

- Whenever possible, shoot for at least three seconds while stable at both the beginning and end of the motion shot. This footage will help stabilize the viewer and is invaluable during editing for transitioning into or out of the sequence.

Figure 7-10: Here I didn't follow my own rules and make sure that my panning path was clear of obstacles. The first shot was great, but I was quickly obscured by a cowboy and then a pole. Shooting from higher up in the grandstands or climbing up the fence could have avoided these problems.

Panning

Follow these rules when panning your camera across a scene:

- Never pan back and forth; pan in one direction and then stop.

- Pan from the waist, moving your body, not your hands. Don't extend the pan beyond your ability to pivot because if you turn your feet, or use your hands, you'll introduce shake.

- When following a subject, try to keep her in the back third of the frame.

- For dramatic effect, start shooting without the subject in the frame, allow the subject to enter the frame, follow her through the panning area, and then let her exit.

- Watch the horizon or some other known level object in your shot as a cue that your camera is off balance.

- Watch the focus—you may need to use manual focus to retain the focus during the entire path of the pan.

Tilt

Follow these rules when tilting your camera up and down:

- Never tilt up and down, tilt in one direction and then stop.

- Tilt at the waist, moving your body, not your hands. Basically, when you bend backwards as far as you can go, stop the tilt motion, because if you use your hands to go higher, you'll introduce shake.

Zooming

Zooming can be used in two ways: first as a tool to follow a subject in the video, second as an effect. As a tool, you might use zoom to keep a subject well framed in the camera as he or she moves closer or further from the camera. As an effect, you might slowly zoom into your child's face as the birthday cake enters the room to capture her glee at all those tasty calories coming her way.

I make this distinction because I feel pretty strongly that using zoom as an effect is best left to experts. It's very difficult to do it well with consumer-level equipment. If you need to zoom in, either stop the shot, zoom in, and restart shooting, or zoom quickly in so that it doesn't take up that much video time.

Here are some rules to follow when zooming to follow motion:

- When zooming to follow motion, it's absolutely critical to keep the camera steady, since the shakes and the zoom may be too much for some stomachs to bear. This means no walking or gross moving around.

- Get to know your zoom controls beforehand. They're very twitchy on most consumer cameras and hard to control. Practice, practice, practice.

- If your camera has manual zoom capabilities, especially up front on the lens, where it's nice and intuitive, use these instead of the button controls.

- Zoom slowly to the desired framing, and then stop, even if it's not ideal. Zooming back and forth to get the perfect frame is distracting.

- Disable digital zoom, or on newer cameras, set it to a moderate level that won't produce distortion.

Dolly, Truck, and Crane

Don't try these at home. There's probably no easy and/or safe way you can pull these effects off smoothly, so just find another way.

Storytelling

The next level after simple recording is storytelling. This adds several important components to the mix.

Tell a Story

As you recall from the last fairy tale you read, stories have beginnings ("once upon a time"), middles (where all the action takes place), and endings ("and they all lived happily ever after"). English majors and classicists may prefer to structure their stories as exposition, rising action, complication, conflict, climax, falling action, resolution, and denouement, which is OK, though perhaps a bit overblown for my daughter's dance recital next week. After all, she's only five and this is the Galax Recreation Center, not Carnegie Hall. Since this is one of the key stops on the Galax Summer Tour, I'm on notice to produce something memorable.

Now, if I was in recording mode, I would simply bring the camcorder with extra tapes and batteries, and then I'd sit in the stands and shoot. However, that would be all conflict and no exposition or denouement.

Given that my wife danced for the Atlanta Ballet, and she sets her sights high, I know she'll be nervous as a cat, and will treat this performance like opening night at the Fox, or perhaps the Kennedy Center for President Bush. So I know there will be plenty of beginning and end, but only if I'm planning ahead.

To a certain degree, the amount of possible footage relates in part to how much I want to torture the poor girl and her mother with the camcorder. We could have pre-event interviews, the bath, the combing of the hair (and associated screams), the getting dressed (tastefully, of course), the packing of the bag, getting into the car, walking into the gym, shooting all the other girls as they come into the gym, and the last-minute hushed instructions from the coach. That should provide me with plenty of beginning stuff to choose from during the editing.

After the show, I can shoot the parent's applause, the instructor's praise, the giggling girls hugging each other goodbye and walking off as a group for the last time (sniff, sniff) until summer gymnastics starts in three weeks, and the trip to the ice cream parlor to celebrate. Then I can shoot my daughter taking off her outfit (tastefully, of course) and talking about how she loved the class, probably shedding some tears because it's over.

I can show her reliving the experience, talking about the highs and lows, her plans for next year, and long-term aspirations (Cirque du Soleil?). So, lesson one in story telling is plan ahead to tell the story. There's really no science to it; every occasion is different.

Storyboards

I don't think you can write a book about video without mentioning the word storyboard; you might be arrested or something. So rather than live in fear for the rest of my life, there it is, out in the open.

Technically, a storyboard is a list of shots with associated drawings, usually on a big white board, that represent the flow of the movie. Hollywood producers use them extensively for two-hour movies while advertising producers use them for 30-second shots. They're invaluable in a professional setting because they help everyone understand the flow of the movie and what's expected for each shot.

I don't know about you, but I'm a terrible drawer and don't have an assistant to follow me around with a stack of storyboards anyway. So generally I make up a short list of shots like the following:

1. Getting ready (doing hair, getting dressed).

2. Pre-event interview ("What's going on today? Who's going to be there? Do you have a message for our sponsors?").

3. The grand entry.

4. Warming up.

5. Coach's pep talk.

6. Events.

7. Closing and awards.

8. Girlie hugs (goodbye).

This doesn't have to be exotic, but thinking about this beforehand, say, a day or two before you leave for vacation, will make sure you get the beginning shots necessary to support the story.

As it turned out, not all the shots happened but the rest went remarkably according to plan. What's lovely about having even a short list is that it allows you to shoot your outlined shots and then be open for opportunistic shots (wait — there's Elvis!) because you've already captured the footage that tells the basic story.

When planning your story, remember to use the different types of shots discussed earlier to help tell the story. The wide shot is often used as an "establishing shot" to help the audience understand they're in a new setting. So somewhere along the way, I'll shoot the outside of the Recreation Center to identify the new location, then a wide shot of the gymnasium to show where all the action will take place. Then, when I shift to medium shots for the action, the viewers will understand where they are.

Another favorite establishing shot for me is a road sign or some other kind of sign that tells the viewers our destination. That's why I took a shot of the Zoo Atlanta sign in Figure 7-11. It's obviously from a different trip, but it shows how a quick shot of a sign like this can instantly tell the viewer where you are and what you're doing. When all else fails, you can simply insert a title during editing, but that's definitely the easy way out.

I also know that medium shots will be my bread and butter, framed to highlight the action. I'll reserve close-ups to show the adulation and motherly love my wife feels for our child, both for artistic and practical reasons — my wife hates the camera, especially if she thinks she's going to end up in a book, or (horror) a Web site.

Shoot to Edit

Shooting to edit means several things. First, if you commit to editing your footage, as opposed to playing it back unedited, you can think "non-linear," shooting a range of shots in and out of order that you can ultimately piece together during editing.

Figure 7-11: With this frame in the front of my movie, no viewer will have any problem figuring out what this movie is about.

A Sample Storyboard for a Birthday Party

This is a script I pulled together. There's nothing magical about creating a script for a birthday party shoot, and this should give some ideas to get started.

Establishing shot (telling the viewers what they're about to see)

- Possibly a shot of an invitation.
- Possibly a shot of the mother asking the toddler, "What day is it today?" "My birpday," she answers.

Beginning

- The mother and father baking the cake, preparing the food, and wrapping the presents.
- The mother and father setting the table, anxiously staring out the window, and waiting for the guests to arrive.
- The birthday girl playing quietly.

Continued

A Sample Storyboard for a Birthday Party *(Continued)*

Middle

- Guests start arriving; children playing.

- Everyone sitting at the table eating.

- The mother lighting the candles and bringing in the cake. The group sings "Happy Birthday," and the birthday girl blows out the candles.

- The children and dad (in our family, anyway) pig out on cake.

- The opening of the presents.

- The children playing.

End

- The birthday girl's best friend's mom calls "Sarah, we have to go."

- Exit shots of all key guests, big hugs, and kisses.

- The parents cleaning up and sighing.

- The birthday girl putting toys away and sighing.

- The birthday girl asleep on her bed with the new toys.

- The parents look in and smile.

[Fade to black. Music wells up and then fades away.]

Cutaways

- A shot of the birthday cake.

- A shot of all presents in a pile.

- Reaction shots of all relevant participants.

- A shot of the dinner table, before and after.

- Close-ups of key presents.

For example, I may want to use a wide shot of the gym to transition the story from the house to the gym, but I need to rush to the door to catch my daughter's grand entrance. So I shoot the entrance and then walk back out and shoot the wide shot, and then reverse the order during editing.

I can shoot multiple takes of certain scenes, knowing that I can later choose the best one for the final production. This works great for birthdays, because my girls seem to love blowing out the candles several times anyway.

Shooting to edit means that I have to capture the footage necessary for editing. This means starting my camera several seconds before I really want to start shooting and shooting for several seconds past the end of the action shot. These before and after segments allow me to transition into and out of scenes gracefully.

Caution

Start the camera as early as possible and always let it run for a few seconds after the shot is done to leave yourself enough room to fade in and out of scenes. By doing this, you will make sure you won't have to cut into scenes during editing.

At this point, you have the footage to tell a good story from beginning to end. In the editing studio (your computer), you can cut and paste, add a few titles and transitions, fade to black, and render out to VHS tape, DVD, or some other format. You've improved from simple recording to simple story telling, and the grandparents will be ecstatic.

However, there is one level higher, what I call movie making. Let's see what that's all about.

Moviemaking

Moviemaking builds on the skills you've learned so far and focuses primarily on the concept of "coverage." You know, what the lion lacked in the Wizard of Oz (sorry).

Coverage is footage shot around the action to provide context for the action. When you have good coverage, it means you filmed all the interesting subjects around the main action, from a range of different angles to provide flexibility during editing. All this is tough with one camera and one person, but even one or two additional shots can make or break a video.

So here are four additional concepts to consider that will help you take your projects to another level.

Cutaways

First is the concept of a cutaway, or a shot that's related to the primary action of the scene, but is definitely ancillary to the primary subject.

There are two common cutaways that should bring the concept home for most viewers. It's the Super Bowl, and Whitney Houston is singing the National Anthem. The camera starts with her, and as she belts out the song, the director cuts to shots of the team captains looking serious, boy scouts saluting, and the fighter squadron flying overhead, scaring the heck out of the folks in the top row.

Just before end of the song, the camera cuts back to Whitney to see if she can still hit the high note on the "land of the free." She does, the crowd goes crazy. All shots except those of Whitney are cutaways.

Another example: It's the evening news, and a local reporter is interviewing a high school kid who just won a prize for his science project. The reporter asks the kid how he got started in science, and as she starts telling the story, the video cuts over to shots of the reporter and the student walking through the lab and examining her project. Perhaps during some of the student's answers, you'll see the reporter nodding in response. These are also cutaways.

Shooting Tips

These tips don't fit neatly into the sections defined herein, but they are definitely something you need to know.

- Don't rush around trying to shoot everything. Plan your shoot and shoot your plan. If you try to do too much, you'll rush your shots and miss the critical ones.

- Remember that you're there to record, not participate. Watch the local little league game and you'll see multiple parents with camcorders shooting and cheering. Obviously, the most critical scenes, Little Sally hitting a home run or Johnny Junior making a diving catch, are ruined if you're jumping up and down and yelling while attempting to shoot.

- Label your tapes. Get in the habit of pasting the blank stickers on your tapes before you put them in your camera. That way, you can label them quickly when you pull them out of the camera, and you'll be able to keep track of what footage is on which tape.

It's easy to understand how the Super Bowl director can get those cutaways — he's got cameras in every nook and cranny in the stadium and can simply press a button and switch to a different camera shot. More interesting is the reporter, who probably went out with only one camera and shooter. To get these cutaways, the shooter filmed the reporter touring the lab before or after the interview, knowing the editing staff would cut the scenes in during editing.

After the interview, the shooter turned the camera on the reporter to catch "noddies" — the reporter nodding in agreement or smiling as the student answers the questions. Sometimes the reporter will actually ask the same questions again on camera so that footage can be cut into the original for a more interactive visual experience.

Cutaways can also be used to hide "blemishes" in the underlying video. Say your family was singing "Silent Night" on Christmas Eve and you panned and zoomed the camera from person to person because you needed to keep the camera rolling to catch the entire song. But, a bit too much eggnog left the camera a touch shakier than you would like during those motions.

So, after the song is over, you take a deep breath, steady yourself and shoot flickering candles, snow on the ground, presents under the tree, little Sally sleeping peacefully by the fireplace. Then you insert these cutaways into the video to hide the camera shakes, keeping the original background audio track with the song playing.

A cutaway can be anything related to the event that's not the primary focus, either an interesting detail or the story behind the story. While shooting the rodeo, for example, I shot several minutes of video while a cowhand was choosing the calf, separating it from the herd, loading it in to the chute, and getting it motivated to run. Certainly not the story I came to see, but it was an interesting piece of background.

Cutaways can be planned or totally spontaneous. Either way, they serve multiple valuable purposes, all of which help make your video appear more professional and more watchable.

Multiple Camera Angles

Another component of coverage is multiple camera angles. This is tough with one camera but can provide a healthy dose of exercise.

Rule number one is don't shoot all of your shots from the same camera angle. Rule number two is that there are no additional rules, except perhaps, to imagine where Spielberg would shoot from if he were there. Every situation is different.

At the rodeo, I shot the calf-roping event from four different angles, from up top, from behind the rider, from the side, and from the other end of the ring, letting the horse and calf come toward me. If I were Spielberg, I would have four shots of the same exact event, which I could interweave as I wished.

Instead, I had four shots of four separate riders, providing the raw footage necessary to visually illustrate the art of calf roping (see Figure 7-12). I had enough shots, along with other cutaways, to provide my editor (a.k.a., moi) with sufficient footage to exercise complete editing flexibility. In short, I had coverage.

Figure 7-12: Four views of calf roping provide gobs of raw material to work with during editing.

When shooting from these various angles, try to avoid footage that will contradict the flow of another shot. For example, in Figure 7-13 on the left, I shot a cowhand getting the calf loaded and ready to run. On the right is a cowboy ready to give chase.

The only problem is that the calf will be running from *left to right*, and then, since I switched sides for the second shot, the cowboy will be chasing from *right to left*. Obviously, this might confuse the user, so I can't put these clips near each other in the final video.

Figure 7-13: On the left, a bull going right. On the right, a cowboy going left. Overall, this is a recipe for viewer confusion.

Shots and Shot Combinations

The pick and roll in basketball is a play where one person sets a pick or stands in the way of the person who's guarding the person dribbling the ball, forcing the defense to react. In the confusion, the person who sets the pick rolls toward the basket, gets the pass from the ball handler, and scores an easy basket.

When shooting your videos, there are several shots and shot combinations like the pick and roll that are used together professionally every day.

REVERSE ANGLE (SHOT/REVERSE SHOT)

The reverse angle shot is used typically during interviews to show both the interviewee and the interviewer. This is shown in Figure 7-14. In a two-camera setup, the director will switch from view to view to catch questions, answers, and responses.

In a single-camera setup, as I discussed earlier, the shooter films the entire interview and then shoots the interviewer nodding or asking the same questions asked in the interview. Then, back at the studio, the editors insert the questions and noddies as appropriate.

The rule here is do not cross the line between the interviewer and interviewee with the camera, keep it on the same side as shown in Figure 7-12. That is, stay on one side or the other, but do not move back and forth across the line, especially when shooting your noddies after the interview is actually over.

Why? Because if you really did have a two-camera setup, which I attempt to simulate here, having cameras on opposite sides of the line would likely bring the other camera into view. In a one-camera setup, the viewer will instinctively sense the discontinuity and wonder where the other camera is. So, in these situations, don't cross the line.

THE OVER-THE-SHOULDER SHOT

The over-the-shoulder shot incorporates both the main subject of the scene and others watching the main subject. Over-the-shoulder shots accomplish several unique objectives.

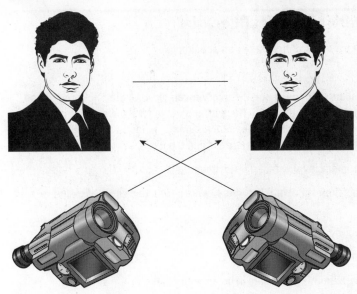

Figure 7-14: When shooting reverse angle shots, don't cross the line between the two subjects.

First, in a group setting, an over-the-shoulder shot lets the viewer know that the subject of the video is speaking to a group of people, providing context about the relationship between the speaker and the audience. As I did in Figure 7-8 (on the left side of the figure), it's also a nice jumping-off point to move to a close-up of what the people are actually looking at. Finally, when there's lots of crowd noise, it helps the viewer understand where all the noise is coming from.

FIRST SHOT, POINT OF VIEW, REACTION SHOT

These shots piece together several sequences into a logical flow and are standard fare in most types of movies. In a horror movie, for example, you see an actor tip-toeing over to the closet after hearing a noise. That's the first shot.

Then, as he opens the closet door, we switch to a shot of what he sees in the closet. It's a white rayon suit, circa *Saturday Night Fever*. That's the point-of-view shot, showing the viewer what the actor is seeing.

The film then cuts back to a shot of the actor, recoiling in horror, and screaming, "No, no, it's not natural fiber." That's the reaction shot.

Take a look at the video from the gymnastics recital (see Figure 7-16). The first of the three shots is my wife, anxiously awaiting our daughter's performance. "What's she watching?" you're thinking to yourself.

Then there's a cut to my daughter, sticking her routine. That's the point-of-view shot, showing you what her momma is watching. Finally, I cut back to mom, smiling her approval and applauding. That's the reaction shot.

How did I shoot this? Well, I couldn't shoot it linearly because I would have to move the camera so quickly that I'd spoil the scene and probably miss the shot. So, I shot my wife when she was concentrating on another little girl, and then I shot her again at the end of the show, when she was beaming at our daughter. Of course, average viewers won't know this; they'll just assume the order of presentation was the precise order of filming (if they think about it at all).

Interview Shoot Checklist

Have an interview coming up? Here's a quick checklist of items to consider:

Equipment and Setup

- To ensure the background will be in focus, place the interviewee close to the background and the camera close to the interviewee. To make the background out of focus, place the interviewee as far from the background as possible and place the camera as far as practical from the interviewee and zoom in (this works better if you're recording the interview with a microphone).

- Use a tripod, and place the camera level with the interviewee.

- Focus by disabling auto-focus, then zoom into the interviewee's eyes and zoom back out to frame the shot.

- Keep the camera rolling throughout (don't stop and start with questions).

- Disable auto-focus and use manual focus.

- White balance before you start shooting (or zoom in on a white object for ten seconds).

- Use AC power if available.

- If you're using a single camera, shoot reaction shots post-interview and follow the rules discussed earlier about not crossing the line between the subjects with the camera.

- Use a microphone and three-point lighting if possible.

- Use headphones to ensure audio quality.

- Quiet on the set — both equipment and people. Shut off fans, air conditioners, computers, white noise, background music, telephones, beepers, and other controllable sources.

Framing

- Observe the rule of thirds — the interviewee should face the interviewer, not the camera, and the frame should be open in the direction the interviewee is facing (see Figure 7-15).

- The subject's eyes should be a third of the way down from the top of the frame (see Figure 7-15).

- If you are shooting a high-energy speaker who has lots of motion, frame the shot so that body parts don't leave the screen.

- Zoom into the speaker with little motion.

Clothing

- Avoid reds and whites.

- Avoid busy patterns like herringbone and paisley, and fine stripes.

- Make sure there's contrast between the background and your subject's clothing (for example, you don't want a brown suit against wood paneling).

- Be sure your subject's eyeglasses aren't reflecting.

Figure 7-15: Rule of thirds in action. I could be a bit further over to the left, but my eyes are precisely a third of the way down the screen.

Background

- Avoid clutter like bookshelves and dense wallpaper patterns.

- Avoid Venetian blinds and backlighting.

- The background should enhance the focus of the interview, not detract from it.

- Remove distracting elements from the shot (like analog computer monitors).

Interview Format

- Script the interview beforehand and share the script with everyone involved if possible, especially if the interviewee and/or interviewer are non-professionals.

Continued

Interview Shoot Checklist *(Continued)*

- The interview should tell a story, containing the following:

  - A beginning — This should include preliminary questions that ask who the person is and why she's here (highlight her background or expertise).

  - A middle — The body of the interview.

  - An ending — This part should include terminating questions like, "What does the future hold in store?" or "Where do you go from here?"

- Ask questions that can't be answered with one word.

Use the Cutaway

- Don't forget the cutaways used to augment spoken answers:

  - The interviewer asking a question.

  - The interviewer nodding, laughing, or otherwise responding to answers.

  - Videos of the interviewee doing something relevant to interview.

Like any pattern, the point-of-view/reaction shot can get repetitive, but if you use it for emphasis during critical scenes, and the other techniques discussed in this chapter where appropriate, your stories will have great beginnings and lots of climax, falling action, resolution, and ultimately a lovely denouement.

Summary

Here are some of the major points covered in this chapter:

1. There are three shooting modes. Recording mode (shooting opportunistically without a plan), story telling mode (shooting with a plan to take certain shots and edit them into a story), and movie making mode (you plan to tell the story with a range of shot combinations that add professionalism to the results).

2. Shoot all videos using the rule of thirds, dividing your screen into thirds like a tick-tack-toe board, and placing the center of the shot on one of the two vertical lines. Let the action dictate the space so that the open two-thirds of the screen is in the direction of where the main character is facing.

3. Three main shots help tell your story. Wide shots help the viewer understand the videos' environment, while close-ups help show reactions to the action. Medium shots, framed to show the main characters and the ongoing action, are the bread and butter of all productions.

4. Limit unintentional camera motion (shaking) by using a tripod or leaning against a solid object while shooting. Limit your use of intentional camera motions like zooms and pans, and optimize usage by rehearsing the motion and using good shooting techniques.

5. Tell a story with your video by planning a beginning, middle, and end. Write a short script that identifies all key shots in the story, and then be sure to get all critical shots.

6. When story telling and movie making, shoot to edit. This means capturing much more footage than you'll actually need to tell the story and thinking non-linearly, where you shoot "out of order" knowing that you can place them into proper order during editing.

7. Cutaways are shots ancillary to the main action that enhance the story and provide great editing flexibility. Common cutaways include the crowd cheering, the coach instructing, the proud mother, rain outside the window, a crackling fireplace, falling snow, or a bird singing on a branch.

8. Movie making involves a range of common shot combinations like reverse angles; over-the-shoulder shots; and shot, point-of-view, and reaction shot. These are fun to plan, shoot, and edit, and they simulate multiple camera shoots, adding an amazing professional touch to your videos.

Figure 7-16: The pick and roll of video: Shot, point-of-view, reaction shot. My daughter really must have stuck that dismount!

Chapter 8

Capturing Good Audio

Audio is the catch-22 of consumer videography. Though critically important to the perceived quality of the overall audio/video experience, it's extremely difficult to capture good quality audio solely by using the microphone on your camcorder. Here I explain why and offer several alternatives for improving audio production quality.

Camcorder Microphone Issues

There are several reasons why it's challenging to pick up good audio with camcorder microphones. First and foremost, camcorder microphones generally have an "omnidirectional" pick-up pattern that gives equal priority to all sounds around the camera. This works well if you're trying to capture ambient noise, but not if you're attempting to prioritize sounds from directly in front of the camera, like a person speaking.

Second, camcorder microphones are attached to the camera — either embedded into the body (as with inexpensive consumer cameras) or attached to a handle (as with prosumer cameras). Embedded microphones are very susceptible to camera noise, like the noise generated by the zoom controls or other internal hums and clicks. All camera-attached microphones are also susceptible to operator noise, whether it be breathing, hand motions over the camera, or just moving around as you're filming.

Still, there are steps you can take to improve the quality of the captured audio. First, and I know this sounds clunky, wear headphones when shooting. They don't need to be studio-quality equipment — even the ear buds that came with your MP3 player will do.

Once donned, these headphones provide immediate feedback about what the camera is "hearing." For example, if roughly moving the zoom controls creates an audible click (a common problem), you'll hear it with headphones, and then you can concentrate on working the controls more smoothly. You'll also be much more sensitive to the sounds you make during shooting, whether it's scuffing your feet as you walk, breathing, or other noises.

Next, understand the limitations of the microphone. If you're at a birthday party and want to capture a quote from the birthday girl in the midst of the melee, you have to get in close; otherwise the omnidirectional microphone will give equal priority to all the other party noises. Of course, if you're wearing headphones, this will be immediately obvious.

As I discussed in the last chapter, police your shoot for extraneous noise. Turn off any background noise that will compete with the true target of your audio-capture capabilities, like appliances and even air conditioning and heating for short periods where audio is critical.

If you're working outside, listen for wind noise and learn how to engage your camera's windscreen when necessary, a feature accessible from your camera's menu that minimizes wind noise. Whenever possible, run a pre-shoot sound check to verify that you're picking up good audio.

Of course, for best results, you'll need a camera that has a number of audio-related features. Let's discuss what they are.

Key Audio-Related Camera Features

If audio quality is a key issue, you should invest in a prosumer camera like the Canon GL2 or Sony VX2000 that has the microphone on the handle (away from the camera body where it picks up less camera noise) and manual gain control so you can adjust incoming volume manually. Even if you're buying an inexpensive consumer camera, there are several features to look for that allow you to boost audio quality.

For example, the Sony DCR-PC150 camera, which resembles the camera in Figure 8-1, has an *intelligent accessory shoe,* or one that can power and send commands to a peripheral like a microphone or light. In contrast, non-intelligent accessory shoes are simple brackets for mounting with no connection to the external device. With an intelligent accessory shoe, you can attach an optional microphone, like the zoom microphone shown in the figure. It also has a microphone input port for an external microphone like those discussed a little later in this chapter. Completing the critical audio-feature troika is a headphone jack so you can listen in.

12- or 16-Bit Audio?

Most DV camcorders offer two audio settings: 16-bit (48 kHz) and 12-bit (32 kHz). Which should you use? Here's a bit of background first.

When originally formulated, DV was designed to provide flexibility for professional videographers by allowing them to record one high-quality 16-bit stream or two 12-bit streams of lesser quality. The theory was that videographers opting for the latter approach could record two streams simultaneously, one from the camcorder microphone and the other from a separate microphone.

As a practical matter, this seldom if ever occurs, especially on Mini-DV camcorders, since few allow this type of recording. So, the original premise behind the 12-bit audio makes little sense, especially if you're editing on a computer that can mix audio tracks much more easily and efficiently than a DV camcorder.

Technically, 16-bit audio will provide higher quality at some slight cost in disk space, but the extra real estate is negligible compared to the space required for the video itself. For this reason, I always record at the higher-quality 16-bit setting.

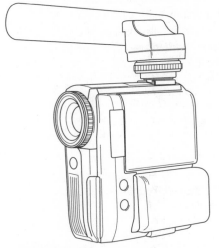

Figure 8-1: Similar to the Sony DCR-PC150, this is a camcorder with a zoom/gun microphone attached to its intelligent accessory shoe.

When I review DV cameras, one feature I focus on is the range of accessories offered by the vendor. Generally, Sony, Canon, and, to a lesser degree, Panasonic offer a range of accessories, including microphones, that truly extend the camera's capabilities in good directions. The easiest and cheapest way to add audio accessories to your camera is through your camera vendor, so check the available accessories before buying.

Going Beyond the Integrated Microphone

All this said, if you are chasing higher-quality audio, chances are that you will have to go beyond the capabilities of the integrated microphone and purchase additional equipment. Generally, you have two options:

- Optional microphones that attach to the camera body.
- Separate microphones that attach via the camera's microphone input.

Let's look at the strengths and weakness of each alternative.

Ambient Noise Considerations

Every location has a unique ambient noise, whether it's air conditioners humming, crowds roaring, or leaves rustling. Back in the studio, if you attempt to mix video shot from a different location with that footage, the lack of similar sound will give you away. For this reason, it's always a good idea to record 60 to 90 seconds of ambient noise at every discrete location where you shoot video you plan to later edit. The procedure is pretty simple; just find a place where you won't be disturbed, turn the camera on, and start recording.

Another trick to recording audio on location is to be sensitive to music, short speeches, and other events that if broken, highlight the fact that you're a one-camera shooter. For example, my children and I recently attended a blue grass festival here in Galax. I was testing cameras and brought one along to catch a song or two.

Visually, there wasn't more than six or seven minutes of footage worth keeping, but it was spread across an evening's worth of music. I could easily cut and paste the video portions together, but if I used the original audio from each segment, the frequent cuts would be distracting.

To avoid this, I recorded two songs in their entirety, which I used as audio background for short video clips cut and pasted in from the night's shoot. That way, the songs play continuously with no break in the audio.

Attachable Microphones

Attachable microphones sold as accessories to the camera are generally inexpensive and convenient. For example, if your microphone is powered through the intelligent accessory shoe, you don't have to worry about buying batteries. Most units communicate through the accessory shoe, and if not, they connect via a simple cable to the microphone port. It's easy to set up, carry, and use.

Obviously, however, if it's attached to the camera, it will suffer some of the same flaws as embedded microphones, like picking up operator noise, though camera noise should be minimal. The most significant problem, however, is that the microphone isn't proximate to a remote speaker, which makes it difficult to capture good audio at a lecture or wedding.

When purchasing any microphone, be sure to ascertain the device's pickup pattern. You already know about omnidirectional microphones, which pick up sound equally from all directions (see Figure 8-2). Here are some other types of microphones and pickup patterns:

- **Unidirectional (or just directional) microphone** — This type of microphone picks up sounds directly in front of the microphone, ignoring ambient sound. The typical unidirectional microphone uses a cardioid pattern (as shown in Figure 8-2) named after the heart-shaped pickup pattern. Microphones with even more focused pickup that eliminate more ambient noise use what's called the hypercardioid pattern. There are also bidirectional pickup patterns for use in interviews and duets, but these typically aren't available in attached microphones.

- **Boundary or PZM microphone** — This microphone lies flat on a surface and has an omnidirectional pickup. Useful for conferences, meetings, and other group activities, it's generally not available as an attached microphone.

■ **Zoom microphone** — This type of microphone adjusts to the zoom ratio of the camera lens. At low zoom ratios, it picks up ambient sound much like an omnidirectional microphone, but at high zoom ratios, the microphone ignores ambient noise and picks up audio from distant sources toward which it is aimed.

■ **Gun/shotgun microphone** — This microphone type is an extreme unidirectional microphone that ignores the ambient and pickup audio from distant sources toward which it is aimed.

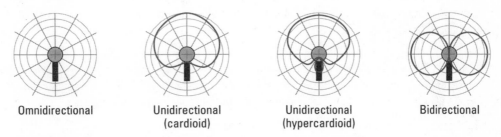

Omnidirectional   Unidirectional (cardioid)   Unidirectional (hypercardioid)   Bidirectional

Figure 8-2: Pickup patterns vary by microphone. Here are the most common.

Many attached microphones offer two pickup patterns. For example, the ECM-HS1 microphone shown in Figure 8-1 operates in both zoom and gun modes, or you can click it off and go with the internal camera microphone.

Trolling for attachable microphones on the Web reveals that Canon's Directional Microphone DM-50 for the Optura Xi is a simple directional microphone that's — according to the Web site www.canon.com — "perfect when you want to record a subject speaking without all the background noise." Like the ECM-HS1, it attaches via the Optura's accessory shoe, so no wires are necessary.

In addition, as stated at www.sharp-usa.com, the Sharp VL-27U camcorder offers a "zoom microphone (VR-8MCN) . . . that automatically adjusts from wide pickup to narrow pickup depending on the zoom ratio selected." Finally, the Sony ECM-MSD1 offers two pickup patterns: 90 degrees for individual speakers and 120 degrees for groups, which makes it perfect for weddings, parties, and other group gatherings.

These descriptions make the purpose of each microphone very clear. Overall, for general close-up work, as in parties, reunions, and other gatherings, where your goal is to eliminate the ambient noise, get a simple directional microphone. Go for the zoom or gun microphone when shooting a distant speaker and other long-range shooting events.

In my experience, these external microphones work very well. However, I keep my ECM-HS1 on gun mode for the most part, because the variance in sound picked up at multiple zoom ratios is very noticeable.

For example, at a recent soccer practice, zooming in to hear what the coach was saying eliminated the ambient sounds of the soccer moms around me, while zooming back in increased the pickup. If you have an event coming up where you need these capabilities, buy early, and practice beforehand to understand how the different pickup patterns will affect your audio.

Separate Microphones

Attachable microphones can only go so far; to produce high-quality audio, you really need a separate microphone. There are generally two types: handheld and lavaliere, the former self-explanatory and the latter a small microphone that attaches to your collar, with a separate receiver that transmits the signal to the camera (see Figure 8-3). Handheld and lavaliere microphones can be either wired directly to the camera or they can send the signal wirelessly.

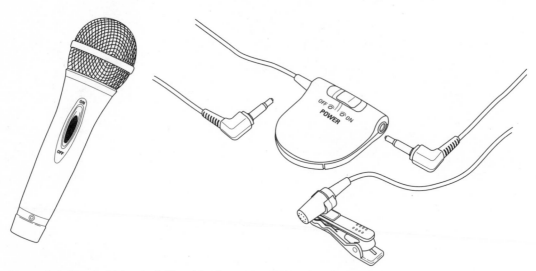

Figure 8-3: Handheld (on the left) and lavaliere microphones (on the right).

Lavaliere microphones work best when you have only one or two speakers, since transferring a small microphone back and forth can get tiresome. They're less obtrusive, and if fastened correctly, lavaliere mics require very little from the user. In contrast, handheld microphones are easy to transfer from speaker to speaker, but they require the speaker to hold them at a fixed distance.

Note

These separate microphones are subject to the same pickup patterns as camera microphones (for example, directional, omnidirectional, and so on), so make sure the device you purchase matches your needs.

Be careful when purchasing an external microphone. Most camcorders supply plug-in power to the external microphones, which means they're looking for unpowered input. This encompasses most inexpensive computer microphones, but once you start getting into more expensive microphones with a mixer, you need to be sure that you're supplying mic-level input, rather than the much more robust line-level input. You also need a system that outputs to a 1/8 stereo miniplug as opposed to a three-pin XLR connector. The bottom line is to purchase from a knowledgeable supplier who has experience outfitting microphones for camcorder use.

Here's a short list of microphone manufacturers to get you started:

Audio-Technica U.S., Inc. at `www.audio-technica.com/index2.html`

Azden Corporation, at `www.azden.com`

Radio Shack Corporation, at `www.radioshack.com`

Sennheiser USA, at `www.sennheiserusa.com`

Shure Incorporated, at `www.shure.com/default.htm`

Sony, at `www.sony.com`

Summary

Here are the key points made in this chapter:

1. To maximize audio quality while shooting, keep the following in mind:

   - Wear headphones so you can hear what's going on.

   - Work within the limits of your microphone.

   - Minimize extraneous noise.

2. If audio is important to you, be sure that the camera you buy has an intelligent accessory shoe, an external microphone port, windscreen control, and a headphone jack.

3. Most camcorders allow you to shoot in either 12-bit or 16-bit audio. Absent a compelling reason for the former, 16-bit is the best default choice.

4. Always record 60 to 90 seconds of ambient noise for any scene in footage that you're likely to heavily edit. This provides the audio background for any audio footage you end up inserting.

5. External microphones have several pickup patterns useful for different activities. These include

   - **Omnidirectional microphone** — Picks up all sounds equally from around the camera.

   - **Boundary or PZM microphone** — Lies flat on a surface and has an omnidirectional pickup pattern.

   - **Unidirectional (or just directional) microphone** — Picks up sounds directly in front of the microphone, ignoring ambient sound.

- **Zoom microphone** — Adjusts to the zoom ratio of the camera lens.

- **Gun/shotgun microphone** — This is an extreme unidirectional microphone that ignores ambient sound and picks up audio from distant sources at which it's aimed.

6. Attachable microphones from your camera vendor are the easiest and cheapest way to extend your camera's audio capabilities. For some shots, however, you'll need either a handheld microphone or a lavaliere microphone. Though widely available from many vendors, not all external microphones can easily be adapted to camcorder use. For this reason, be sure to purchase from a knowledgeable vendor.

Chapter 9

Shooting for Digital Distribution

When producing video for distribution on VHS tape, visual quality is limited only by the quality of your equipment and your creativity. In contrast, when producing video for digital distribution, whether via DVD, CD-ROM, a local area network, or the Internet, you're limited by three additional critical digital realities that can dramatically degrade output quality.

The three digital realities are bandwidth, lossy compression, and inter-frame compression. Though they definitely have that "these are way too technical for anything I'll be doing" ring to them, if you plan on distributing your videos in any digital format other than DVD or CD-ROM, you definitely need to read on.

Understand and work within these realities, and you'll produce optimum quality for your chosen distribution medium. Ignore them, and you'll almost certainly be disappointed with your results.

So, as Jay Leno might say (and does, nearly every night), let's get to it.

Reality 1: Bandwidth Matters

Bandwidth is the size of the data pipe between your video data and the person who accesses it remotely (remote viewer), typically expressed as the amount of data transmitted per second (see Figure 9-1). For example, a modem has a bandwidth of 56 kilobits per second (kbps), a DSL or cable modem has a bandwidth of 400 kbps or higher, and a local area network (LAN) has a data rate of 100 megabits per second (mbps).

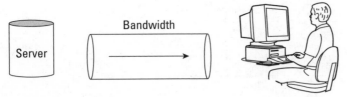

Figure 9-1: Bandwidth is the size of the pipe between your video data (here on a server) and the remote viewer.

Whereas most communications-oriented mediums like modems, cable modems, and LANs are expressed in bits per second (or kilo-, mega-, or gigabits per second), the bandwidth of optical media, like CD-ROMs and DVD-ROMs, is expressed in *bytes* per second (or kilo-, mega-, or gigabytes per second). This makes it tough sometimes to compare throughputs of networked and optical media.

The formula, of course, for converting bits to bytes, is that 8 bits equals 1 byte. This yields some fairly interesting observations.

For example, a single-speed 1X CD-ROM drive, ancient by any standard, transmits 150 kilobytes per second (KB/sec). In contrast, the 400-mbps cable modem that costs you $49 a month only delivers about 50K/sec, about one-third the bandwidth of that ancient CD-ROM.

As you saw in Chapter 5, 1X DVD equals about 1.350 megabytes per second (MB/sec) or a staggering 10.8 megabits per second (mbps). Since current DVD drives can read at up to 4X DVD, that's 43.2 mbps or 108 times faster than that cable modem you thought was a total speed demon.

At a high level, CD/DVD bandwidths are huge, while Internet bandwidths are small. As you'll see, this dramatically affects the quality of video you can deliver over the respective mediums.

Understanding Data Rate

Data rate is the term that describes the temporal size of a video file, usually, as with equipment and network bandwidths, expressed in data per second. For example, DV video has a data rate of 3.6MB/sec.

When you distribute your files digitally, you as·producers choose the data rate for your files, using screens like those shown in the following figure. Figure 9-2 is a screen from Adobe's MPEG Export utility.

I'll explain all the encoding concepts in Chapter 16, but for now I want you to notice the Constant bitrate settings in the upper-right corner of Figure 9-2. Here, I'm simply telling the encoder to produce a file with a bit rate of 8,000 kbps. Every time you produce an MPEG file, you'll make a similar selection.

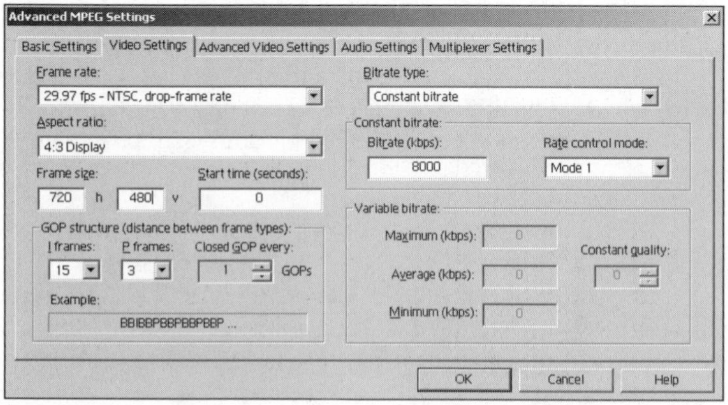

Figure 9-2: The data rate setting from the Adobe Premiere MPEG export screen, encoding to a constant bit rate of 8,000 kbps.

Figure 9-3 shows the business end of a RealSystem encoding tool. Once again, I'll discuss the key details in Chapter 16, but what I want you to focus on here are the Target Audience Settings on the left. Here, Real lets you select a target and then automatically chooses the data rate for that file based upon that target. Some Real tools actually let you go in and fiddle with the data rate setting, but most users are better off using the default setting.

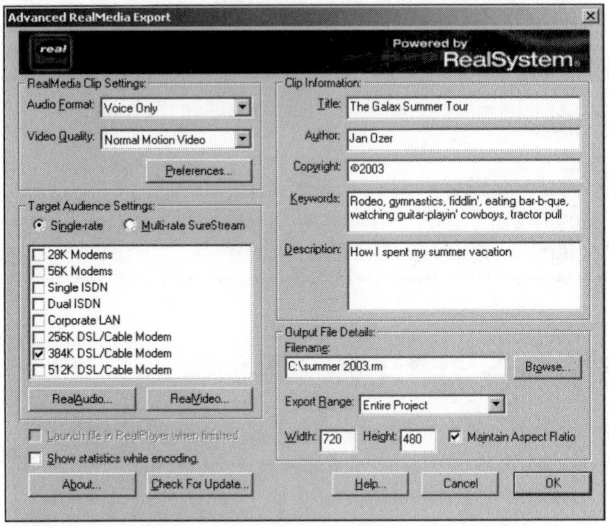

Figure 9-3: Encoding for delivery via RealVideo. Here you select target audience, not a specific data rate.

If you were the encoding tool and saw that I selected a target audience of 384 kbps, you'd probably be thinking something like, "Well, Jan wants to post this video to a Web site where someone will view it with a 384-kbps cable connection. At this bandwidth, this means she can retrieve about 384 kbps of data per second."

Then you'd continue. "Well, I'm sure Jan wants it to play smoothly on that connection (it's probably his mother or someone important like that), so I better make the data rate of the file smaller than the bandwidth of the cable connection, say 350 kbps. Otherwise, if the data rate is too big, the cable connection won't be able to retrieve data fast enough to play the video smoothly and it will stop and start like a bucking bronco, which Jan's mom will certainly mention during their next phone call."

Simply stated, the Golden Rule for distributors of digital video is to produce files with a data rate less than the bandwidth of the smallest pipe between the data and the remote viewer. This will ensure that the file plays smoothly. If the data rate is higher than the bandwidth of the biggest pipe, quality will degrade, the video will stop playing, or both.

A bit more theory, and then we'll come back to the Golden Rule and some notable exceptions.

Er, What's a Codec?

I haven't mentioned the word codec yet, but since I will in a moment, I thought I'd define it. Codec is the contraction of **co**mpressor/**dec**ompressor, or en**co**de/**dec**ode, depending upon whom you ask. Basically, every audio or video compression technology has two components, an encoder you use in the lab to compress the file, and a decoder that the remote viewer uses to decode the file. So every compression technology is a codec, and every codec is a compression technology.

Codecs you know and love include MPEG-1, MPEG-2, MP3, MPEG-4, RealAudio, RealVideo, Sorenson, and Microsoft's Windows Media Video and Audio. As long as we're on the topic, DV is a codec as well, and gray hairs like me remember Cinepak and Indeo, the most popular codecs in the mid-1990s, with affection.

Interestingly, QuickTime and Video for Windows are not codecs but architectures for the development of video-related products like capture cards, video editors, and codecs. Hence, Sorenson and Cinepak are QuickTime codecs, but QuickTime itself is not a codec.

Reality 2: Video Compression Is Lossy

At a high level, there are two types of compression technologies, *lossless* and *lossy*, determined by comparing the original file and the decompressed file. Lossless compression technologies like PKZip produce a decompressed file that's the same as the original, with no loss in quality. Hence, the lossless moniker.

In contrast, lossy technologies like JPEG produce a file that looks like the original but isn't exactly the same. Lossy technologies work by throwing away hopefully redundant information that isn't required to reproduce the original files. At higher and higher compression ratios, they throw more and more information away, which makes it difficult to reproduce the original image with accuracy. This is shown in Figure 9-4.

The great thing about lossless compression technologies, of course, is their accuracy. Unfortunately, especially with real-world still images and video, lossless technologies produce less than 2:1 compression (compressing the original file down to half the original size). However, this is inadequate for virtually all video distribution applications.

I'll spare you the math, but depending upon factors like frame resolution (pixel height and width) and frame rate, you have to compress a video file up to 100:1 to achieve your target data rate. That's why all video compression technologies, or codecs, like MPEG-1, MPEG-2, RealVideo, Sorenson, and Windows Media are all lossy technologies.

As you can see in Figure 9-4, lossy compression technologies are scalable and can achieve virtually any file size. The obvious price is quality.

Simply stated, the immutable rule of lossy compression is that the more you compress, the more you lose. The lower the data rate you assign to the file, the worse it's going to look. Using the control shown in Figure 9-3, if you produce a file targeted toward 56-kbps modems, it will look worse than files produced for 384-kbps DSL modems.

But just because a person connects to the Internet via a 56-kbps modem doesn't mean you have to encode the file at 56 kbps. Here's why.

Original　　　　38:1 compression　　　　75:1 compression

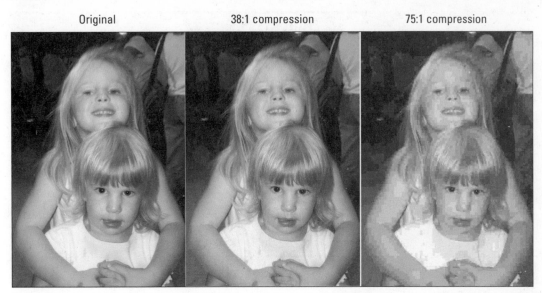

Figure 9-4: At 38:1 compression, JPEG holds up well, but it starts breaking down seriously at 75:1.

Streaming Data

The Golden Rule (the file data rate must be less than the bandwidth of the smallest pipe between video file and viewer) applies only to files that are transmitted via a technique called *streaming*. Streaming is the concept of sending data immediately to start video playback and then maintaining the data stream continuously to enable smooth playback.

Since the playback starts immediately and is designed to be continuous, the data rate of the video file must be less than the bandwidth of the modem or other connection mechanism. Otherwise, the data doesn't get there in time, and the show is over, at least temporarily.

Contrast this with *download-and-play* delivery, the first technique used to transmit video files over the Web. Here, the video is downloaded to your computer fully before you can start playback. There might be a hefty delay during that download, but you've eliminated the modem bandwidth limitation, so you can encode the video to much higher data rates.

Download and play has an archaic ring to it, but if you think about it, this is the technique used when you deliver video via e-mail, since the file must be fully downloaded and saved separately to disk before playback can begin. Accordingly, even if grandma connects via a 56-kbps modem, that doesn't mean you have to encode to a target data rate of 56 kbps. Instead, you can encode at 200–300 kbps and tell her to cool her jets and wait for the e-mail to download.

Interestingly, there's a hybrid between streaming and download and play called *progressive download* that has been used quite successfully by Apple's QuickTime. Here, the video starts to play immediately but stops if the viewer doesn't receive sufficient data.

What's unique about this approach is that the video data retrieved from the remote site is stored on your hard drive, so even if the first time through it starts and stops frequently, ultimately, once the data is on your hard drive, it will play smoothly. Using this technique, movie studios can post huge files that could never, ever stream in real time via cable modem or DSL, knowing that ultimately they will look good when played back from your hard drive. Since they're not designed to stream, they don't need to be highly compressed, which is the secret behind QuickTime's high-quality trailers. Of course, this technique works best for short videos that the remote viewer *really, really* wants to see. Renee Zellwegger? Yes. A video advertisement for a new line of refrigerators? Probably not.

So the key takeaways up until now are as follows:

- When streaming, the data rate of the video file must be less than the bandwidth of the smallest pipe between the video data and remote viewer.

- Video codecs are all lossy technologies, so the more you squeeze, the more you lose. The smaller the pipe you stream through, the lower the video quality.

- When you're not streaming (for example, when distributing your file via e-mail), you can encode at data rates higher than the connection bandwidth of the remote viewer.

Reality 3: Inter-Frame Compression Means Motion Degrades Quality

Which type of videos compress more effectively: talking head videos or videos with lots of dynamic motion? Most readers will reflexively say talking heads (hey, it's my fourth book, I know these things), and these readers would be right. Here I talk about why and how this impacts the way you have to shoot and edit your videos for maximum quality.

Most codecs use two types of compression to achieve their target data rate. First is *intra*-frame compression, which is compression performed solely with regard to information within that frame. Second is *inter*-frame compression, a technique used to remove redundancies between frames. Figure 9-5 shows how.

Inter-frame technologies use a system of key and delta (also called "difference") frames to compress multiple frames. Key frames are stored in their entirety and encoded using only intra-frame techniques. In contrast, encoders use inter-frame compression to eliminate the redundancies between the key and delta frames and then store only the differences between the two frames, once again encoded using an intra-frame technique.

In the animation file (called Interframe.flc) included on the CD accompanying this book, "Mikey the Microprocessor" (don't ask) is the perfect talking head, moving only his mouth and eyes during the short animation. While encoding, the codec will first store the entire key frame, as shown on the bottom left of Figure 9-5, and then the difference between the key and delta frames.

On the CD-ROM

Note that you can play the animated Interframe.flc file with your QuickTime player.

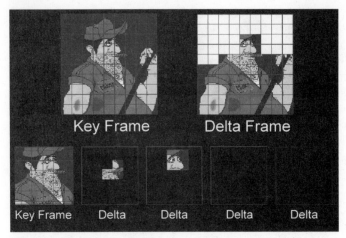

Figure 9-5: Inter-frame compression uses key and delta frames to eliminate redundancies between frames, a high-quality technique that works best with low-motion video.

Operationally, the encoder breaks each frame into blocks and then compares the blocks in the key and delta frames, as shown on the top row of Figure 9-5. If they're identical, the blocks are discarded as redundant. If different, they're stored and then encoded using an inter-frame technique.

Quick question: Is inter-frame compression lossless or lossy? Well, with the animation shown in Figure 9-6, it's actually lossless, since you can create the original video from the key frame and information stored in the delta frames.

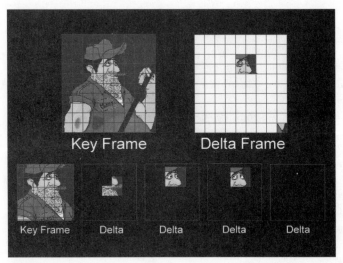

Figure 9-6: Inter-frame compression uses a system of key and delta frames to remove redundancies between the frames.

With real-world videos, inter-frame compression isn't lossless, because minor variations indistin-guishable to our eyes make it extremely unlikely that blocks on consecutive frames will be 100 per-cent identical, bit for bit. So inter-frame codecs accept less than 100 percent matches in their search for redundancy, which prevents inter-frame compression from being completely lossless.

However, inter-frame compression is a lot more lossless that intra-frame compression. In highly static shots, like talking heads, with large ranges of redundant regions, inter-frame compression can accomplish the bulk of the necessary compression, which translates to high quality. In contrast, when there's too much motion, inter-frame redundancies are rare, so intra-frame technologies have to carry the load.

How much difference does this make? Well, it depends upon a bunch of factors that I'll explore in more detail in a moment. However, Figure 9-7 tells the story.

Figure 9-7: Talking head videos compress well because high inter-frame redundancies maximize inter-frame compression. High motion videos have little redundancies, forcing intra-frame to kick in with poor results.

Both videos in Figure 9-7 were compressed with the same codec to the same data rate. The video on the left looks great, because motion is extremely limited. On the right, the spinning motion of the merry-go-round eliminates inter-frame redundancy, forcing intra-frame compression to carry the load. The result? Distorted ugly video.

There are a few other points you should understand. First, in the real world, inter-frame com-pression is much more complex than that shown in Figure 9-5. For example, MPEG-1 and MPEG-2 use two types of delta frames, called Predictive and Bi-Directionally Interpolated frames, the latter of which searches for redundancies in frames both before and after its location.

In addition, more sophisticated encoding engines can search for redundant blocks in various locations in the delta frames, increasing the likelihood of finding a match. This is one of the key rea-sons that more expensive MPEG-2 encoders used to encode Hollywood movies produce better results than the encoder on a $100 authoring program or in an $800 digital camera that stores video in MPEG-2 format.

Nonetheless, the key takeaways are the same:

■ Inter-frame compression, when available, typically produces better quality than intra-frame compression.

■ Motion is the enemy of inter-frame compression. Higher motion video reduces inter-frame redundancy, which forces the comparatively more lossy intra-frame compression to carry the load, resulting in lower-quality video.

Applying Inter-Frame Theory to Your Videos

All that said, where does this inter-frame compression stuff matter? Take a look at Figure 9-8.

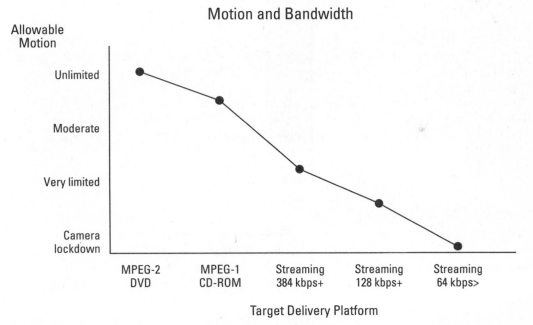

Figure 9-8: Allowable motion in your video by delivery platform.

Basically, the point of Figure 9-8 is that your delivery platform determines the amount of allowable motion. If you're producing for delivery on DVD via MPEG-2 compression, you're in great shape. Even using a $49 DVD-authoring tool, you should be able to achieve relatively artifact-free video irrespective of your camera techniques, special effects, and other sources of motion.

On the other hand, as you shift your bandwidth target lower, motion creates a more significant problem. For example, when streaming video at 64 kbps and below, you have to lock down the camera on a tripod and limit on-screen motion significantly or video quality will degrade significantly.

Whatever platform you're targeting, you'll improve quality if you limit motion during filming and editing. At the very least, you should eliminate hidden sources of motion, like those discussed in the following sections, to maximize the quality of the motion integral to the story that you're telling.

Sources of Motion to Watch Out For

So, you know motion is the enemy, and now you're out on a search-and-destroy mission. If you're shooting for low bandwidth distribution, there are several obvious and some not so obvious places to find motion. Here are the key places to look.

TRIPOD

This is an obvious one, especially for those using a small, consumer camcorder that's almost impossible to hold steady. Even shoulder-mounted cameras produce small amounts of motion that can seriously degrade image quality.

For example, when I was working at Iterated Systems, a friend got me a tape of Deion "Prime Time" Sanders interviewing Barry Bonds, as well as the rights to use the video at a trade show in Atlanta. We were pretty ecstatic, because Prime Time was pretty high-profile back then and we thought it would be a great draw at the booth. Though the video looked perfect to the naked eye, it compressed horribly.

Studying the captured video, we found that each frame shifted one or two pixels in different directions from the previous frame. With our relatively primitive codec of the day (this was 1991), this limited our ability to find inter-frame redundancies, with the resultant drop in quality.

We traced this back to the fact that it was filmed with a shoulder-mounted camera, not a tripod. Though the video was perfect for television, it was unsuitable for high-quality compression.

The obvious answer is a tripod or some other stationary object for shooting.

ZOOMING, PANNING, AND TILTING

Zooming and panning, however slow and well-controlled, change every pixel and every frame, virtually eliminating inter-frame redundancies. In Chapter 7 you learned to severely limit these effects; if you're transmitting your video at low bit rates, you should eliminate them entirely.

CONSIDER THE BACKGROUND

When filming for low bit-rate distribution, working with a "compression-friendly" background becomes paramount. Here are some tips to help you accomplish this.

Keep these things in mind when considering your lighting:

- Use flat lighting. Graduated lighting may produce banding (see Figure 9-9) where similarly colored regions band together.

- Make sure your scene is very well lit. If it's not, your camera will boost the gain to compensate, which creates noise. In addition, some streaming codecs darken the video during encoding, so it's better to be a touch overexposed prior to compression.

- Try to eliminate shadows and lighting hotspots from direct beams.

Figure 9-9: Graduated lighting may produce banding, as shown above.

Here are some additional background care and feeding tips:

- Use a bland, basic background. Books and complex wallpaper are out. Trees and bushes (or anything that can blow in the wind) are bad. Venetian blinds are a disaster.

- Experiment with a black light-absorbing background fabric to minimize background detail.

- Use camera techniques to blur the background when shooting for streaming and other highly compressed distribution formats. You can accomplish this in one of three ways:

  - If your camera has manual aperture controls, open the aperture to narrow the depth of field (see Figure 9-10).

  - If your camera doesn't have a manual aperture control but does have a "portrait" pro-grammed mode, try the portrait mode, which often accomplishes the same effect:

  - Otherwise, move the subject away from the background and the camera as far away as possible from the subject. Then zoom in to frame the subject, which should blur the background considerably. Of course, you'll probably need a remote microphone, or your audio quality will suffer dramatically.

Open aperture   Closed aperture

Figure 9-10: Opening up the aperture blurs the background. Here I'm focusing on the model on the right, whose hair you can just see on the right of each frame. If you don't have manual controls, try portrait mode on your camcorder, which often has the same effect.

SHOOTING FOR THE SMALL SCREEN

In Chapter 7 I spoke of wide-angle establishing shots, and full-screen medium shots. Forget these for streaming. Especially for low bandwidth targets, you need to frame your shots very tightly around the target, and if you have two people in the frame, get them as close together as possible.

In addition, whenever the visual image is degraded, as it almost always is during streaming, high-quality audio becomes even more important. As described in Chapter 9, usually this means using a microphone and monitoring audio capture during shooting, and making sure the incoming audio is as loud as possible without distortion.

In a business setting, use a three-CCD camera whenever possible, since the benefit of high-quality input is exaggerated when compression is extreme. In addition, these cameras provide advanced controls for capturing and monitoring audio, simplifying these tasks.

Lose the background music track whenever possible. Like motion in video, the more complex a sound is, the more difficult it is to compress. Most streaming codecs are extremely effective at encoding well-recorded speech, even at extraordinarily low bit rates. Throw a background music track or special effects into the mix, and audio quality will suffer.

SHOOT SPECIFICALLY FOR THE WEB WHEN POSSIBLE

While many of the preceding rules are simply common sense (like "always use a tripod if possible"), many contradict otherwise good choices for producing interesting video like restricting action and using bland lighting and backgrounds. For this reason, if you plan to distribute your video at low data rates, it's best to shoot exclusively for this medium whenever possible.

Along these lines, the most effective method for producing high quality at low bit rates is to use blue-screen techniques to overlay the video over a still or black background, as illustrated in Figure 9-11.

| Motion background | Still background | Blue screen | Black matte |

Figure 9-11: Blue-screen techniques can improve quality for streaming. The three images on the right were produced using this technique.

Briefly, I started with the blue-screen video that is second from the right. Then, using Adobe Premiere (see Chapter 14 for details), I overlayed the video against three backgrounds and then encoded the files to similar parameters. Here are the details:

- **Motion background.** Basically, I shot a wall in my office to get some moving footage and then keyed the subject over the moving video. This most closely approximates the results I would expect from a regular video, since both the subject and background are live videos.

- **Still background.** Here I took a single frame from the wall video and stretched it out as background for the overlayed video. This totally eliminated any motion in the background video, allowing the codec to focus solely on the subject, which is noticeably better in quality than the moving background. It's a bit of a mindbender, but small fluctuations in lighting and who knows what else limit the redundancies found by the encoder. This proved the concept: It's better to shoot over a blue-screen background and overlay over a still image than encode regular video.

- **Original blue screen.** Here, I just encoded the original video. Note that quality is slightly lower than the still background.

- **Black matte.** Here, I overlayed the video over a plain black matte, which produced the best result of all. Clearly, limiting the work the encoder has to do in the background produces the best overall result.

Test Early and Often

The best advice I can give all producers seeking to distribute at low bit rates is to test their shoots at the target-encoding parameters as early and often as possible. In fact, with notebooks like my Dell Latitude, you can actually capture and encode on the shoot.

What about Editing?

You should also modify your editing to ensure that your video compresses well and looks best on the small screen. Some suggestions include:

- Use cut transitions or wipes, which introduce very little motion. Avoid slides and pushes, which introduce significant motion, as well as 3D effects like page peels.

- Avoid motion and other effects whenever possible. For example, don't scroll titles in and out of the screen, and don't move other objects like 3D logos or picture-in-picture effects on and off the screen.

- When creating titles, use larger than normal fonts, as well as simple fonts, and ensure that there's high contrast between the font and background colors. If the colors are similar, they will blend together during compression. Consider leaving the title on-screen longer than normal because it may take a few seconds for it to become clear and readable.

- Observe whether encoding has darkened your video significantly. If so, consider using a brightening or gamma filter to boost brightness to counteract this effect.

- Basically, the best statement I've seen on this topic comes from Tim Kennedy of Streaming Media World, who said:

  "As you mourn the loss of your effects, remember what streaming your content is all about. Your goal is to communicate a message. Effects cause unnecessary change in your streaming video. They force the video stream to put more resources into something other than what the true subject is of your video. Your subject is what communicates that message. Lose the effects. Focus on the goal." (See `http://smw.internet.com/video/tutor/streambasics2/index4.html`.)

The problem is that some errors aren't obvious until you encode. For example, I didn't notice the banding artifact shown in Figure 9-9 until weeks after the shoot. The video, professionally shot on BetaSP (this was 1994), looked beautiful on all the monitors and in the editing suite. It wasn't until we actually encoded that the problems became obvious. Then, it was too late to fix, and we basically had to start over.

Summary

Here are the key points covered in this chapter.

1. Bandwidth is the size of the pipe between your data and the remote viewer.

2. All compressed files have a data rate defining the amount of audio/video data per second in the file. The Golden Rule for distributors of digital video is to produce files with a data rate less than the bandwidth of the smallest pipe between the data and the remote viewer.

3. The Golden Rule doesn't apply to files that aren't streamed, such as files distributed via download, e-mail, or by progressive download.

4. Video codecs are all lossy technologies that decrease in quality as file sizes get smaller.

5. Inter-frame compression uses redundancies between frames to compress, which is generally more effective than intra-frame compression, but works best when motion in the video is minimal.

6. Motion is the enemy of inter-frame compression. To produce the best video quality, minimize motion in your original videos and don't introduce motion during editing.

7. Similarly, audio codecs work best with a clear distinct signal, which means nix the background music and sound effects for streaming audio.

Part III

Video Editing and Production

Chapter 10

Capture for Video Editing

PC MAGAZINE
www.pcmag.com

Video capture is the process of transferring video from your camcorder to your computer. Back in the bad old days, video capture was a train wreck waiting to happen, since computers and disk drives were comparatively slow, disk capacity tremendously expensive, and operating systems almost hostile to multimedia. Capture was an art worthy of long chapters on tweaking parameters and system components to optimize production quality.

On today's computers, much faster all around, with capacious storage and video-centric operating systems, DV capture is one-button simple, and analog capture, once you understand the basics, is only slightly more complicated. Video capture has morphed from art to science, and it ain't rocket science at that. So let's get the video to disk and start the fun stuff, which is video editing.

Operationally, video capture is typically controlled by the video editor, and all the options discussed in this chapter are exposed through controls provided in your editing software.

Capture Concepts

Let's start with some concepts that impact all capture tasks, both analog and digital. When capturing video from a DV camera, capture is more like a file transfer, since the same file stored digitally in the camera is simply transferred to the computer. Some folks call it capture, some transfer. I'll use the former for consistency.

In contrast, transferring video from an analog camcorder to computer is a two-step process. First is *digitization*, or *analog-to-digital conversion*, where the analog signal is converted to neat little digital zeros and ones. Then, in most instances, the video is also compressed, usually into MPEG-2 format, but also into MPEG-1, and in the case of some FireWire devices, DV.

Interestingly, this process mirrors what happens on a digital camcorder, which performs its own analog-to-digital conversion and then compresses the digital file into DV format. Once again, analog capture also has many names, like digitization and A-to-D conversion, but I'll stick to the capture nomenclature.

Glossary of Capture Terms

During capture, especially analog capture, you'll encounter a range of options that I haven't yet discussed. I'll identify how and when to use these options in the next section, but for now, here's a brief glossary.

- **Video format.** This is the format used to store the video. Generally this is synonymous with codec, for **co**mpressor/**dec**ompressor, since virtually all capture formats are also compressed.

- **Capture resolution.** This is the height and width of the video expressed in pixels. DV has a resolution of 720x480 pixels, as does MPEG-2. As with all DV capture options, which must adhere to a fixed standard, once you decide to capture in DV format, you won't be able to adjust capture resolution. MPEG-1 has a resolution of 320x240 or 352x240 pixels, depending upon the capture device. If you have a choice, use 320x240 unless you're creating a VideoCD or SuperVideoCD (these are covered in Chapter 19).

- **Frame rate.** This is the number of frames per second stored with the captured video. The default for MPEG-2, MPEG-1, and DV is 29.97, which is the number of frames per second in the NTSC standard. Alternatively, when capturing in some alternative formats, like Indeo, you can choose your own frame rate.

- **Video data rate.** This is the amount of data per second stored with the compressed file. MPEG-1 and -2 are scalable standards that may allow you to adjust the capture data rate upward and downward. In contrast, the DV data rate is fixed at 3.6MB/sec.

- **Audio format.** Audio may also be stored in a compressed format, usually MPEG, or uncompressed, usually in some variant of Pulse Code Modulation (PCM format).

- **Audio data rate.** As with video, this is the amount of data stored per second with the audio file. When storing in PCM formats, you often select the audio data rate automatically once you choose your audio storage parameters. Specifically, first you'll choose the audio sample rate, typically 11, 22, or 44 kHz, which is 11K, 22K, or 44K per second. Then, you select whether to store the video in 8- or 16-bit mode, with the latter doubling the data rate, and mono or stereo, with the latter choice doubling the data rate again. For example, CD-ROM quality audio is 44 kHz, 16-bit stereo, which requires 176K/sec (44x2x2). When not capturing compressed, CD-ROM quality is almost always the best choice.

If these sound confusing, don't despair. Most video editors have presets like good, better, and best that you can select to make all these choices for you, simplifying the capture task considerably.

Capture Options

Since DV capture is essentially a file transfer, there are few capture options, if any, on most programs. Some programs enable capture to MPEG format, and some high-end programs allow you to adjust the incoming audio volume but that's about it.

In contrast, when capturing analog video, there's a lot more going on. You have to tell the computer which format to store the video in and choose parameters like data rate, resolution, frame rate, audio format rate, and data rate. In addition, you may have to tune the incoming video signal for brightness and color accuracy and adjust the audio volume. This is why analog capture is more complicated than DV, though many vendors use presets to make it extremely simple.

Scene Detection

Scene detection refers to the ability of video-editing software to identify different scenes in the source video. For example, during my daughter's recent gymnastics exhibition, I shot about an hour of video, pretty much the entire event. In the bad old days before scene detection, I would have had to watch the entire video, select the scenes I wanted in the final production, and then capture these manually. Obviously, this was a lengthy process. With scene detection, my editing software can identify the various scenes that I shot and separate them in the capture album, which saves a ton of time.

There are two basic types of scene detection. As I discussed in Chapter 7 (see the "Taking Care of Time Code" sidebar), DV tapes store a time and date code that relates to when the video was actually shot. Editing software scans these codes to identify breaks that indicate that you stopped and restarted shooting. Scene detection based upon these date codes is simple, fast, and automatic, but unfortunately it's available only when capturing from DV cameras.

The other type of scene detection is content-based scene detection. Here the video editor scans frame by frame to identify gross changes between the frames that may indicate that you changed scenes. Unfortunately, it may also mean someone walked in front of the camera or that you just followed little Sally from the house into the yard. Some editors provide threshold parameters that let you adjust what they consider a scene change, which is useful, but content-based scene detection is seldom as accurate as time-code-based techniques.

Device Control

Another lovely feature of DV cameras is that the same cable that carries the video to and from the computer also carries commands for stopping, starting, rewinding, and fast-forwarding the camera. Once you hook up your camera to your computer, you can drive capture solely through the software. This also enables advanced functions like batch capture, where you can set in and out points in the DV tape and have the editing software go fetch.

Though there are some standards for device control of analog cameras, few consumer video editors support them. For this reason, when capturing analog video, you do it the old-fashioned way — press play on the camcorder, press capture in the editor, and stop when appropriate. Batch capture is not in the cards.

Dropped Frames

Dropped frames occur when the capture computer can't store the video to disk fast enough. Technically, the capture software simply repeats the last successfully captured frame over and over until the computer can catch up, which creates obvious stutters in the video.

Back in the day, dropped frames meant that you had to dial down the capture data rate and store less video per second to disk, or some other draconian measure. Today, it's more an indication that something's gone awry in your setup, since virtually all computers are more than up to the task. Once a producer's nightmare, dropped frames are now simply something to watch for when capturing both analog and DV video.

Capture Directory

Virtually all video editors allow you to select the directory (also called a folder) for your captured video. The default setting for most programs are the Windows XP defaults (see Figure 10-1), which I absolutely detest because they're not on my capture drive and make the files extraordinarily difficult to find to reuse or delete. For this reason, I create a separate directory for each project I work on and store all project assets in this directory.

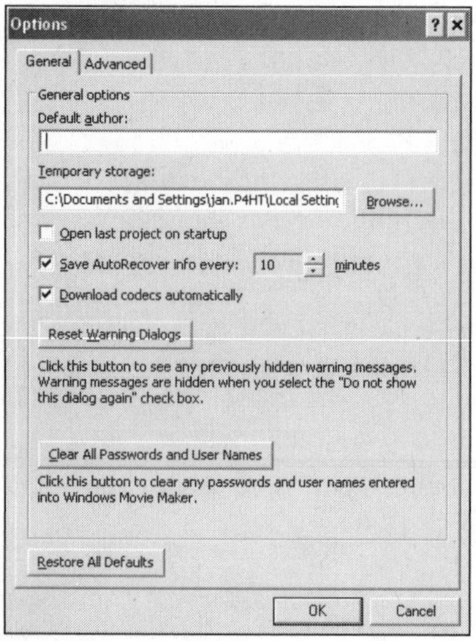

Figure 10-1: Not surprisingly, Movie Maker 2 adheres to Microsoft's file placement strategy, by default loading the files into a subdirectory that makes them impossible to find. I always switch to a project-specific folder on the root of either my capture drive or system drive for a laptop.

As you'll see, Movie Maker 2 gives you the option to select a target capture directory at the start of the capture process. Most other programs don't, so get in the habit of setting the target before you start capturing.

Defragmenting Your Hard Drive

I covered this in Chapter 6, but let's quickly review. When a disk drive stores large video files, it attempts to place them in contiguous sectors on the hard disk, which is most efficient for capture and editing. However, over time, as you add and delete files, large open spaces become less available, and the disk starts spreading large files in multiple areas. As you would expect, this slows performance significantly.

Deleting files is only a partial solution, since it's like throwing away every other piece of paper on your desk — it cleans things up a bit, but you're still left with a ton of clutter. For this reason, Windows includes a disk defragmenter tool with all recent versions, usually found by clicking Start → Accessories → System Tools → Disk Defragmenter. When you load the program, you can first analyze your disk, which tells you whether you need to defragment or not. If so, budget plenty of time, since this can take hours depending upon factors like the size of the drive, the size of files placed on disk, and disk speed.

I'm almost embarrassed to show you this, but Figure 10-2 shows the capture drive on my main test computer. As you can see, on a 112GB drive, I only have 1 percent of free space remaining, and one file in particular, the top VOB file (which stands for Video Object, which is the format used when writing DVDs) that I recently built to record to DVD, was actually stored in 2,057 different fragments. It's almost shocking that the disk burned successfully. Definitely time to delete some files and defragment.

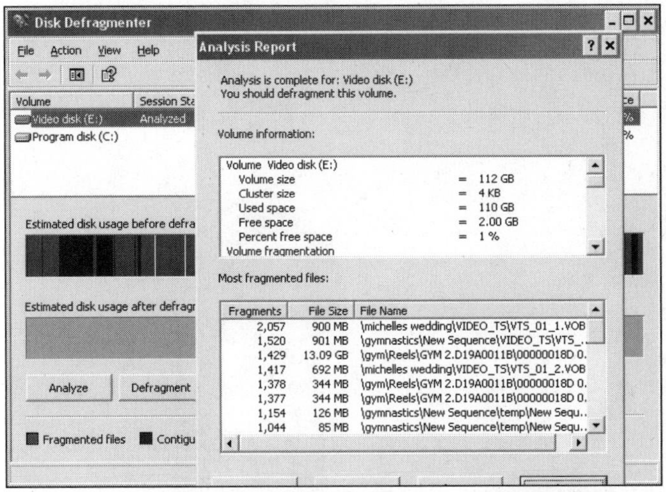

Figure 10-2: Can't let Mama see my disk in this condition — she might send me to bed without dinner. It's definitely time to defragment.

I detest deleting large video files, since I always feel like I'm deleting memories and eliminating that one last chance to tweak the production into perfection. So I sigh and remind myself that I can copy the DVD I produced, or I can recapture the final production from the DV tape where it's stored and start deleting.

Tip

Most well-mannered capture programs check for and monitor remaining disk capacity during capture and end the capture before you run out of space. Others don't and may crash when disk capacity is reached. Either way, check disk capacity before you start capturing. When capturing DV, it takes roughly 216MB per minute of video or about 13GB for a complete one-hour tape.

DV Capture

Let's explore two ways to capture DV, first manually, using Movie Maker 2, and then batch capture with Ulead's VideoStudio. First, however, you have to get connected.

Connecting for DV Capture

To capture DV video to your computer, you'll need the following:

- Either a FireWire port in your computer or a separate card like that shown in Figure 10-3.
- A FireWire cable like that shown in Figure 10-3.
- Video-editing software to drive the process.

As it turns out, the cable is the only tricky part. Virtually all DV cameras use the same 4-pin connector used by my trusty Sony DCR-PC7, and most FireWire cards, like that shown in Figure 10-3, use the larger 6-pin adapter. This makes the 4-pin/6-pin FireWire cable perfect for the task at hand.

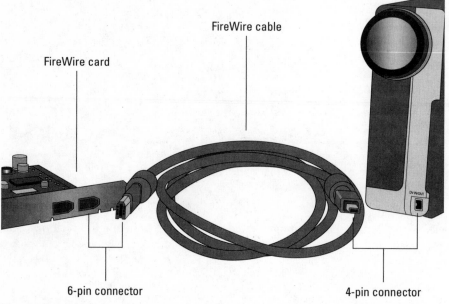

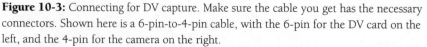

Figure 10-3: Connecting for DV capture. Make sure the cable you get has the necessary connectors. Shown here is a 6-pin-to-4-pin cable, with the 6-pin for the DV card on the left, and the 4-pin for the camera on the right.

However, my Dell Latitude laptop uses a 4-pin connector, so I need a 4-pin/4-pin FireWire cable to connect up to my Dell. These are available, so it's no problem, but if you have to buy a cable or cables for your various capture systems, make sure you get the appropriate connectors.

Capturing DV Manually

Once the cables are plugged in, you're ready to go. Turn your DV camcorder into VCR mode, and follow the Windows Movie Maker 2 wizard.

1. Click "Capture from video device" on the upper left. If the Movie Tasks bar isn't showing, click the Tasks icon beneath the menu on the upper left.

2. You should now see a screen where your DV camera should be identified in the available devices. If not, check that your camcorder is on and in VCR mode, and reseat the cables in the camcorder and FireWire card or port. If that doesn't fix the problem, check the documentation that came with your FireWire card or computer.

3. On the next screen that appears, Microsoft gives you the option to enter a capture filename and subdirectory. If you you're going to change from the default location, this is your last chance.

4. In the next screen (shown in Figure 10-4), Microsoft recommends that you capture in "The best quality for playback on my computer." This will encode your video into Microsoft's Windows Media format, which is best for immediate playback, but anathema if you plan to edit your video. For this reason, I recommend that you choose the DV format.

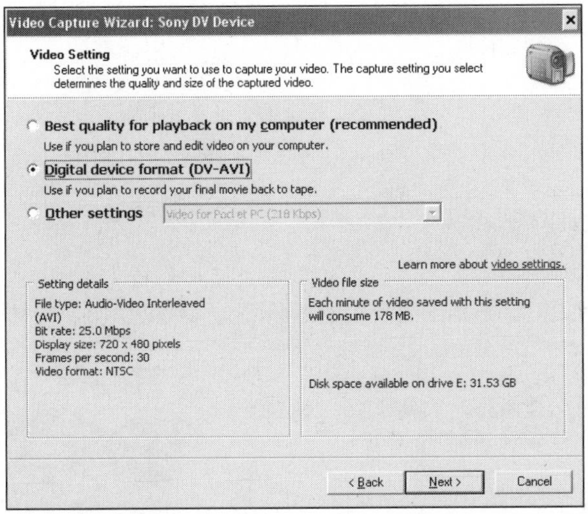

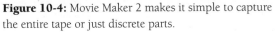

Figure 10-4: Movie Maker 2 makes it simple to capture
the entire tape or just discrete parts.

5. In the next screen that appears, Microsoft lets you capture the entire tape automatically, or you can pick and choose your segments. Since I shot an hour of video at this event, I'm going with the former. You can also elect to preview the video during capture or not. Most computers should have absolutely no problem doing so, but if your captured files don't play smoothly—indicating dropped frames during capture—uncheck the preview box.

6. In the next screen (as shown in Figure 10-5), I'm in the midst of a capture. See that "Create clips" checkbox in the lower-left corner? That's how you enable scene detection. If you roll through the entire tape, the Finish button will become enabled to exit this menu. You can also click Stop at any time and then elect to either save the captured file or delete it.

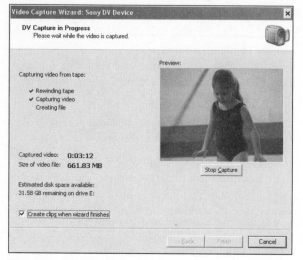

Figure 10-5: Movie Maker 2 during video capture. Check the Create clips control, and Movie Maker 2 will break your video into scenes based upon DV time code.

Pretty simple, eh? Figure 10-6 shows all the captured clips, separately nestled in Movie Maker 2's collections folder. Note that while Movie Maker 2 makes it look like all the clips are separately captured, it's actually one big file, with picons (picture icons) captured from the start of each scene.

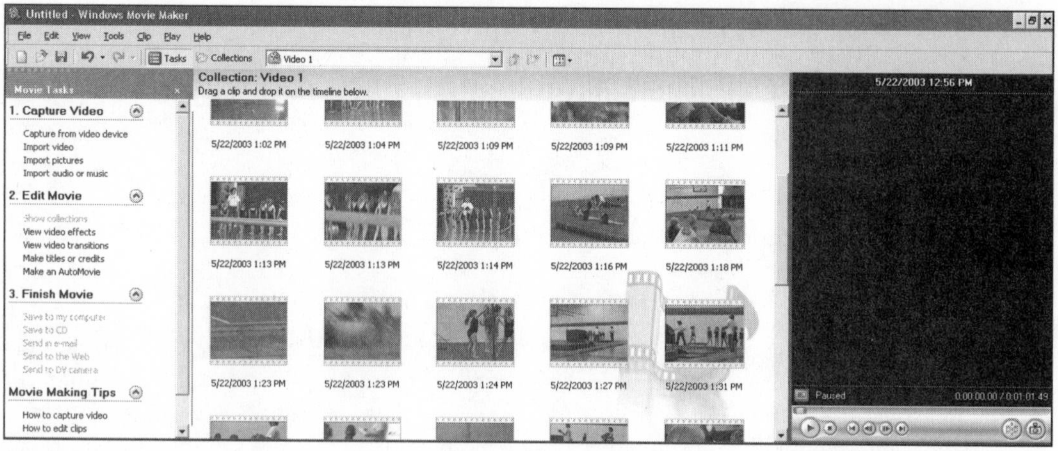

Figure 10-6: The results of our DV capture with scene detection enabled. I told you this stuff was easy.

Most consumer video editors work very similarly, though many don't offer Movie Maker 2's useful wizard. When using other programs, remember that you'll need to set the following parameters to get it right:

- Capture directory

- Capture format (always DV if available and you plan on editing your video)

- Scene detection enable/disable

- Capture filename

Note

Note that audio is interleaved into the same stream as the audio, so it's almost impossible to store one without the other. Also note that some video editors don't play the audio during capture, which is definitely scary. Usually, each time I start capturing with a new program, I'll capture a short file, play it back to make sure everything is OK, and then proceed with my longer capture.

Batch Capturing DV Files — Ulead VideoStudio

Batch capture provides the ability to manually scan your DV tapes selecting in and out points for the various scenes that you'd like to capture. Then you press the proverbial button, walk away, get the proverbial cup of coffee, and let the program capture all the scenes for you.

Batch capture works well when scene detection doesn't. For example, if you were shooting a lecture and shot one hour straight, time-code-based scene detection would be useless. Ditto for VHS tapes captured over to DV using your camera's analog input capabilities.

Batch capture is a staple on prosumer and professional packages, and Ulead also includes it in its latest release of VideoStudio. Here's how it works:

1. In the VideoStudio interface, you select Capture and then Batch Capture. This takes you to the screen in Figure 10-7.

Figure 10-7: Ulead's batch capture function is a nice feature for projects where automatic scene detection isn't effective.

2. Under the preview window, press the Play button to start the video, then press F3 to "mark in" scene starting points and F4 to "mark out" scene ending points. Remember to mark in a few seconds early and mark out a few seconds late to provide leeway while editing. If you need to stop and rewind the video to get it right, just use the controls under the preview window.

3. When you've marked all the desired clips, click Capture Video.

4. VideoStudio will rewind the tape and get busy. A dialog box appears and tells you where VideoStudio stored the files, and that capture proceeded with no dropped frames. Note that Ulead stores each file separately, naming them automatically.

5. VideoStudio automatically inserts the clips into the program's editing storyboard, so once you're finished capturing, you can immediately start editing (see Figure 10-8).

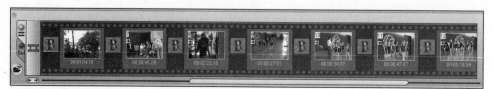

Figure 10-8: Once you're finished capturing, you can start editing right away.

Note

Note that many video-editing programs get confused during capture if the time codes in your video aren't continuous, especially programs attempting to batch capture. See the "Taking Care of Time Code" sidebar in Chapter 7.

Analog Capture

Analog capture is your only option when capturing from an analog camcorder or VCR, and it's also useful when capturing from DV cameras to external MPEG-2 devices like Adaptec's VideOh! DVD for fast conversion to DVD. There are two critical rules to understand when working with analog video.

First, always capture the best available analog format. Figure 10-9 shows the connectors on a typical Hi8 camera. The two video connectors are S-Video and composite. As the number of holes suggests, the S-Video signal delivers higher quality information, so use S-Video when available. Most camcorders have it; most consumer VHS recorders do not.

That Whole Windows File Size Limitation Thing

The original Windows operating system couldn't store a file larger than 2GB, since at the time it was developed, no one could conceive of the need to store a file that big. Not to mention that the average hard drive was only a few hundred megabytes at best. Don't get smug, you Mac fanatics, the original Macintosh had the same limits.

Today, however, if you're running Windows XP or Windows 2000, and your capture drive is formatted using the NTFS (Windows NT File System), you can capture files up to the limits of the disk, which makes life really simple. If your disk is formatted in FAT32, you may be limited to 4GB — about 19 minutes of DV Video.

Different programs handle this differently, with some cutting off capture when you hit the limit; some keep on chugging and automatically create multiple files in the background.

If you were looking for an excuse to upgrade to Windows XP or later, and you plan on doing a lot of editing, avoiding this limitation is definitely a good one. Just remember to format your disk using the NTFS technique, which will be one of the key questions the XP installation wizard asks during setup.

The second rule is always capture at the eventual output resolution, or larger, but never smaller. For example, suppose you were capturing video for converting to Windows Media format and e-mailing to your brother-in-law. As I'll discuss in more detail in Chapter 16, you probably want the video encoded at a resolution of 320x240. During capture, it's acceptable to capture at that resolution, or higher, say full DV or MPEG-2.

Conversely, suppose you were capturing to output to DVD, which requires MPEG-2 at a resolution of 720x480. Capturing at 320x240 would force you to zoom the video upward to 720x480 during encoding, which is bad practice because it degrades video quality. So, capture at full resolution, if available.

If you're capturing for output to multiple formats (DVD and e-mail), capture at the higher resolution, and, if you're not sure, always capture at the highest possible resolution.

Setting Up for Analog Capture

The cables and connectors you'll need to hook up for analog capture depend totally upon your analog source and capture device. I'll cover two scenarios that hopefully will provide some useful guidance.

ANALOG CAMERA TO CAPTURE CARD AND SOUNDCARD

In our first scenario, I'll connect an analog camera, with outputs like that shown in Figure 10-9, to an analog-capture card (similar to Pinnacle's DC-10) shown in Figure 10-10. On the capture card, you can see two separate connectors for S-Video and composite video, one to accept the incoming video and the other to connect back to the camera for printing to tape (see Chapter 16). In situations like these, where the analog-capture device doesn't have audio inputs, I'll input audio through the system soundcard.

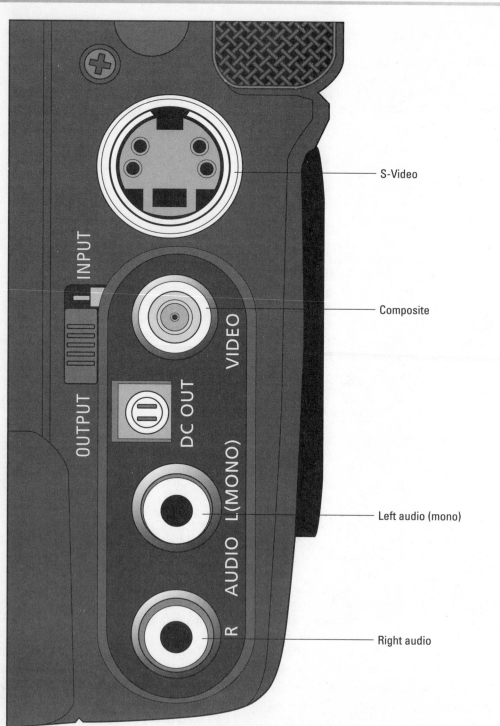

Figure 10-9: Here you see a typical analog Hi8 camera, showing the two video (S-Video and composite) connectors and the two stereo audio connectors. When available, always use S-Video.

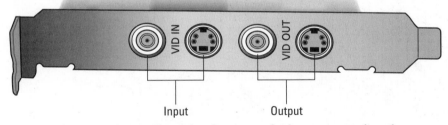

Figure 10-10: An analog-capture card with two sets of video connectors, but what about audio?

Since I have S-Video available, I would use the cable shown in Figure 10-11 to make the connection. If not, I'd use the composite connector on the cable shown in Figure 10-12, leaving two connectors for stereo audio.

Figure 10-11: The S-Video cable.

Figure 10-12: The three-headed RCA cable for composite video and stereo audio.

Few, if any soundcards accept dual RCA connectors, however, leaving us with the problem of converting our separate audio connectors to a single stereo connector. Two potential answers are shown in Figure 10-13. These are called Y connectors, with a stereo male adapter and twin female RCA adapters, and you can typically find them at Radio Shack or at www.cables.com. Or, you can simply find a cable with two RCA male adapters, and one male stereo audio connector.

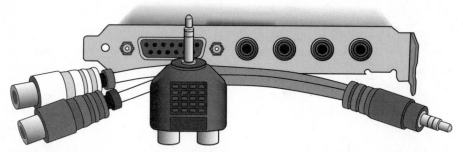

Figure 10-13: Y connectors accept dual RCA connections and output stereo audio. Though the form factors are different, both connectors do the same thing. You can't see it here, but they're color-coded, red for right and white for left. Plug in the analog audio outputs from your camcorder into the two jacks and the stereo connector into the appropriate port in your soundcard.

When connecting the cables, note that most connectors on cables and cameras are color-coded, with yellow for composite video, white for left or mono-only audio, and red for right audio.

DV CAMERA TO EXTERNAL MPEG-2 DEVICE

The other setup scenario I'll explore is connecting a DV camera, like that shown in Figure 10-14, with an external MPEG-2 capture device, like that shown in Figure 10-15. The fox in the woodpile in this example is that the camera has one output port for stereo audio and composite video. This requires a specialty cable like that shown in Figure 10-16, which has a one to three configuration, representing composite video and stereo audio.

Fortunately, virtually every camera vendor that uses this configuration includes a specialty cable in the box. Unlike any other cable or connector you've looked at so far, however, these are often customized to the specific device, so if you lose the cable, you may have to buy another from the camera vendor.

So, to connect the dots here, you would use the S-Video cable shown in Figure 10-11, and the specialty cable shown in Figure 10-16.

Capturing Analog Video

I'll run our analog test capture using Pinnacle Studio and Pinnacle MovieBox USB, an external box that captures in MPEG-1 and MPEG-2 formats. First I'll choose the capture parameters, and then I'll tune the incoming audio and video.

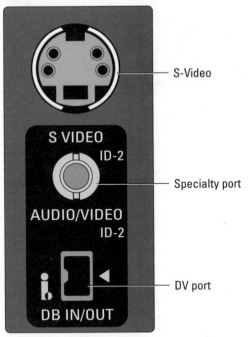

S-Video

Specialty port

DV port

Figure 10-14: The analog output ports for a low-end DV camcorder.

Figure 10-15: An external MPEG-2 capture device.

CHOOSING YOUR ANALOG CAPTURE PARAMETERS

Even though you already went through many of these same steps for the batch capture using Ulead VideoStudio, let's run through them again to see how to operate in another program. In Pinnacle Studio, you select the Capture tab on the upper left to move into capture mode.

1. Most programs don't offer the same type of wizard that Microsoft provides with Movie Maker 2, so you have to hunt for all the relevant settings. My first stop is always setting the folder for the captured video.

Figure 10-16: A specialty cable that outputs composite video and stereo audio from the specialty port shown in Figure 10-14.

2. In the box shown in Figure 10-17, I choose my scene detection option. Since content-based scene detection is iffy, I'll simply watch the video and choose scenes by hitting the space bar. No time-code-based scene detection is available (of course) because I'm capturing analog, not DV.

3. Now I choose the capture format and other capture parameters. Studio has three presets (DVD, SuperVideo CD, and VideoCD). If I plan to output to these optical formats, I definitely want to use the preset for capture. On the other hand, if I'm capturing to edit and distribute in a non-optical format, here are considerations for each capture parameter.

   ▪ **Format.** This parameter is very device-specific, running the gamut from uncompressed YUV formats (don't ask) to MPEG. The most common choices are DV, MPEG, and Motion JPEG, essentially a series of files compressed in JPEG format. Generally, your goal when capturing for editing is to capture at the best quality possible. Since MPEG formats are more highly compressed than Motion JPEG or DV (which is a variant of Motion JPEG), you generally should eschew MPEG if either of the latter two are available (refer to Figure 10-18).

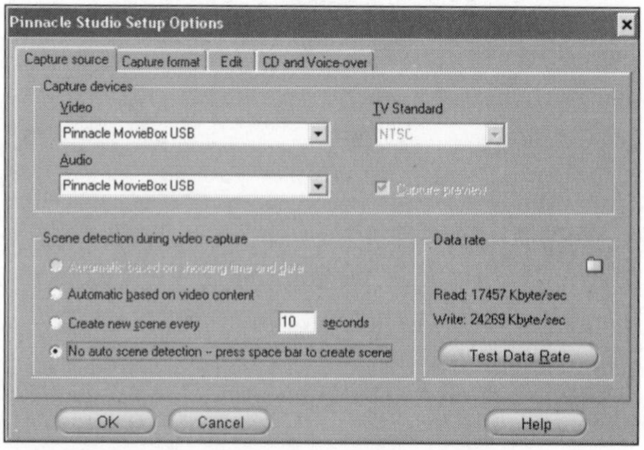

Figure 10-17: Choosing scene detection options in Pinnacle Studio.

Figure 10-18: Choosing
your format.

- **Resolution.** Once again, either choose the ultimate target resolution for the video you're producing or a larger resolution.

- **Data rate.** Since most formats are compressed, higher data rates should deliver more quality. Push it to the limit and try to capture; if you start dropping frames, you can always dial it down.

- **Audio capture parameters.** MovieBox captures all audio as MPEG-2 Layer 2 compressed audio. If your capture software gives you an option, capture at full CD quality (44 kHz, 16-bit, stereo). While you may want to reduce this before you distribute, you can handle that during final rendering.

- **Frame rate.** Studio doesn't expose the frame rate as a selectable capture parameter since MPEG files are always 29.97 frames per second (fps). In general, you should always capture at 29.97 frames per second.

INCOMING SIGNAL

With these parameters selected, it's time to enter the main capture interface (see Figure 10-19). Here I select S-Video input and elect to capture audio.

Most important are the adjustments to the incoming video. Studio offers the usual cast of adjustments, including brightness, contrast, sharpness, hue, and saturation. As shown in Figure 10-20, finding the optimal parameters can make a huge difference.

On the left is the unadjusted image, which is clearly too dark, a situation that compression will typically only worsen. On the right is the image post-correction, which is much brighter. True, you can make these adjustments during editing, but this increases production time and can degrade the image. Take the time to get it right during capture.

TUNING THE INCOMING SIGNAL

With these parameters selected, it's time to enter the main capture interface (see Figure 10-19). Here I select S-Video input and elect to capture audio.

Most important are the adjustments to the incoming video. Studio offers the usual cast of adjustments, including brightness, contrast, sharpness, hue, and saturation. As shown in Figure 10-20, finding the optimal parameters can make a huge difference.

Choose video input   Enable/disable audio capture

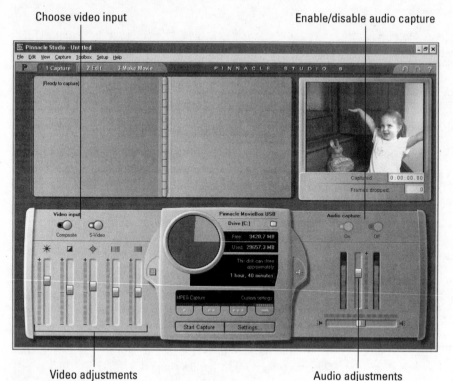

Video adjustments   Audio adjustments

Figure 10-19: Pinnacle Studio's analog capture control screen, with video adjustments on the left and audio controls on the right.

On the left is the unadjusted image, which is clearly too dark, a situation that compression will typically only worsen. On the right is the image post-correction, which is much brighter. True, you can make these adjustments during editing, but this increases production time and can degrade the image. Take the time to get it right during capture.

Before capture, you should also monitor the presence and volume of the incoming audio, trusting Studio's volume meter more than you trust your own ears. That's because the volume you hear can be affected by factors like volume levels in our Windows settings or the volume set on our speakers. It's always good to check both of these before capture to make sure they are within normal limits.

To access and adjust the Windows volume meter, select Start → Programs → Accessories → Entertainment → Volume Control, which should bring up a control that looks like Figure 10-21.

When adjusting the incoming volume, try to keep it in the middle range, as shown in Figure 10-19. If you set the volume too low, compression may make it inaudible. If you set it too high, clipping can result, which produces a metallic click each time the audio strays into the highest range.

When all this is set, press play on your camcorder, watch the video play in the preview window, press Start in Studio, and you're off. Remember that in this case, I selected manual scene-change detection, so click the space bar every time you want to start a new scene.

Original image   Adjusted image

Figure 10-20: Take the time to adjust the incoming video for brightness and color, which will save editing time and improve output quality.

During capture, most programs monitor dropped frames, and they either stop capture if frames drop or simply post a message on-screen. Typically, one or two dropped frames are pretty unnoticeable, but if you see chunks of 10 or 20, it means you've got a problem and the captured video will likely be unusable. Check the pre-capture configuration items described in Chapter 6 to attempt to correct it.

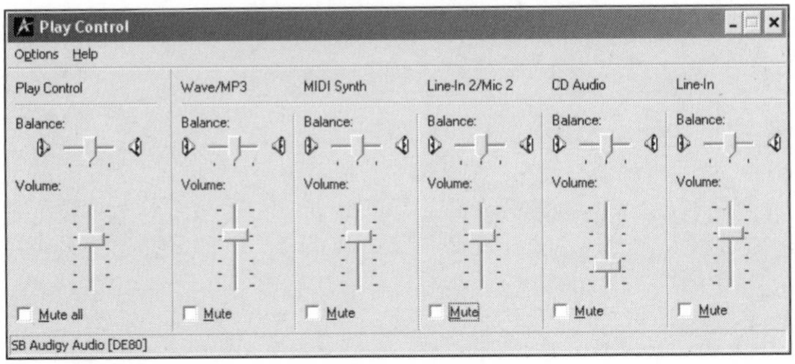

Figure 10-21: These are Windows volume settings that control what you hear from your speakers. Make sure that both Wave/MP3 and Master (titled Play Control, all the way to the left) are unchecked and turned up to between 40 and 60 percent.

POST-CAPTURE

If it's your first capture with the program, or even the first capture of the session, I recommend stopping the capture after a minute or two and playing the video to ensure that brightness, color, and audio volume are all correct. Nothing is more frustrating than waiting for an hour while a tape gets captured, only to learn that the video is worthless.

Note

In most instances, you can capture with one video-editing program and then edit in another, so long as you're on the same computer. However, if you transfer the video to another computer, you may experience problems, especially when capturing in formats other than MPEG or DV, which typically are proprietary to the capture device. Since these codecs necessary to play the captured video are installed with the capture card, these files won't display on other computers. If you want to capture on one computer and edit on another, convert the captured file to DV or MPEG format before transferring the video.

In Studio, you have to click the Edit button to enter edit mode (you can't play the video in capture mode) and then double-click any scene stored in the album. As shown in Figure 10-22, Studio will start the video playing in the player on the right.

Figure 10-22: Test your captured files as soon as possible to ensure audio/visual quality.

If possible, reduce the video to the final target format as soon as possible after capture. So if you're distributing in RealVideo format, encode a representative sample in RealVideo as soon as possible. If the encoding drops brightness significantly, or otherwise produces anomalies, you may need to adjust for this during capture.

Cross-Reference

See Chapter 16 for details on rendering.

Summary

Here is a summary of the key points from this chapter:

1. When capturing DV video, here are the parameters you need to locate and set:

   - **Capture subdirectory.** Generally it's best to select a folder on the root directory of your capture drive or system drive if you don't have a separate drive.

   - **Capture filename.**

   - **Capture format.** Use DV if available unless you have a very compelling reason not to.

   - **Scene detection.** Use time-code-based scene detection unless it wouldn't be helpful, as in the case where you filmed continuously for the entire tape.

2. When capturing analog video, here are the parameters you need to locate and set:

   - **Capture subdirectory.** Generally it's best to select a folder on the root directory of your capture drive, or system drive if you don't have a separate drive.

   - **Capture format.** Use DV if available, then Motion JPEG, if available, and MPEG-2 as the last resort.

   - **Data rate.** If it's adjustable, then you're dealing with a compressed format, and higher data rates will deliver better quality.

   - **Resolution.** Always capture at or larger than the target distribution resolution. If distributing in multiple formats, use the largest resolution available.

   - **Audio parameters.** Capture at CD quality (44 kHz, 16-bit, stereo) if you have the option.

   - **Frame rate.** Capture at or above the target distribution frame rate. Use 29.97 or 30 fps when in doubt and adjust during final rendering.

   - **Scene detection.** Use time-code-based scene detection unless it wouldn't be helpful, as in the case where you filmed continuously for the entire tape.

3. The most critical aspect of analog capture is getting the incoming audio/video parameters tuned correctly. Do this for each project and each major scene change within each project.

4. Capture a few quick scenes and then check the files before capturing the entire tape. Not much can go wrong with DV capture, but analog capture errors can sneak up and byte you (OK, sorry about that).

Chapter 11

Basic Editing Techniques

The one constant about good video is change. We're not talking just MTV either. Check out the nightly news, *60 Minutes*, and *Good Morning America*, and focus on the length of time that the video remains constant before a scene change, a zoom, a pan, a switch to a different camera, or a graphics update. If you see a stretch of 15 to 20 seconds of static video, I'd be shocked.

This is the video environment we live in and what the folks who will watch your video expect. Without question, your job is much tougher than television producers, because you don't have multiple cameras and camera operators, a control room, and a video-editing suite — or perky Katie Couric or Geraldo (heaven forbid). All you have is your DV camera, a sub-$100 video editor, and the people and places that make you want to shoot videos to remember.

Oh, yes, and you've got your imagination and ceaseless desire to create something worth watching, that captures that moment in space and time that you're filming to preserve, and, if you're me at least, to produce a laugh and a smile. To have the people who ridiculed you for dragging that camera, tripod, and hideous black bag around (usually your spouse, children, or other loved ones), look up and ruefully admit that you were right, it was all worth it.

Hey, a man can dream, can't he?

So, you've shot your video, and the moment is past. Now it's time to actually create your movie, to convert your raw material into something worth watching. The wonderful news is that your $49 video editor has features and performance that a Hollywood film producer would have killed for a scant 20 or 30 years ago. Clearly, you have more than enough firepower to deliver a blockbuster.

What you absolutely must remember is that you're not just here to trim your clips, add transitions and titles, render your video, and go home. You're here to carve your video into small digestible chunks and weave them into a dynamic presentation that grabs the viewer's attention and won't let go until the closing credits (scrolling, of course).

The truly amazing part is that it isn't hard. You don't have to be particularly artistic or technical or have a filmmaker's degree. You just have to understand the goal, identify the relevant tools at your disposal, and use them to their best effect.

I'll give you an example. A few months ago, I was at Saint Simon's Island for a family wedding. It was a touch too cold to go swimming, but my daughters wanted to torture their parents by getting in bathing suits and running close to the edge of the pool, teetering on the stairs and falling once or twice to scrape their knees and elbows, right where it would bleed through to ruin their new white dresses. You know the drill.

Grandmommy and Granddaddy were there, smiling at our discomfort, so naturally I took out the DV camcorder and started shooting. Pure Recording mode, nothing really going on, but time with kids and grandparents is a diminishing asset to be preserved. And I shot about 10 minutes of video that's as fundamentally unwatchable as any video ever shot. We're talking Malcolm McDowell in *A Clockwork Orange* pin-your-eyes-open painful.

So, what to do? Well, taking a cue from MTV, when you have fundamentally unwatchable video, make a music video out of it.

Working in Pinnacle Studio, I divided about five minutes of the most intensive pool torture into approximately 10-second clips and shuffled them about into random order. Then, I sped up each clip to double time to create a Chaplin-like effect and added a Beach Blanket Bingo-esqe soundtrack from Sonic Desktop's SmartSound collection.

This process changed five minutes of unwatchable video into 30 scenes totaling 150 seconds, with catchy background music that strangely appears well synchronized in spots, though in reality it was random. True, I still had five additional minutes to deal with, but there was more conversation and interaction in these, so they were more fundamentally interesting and less radical methods would do.

Other sections of the video I shot that weekend were equally unpalatable as originally shot, mostly footage of the ceremony and conversations at the wedding reception. Here, I divided each conversation into the smallest digestible vignette possible and separated them with simple dissolve transitions. Instead of watching 10 minutes of continuous dialog, viewers see multiple short stories, which help satisfy their need for diversity and change.

What's the moral? The one constant of good video is change. That's the one characteristic users demand.

Fortunately, you have many tools that deliver change. You've got background music, special effects, transitions, and titles. You have a razor tool that can cut your videos into a thousand discrete chunks, and there's video overlay, animations, and slideshows. There are also tools that can take your source videos and create MTV-like music videos for you, or you can do it yourself.

Cross-Reference

Take a look at Chapter 12 to learn how to add audio such as background music to your production. See Chapter 13 for more on video overlay, still-image animation, slideshows, and color correction. Lastly, turn to Chapter 14 for a discussion of automated tools that can turn source video into a music video.

None of these are hard to apply or master, or even time-consuming once you get the hang of it. You just have to be relentless in your efforts to inject change on a regular basis.

Two caveats. First, in this relentless pursuit of change, you have to be tasteful. Of course this is a dynamic metric that changes with content and audience, but a raucous sound effect or random flashy transition generally degrades perceived quality of your video.

Second, I recognize that not all projects require this kind of attention. Sometimes you just want to bang out a quick video to e-mail to the in-laws. I'll cover that type of production as well, though once you learn the basic tools, it's easy to apply them to any project, irrespective of length.

So, here you learn to access the basic editing tools to trim videos into digestible chunks, how to create slideshows, and how to insert transitions, some basic special effects, and titles.

Meet Your Video Editor

Let's start with a brief introduction to your video editor. Though all video editors look and work slightly differently, they generally share these four basic windows:

- **Libraries or albums.** These contain all assets imported into the project and the collections of transitions, special effects, title presets, and other effects included with the program. This is the upper-right window of Figure 11-1, with icons from the various scenes captured in the video.

- **Preview window.** This is where you preview the movie that you're building, both the raw clips and special effects like transitions and titles. Often this window does double duty as a "trim" window, which allows you to cut and paste your videos (see Figure 11-1).

- **Movie construction window.** This is where you assemble the components of your production. Most programs have at least two views, a storyboard and timeline view, explained in more detail later in this chapter.

- **Context-sensitive tools.** Most editors show context-sensitive tools in a control window depending upon the function then being performed. In Figure 11-1, VideoStudio shows basic trim controls and fade in and fade out controls on the upper left. These change as you move through the production steps shown in the top menu bar.

Working in the Library

All libraries work a bit differently, and learning how yours works can make the difference between keeping key project assets at your fingertips or looking for them anew each time you run your editor. Sounds dull, but you'll save lots of time in the long run if you spend a few minutes on the points outlined in the following sections.

ASSET MANAGEMENT

The most important library function to learn is how the library function handles your captured videos and other assets. There are basically two approaches.

Most consumer packages like Microsoft's Movie Maker 2, VideoStudio, and Pinnacle Studio simply display the assets available in the currently selected subdirectory. While references to files actually included in the project are saved with the project, the library only displays the files and scenes contained in the currently loaded directory, as shown in Figure 11-2.

Figure 11-1: Ulead VideoStudio 7 is known for its logical interface dominated by a lovely preview window.

The other approach, prevalent in professional programs, is to store all files inserted into the project in a storage bin where you can easily find them. This is shown in Figure 11-3, taken from Adobe Premiere. As you can see, you can even create multiple bins for various sections of the project.

I actually prefer this approach, since it simplifies asset management, but most consumer editors go the other route, which makes it easy to lose track of your project assets. To avoid this confusion, I typically create a separate directory for each project, capture all videos into that subdirectory, and place all still images and other project assets in separate folders within this project directory.

SPLITTING, COMBINING, AND LABELING SCENES

If you're working with a DV camera, most likely you've captured with scene detection enabled, resulting in multiple clips in the video library. Even if you're capturing from analog sources, most video editors can also break up scenes based upon content, again resulting in multiple files.

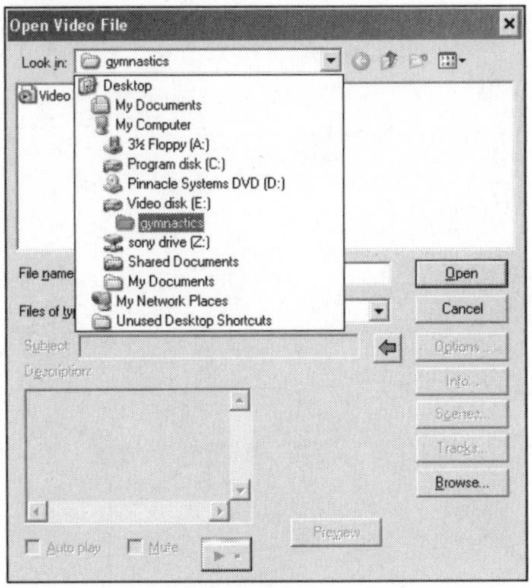

Figure 11-2: Most consumer video editors have no project bin that stores all assets. Their libraries simply display the files in the currently loaded directory.

Virtually all video editors provide the ability to split these scenes further or combine them (see Figure 11-4). This is useful in several instances, particularly when you're looking to consolidate videos for presentation on DVD.

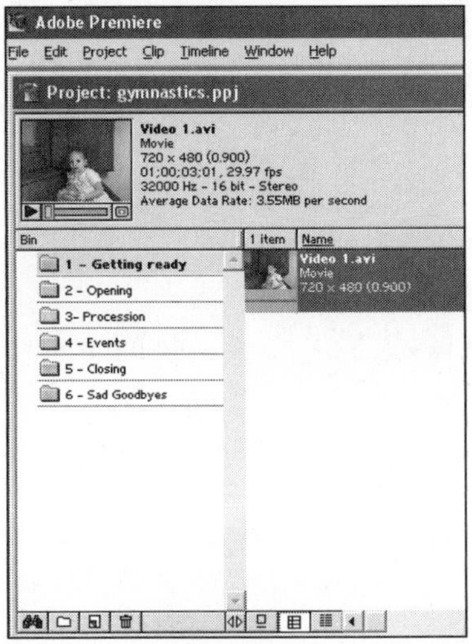

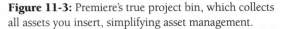

Figure 11-3: Premiere's true project bin, which collects all assets you insert, simplifying asset management.

For example, Pinnacle Studio has the lovely ability to create chapter points for all scenes in the movie window and then automatically produce menus with links to these chapter points. I'll discuss what all this means in Chapters 17 and 19, but essentially, it allows you to drag your videos into the movie window, press the proverbial button, and produce a DVD, no muss, no fuss.

Generally, however, with scene detection enabled, you have too many videos in the album to practically serve as DVD menu items. For example, during a recent trip to Zoo Atlanta, I ended up with about 118 scenes as originally captured. However, I grouped these by animal visited and other major sections and ultimately reduced the total scenes in the album to under 20, which fit on three DVD menus, producing an easily navigable disc.

Figure 11-4: Combining videos helps make them more manageable, especially for DVD projects (this is from Microsoft Movie Maker 2).

Most video editors also allow you to label scenes in the album, making them easier to find and later use (see Figure 11-5). Often this is necessary when project development spans several days or when you're assembling videos shot in the distant past.

The Preview Window

The preview window is where you'll preview the fruits of your editing labors. Most preview windows are driven by VCR-like controls, with a scrubber bar you can grab and pull with your mouse for faster navigation (see Figure 11-6). Many preview windows, like VideoStudio's, also function as a trim window, where you can precisely trim your videos. More on that in a moment.

Figure 11-5: Renaming videos automatically labeled by Movie Maker 2.

Editor Basics

Most video editors operate similarly in many key respects. Here are some highlights that you should anticipate:

- The editor probably saves your work in a project file, including all references to files actually included in the project. Like word processors and other programs, this allows you to stop editing and shut the computer down and then return and pick up where you left off.

- Edits will be "non-destructive" and don't actually change the video, audio, or images captured to disk. For example, if you capture a 10-minute video, load it into your editor, and then split it into two five-minute files, the original captured file is unchanged. Your edits will only be implemented on the file that you render at the conclusion of the project.

- When you drag video into the project or move it on the timeline, the audio will typically follow. To separate the two, which is useful in a variety of circumstances, you'll have to manually break the link, which programs accomplish in different ways. More later in the section "The Art of Insert Editing."

- Most editors have multiple levels of undo and redo so you can experiment at will.

- Most editors have presets for items like transition duration, and the duration of still images placed in the project. While you'll be able to change these manually for each transition and image, it's often easier to change the preset before you get started.

Figure 11-6: VideoStudio's capacious preview window is driven by VCR-like controls and doubles as a trim window. The scrubber control is that little horizontal capsule beneath the window that you can click and drag to any location in the video.

The Movie Construction Window

The movie construction window is called different names in different programs, but it's always easy to find, since it contains either a storyboard, timeline interface, or both. This is where you'll insert and edit your clips and where you'll spend the bulk of your editing time. Since they're so integral to your editing efforts, let's take a moment and explore the concepts of storyboard and timeline.

WHAT'S THE STORY(BOARD)?

As discussed in Chapter 7, a physical storyboard is a list of shots with associated drawings, usually on a big white board, that represent the flow of the movie. Hollywood producers use them extensively for feature-length movies, while advertising types use them for 30-second shots. They're invaluable in a professional setting because they help everyone understand the flow of the movie and what's expected for each shot.

In the context of a video editor, a storyboard works the same way. As shown in Figure 11-7, it allows you to order and reorder your videos at will. To get started, you simply select the desired scene in the video library with your pointer, hold down the left mouse button, and drag it to the desired spot. Usually you'll see some form of feedback, like the plus sign, indicating that it's OK to release the mouse and drop the scene into the box.

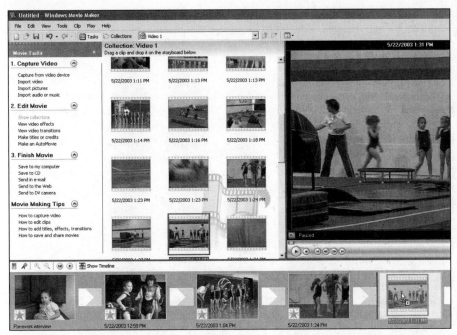

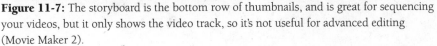

Figure 11-7: The storyboard is the bottom row of thumbnails, and is great for sequencing your videos, but it only shows the video track, so it's not useful for advanced editing (Movie Maker 2).

You typically can reorder scenes within the storyboard the same way—grabbing and dropping them into different boxes—and the editor automatically adjusts all subsequent videos as necessary. Click the play button on your preview window, and you can see how your assets flow from one to the next.

Storyboards are great for very simple projects because they're more intuitive than a timeline. They're also useful in more complicated projects when experimenting with different video sequencing because they clearly show each scene, while timelines often obscure scenes, especially shorter ones.

On the other hand, storyboards don't show the time dimension very well, and though transitions are effectively presented, other effects, like titles, background music, or narrations, that often span multiple scenes, aren't shown at all. For this reason, most video editors start in the storyboard and then switch to the timeline, or they ignore the storyboard altogether.

Note

Virtually all consumer products toggle between timeline and storyboard views, essentially offering alternative views of your project. That is, any edits you make in the timeline view will show up in the storyboard view, and vice versa.

In contrast, most advanced products like Premiere and Pinnacle Edition offer a storyboard function that's totally separate from the timeline. You can sequence your assets in the storyboard and then drag them into the timeline, but edits made in the timeline don't show up in the storyboard.

THE TIMELINE

If you study Figure 11-7 closely, just above the second figure from the left at the bottom of the screen, you'll see a "Show Timeline" button. Most consumer editors have a similar button that toggles you into timeline view.

Figure 11-8 shows the timeline view in Pinnacle Studio, which is very representative of the timeline used by most consumer editors. The first characteristic to notice is the time bar just atop the video thumbnails. This shows project duration, with over four minutes of video shown in Figure 11-8.

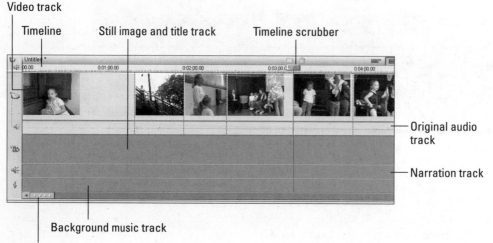

Figure 11-8: Pinnacle Studio's timeline view.

Note that each thumbnail image represents a separate scene, and that in contrast to the storyboard, which shows each scene equally, timelines allocate space according to duration. This means that longer videos take up more space visually while shorter videos take less space. More on this in a moment.

Next, notice the multiple tracks on the timeline. Studio offers five tracks as follows:

- One track for the video and another track for the "Original" audio, which is the audio actually captured with the video file.

- A title track for still images and titles.

- Two tracks for additional audio, nominally for narration and a music soundtrack, but they are capable of handling any type of audio file.

This is reasonably characteristic of most consumer editors. For example, Movie Maker offers a separate transition track but only two total audio tracks, while VideoStudio offers a separate overlay track and title track, as well as three total audio tracks.

In Chapter 14, we'll spend more time with advanced editors that offer up to 99 separate tracks of audio and video, but don't let this minimize your image of the creative potential offered by consumer editors. Other than a few advanced functions like blue-screen video that most consumers can't easily shoot anyway, consumer editors can perform most basic edits that professional tools can do, within a much more accessible interface.

Timelines can look imposing to beginning users, but they're really not once you understand a few consistent principles. First, all timelines shrink and expand to allow for different views. For example, in Figure 11-8, you see only about four minutes of video, while in Figure 11-9 you can see 55 minutes of video.

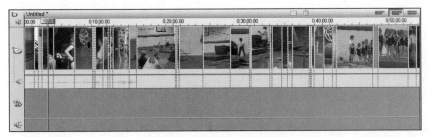

Figure 11-9: Studio's timeline fully zoomed out, showing 55 minutes of video.

During the course of building a project, you'll zoom in and out on the timeline at least a gazillion times, maybe more. For example, you'll zoom in to create titles for specific videos or to add transitions between clips. Then you might zoom out to see five or ten minutes at a time to add a background audio track.

For this reason, it's crucial to identify where the zoom controls are and how they work. Figure 11-10 shows a sampling of how programs accomplish this, with Studio's right menu commands, and the Zoom in and Zoom out buttons used by Movie Maker and VideoStudio. Note Studio's ability to show the entire movie in one right click, a nice convenience shared by most other products.

Figure 11-10: All timelines offer controls for zooming into the timeline, showing more clip detail, or zooming out from the timeline, to show the big picture.

Second, as shown in Figure 11-8, all timelines have a *slider*, usually located at the bottom of the timeline, that moves the window through the project. For example, to see videos located to the right of the videos then displayed, you would click the slider with your pointer, hold down the left mouse button, and drag the slider to the right.

All timelines also have a *scrubber* that represents the point in the video then shown in the preview window, also called the *edit line*. To play a video scene in the preview window, you click the scrubber with your pointer, hold down the left mouse button, drag it to the desired location, and then press play in the preview window.

Once you understand how to zoom, slide, and scrub through your videos, you're well on your way to "getting" how the timeline works.

PROJECT FLOW AND ORGANIZATION

A few points here on project flow and organization. Generally, when you're building a project, you trim your clips, add transitions and titles, apply special effects, and then add your audio last. This is because audio placement is often location-sensitive, like in the case of a narration tied to a video track. Since trimming clips and adding transitions can change the location of those clips on the timeline, you only want to add audio when the visual portion is set.

Second, you want to build your project completely and then render. You typically don't want to create and then render portion by portion because rendering almost always involves lossy compression, which degrades quality. If you render section by section, then join the rendered clips and then re-render them, you can degrade quality. It's like photocopying a photocopy. Projects are best rendered once and only once.

I recognize that this complicates longer projects, which would be lovely to build section by section. As discussed in Chapter 3, this type of functionality is only available on prosumer editors, like Pinnacle Edition (see Figure 11-11), which allow you to build the sequences individually and then join them together at the end. Not only does this simplify design, it also simplifies the use of repetitive sections like opening and closing credits.

Figure 11-11: Prosumer products like Pinnacle Edition allow you to build your sequences separately, simplifying production. Click on each sequence on the right, and Edition opens a separate timeline for that sequence.

There is one set of circumstances where it's safe to build and render your project section by section, which I used to good effect with the wedding video discussed at the beginning of the chapter. Specifically:

- If you're rendering your project to DV video (typically for output to tape), *and*

- You don't plan on adding any project-wide effects after combining the clips that would require re-rendering

Then it's safe to render section by section. However, if you're creating the same project for ultimate burning to DVD, note that DV compression adds another lossy layer and simply isn't advisable. In addition, each rendered DV section will require an additional 216MB per minute, which can quickly add up.

OK, that's the 50,000-foot view; now it's time to dig in and start working. To set the table, you've captured all of your video, and it's sitting there in the library begging to be turned into a cohesive production.

Splitting and Trimming Your Clips

Step one is to find and prepare the scenes that actually make it into the final production. This involves two discrete steps: *splitting*, where you split one scene into multiple parts, and *trimming*, where you trim away the unneeded footage from the beginning and end of the clip to isolate the raw material that comprises your final video.

As previously mentioned, most editors allow you to split clips in the library window, while virtually all editors allow you to split on the timeline. Trimming usually occurs in a separate trim window and/or on the timeline.

Without question, the splitting and trimming phase is the most important stage of editing. Like preparing a fine meal, this is where you trim the fat and excess leaves, stalks, and pits, and cut the protein, veggies, and fruit into bite-size pieces. You can add spices, special sauces, and candlelight to your heart's desire, but if your raw ingredients are lacking, the meal will be substandard.

The same holds true with video. You have many tools to garnish the video, but unless you've isolated the most truly interesting clips and excised the rest, overall quality is compromised.

While the situations clearly aren't parallel, it's instructive to note that in shooting *Gone with the Wind,* the director shot 449,000 feet of color film that was ultimately edited down to 20,300 feet for the 3-hour-and-45-minute film. That's a ratio of less than 5 percent. Applying the same ratio, if you shot 60 minutes of video, that would translate down to a usable 3 minutes.

Note

I'm not suggesting that you apply this 5 percent ratio to your vacation footage. However, it is instructive to note that most great videos are produced by leaving the vast majority of film on the cutting room floor.

Obviously, given the different types of videos that you'll shoot and their varying purposes, deriving a fixed, unwavering rule about how and what to trim is impossible. Your task also differs slightly depending upon the approach you took during shooting. Here, I'm referring back to the three modes discussed in Chapter 7.

Trimming in Recording Mode

If you were in recording mode, for example, just shooting as the events unfolded around you, your goal during trimming is to find the vignettes worth watching and to weave them into a reasonably cohesive presentation. You obviously have to honor the moment, but you also satisfy the viewer's need for frequent change and entertainment.

For example, during the Saint Simon's wedding mentioned at the start of this chapter, I was in recording mode, just capturing the weekend. While editing, I trimmed sequences unrelated to the ceremony as closely as possible, but I left a good bit of the ceremony untouched. My primary focus was to trim the extraneous footage to find the nuggets. Once again, general rules are just that, but here are some rules that I try to follow, using techniques demonstrated in the following sections:

- Reduce each sequence to the smallest possible vignette, whether a comment, joke, story, exercise routine, or sports play. Four 15-second sequences separated by transitions are infinitely more palatable than the original uncut 80-second sequence (see Figure 11-27 later in the chapter, where I trimmed an 80-second continuous sequence into four much shorter vignettes).

- Understand when *sound synchronization* is important and when it isn't. For example, pre- and post-wedding processionals take a while, and the full, unedited version may be uninteresting to many viewers. Unfortunately, since the background music is generally continuous, if you simply split and then trim the audio with the video, you introduce obvious audio breaks, which highlights the fact that you're contracting the video.

  Using a technique called *insert editing*, you can maintain one consistent audio track while shortening the video considerably, which makes the contractions easier on the eye and ear. Sounds difficult, but as you'll see later in this chapter, it's really pretty simple.

- Understand when *background audio* is important and when it isn't. When background audio doesn't matter, consider converting the sequences to a music video, either manually or through programs like muvee or functions in programs like Roxio VideoWave, Microsoft Movie Maker, and Pinnacle Studio.

  For example, you just came back from New York City and have 10 minutes of awesome footage of the sights. Or perhaps you've got random scenes from summer at the beach, Yellowstone National Park, or Disney World. These would typically be much more palatable viewed in short clips accompanied by music, and you can speed up or slow down the video to achieve dramatic or comic effect. I show you how to do this manually, later in this chapter, as well as explore the automated functions in Chapter 15.

- Motion within the video itself makes it easier to watch, reducing the need to introduce change. If people are marching, dancing, or otherwise moving, you can inject change at a less frequent pace.

- Excise all violent camera motion.

- If there isn't any motion on-screen for more than a second or two, consider trimming those frames. Be merciless — a few seconds saved here and there can really add up.

Trimming in Story-Telling and Movie-Making Modes

If you're in story-telling mode, you have a basic script in mind, and you know there are certain scenes that you must isolate and include to tell the story. You have to create the story beginning, set each scene with an establishing shot, tell your story, and then end it. Your task is a bit easier because you shot with purpose, and even before you start editing, you have a pretty good idea of how the video will fit together.

If you're in movie-making mode — shooting to tell the story and to obtain coverage for some cool movie-making combinations, your task is even easier because you know exactly what you're looking for in your raw video. This was the mode I used to shoot my daughter's gymnastics presentation. I had a script in mind and certain combinations that I was looking to create. Rather than trying to trim the fat during editing, I was trying to find the key nuggets that fit my purposes. The rest would end up on the cutting room floor.

But enough chatter, let's get busy.

The Mechanics of Splitting

Simply stated, you'll *split* a clip when one clip contains more than one scene that you would like to isolate. Then you'll *trim* the individual scenes to remove the unnecessary frames at the beginning and end of the video.

For example, Figure 11-12 shows a clip on the timeline in Movie Maker 2. This is the pre-event interview, where I asked my daughter Whatley questions about why the day was special. As you can see, the entire scene lasted about one minute and 20 seconds. My goal was to isolate each question and answer by *splitting* the scene into separate parts, and then *trimming* each scene to isolate only the most usable sections.

To split the clip:

1. Grab the timeline or player scrubber with the pointer and move the edit line to the desired split location. Usually, this is the first frame of the new clip you're seeking to create.

2. Use the split key that's shown just below the preview window in Figure 11-12. Virtually all editors have a button or control like this, often a pair of scissors (Ulead VideoStudio) or razorblade (Pinnacle Studio). Figure out where this control is early, because you'll be using it often.

As you can see in Figure 11-13, the single clip now has two components. At this point, you would create as many splits as necessary to isolate the desired segments.

VIDEOSTUDIO'S EXTRACT VIDEO CONTROL

Ulead took splitting to a new level with VideoStudio 7 when they introduced the Extract Video Control, which works exceptionally well in several types of editing tasks, particularly when automatic scene detection is not effective (see Figure 11-14).

This can occur when you shoot continuously for long periods, so there are few time and date changes to detect, or when editing analog footage that doesn't have time and date code information. For example, I often edit yoga and Tai Kwon Do stretching tapes to eliminate certain exercises that disagree with my chronically sore back or lengthy verbal explanations of poses I've already learned.

Figure 11-12: To split a clip, move the timeline or player scrubber to the desired location and press the split control, which is on the bottom right of the preview window.

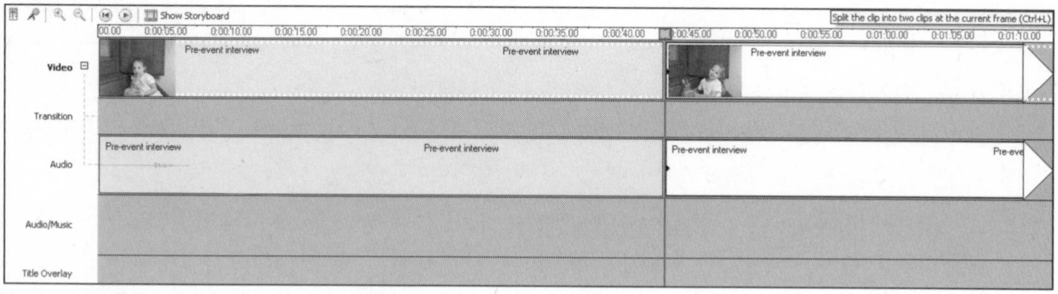

Figure 11-13: Mission accomplished, a clip split into two. Now you can trim the fat and emerge with two crisp vignettes.

Since most of my tapes are analog, time-code-based scene detection isn't available, and techniques that generate scenes based upon content produce too many scenes. Using VideoStudio's Extract Video function, I can scroll through the video choosing start and end points for scenes to either include or exclude in the final video. This really speeds the splitting process, and hopefully other programs will copy this feature in the near future.

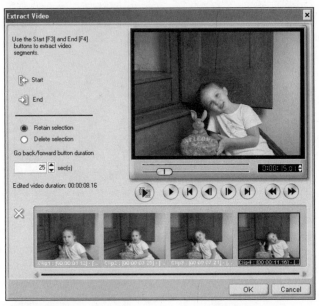

Figure 11-14: VideoStudio's Extract Video lets you scroll through your video selecting scenes to retain or delete.

The Mechanics of Trimming

Once you've isolated the clips you want to include, whether through scene detection or splitting, the next stage is to trim unwanted frames from the beginning and end of the clip.

There are generally four approaches to trimming, as shown in the following sections. I'll introduce them in the order most commonly supported by the various programs we're considering.

TRIMMING ON THE TIMELINE

Figure 11-15 shows Movie Maker 2 in timeline mode. Here's how to trim the clip using timeline controls:

1. Touch the clip to trim. Typically, the program highlights the clip in some way; as you can see in Figure 11-15, Movie Maker darkens the clip.

2. Hover the mouse over the edge to be trimmed. The cursor changes shape, usually to an arrow, allowing you to click the left mouse button to grab the edge and drag it to the left.

3. When dragging, watch the preview window until it displays the target end frame. Note that you may have to move the project scrubber to preview the final frame, an unfortunate lapse in some programs. Others, like Pinnacle Studio, follow the dragged video precisely. Then release the mouse, and the clip shortens accordingly.

Figure 11-15: Virtually all programs support trimming on the timeline, which is fast and easy, but sometimes this method lacks precision.

Initially, when the clip is at its full, original length, you won't be able to drag the edge to the right to increase clip duration, since you can't make the clip longer than it actually is. However, once you trim some frames from the edge, you should be able to drag the clip both ways to find the target frame.

Trimming on the timeline is fast and easy, but it sometimes lacks frame-by-frame precision. That's why I appreciate programs that offer a separate trimming window with frame-accurate controls. That's your next stop.

TRIMMING IN THE TRIM WINDOW

Trimming windows offers the frame accuracy lacking in trimming on the timeline and may be slightly easier for novices to understand. Using Pinnacle Studio as a guide, here's how it works (see Figure 11-16):

1. Select the target clip to make it active.

2. Each program uses a different procedure to activate the trim window. In Studio, for example, you can double-click on the clip or click the small camcorder icon on the top left of the timeline.

3. Your key task in the trim window is to select the adjusted start and end frames of the trimmed clip. The two best ways to accomplish this are to

    a. Use the transport controls to move the timeline scrubber to the target start frame, and click the Set start time icon on the left. Then use transport controls to move the timeline scrubber to the target end frame, and click the Set end time icon on the right.

    b. Drag the Start frame caliper to the desired start frame and the desired End frame caliper to the desired end frame.

4. Exit the trim window by clicking the camcorder icon or the X in the upper-right corner of the trim window.

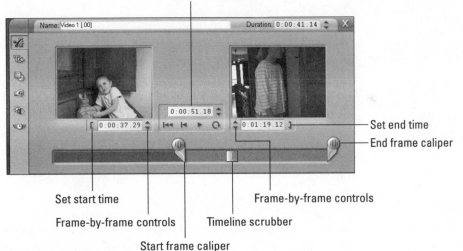

Figure 11-16: Studio's trim window offers precision editing.

As shown in Figure 11-17, Ulead's VideoStudio uses a two-bar system for its trim controls, which are located beneath the preview window. The bottom bar is the jog bar, with controls for moving through the video, and the top bar is the trim bar, which actually effectuates the trim.

Once again, you can trim the video by using transport controls to move to the desired locations and then click Mark in and Mark out controls, or directly grab and pull the trim controls to the desired locations.

Figure 11-17: Ulead's trim controls sit beneath the program's massive preview window.

Note

Virtually all consumer class editors will *snap* videos located behind the trimmed video on the timeline back and forth in concert with your trims, so you don't have to worry about introducing gaps into your projects. Ditto for videos that you delete on the timeline, where all videos located after the deleted video will snap back to fill the gap. However, many prosumer editors don't automatically snap videos to close the gap, at least by default, so you need to be much more careful when trimming.

DUAL-PANEL TRIM WINDOWS

As you would expect, prosumer programs like Adobe Premiere, Ulead MediaStudio Pro, and Pinnacle Edition (see Figure 11-18) provide even higher levels of precision with a dual-panel trim window that includes both effected clips. This allows you to see the precise end frame of the first clip and start frame of the second clip.

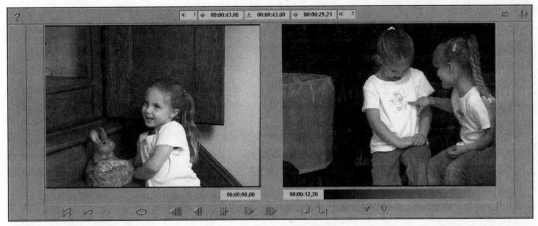

Figure 11-18: Pinnacle Edition's dual-panel trim window provides precise control over the transition point between the two clips.

Here you can adjust the trim points of each clip separately or enter a *slip trim mode* that adjusts the transition point between the two clips without changing overall production length. I'll describe this further in the next section using Pinnacle Studio.

SLIP TRIM OR ROLLING EDITS

The fourth edit mode is called slip trim or rolling edits, and this method is frequently used for commercial projects and is often useful for consumer projects. Here's the situation. You're in charge of producing a 60-second commercial, which means 60 seconds exactly, not one frame more or less. However, in reviewing your very nearly finished project, you notice that the transition between two clips is a bit off, say by five frames. What you'd like to do is extend the first clip by five frames and shorten the second clip by the same five frames to maintain the target length.

With a normal trim edit, if you extended the first clip forward by five frames, you'd have to separately adjust the second clip backwards by the same five frames. By using a slip trim or rolling edit, you can accomplish both edits at once. Here's how it works in Pinnacle Studio (refer to Figure 11-19):

1. Holding down the Shift key, touch the first clip with the pointer, and then the second. Both should become highlighted.

2. Move the pointer between the two clips. Instead of the normal double-arrow pointer, you'll see the rolling edit pointer.

3. Click the left mouse button to grab the transition point and drag it to the new target location.

Figure 11-19: The slip trim or rolling edit in Pinnacle Studio. Activate both clips by touching them while holding the Shift key, and move the pointer between them, which should convert the pointer to the tool shown above. Click the left mouse button and drag in either direction.

This tool can be invaluable when making late-stage adjustments after producing multiple clip sequences like narration or background audio.

THE SCIENCE OF MAKING HEADS AND TAILS

When trimming your clips, it's critical to comprehend the impact of fades and transitions on the final video. It's helpful to use the terms head and tails to understand how and why.

Figure 11-20 shows three clips on the Premiere timeline. In the project, I fade into the first clip, use a two-second dissolve transition between the two clips, and then fade to black after the third clip. Both the fade in and fade out take two seconds.

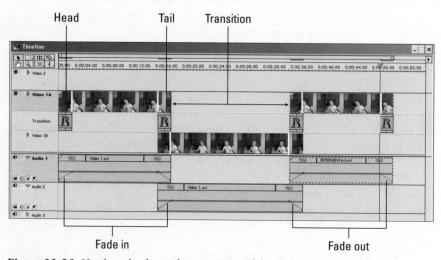

Figure 11-20: Heads and tails are those portions of the clip consumed by transitions and fades.

You'll also notice on the audio track that I fade (increasing volume from 0 percent to 100 percent) into the first clip with a cross-fade between the transitions (decreasing first clip volume from 100 percent to 0 percent while increasing the second clip volume from 0 percent to 100 percent) and fade out of the third clip (decreasing volume from 100 percent to 0 percent).

Consider the first clip where I'm fading in the video from black over two seconds and fading in the audio. These fades mean that a good portion of the first two seconds of video won't be visible and a similar portion of the audio won't be audible. So if I trim the video so Whatley starts talking on the first or second frame, her initial words won't be visible or audible after applying the fades.

For this reason, during trimming, I leave at least a two-second *head,* which represents those frames that won't be viewable or audible due to the applied effect. Otherwise Whatley won't be seen or heard, suitable for children in the 1800s but certainly not a crowd pleaser today.

The *tail* works the same way but at the other end. If I trimmed the clip so that Whatley stops talking on the very last frame, these won't be seen or heard as I transition into the next clip. For this reason, I would trim at least two seconds beyond the last frame I actually want to see and hear. This would be the tail.

When trimming, it's useful to identify the desired start and end frames that you want visible in the finished video. Adjust these by the anticipated duration of the fade or transition effect to identify the proper start and end points for your trim.

If you forget about heads and tails during editing, it's not a big deal, since you can always adjust the trim points after applying the transition effects. It's much more significant during shooting, since if you don't have sufficient heads or tails on tape, you're out of luck. That's why it's always good to start shooting early and to continue for several seconds after the scene. During capture, it's also helpful to make sure you have sufficient heads and tails surrounding the target scene.

Finally, if you're using Premiere Pro, as opposed to Premiere 6.5, shown in Figure 11-20, you may be wondering where the 1A and 1B tracks are. Actually, they're gone, as Adobe dropped this "A/B Roll" style of editing for several good reasons, including the new ability to apply transitions on all tracks, not just 1A and 1B. You still need to plan for your heads and tails, of course, since transitions and fades work the same way under the hood, but the visual feedback of how heads and tails are used is much more limited.

THE ART OF INSERT EDITING

When transitioning from clip to clip within the same basic scene, your goal is to move through the clips with little fanfare, allowing the viewer to simply flow with the experience. For example, if you were watching *Law and Order*, during the late courtroom scene, the shots would switch from the indignant district attorney to the petulant defense attorney to the bored judge and defiant defendant using quick cuts to minimize the disruption.

Of course, during shooting, the producers probably used four cameras and switched between them during editing. You don't have that luxury, but you can achieve the same effect if you shoot and edit carefully, and use an unbroken audio track as an accomplice in your deception.

Similarly, when you're trying to contract scenes to make them more palatable to your viewers, frequent breaks in the audio track bring attention to your efforts. On the other hand, if you can shorten the video while maintaining the background audio, your contractions are almost unnoticeable. A technique called the insert edit makes both of these possible.

Once you learn how and when to use the insert edit, you will instantly boost the perceived quality of your productions to a much higher level, and you'll have a heck of a lot of fun doing it.

First Shot, Point of View, Reaction

So, without further ado, here's the insert edit. Let's start with the first case: I'm shooting my daughter's gymnastics routines and want to weave four elements into one cohesive stream. This is the classic shot, point of view, reaction shot discussed in Chapter 7, which includes the following four components:

1. My wife, watching the proceedings (shot).

2. Whatley's trampoline routine (point of view — what my wife is watching).

3. My wife smiling and applauding (reaction).

4. The crowd applauding (reaction).

Each of these shots is shown in Figure 11-21. Since I only had one camera, I have to pull shots 1, 3, and 4 from other parts of the captured video. To be more specific, I shot all of Whatley's sequences in their entirety. When other girls were on stage, I shot my wife and crowd scenes because I knew I would need these shots to produce this effect. Quick tip — if you want to catch your spouse cheering wildly, shoot her/him when the child of the person whom they're sitting next to is performing.

Of course, the fact that I pieced these clips together from non-contiguous sections would be patently obvious to the viewer if the soundtrack broke between each scene; to avoid this, I used the soundtrack from scene 2 for the entire sequence, replacing the actual video (but not the audio) with the other video sequences.

Figure 11-21: The four shots I'm weaving into one sequence, using audio from the second and video from all four.

In theory, this seems relatively simple, but each product accomplishes this type of effect differently. Specifically, as previously mentioned, all video editors maintain synchronization between audio and video tracks until you take some action to break the synchronization. In most prosumer products, you simply unlink the two via simple menu commands. Then you're free to cut, paste, trim, and otherwise edit each track separately.

Note

Consumer products generally use slightly more complicated approaches to editing the audio track independently of the video, and not all can handle insert editing. For example, Roxio's VideoWave Movie Creator is a storyboard-only product that can't accomplish this, a limitation most storyboard-only products share.

With VideoStudio, you use a right-click command called Split Audio, which moves the audio captured with the video to the narration track and allows you to edit audio and video separately. With Pinnacle Studio, you lock the audio track (see Figure 11-22), which allows you to edit the video track at will without impacting the audio.

Figure 11-22: Studio's locked audio track lets me edit the video tracks at will, without impacting synchronization. You lock and unlock the tracks by pressing the icon to the left of the track.

Once locked, I simply used Studio's razor blade tool to split the main clip and delete the unnecessary segments, creating gaps that I filled with the desired frames from the other clips as shown in Figure 11-23.

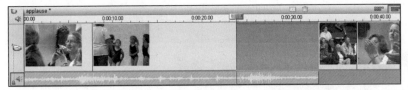

Figure 11-23: Once the audio track was locked, I could cut and paste video at will. Here we are about halfway through.

Figure 11-24 shows the final creation. As you can see, the audio track beneath the four segments is unbroken. The sharp-eyed among you will notice the applause and clapping sound effects perched below the final two sections, which supplemented the capacious output of my wife and the crowd. I figured that if I wasn't holding the camera, I would have added at least that much. Like they say, all's fair when you're doing the editing.

Note that I didn't use a transition between these clips, since that would suggest a temporal change when I was seeking to create the opposite effect. I discuss what transitions are and how and when to use them a little later in the chapter.

Trimming to Please

As previously discussed, when sound synchronization isn't important, you can cut huge chunks out of a video without the viewer noticing, increasing both the pace and the pace of change. For example, at the Saint Simons wedding, the opening processional consumed almost six minutes of video, reasonable for a professional videographer preserving the moment, but unwieldy for other viewers who just wanted to see the highlights.

Figure 11-24: Note the unbroken audio track with four separate video tracks atop. I have three different shots from four different times that look like they were shot simultaneously by multiple cameras.

Using VideoStudio, I used the Split Audio command to separate the tracks (see Figure 11-25) and simply split and trimmed the video to the most efficient chunks, paring the video down to under two minutes and 30 seconds, primarily by cutting out segments of ushers, bridesmaids, and flower girls waiting to walk down the aisle (see Figure 11-26). While the people who choreographed the wedding may notice the difference, most viewers would not; since the continuous audio sends a message that nothing has been cut. All told, I saved over three and a half minutes of viewing time, over 50 percent.

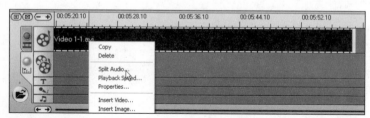

Figure 11-25: VideoStudio's Split Audio command separates the audio and video stream so you can edit them separately.

Finally, Figure 11-27 shows a video of my daughter and her fellow bridesmaid answering my questions after the ceremony. This was about 80 seconds of video, pared down to about 40 seconds by splitting and trimming the separate chunks to cut out the fat. Insert editing wasn't an issue, because I needed to preserve the original audio track.

Note that in Figures 11-24 and 11-26 I didn't use a transition between the clips, but in Figure 11-27, I inserted a dissolve transition between each clip for two reasons. In the first two cases, I was trying to hoodwink the viewer into thinking I had a multiple camera setup and/or that critical segments of the video weren't being cut. In both these cases, a transition would highlight exactly what I was hoping the viewer would ignore.

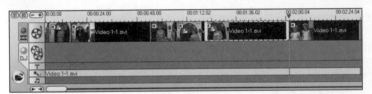

Figure 11-26: Then I used the split and trim commands to eliminate over 50 percent of the video, which the continuous background audio will make unnoticeable to most observers.

In Figure 11-27, I was clearly cutting segments from the video, and I wanted the viewer to notice this, because it highlights the impression that I was consolidating huge chunks of video to just show the nuggets. In addition, because the pictures were static—same characters, same setting—viewers can miss the simple cuts and be confused at the change. Thus, the simple dissolve between each segment.

Figure 11-27: Here I was in pure contraction mode, cutting 80 seconds of video down to about 40. Doesn't sound like a lot, but it adds up, and the more chaff you cut out, the more the viewer appreciates the wheat.

As you can see, it's difficult talking about trimming and splitting without discussing transitions because they are so intertwined. So, without further ado, let's er, transition into transitions.

Using Video Transitions

Transitions are visual effects that help shift the viewer from one scene to the next. Probably the most common transition is a cut, which is actually the lack of a transition between scenes where one scene simply stops and the next starts. After that, the most common transitions are a dissolve, where one scene blends in with the next briefly before the second emerges clearly on its own, and a fade to or from black, where the screen fades to black and then the new scene fades in.

Though technically transitions are used between clips as you'll see, mechanically they're also often used at the start or end of a clip. For example, to fade to black at the end of a clip with most consumer editors, you apply a fade transition to the end of the clip. Ditto for fading in from black, where you apply a fade transition to the beginning of the clip.

Next time you're watching television or a movie, notice how transitions are commonly used in these media. For the most part, when simply switching between different camera angles during the same general scene, most directors do not use a transition. They simply cut from camera to camera, and then, when the scene changes, a dissolve or fade will help the viewer understand that a temporal change has occurred.

This is the concept of the *motivated* transition, a transition used to serve a particular purpose. When transitions are motivated, they can significantly enhance the entertainment value of the video. However, when used indiscriminately, they have the opposite effect. This means that there is a huge difference between knowing how to use a transition and knowing how to use it well.

Let's start with a look at the mechanics of applying and customizing transitions. Then you can take a look at the art and exactly what makes a transition "motivated."

The Mechanics of Transitions

If you're just getting started, the easiest way to begin working with transitions is in storyboard view, so I'll start in this view in Movie Maker (see Figure 11-28).

Like most editors, Movie Maker stores transitions in the same library space as it stores the video clips. Usually the transition album or library is simple to find; if not, consult your manual.

Once you find them, you'll find that most editors allow you to do the following:

- **Preview a transition before selection.** Double-click on the transition, and it plays in the preview window (as shown in Figure 11-28).

- **Select a transition.** Drag it into the box between the two clips.

- **Preview a transition after selection.** Press play under the preview window immediately after inserting the transition, and/or click the box and then press play.

- **Choose another transition.** Drag and place it over the previous transition.

It's all pretty simple. From there, the editors differ significantly regarding how and how much you can customize a transition.

For example, with Movie Maker 2, you have to enter the timeline, click the plus sign on the left of the video track label to expose the transition track, and then trim like you would a video clip (see Figure 11-29).

Most other editors offer separate transition controls with greater precision. For example, VideoStudio lets you control duration by entering in a specific time, and depending upon the transition, also allows you to insert a border, select the border color, choose edge type, and effect direction (see Figure 11-30).

As I'll discuss in more detail later in the chapter, Pinnacle Studio trumps all consumer editors in terms of the breadth and customizability of their transitions, especially if you upgrade to Plus and Pro versions of their transition tool, Hollywood FX. In addition to the same type of duration controls that Ulead offers, Studio provides advanced editing tools that allow you to customize the transition in three dimensions as well as a host of other effect-dependent characteristics (see Figure 11-31). Most users won't need this level of customizability, but it's nice to know that it's there.

Note that transitions can generally be used between any media on the timeline, whether video, still images, or animation. Depending upon the program, transitions are also used on the title track to fade into and out of titles.

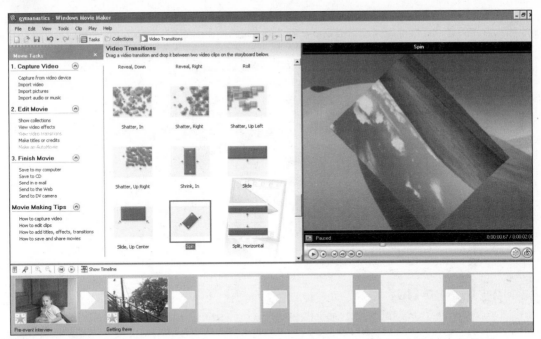

Figure 11-28: Transitions are simpler to understand in storyboard view; just grab and drag into the box between the clips.

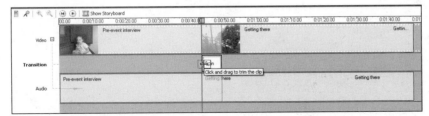

Figure 11-29: Movie Maker 2 only lets you change transition duration and then only by dragging the edges.

Figure 11-30: VideoStudio provides more creative options and better precision over duration.

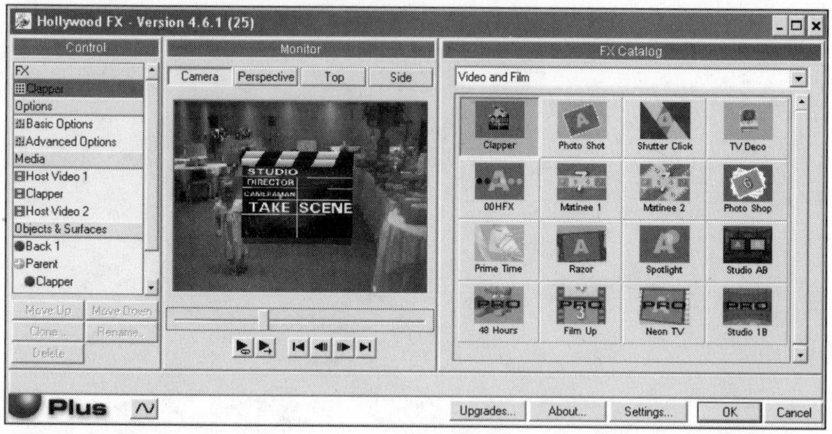

Figure 11-31 screenshot showing the Hollywood FX - Version 4.6.1 (25) interface with Control, Monitor, and FX Catalog panels.

Figure 11-31: Though you may pay a bit extra for Pinnacle Studio's Hollywood FX, it will expand your creative options immensely.

Fading In and Out

Virtually all producers use this effect, so let's examine how to make it work. Just to recap, fading to black is best used to signal to the viewer that a significant change is about to occur. For example, in the Saint Simon's wedding weekend video, I faded to black between all major segments, which occurred over three days and several different venues. In contrast, in the gymnastics movie, which occurred over the course of only a few hours, I dissolved between major scene changes and only faded to black at the end.

Editors produce the fade effect in different ways, so to make sure you'll know where to find it in your editor, let's review the three basic approaches to fading to black, as outlined in the following sections.

FADE AS A TRANSITION IN PINNACLE STUDIO

This is the simplest approach. As you can see in Figure 11-32, you drag the fade transition down behind the last clip on the timeline, and you're done.

FADE AS A VIDEO EFFECT IN MOVIE MAKER 2

As you can see in Figure 11-33, Microsoft Movie Maker 2 includes a separate "Fade Out, To Black" effect. Simply drag this to the last clip on the timeline and consider yourself faded. This is also pretty easy, assuming that you know where to look.

DISSOLVING INTO A BLACK IMAGE

This is the most complicated approach. Basically, you must create a black scene after the final clip and then apply a dissolve transition between them (see Figure 11-34). VideoStudio simplifies this with a library of colored slides you can drag down to the storyboard, but this involves another step not necessarily intuitive to many users.

Figure 11-32: Using the fade as a transition in Pinnacle Studio. Drag it down, and you're done.

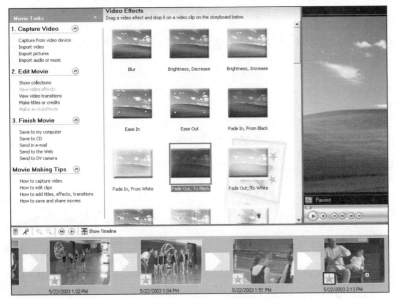

Figure 11-33: Using fade as an effect in Movie Maker 2. Drag it down, and you're done.

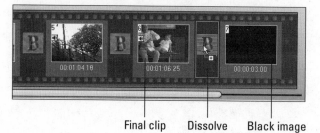

Final clip Dissolve Black image

Figure 11-34: Using fade as a dissolve between the final video and a black slide (VideoStudio).

Fading in, of course, would be just the reverse. In VideoStudio, you would drag the fade in transition *before* the first clip, in Movie Maker 2 you would drag the "Fade In, From Black" effect onto the first clip, while in VideoStudio you would drag a black slide before the first clip and then dissolve between them.

The Art of the Motivated Transition

It goes without saying that transition use should conform to the tone of the underlying video. With business or serious (graduation, confirmation, and such) videos, I would almost always stick with cuts, dissolves, and fades.

As the tone lightens, however, transitions properly used, or *motivated*, can be invaluable. The concept of the motivated transition is a favorite of mine, though it's somewhat elusive.

A transition (or other effect) is motivated when it relates to the content and/or audience of the underlying video material. It's helpful, sometimes, to liken the concept to how you would use clip art in a book or presentation. For example, imagine you were creating an illustrated book instead of a movie. You have your typewritten words and your clipart collection. Assume you were describing the scene where little Sally was about to go skiing for the first time. As you write about the scene, your clipart choices might be

- A picture of a snowy ski slope, which is motivated and enhancing.

- A picture of a frying pan — unmotivated and confusing (at best) or irritating (most likely).

- No picture at all — not quite a snowy ski slope, but not negative either.

Clearly, here, if you had a picture of a snowy slope or some other, similar image, you would use it, but you wouldn't use the frying pan just because it's available, you'd probably go without.

Now let's apply this to video transitions. You have a sequence where your girls are getting bundled up and ready to go outside into the snow. When you transition from the bundling-up scene to the first scene outside, you could apply

- A snowflake transition (see Figure 11-35) — this is motivated and probably amusing.

- A zigzag fade transition — this is unmotivated and probably irritating.

- A cut or dissolve — this would be appropriate and unobtrusive.

In this situation, the snowflake can be a fun, visual bauble that helps promote the mood of the day, where the zigzag fade is just showing off. My advice here is that if you can't find a motivated transition, stick to a simple cut or dissolve.

Figure 11-35: Applying a motivated transition in Pinnacle Studio, the always-lovely snowflake transition.

Other examples of motivated transitions that I have known and loved are

- The scene clapper shown back in Figure 11-31. During the wedding, my wife was rehearsing with the flower girls, and I used this between takes.

- After the close of the processional, instead of a fade, I used the album transition shown in Figure 11-36.

- In Halloween videos, I've used fog transitions between the clips.

- When transitioning to scenes involving water, I've used a ripple transition.

- For birthday videos, I've had scenes curl up into balloons and float away.

Even when using motivated transitions, remember that cute gets old fast. Used once or twice, they're nice. Three times or more, and you bore everyone in the room.

Once again, in this regard, Pinnacle's Hollywood FX clearly stands above the rest of the available consumer and prosumer editors, with a superior collection of occasion-specific (weddings, birthdays, and sporting events) transitions that guarantee you'll have a motivated transition or two to serve to your viewer.

Figure 11-36: Closing the album on the wedding procession. Pinnacle Studio gives you many motivated transitions that add significant value to your presentation.

Designing Titles

Titles are the third troika of this basic editing chapter and are typically used more to transmit information than as a design enhancement. That said, titles can be used in a variety of ways, and title design tools vary greatly from product to product.

For example, you can use titles in two different ways:

- As a *full-screen image*, generally placed on the same track as the video
- As an *overlay*, where the title displays *over* a video

When producing titles, most editors give you control over the following elements:

- Background image (if full-screen title)
- Text attributes
- Duration
- Animation, or how the title appears and disappears from the video

So let's let these variables serve as the outline for this section.

Full Screen versus Overlay

Figure 11-37 shows a full-screen title in Movie Maker 2. As you can see, the full-screen title is on the video timeline, and as with videos and still images, you can adjust duration by clicking and dragging an edge with your cursor. You can also easily move the title by grabbing it in the middle and simply moving it to the new location.

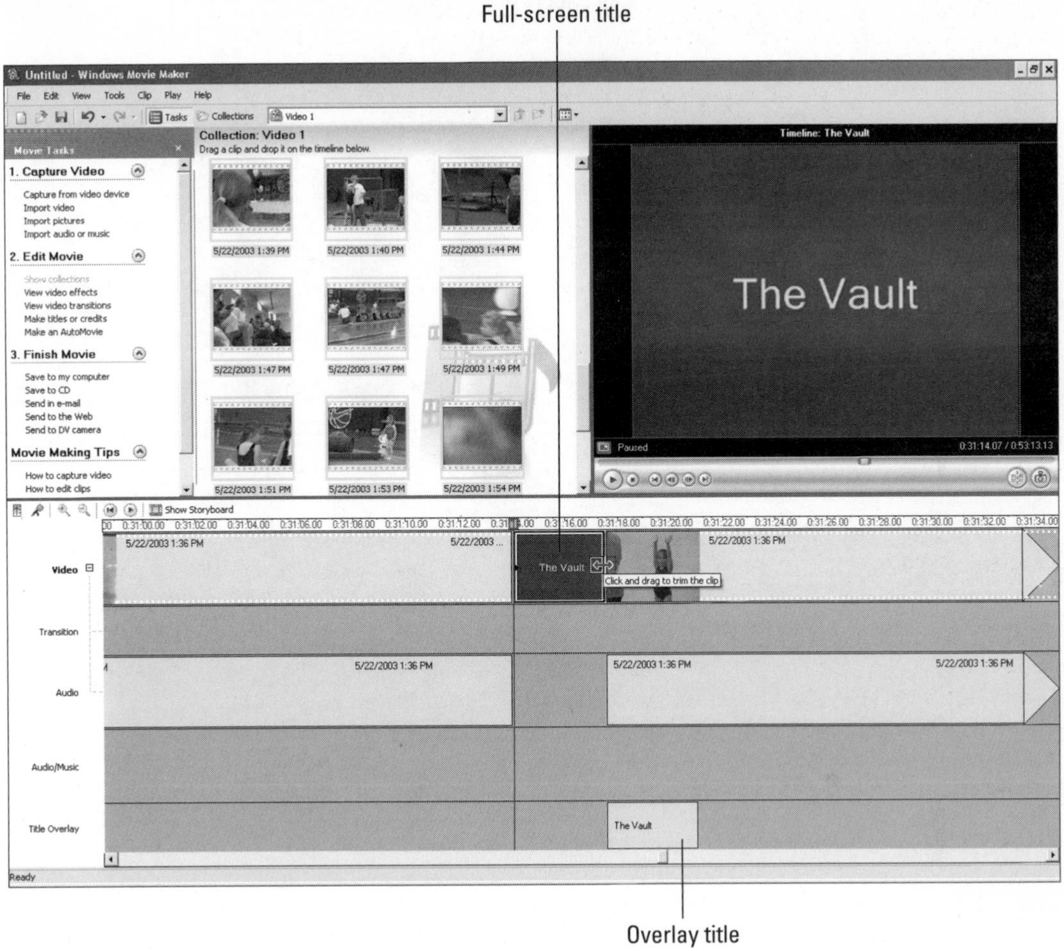

Full-screen title

Figure 11-37: A full-screen title in all of its blue glory.

Figure 11-38 shows the same title as an overlay, where it sits on the overlay track. Many programs let you select between a full-screen and an overlay title during the creation process, or let you drag a template to the desired track.

Others won't let you place titles directly on the video track. For example, with VideoStudio, to create a full-screen title, you drag a still image from a color swatch library in the desired background color, and then drag your title to the title track. It's a touch more complicated but easy once you know the mechanics.

Building Titles

Though title design tools vary among the products, the operational procedure is generally similar. You typically enter the title editor via menu commands or double-click the title track to load the editor. Once there, you'll have various controls for creating, styling, and positioning your text.

Figure 11-38: An overlay title, where the background video shows through.

Pinnacle Studio's titling function provides a superset of most controls provided by the various editors (see Figure 11-39). Note the box about 30 pixels in from all four sides of the screen, which is the title safe zone. As you may recall from Chapter 7, any title components beyond these edges may be cut off as overscan when displayed to an analog monitor.

Most editors provide access to all system fonts and the normal alignment and positioning controls, while Studio goes a bit further with text styles, shown to the right of the main window. These are great for the text-design-challenged, a group I definitely belong to.

Studio also allows you to align the text precisely with PowerPoint-like text-creation capabilities. With other editors, you typically align your text vertically using the carriage return and horizontally with a combination of alignment controls and spaces, which is more cumbersome.

Once you've created, sized, colored, and aligned your text, there's generally a "Done," "OK," or similar control to exit the title designer and return to editing. The finished menu appears in your timeline where you can move and adjust duration as described previously.

Many programs also have canned titles that you can easily drag and drop into your production like those shown in Figure 11-40. These are a great way to get started; just drag them in and edit them as desired.

Title safe zone   Text styles

Figure 11-39: Pinnacle Studio's Title Editor is highly functional with lovely style presets and great alignment controls.

Figure 11-40: Ulead's canned titles provide an easy way to get started; just drag them in and use as is or customize them to meet your own needs.

Animating Titles

Title animation tools enable you to fly, fade, slide, zoom, or otherwise make your text appear on-screen, and then disappear. These are most commonly used to fade into and out of text titles — a nice effect — and, of course, for closing credits.

With Ulead VideoStudio, you simply select Cross-fade in the animation control in the title designer, and you're done (see Figure 11-41). Other products, like Pinnacle Studio, use fade transitions to fade text in and out. Microsoft offers the simple fade effect and a whole lot more, with very cool effects like the typewriter, which displays each letter one by one.

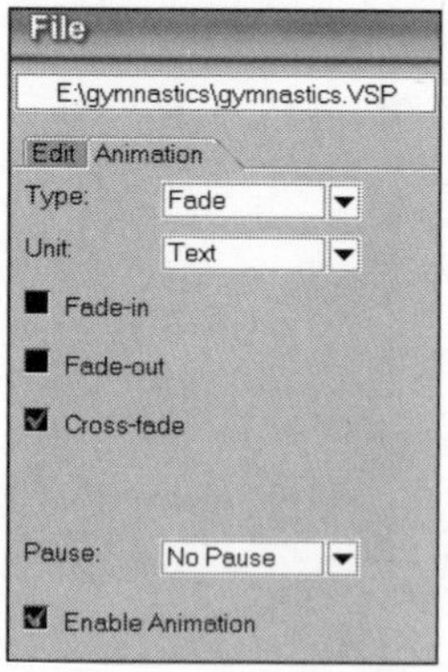

Figure 11-41: Ulead's simple controls for fading a title in and out.

Most editors also provide facilities for scrolling credits for the end of your video, like those shown in Figure 11-42. Simply insert the appropriate titles and names, and you're on your way. As with most titles, you can display over a single color (as shown in the figure), or customize the title with a background image.

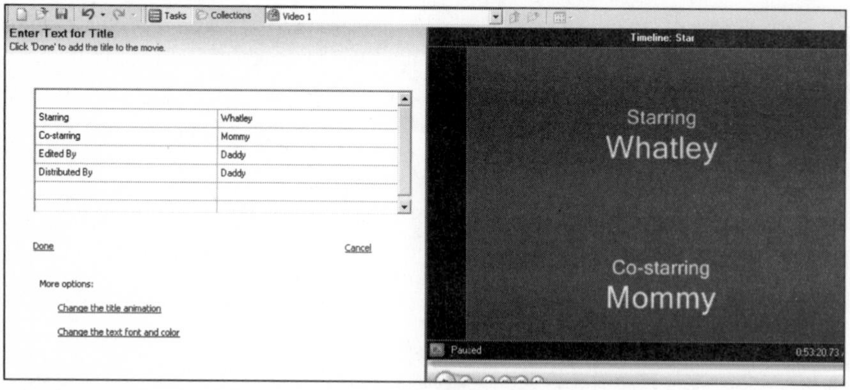

Figure 11-42: Microsoft's excellent scrolling credits tool.

Growing Your Own Music Video

When background music and sound synchronization don't matter, you can create your own music videos or use the tools discussed in Chapter 15. In the wedding I shot on Saint Simon's Island, I had about seven minutes of my two girls and two other little girls dancing to a number of different songs.

Remember, I wasn't the official wedding videographer, who is faced with a much different job and target audience. I was just trying to figure out some way to make seven minutes of video less boring and more watchable.

Overall, the project incorporates a lot of techniques and technologies discussed elsewhere, but the most critical part was the splitting, so I'll discuss it here.

Here are the steps I took:

1. The starting point (see Figure 11-43): Six minutes and 40 seconds of little girls dancing.

Figure 11-43: Here's the starting point, one almost-seven-minute clip.

2. Step one (see Figure 11-44): Use Studio's Subdivide Scenes command to split the video into 10-second segments.

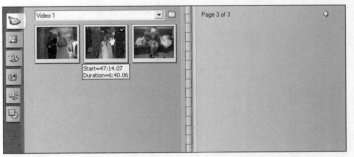

Figure 11-44: Start by subdividing the clips in the album (or on the timeline if more convenient in your editor).

3. Step two (see Figure 11-45): Splitting the clips produced about 40 separate segments, which I dragged down to the storyboard and started dragging randomly around to

minimize the number of actual contiguous segments shown. I also deleted some segments and trimmed some clips to eliminate unrelated frames.

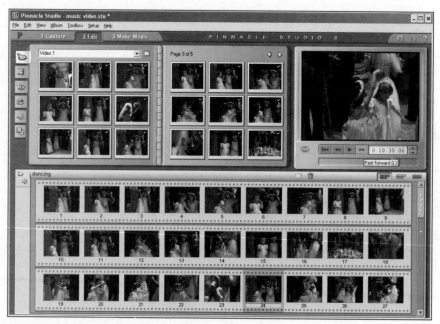

Figure 11-45: Yikes! Here's all the separate clips I created. I used the mouse to drag them around and place them in random order.

4. Step three (see Figure 11-46): Using Studio's motion control, I sped each clip up to twice the normal speed. Virtually all consumer editors share this feature, which can also create slow-motion video.

Figure 11-46: Speed 'em up by 200% (2X).

5. Step four (see Figure 11-47): Using Studio's SmartSound feature, I chose a Latino beat background audio track and added it to the movie. I could have used a track ripped from a CD-ROM, an MP3 file, or any other audio file (see Chapter 12).

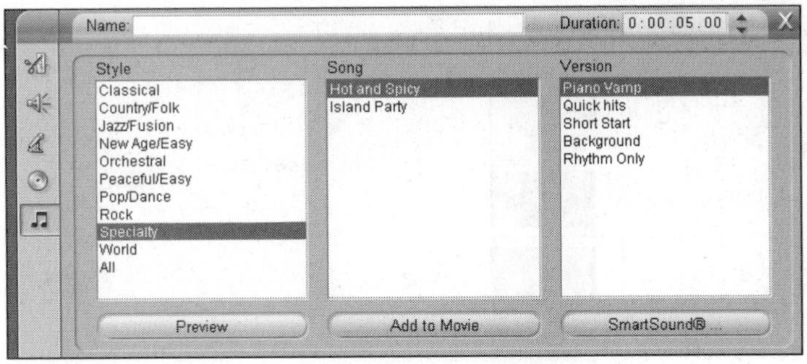

Figure 11-47: Pick out some Hot and Spicy background music from SmartSound.

6. Step five (see Figure 11-48): I experimented with and without transitions, and ultimately I decided to go with fast dissolves between the clips.

Figure 11-48: Add one-second dissolves between the clips.

7. The finished project (see Figure 11-49): As you can see, I contracted almost seven minutes of unwatchable video down to about two minutes and 20 seconds, delighting all viewers. This procedure should work well for any series of clips about a related topic where the original background audio isn't important and can be replaced by music.

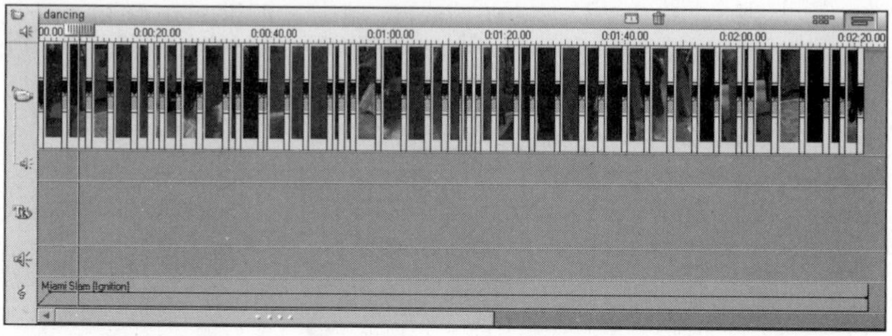

Figure 11-49: The finished project, now 2:20 long, about one-third the length of the original video and much more watchable.

Summary

Here is a summary of the key points made in this chapter:

1. Creating watchable video is largely about introducing frequent change into your productions. If you doubt this, watch any show on television or any movie, and notice how long they remain on one static shot.

2. Invest time up front learning how your library works, where and how it stores the assets and available editing controls. This will save time in the long term.

3. Most editors offer both storyboard and timeline views. Storyboards are better for determining the original sequence of your assets, while timelines are better for adding titles and transitions, background music, and other advanced editing.

4. Probably 80 percent of all editing time is spent in trimming and splitting your clips. Learn how your program accomplishes this early.

5. When trimming and splitting, remember to plan for transitions and fades, which can obscure frames and audio at the beginning and ends of your clips.

6. Insert editing is fun and adds significant production value to your clips. Learn what it is and how it works with your editor, and start planning for it when shooting.

7. Transitions ease the flow from one clip to another. Most professionals use either dissolves or cuts 99 percent of the time. Once again, let network television or movies be your guide. Other than these, the best transitions are "motivated" and relate to the content of your video.

8. Titles are typically available as full-screen images or overlays that show through over other videos. Though most programs provide ample controls for adding motion to titles, simple and elegant beats showy and distracting 99 percent of the time.

9. When the original background audio isn't important to the video content, consider converting your footage to a music video. Several tools that automate this are discussed in Chapter 15, or you can do it yourself as shown in this chapter.

Chapter 12

Working with Audio

Audio, done well, is a highly compelling addition to any video project. Back in Chapter 8, you learned the basics of capturing high-quality audio with the video. Here I explore adding audio from other sources involving narration, background music, and sound effects.

Then I'll discuss how to edit audio on the timeline, learning how to fade in and out and to mix the various tracks for maximum effect. I'll conclude with a quick look at some tools that can help fix problems with your audio, like mechanical hums or audio recorded at different volume levels.

Creating Narrations

In many operations described in this book, learning how to use your software is the key element to success. Not so with narrations, which are extremely simple to produce from a software perspective, even with consumer-class equipment. The hard part is preparing both the narration and the recording studio to get fluid, crisp, and high-quality recordings.

I'll start with the mechanics and then move to the finer points.

Getting Connected

To record high-quality narrations, you'll need two pieces of equipment: a microphone and a headset. If you use external speakers, you may generate feedback, that irritating, screeching noise resulting when audio from the speaker goes back through the microphone.

Figure 12-1 shows the two approaches: one unit that includes both headset and microphone or two separate devices. Note that the Labtec microphone is a USB device, while the combination device plugs into your soundcard.

In my experience, matching a microphone with a soundcard is a hit-and-miss thing. In other words, microphones that worked well on one system might not work well on another, producing excess background noise or hum. Even the Labtec USB microphone, which bypasses the system soundcard altogether, worked well on my home-grown Intel Pentium 4 computer but produced excessive hum when recording on my Dell notebook.

So, when you buy a microphone, make sure you can return it if it doesn't work well, and try it on multiple computers before you send it back. Once you've found a combination that works well for you, don't upgrade willy-nilly to the next piece of new gear you see, since it may not work as well.

Before buying, you may want to check `www.epinions.com`, which is a decent source of microphone reviews. For example, the Labtec 704 in Figure 12-1 received five stars in the two listed reviews on the site.

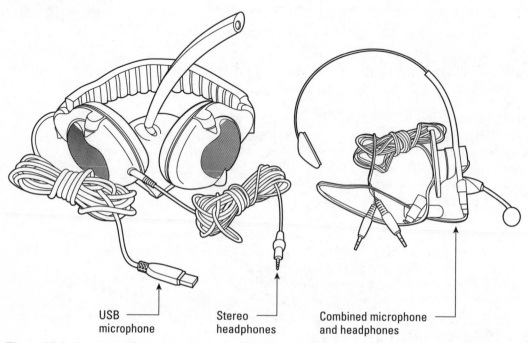

USB microphone   Stereo headphones   Combined microphone and headphones

Figure 12-1: Two approaches to microphone and headset: one integrated, which I prefer, and the other not.

To connect a standard microphone to your computer, simply find the microphone port on your sound board or notebook computer and plug it in. Typically, combination devices label the microphone red and the speaker plug black, though this isn't universal. Note that line-in *will not work well,* since the computer expects a different signal from powered sources. So, be sure to find the microphone port.

It's the same deal for USB microphones; simply plug it into your computer's USB port. Typically, no drivers are required for either device, so they both should be Plug and Play.

Preparing the Studio

Virtually all professional narrations are produced in a sound-proofed room with echo-canceling foam for wallpaper. While you don't have to duplicate this to achieve high-quality results, lawn mowers, dishwashers, and other loud household appliances have been known to ruin many a good recording.

So, to minimize extraneous noise in your home or office, be sure to

- Shut down all unneeded equipment (printers, other computers, routers, and so on).

- Shut down the air conditioning, heating system, or fan.

- Turn off major appliances like washing machines or dishwashers.

- If you have fluorescent lights, turn these off as well. Your monitor should provide sufficient light even if alternative sources aren't available.

- If your computer is loud, consider placing pillows that shield you from the noise produced by the ventilation fan. Blocking the fan totally, of course, would be a bad strategy unless you want things to get real quiet when your computer overheats and quits working.

Scripting Your Narration

Unless you're James Earl Jones or Tom Brokaw, narrations can be easy to create or sound professional, but not both. It's easy to simply pull the trigger and start talking, but unless you're unusually gifted, you'll experience your share of ums, ahs, and misspoken words. Audio is really a cruel medium because it plays back exactly what you say and how you say it. There's nowhere to run, nowhere to hide.

If high quality is your goal, scripting is your best tool. However, creating a script is time-consuming and reading a script well is surprisingly difficult, especially if it exceeds 60 seconds or more.

Here are some rules to consider when creating and recording your script:

- Use conversational language comprised of easily pronounceable words. Read the script out loud frequently to identify any rough spots that are hard to pronounce.

- Use short sentences and short sections no more than 60 to 90 seconds. Otherwise, the script will be extremely difficult to read.

- Use very large fonts that produce five or six words per line so the script is easy to read during recording.

- When recording, avoid drinking either very cold or very hot drinks, which can mess with your vocal cords.

- Your natural tendency will be to start speeding up to get to the end of the narration, which is very apparent to the listener. Take it slow.

- Try not to sound like you're simply reading the lines. If you didn't write the script, this means you'll have to read it several times until the words become your own.

- It sounds silly, but you'll perform better if you're in a good mood. Write little notes to yourself on the script (gosh, I'm happy to be here) and get in the habit of smiling before you read each segment. It wouldn't hurt to have a mirror there so you can monitor your mood. You'll be surprised how much difference it makes.

- Take frequent short breaks, and count on multiple takes to get it right.

If this sounds like a lot of work, it is, as I mentioned at the beginning of this chapter. However, I'm not suggesting that all narrations should be scripted and are unacceptable unless perfect.

Rather, I'm suggesting that in most instances if you strive for perfection, you'll either take a lot longer than you'd like or quickly lower your standards. Take comfort in the fact that while all imperfections will sound glaring to you, probably no one else will notice them at all.

Recording the Narration

That's enough planning and fussing. Let's record some audio. For this section, I'm going to use Movie Maker 2, which operates similarly to other consumer-class editors and record a narration for my daughter's exercise bar routine.

My goal is to sound like a gymnastics or ice-skating announcer, speaking in hushed tones as I describe her routine. It's pretty silly, which is OK since the primary audience is a five-year-old, plus I can work in some praise that I felt but couldn't share during the event ("look at that extension, the tuck, the pointed legs. What a beautiful routine!"). Note that my goal is not to replace the background audio shot with the video, the sounds of the gym and applause, but to mix the narration with these ambient sounds.

Here are the steps that Movie Maker 2 requires:

1. Choose Tools → Options to select the Options menu. I want to put this clip where I can find it later, say in the project folder I created during capture (refer to Figure 12-2).

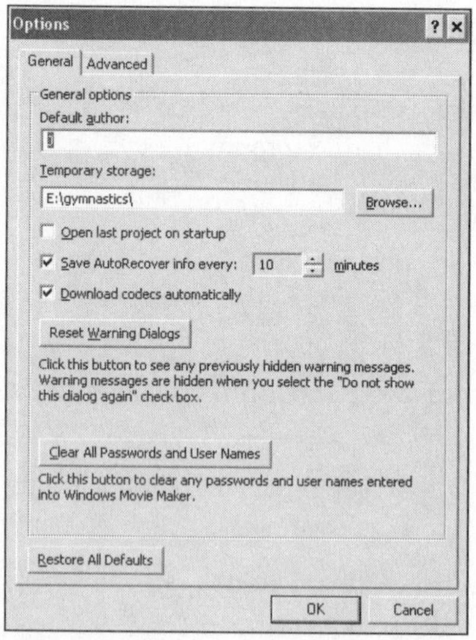

Figure 12-2: Here's where you designate your project folder.

2. Move the timeline scrubber (the tool you use to move through your video on the timeline) to where the narration should be inserted in the timeline (shown in Figure 12-3). As with most programs, the timeline must be open at that spot; otherwise you won't be able to record.

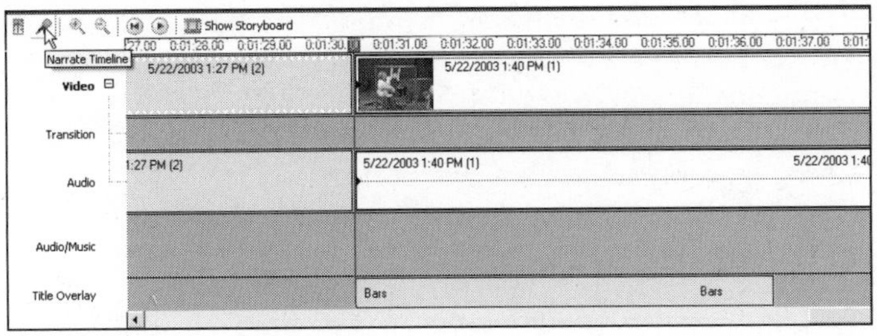

Figure 12-3: Move the timeline scrubber to the point where you want the narration to start on the timeline.

3. Click the microphone icon (shown in the upper-left corner of Figure 12-3) to open the recording interface.

4. Click Show more options to open the advanced options as shown in Figure 12-4.

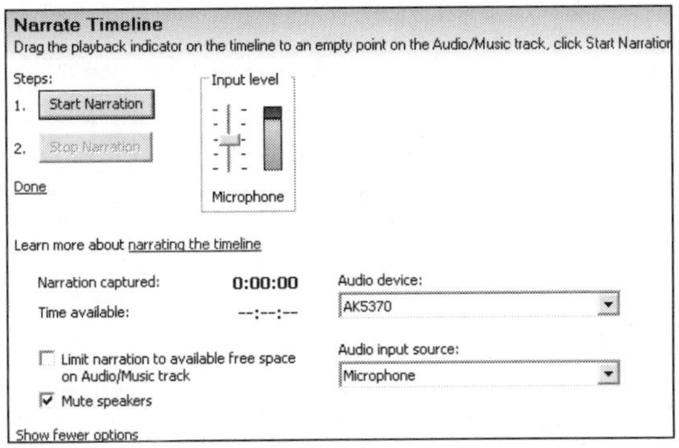

Figure 12-4: The advanced options in the Narrate Timeline box.

5. If you don't have a headset, check the Mute speakers checkbox so you can play the video while you're recording without sound coming from the speakers. You can also elect to limit narration to the free space on the timeline, a convenient option (see Figure 12-4).

6. Practice speaking into the microphone while watching the input levels shown in Figure 12-4 and adjusting the volume control. It's tough to see in grayscale, but your goal is to keep the level between 60 and 80 percent of the maximum. As with capturing analog video, if you move into the top zone, you risk clipping, a clicking noise produced by audio that's too loud.

Try to avoid getting your mouth too close to the microphone, which can produce distortion with hard consonants like P and B.

At this point, the volume meter is live, so if it's jumping around while you're sitting there quietly, it's hearing some background noise that you're not. Try to find the source before you start recording.

7. Once you've achieved the proper level, click Start Narration to begin recording, and Stop Narration to end recording (see Figure 12-4).

8. Movie Maker 2 will prompt you for a filename or otherwise name the file for you. Click Save to save the file.

As you can see from Figure 12-5 Movie Maker 2 inserts the narration neatly at the edit line.

Figure 12-5: The narration inserted in the edit line in Movie Maker 2.

Let's analyze how I did. The best evaluation source is the waveform that represents the file I just created during recording on my home-grown Pentium 4 desktop. I imported this and a narration recorded on my Dell laptop into Sound Forge, an audio editor from Sony. Most programs don't show this level of detail, but it's instructive, so let's have a quick look. As shown in Figure 12-6, the home-grown workstation results are on the bottom, and the Dell's are on top.

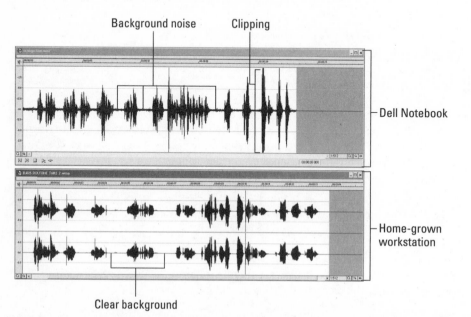

Figure 12-6: The bottom track is relatively noise-free and has good volume levels, while the top is very noisy. Same microphone, different computers. Go figure!

Several items are worthy of note. Most important is that on the bottom, the height of the waveform is close to the desired 60 to 80 percent range, so the volume should be acceptable. Second, where there's no audio, the line is perfectly flat, which indicates that the microphone is not picking up any background noise.

The only negative in the waveform is the small line about 10 seconds in that reaches from top to bottom. I said the word "beautiful" with my mouth too close to the microphone, and the microphone distorted that hard B. I probably should re-record, but heeding my own words about striving for perfection, I'll let it go and move on to the next narration.

Anyway, contrast this file with the waveform produced on the Dell, which looks fuzzy wherever there are no peaks in the waveform, despite shutting off all equipment in my office and working by the light of the notebook's LCD screen. This indicates some electrical incompatibility between the device microphone and my notebook, or perhaps a user error. Whatever it is, it doesn't bode well for quality. I'll discuss alternatives for eliminating this noise later in this chapter.

Also note the line about 20 seconds in that looks flat on the top and on the bottom. This is "clipping," where the extreme upper and lower ranges are simply cut off because I was speaking too loudly or the volume was set too high. While I could eliminate the clipping by recording again at a lower volume, the fuzziness was there to stay, so I opted to change computers. This is no slight against the Dell, because, as I said earlier, not all microphones work equally well with all computers.

Note

Microsoft Movie Maker 2 saves all narration files in Windows Media Audio format, which many other video editors don't recognize. If you plan on using the files again in another production, you'll either have to convert them with an audio editor or re-record.

Ripping CD Audio Tracks

For the uninitiated, ripping is the act of reading a file from CD and converting it to a format you can store on disk and play back on your computer or portable MP3 or similar player. Though this may change in some upcoming releases, the sad fact is that in general, video editors do a pretty poor job ripping CD tracks to include in your video productions.

For example, few, if any, current video editors can access Gracenote's free CDDB online database (CDDB stands for CD database) to auto-insert track names and titles, so you'll have to name all of your own tracks. In addition, some programs don't actually rip the track until you're ready to produce, which is a logistical problem if the CD is back in your car or upstairs in the library.

Therefore, most producers are better off using a free tool like Microsoft's Windows Media Player, MusicMatch's Jukebox, or RealNetwork's RealOne to rip tracks from CDs. These programs can name the tracks for you, immediately rip them to disk faster than real time, and save them in a library so you can access them for casual playback as well as for your video projects.

The only caveat is to make sure you're using a format compatible with your video editor. Most video editors can accept MP3 and uncompressed WAV files, but fewer accept Microsoft Windows Media files, and very few accept RealAudio files. Nonetheless, since RealOne provides access to both WAV and MP3 files without charge, I'll use RealOne to demonstrate ripping. If you don't have a copy, surf on over to www.real.com and download it.

If this is the first time you've used a track ripped by a third-party program in a video production, try to load the file into your video editor as soon as possible. Even if an editor supports MP3, it may require specific parameters, a fact you're better off discovering after you've only ripped one file than after ripping an entire soundtrack.

My wife would absolutely shoot me if I used a Springsteen song in a gymnastics video, so we'll go with The Indigo Girls' album, *Shaming of the Sun*. "Shame on You" is a nice bouncy tune that would serve well as the background for a montage of gymnastics routines.

The following steps show the series of commands used to rip a track in RealOne. Let's walk through it:

1. Place the CD-ROM in the drive. As promised, Figure 12-7 shows that RealOne recognizes the CD and automatically inserts all song names, saving loads of time. Keep in mind that this only works if you're online.

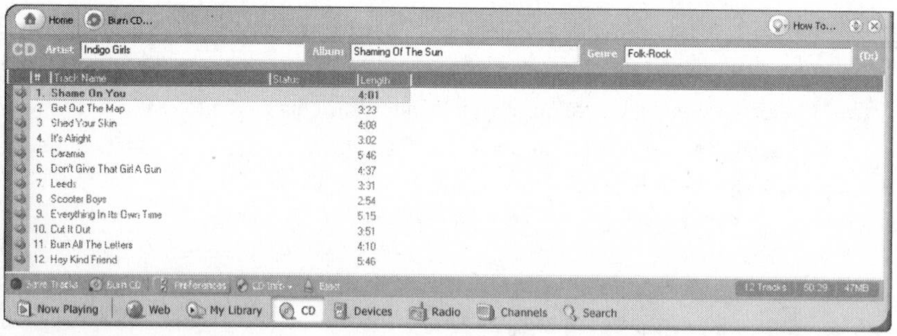

Figure 12-7: Ripping tracks in RealOne is fast, easy, and flexible. Notice that RealOne has populated the track names for me by checking the CDDB database.

2. In the General options box, I perform the now familiar task of changing the storage subdirectory so I can find my music files.

3. Next, I select the audio format. MP3 (as shown in Figure 12-8) is the most economical format from a drive standpoint, offers good quality, and should work in most editors. If you can choose the bit rate, stay higher than 128 kbps. On the other hand, WAV is the safest, which RealOne rips in full CD-ROM format at 176 kbps.

4. After that, click Save Tracks (shown on the bottom left of Figure 12-7). RealOne provides one last chance to change parameters and then starts ripping.

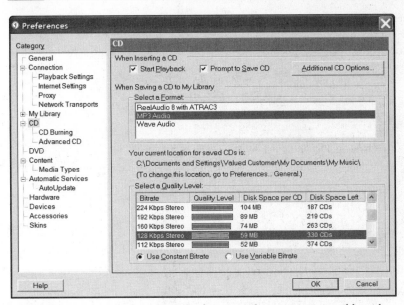

Figure 12-8: When selecting the audio format, make sure it's compatible with your video editor; MP3 and WAV are your safest choices.

Smart Sound Background Music

I covered this in the last chapter in the context of creating your own music video, but let's touch on it again here. A company called SmartSound (formerly Sonic Desktop) produces a program either called SmartSound (when bundled with third-party video editors) or called Movie Maestro or Sonicfire Pro (when sold as a standalone product through retail channels) that creates custom-length, theme-based background music tracks.

Let's explore that for a moment. The term *custom-length* means tuned to the specific length of the video, whether 30 seconds or 10 minutes, with an appropriate (meaning non-abrupt) beginning and ending. So it actually sounds custom-made for your production.

Second, it's theme-based. So if you're creating a video about a trip to Hawaii, there's a Hawaiian Holiday theme. The company includes a small but useful offering of music in the base product, which you can supplement with additional (for a fee) tracks direct from the company.

It's hard to describe the positive impact of appropriate background music, but think Elton John and *Lion King*, or Rogers and Hammerstein and *The King and I*. There's no question that a good soundtrack can be quite striking, even on less-ambitious projects.

For example, during the wedding I frequently referred to in the last chapter, I created two custom music video clips, one of my children running around the pool, the other of the children dancing at the reception. As you may recall, I cut the base footage into 10-second chunks, sped them up to 2X speed, distributed the chunks in random order, and added background music via SmartSound.

For the pool scene, I used a Beach-Boy-esque ditty that sounded like it came off the radio in the mid-1960s with the vocals stripped. For the dance scene, I used a Latin beat that sounded custom-made for the girls dancing at 2X original speed. The results were simply fantastic.

SmartSound is easiest to use when accessed directly from within the video editor, as you can do with Pinnacle Studio. You simply highlight the target video tracks, bring up the SmartSound menu (see Figure 12-9), select the appropriate music, and click Add to Movie. Studio adds the audio and treats it like any other audio file thereafter.

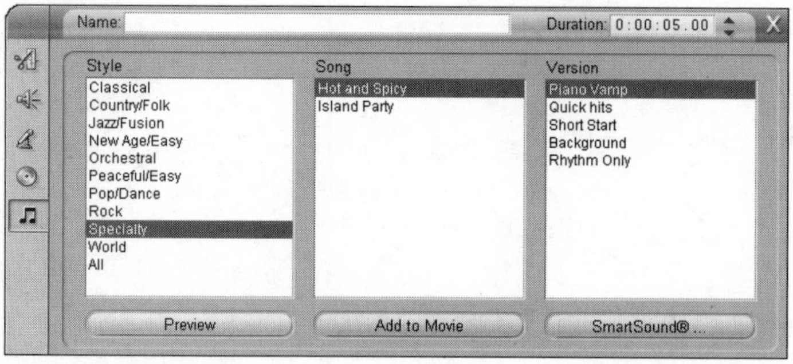

Figure 12-9: Choosing SmartSound tracks from within Pinnacle Studio.

However, if your editor doesn't bundle SmartSound, you can still access their collection, but you'll have to finish and render your project first. Then, you load it into SmartSound and follow these steps:

1. Select "Choose Movie" from the menu to load the rendered movie (refer to Figure 12-10).

Figure 12-10: Using Sonicfire Pro to create background soundtracks for your videos.

2. Click the Assistant icon to load the Assistant.

3. A series of screens will walk you through the steps of selecting and previewing your background audio tracks. Note that if you're online, you can choose to search SmartSound's database of music and purchase single tracks for around $19.95 or complete CDs for up to $99.95. It's a bit steep for casual use but perfect for high-profile events like weddings, bar mitzvahs, and graduations that require a special touch.

4. After you've chosen your music, you can insert it for the entire duration or any segment and incorporate several different tracks into your production.

5. Once you add the background audio tracks, you can use a simple volume slider to adjust soundtrack volume (see Figure 12-10) and then output either the finished movie or the soundtrack (see Figure 12-11). I recommend exporting the soundtrack only, which contains only the new music and does not mix the other audio tracks from the production. Then you can import the background track into your editor and produce normally. If you follow this approach, you should hold all volume adjustments in the soundtrack until you import the file into your movie.

Figure 12-11: Output options.

Adding Sound Effects

Many programs ship with libraries of sound effects, and certainly they are widely available elsewhere. For example, PowerPoint includes a small library of sound effects.

While I'm not big on animal sounds or other zany noises, I have been known to "sweeten" the applause my children receive for their athletic endeavors if I feel the audience has been unappreciative. Hey, done right, no one can tell the difference, and 20 years from now, they'll think they were performing in Madison Square Garden.

Most programs treat sound effects like any other audio file, so they're simple to import and edit as discussed in the following sections. The only potential downside is that you're consuming a track you would otherwise preserve for narration or background music.

Getting Audio to the Timeline

When you create audio within a program, either by narration, ripping CDs, or via SmartSound, typically the program inserts it into the proper track. When importing audio assets created elsewhere into the project, you'll have to do this manually.

As discussed in the last chapter, all editors have asset libraries, usually specific to asset types like audio, video, and still images. To insert assets into the project, locate the library, load the file into the library, and then drag it down into the project.

For example, Figure 12-12 shows Pinnacle Studio's audio library accessed by choosing the speaker icon on the left of the album screen. Load files using the folder atop the library window, and then you can drag it down into one of the two bottom tracks.

Like most editors, Studio will prevent you from loading files on tracks where they don't belong. For example, you couldn't load an audio track on Studio's video timeline. If your editing program won't let you drop the audio file on a particular track, it's probably the wrong track.

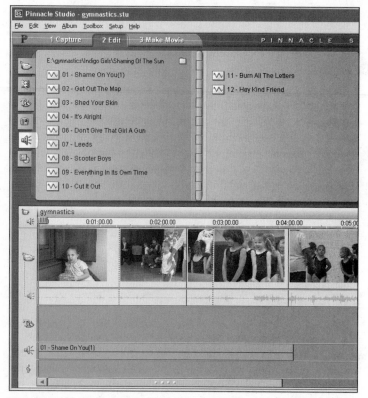

Figure 12-12: Studio's audio library. Use the folder icon to point the program toward the directory containing the audio files.

VideoStudio follows the same approach as Studio, with specific libraries for each asset category. In contrast, Microsoft's Movie Maker 2 uses a unified collections window with a specific task for loading audio files.

Adjusting Track Volume

All video editors provide the ability to adjust the volume of a single audio track and to fade in at the beginning and out at the end of the clip, though predictably, they get there in different ways. As shown on the left in Figure 12-13, you access Microsoft's commands via right-mouse-click commands and then you just follow the appropriate controls. VideoStudio provides a similar, but more visual approach, as shown on the right of Figure 12-13.

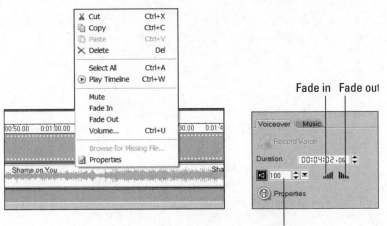

Figure 12-13: Volume adjustments for Microsoft's Movie Maker 2 on the left and Ulead's Video Studio on the right.

As shown in Figure 12-14, Pinnacle Studio offers more options. First, each track includes rubber-band controls that you can modify manually or via slider controls. For example, if you study Figure 12-14, you'll see three audio tracks: the original audio, the recorded narration, and the background music track.

The solid line in each audio track represents volume at that location. As you can see, I lowered the volume for both the original audio track and the background music track where I inserted narration files marked "trampoline" and "BARS ROUTINE." Obviously, this allows the narration to be heard over other audio sources.

To do this manually, you simply touch the rubber-band control to create a control point, and then drag that point upward or downward. This is the most frequent approach taken by prosumer video-editing programs.

In addition, on the upper left is Studio's volume mixer, which offers fade controls and global volume adjustments for each track and a volume meter that adjusts the rubber-band controls at the current edit line. What's unique about this control in the consumer space is that it works in real time, just like professional mixers.

Specifically, you can play the audio and use the sliders to adjust the volume on all three tracks in real time, with your edits showing up in the rubber-band controls where you can modify them further. This is pretty nifty for producers who like to use multiple audio tracks.

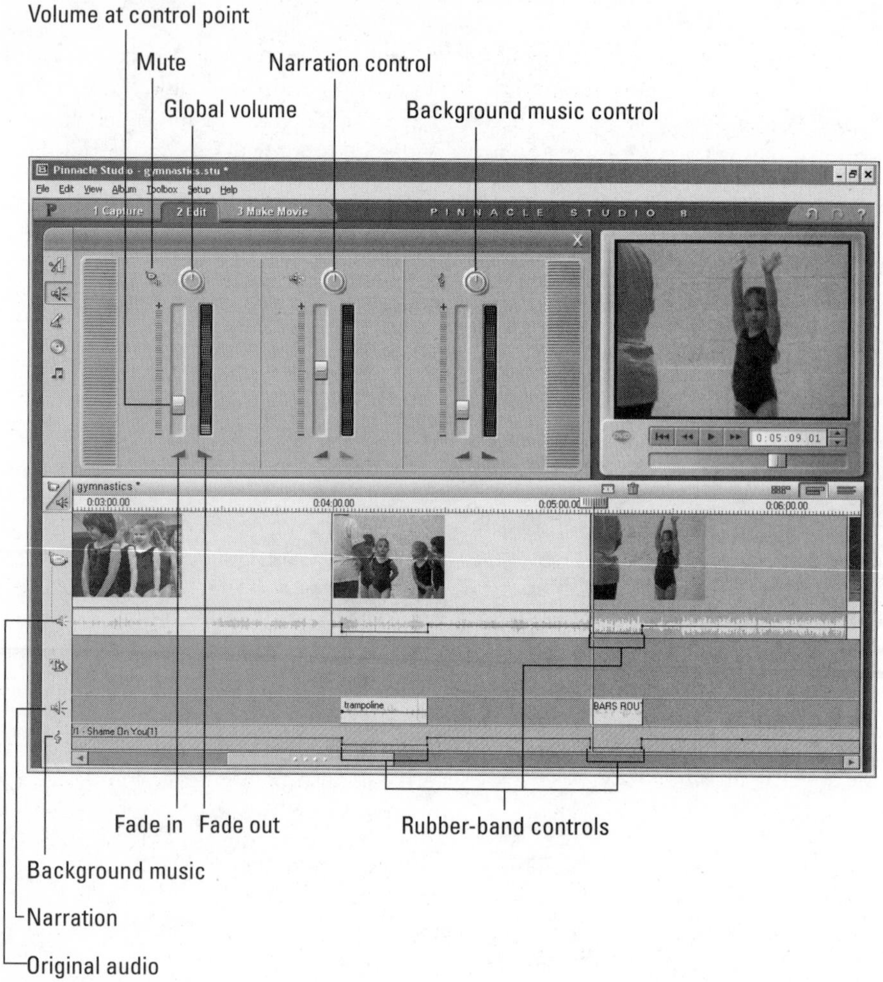

Volume at control point

Mute   Narration control

Global volume   Background music control

Fade in Fade out   Rubber-band controls

Background music

Narration

Original audio

Figure 12-14: Pinnacle Studio uses rubber-band controls on the timeline and a real-time audio mixer, a great offering for audio-centric productions.

Editing Audio on the Timeline

Typically editors trim and otherwise edit audio and video similarly. For example, with Movie Maker, you trim audio duration on the timeline by selecting the track, holding your pointer over the edge, and grabbing and pulling the edge to shorten or lengthen the track (see Figure 12-15). To change location, simply touch the track, grab it anywhere except for an edge, and move it to the desired location.

All other editors use these same basic procedures. Pinnacle Studio also provides a separate audio trim window, but most users can get it done on the timeline.

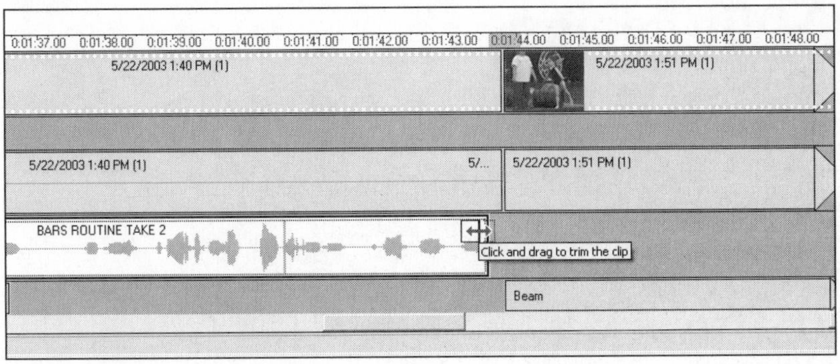

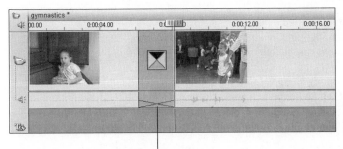

Figure 12-15: To shorten or lengthen an audio clip in Movie Maker, click it, grab an edge, and adjust as desired.

Inserting Cross-Fades into Transitions

As discussed in the last chapter, transitions are video effects that smooth the passing from one clip to another. For example, you may insert a dissolve transition between clips to show the slight passage of time or a fade out/fade in to show a longer passage. Either way, whenever you insert a video transition, you probably want your audio to transition smoothly as well.

You accomplish this with an audio cross-fade, transitioning the audio in the first clip from 100 to 0 percent volume while transitioning the volume in the second clip from 0 to 100 percent. Nothing exotic, you just need to know your editor's strategy for getting this done.

For example, for Movie Maker and VideoStudio, you use the same commands that were shown in Figure 12-13, manually fading each track in and each track out. In contrast, whenever you insert any transition between clips, Studio inserts the cross-fade for you (see Figure 12-16).

Note that if you cut from clip to clip, rather than using a transition, you shouldn't cross-fade. Appropriately, Studio doesn't insert a cross-fade under these circumstances.

Audio cross-fade

Figure 12-16: Studio creates audio cross-fades for all transitions.

Advanced Audio Topics

These are the basics of audio editing, so let's have a quick look at some prosumer features that should start trickling down into consumer space fairly soon. Let's start with a topic near and dear to all videographers' hearts: noise removal.

Noise Removal

Noise is a constant problem in video productions and narration, whether from poor-quality equipment or background noises like air conditioning or an electric fan. Let's use the noisy waveform that was shown in Figure 12-6 as our benchmark. As you may recall, the noise in this waveform was caused by an electrical interference produced by a bad fit between microphone and computer. Let's call it machine hum.

If you listen to the file, which is available on the CD-ROM, you'll notice that the noise is most noticeable when I'm not talking. There are two basic approaches to removing this noise, one is simple, the other is complex. I'll show you how both work.

On the CD-ROM

The audio file is called trampoline.wav and can be found in the Chapter 12 subdirectory on the CD accompanying this book.

The simple approach is through a *noise gate* (see Figure 12-17). A noise gate lets you set a threshold level (-20 dB in the figure), and considers any audio under that volume to be "noise" that it simply deletes. In Figure 12-17, attack time refers to how quickly the filter kicks in once the threshold is reached, while release time defines how quickly the filter stops after the sound is greater than the threshold, and the filter ceases operation.

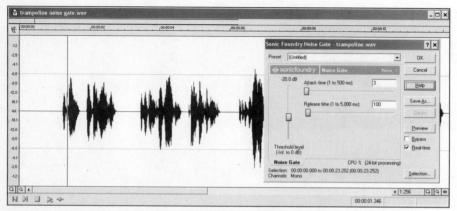

Figure 12-17: A noise-gate filter simply drops all audio below a certain threshold down to zero. This *looks* wonderful in the waveform but *sounds* abnormal.

If you compare the waveform shown in Figure 12-17 with the top waveform in Figure 12-6, you'll see that most of the machine hum is gone. However, since the noise gate only impacts those regions that meet the threshold requirement, Sound Forge didn't remove machine hum for other segments, like when I was speaking.

The listener hears the hum while I'm speaking and knows there's some kind of background noise, but once I stop speaking, it goes away, which sounds anomalous. Accordingly, though this process *looks* very effective when you compare waveforms, it's not when you actually hear it.

On the CD-ROM

Listen to the file called trampoline noise gate.wav on the CD-ROM to hear what I mean.

The complex approach is one that attempts to remove the machine hum from the entire audio track. That's true "noise removal," and Figures 12-18 through 12-20 show how it works.

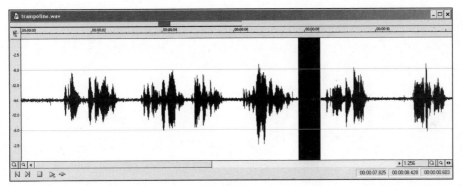

Figure 12-18: True noise removal doesn't look quite as effective, but sounds much better.

Figure 12-18 shows the original WAV file. As you can see, I've selected a region within the file where I was not speaking, essentially telling Sound Forge "look, this is what the machine noise is." Figure 12-19 shows a "noise print" of the area that I've selected. Sound Forge then seeks to remove this spectrum of sound from the entire track.

If you compare Figure 12-20 with Figure 12-17, you'll see the latter looks much cleaner. However, if you listen to trampoline noise reduction.wav on the CD-ROM, you'll note that it sounds much more realistic. This same approach works well for tape noise and click and pop removal from audio recorded from a turntable.

On the CD-ROM

Now compare the file trampoline noise-gate.wav to the file trampoline noise reduction.wav to see the difference between using a noise-gate filter and a noise-reduction approach.

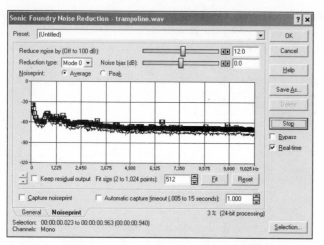

Figure 12-19: Sound Forge makes a noise print of the background noise.

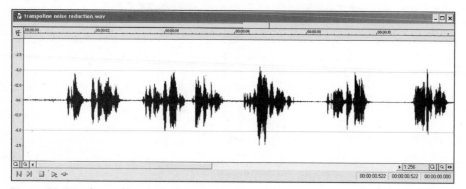

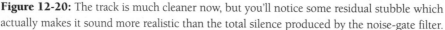

Figure 12-20: The track is much cleaner now, but you'll notice some residual stubble which actually makes it sound more realistic than the total silence produced by the noise-gate filter.

Note that you should never assume that even a sophisticated tool like Sony's Noise Removal filter will be able to eliminate background noises from your recorded video or audio. While it usually works with any consistent background noise, it's not 100 percent by any means. The most prudent course is to eliminate all extraneous noises while recording and monitor audio quality with headphones while shooting or narrating.

The following sections take a quick look at two other features that should soon become standard on consumer audio editors.

Equalization

Equalization is adjusting the different frequency bands in an audio file to highlight certain sounds, much like the graphic equalization controls used on fancy stereo systems (see Figure 12-21). These let you customize the audio precisely to achieve the desired sound.

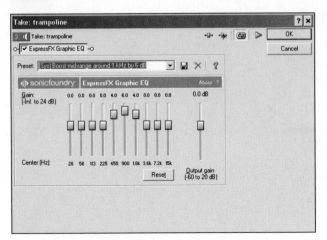

Figure 12-21: Equalization controls on Sony Vegas — not quite as sexy as subtly lit buttons on a stereo system, but they serve the same purpose.

As you can see in Figure 12-21, you adjust the controls for each frequency upward or downward to customize the sound. In addition, most programs supply presets for different types of productions. In the figure, the preset is "Boost mid-range around 1 kHz by 6 dB." I'm sure that consumer editors will likely provide much more user-friendly language, like mixed music and speech, but that remains to be seen.

Normalization

Normalization provides the ability to ensure that all audio tracks in your production play at the same volume, an invaluable tool when using audio tracks from different sources. You can also use normalization to increase the volume of a poorly recorded track to maximum value without distortion.

Figure 12-22 shows the normalization control from Sound Forge using peak-level normalization. You set the level (100% in Figure 12-22) and Sound Forge increases volume so that the highest point in the track reaches 100 percent. Then you apply the same filter to all tracks, performing a similar adjustment and ensuring consistent volume over the entire production.

Audio Panning

Stereo panning refers to the ability to adjust audio so that the listener hears the audio from one speaker or the other (at the extreme) or to unevenly distribute playback over the two speakers. Figure 12-23 is the Pan control from Ulead's MediaStudio program with start and ending controls for each stereo track.

To pan the sound of a train moving from left to right, you would use the controls as shown, with 100 percent of the sound starting on the left side (and 0 percent on the right), and 100 percent of the sound ending up on the right (and 0 percent on the left). The transformation curve controls determine how quickly the sound level changes and work differently from program to program.

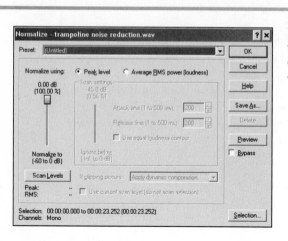

Figure 12-22: Sound Forge's normalization filter, which boosts volume as much as possible without distortion and can help ensure consistent volume on tracks from multiple sources.

Here's what we can learn from MediaStudio's help files:

- **Linear.** This causes the sound level to change at a constant rate over time. Choose this if you want to do a gradual fade.

- **Exponential.** This type of fade-in causes sound levels to start out slowly and end very quickly, while an exponential fade-out causes sound levels to start out fast and end very slowly.

- **Logarithmic.** This type of fade-in starts quickly and then levels out slowly, while a logarithmic fade-out starts very slowly and then drops suddenly.

Note

Notice the play and stop controls (the buttons with a black triangle and square) on the lower right of the Pan dialog box. These controls let you preview your settings and adjust them before actually adding the effect to the clip.

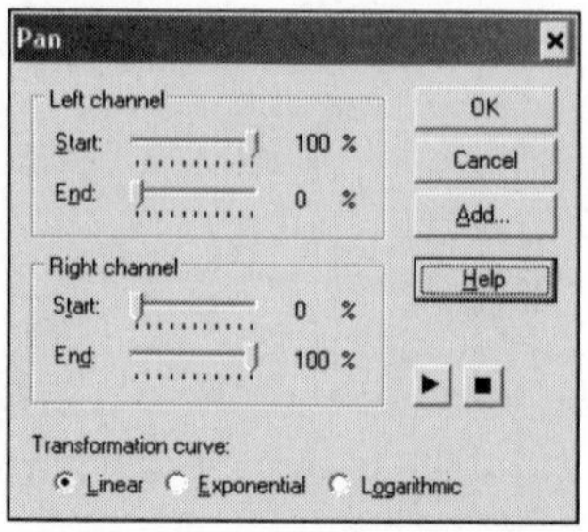

Figure 12-23: MediaStudio Pro's Pan control allows you to control how the audio track is distributed over the stereo speakers.

For example, Linear changes the sound at a constant rate, which would approximate a person walking from right to left, but not a train, which would quickly approach from the left and then slowly fade to the right. Looking at the three alternatives, it appears that an exponential curve would work best, but it's a trial-and-error type of operation.

Taking this one very happy step forward is Sony Vegas with full surround-sound control (see Figure 12-24). This allows DVD developers to assign each audio track a speaker position over the 5.1 surround spectrum and change that position over time. In the figure, I'm assigning track 2 a position almost directly in front of the front right speaker.

Figure 12-24: Vegas' Surround Panner lets you position each audio track in the surround spectrum.

While surround capabilities won't show up on consumer editors for a while, it's a key feature if you're creating DVDs for playback on surround-sound systems. In addition, since Windows Media Audio now supports 5.1 Surround, it's a fun feature for high-end users developing immersive audio experiences for their own listening pleasure.

Other Effects

Other prosumer effects available today that should soon appear on consumer editors include the following:

- **Time stretch.** This allows you to shorten or lengthen audio tracks without distorting track pitch.

- **Stadium and similar effects.** These adjust the sound to make it seem as if created in a stadium, large room, or other surrounding.

- **Echo.** This creates an echo in the audio track.

You get the idea. Video special effects were the battleground of video editors in 2001 through 2003; audio special effects will start gaining prominence in 2004 and thereafter.

Summary

Here is a summary of the key points in this chapter:

1. Most consumer video-editing programs have narration tracks and tools for creating and inserting narration into your video productions. Narration requires a microphone and usually a headset to ensure high-quality recording. Narrations work best when scripted and recorded in quiet surroundings.

2. Most programs also include facilities for ripping tracks from CD-ROMs. In general, they're inferior to free tools like Microsoft's Media Player, MusicMatch's Jukebox, and RealNetwork's RealOne, which offer features like automatic track naming and flexible file conversion facilities. All video editors accept WAV and MP3 files, with Windows Media Audio files accepted by some, and RealNetworks files accepted by very few.

3. You can create your own custom-length, theme-based background music with software from SmartSound. It's easiest when the software is integrated into the base program, as with Pinnacle Studio. When working with video editors, you can achieve the same results by purchasing Sonicfire Pro or Movie Maestro directly from SmartSound.

4. Most video editors have audio-specific libraries or albums to import audio files for dragging into the timeline. Once on the timeline, you get controls for adjusting volume, and fading into and out of the clip, though they're implemented differently on each program. Very few consumer tools, other than Pinnacle Studio, provide a multi-track, real-time audio mixer that really simplifies the use of multiple audio files.

5. Most video editors use the same editing paradigm for audio as for video. You should be able to trim audio on the timeline and split the clips using the same types of controls as with video.

6. Use cross-fades to transition audio from one track to another whenever you use a video transition. Once again, each program will do this differently.

7. There are two general techniques for eliminating mechanical hums and similar background noise: noise gates and noise removal. The latter is superior but generally is only available on very expensive programs.

8. Two other functions will soon appear on consumer video editors: equalization, which allows producers to manipulate specific frequencies in the audio to achieve the desired sound, and normalization, which allows producers to make all audio files in the production the same volume.

Chapter 13

Working with Still Images

I first used a digital still-image camera in 1997 when my wife and I traveled to Egypt to visit Cairo and the Valley of the Kings. It was a bulky loaner from a *PC Mag* staffer that captured about 20 640x480 still images before it needed downloading to my notebook computer.

My most immediate problem after coming home was a vacation picture face-off with a friendly couple who had just returned from two weeks in China. She was a great amateur photographer who had taken evening courses on still-image photography. My wife was an enthusiastic amateur who had five or six rolls of printed film.

I had about 70 digital photographs and no way to print them. Even if I had a printer, at such low resolutions, they would have looked terrible. So, the Saturday afternoon before our dinner, I spent about five hours in Premiere creating my first video slideshow.

As it happened, I had taught a digital video course the week before I left for Egypt, and a class participant showed me how to do an image pan in Premiere. As you'll see a little later in the chapter, this effect allows you to move the video view port around an image, a la Ken Burns of *Civil War* and *Baseball* fame.

So I integrated several of these effects into the 36-second slideshow chronicling the actual trip to Cairo, door to beer chaser, so to speak. Then I synchronized the slides to the Bangle's "Walk Like an Egyptian," rendered several files to find the ideal parameters, then grabbed my laptop and power cord and left for home.

On the CD-ROM

The slideshow itself is on the CD-ROM in the Chapter 13 folder (Walk like an Egyptian.avi), missing the background music due to the obvious rights issues. When you watch, hum along and imagine how great it must have been.

Actually, it was pretty cool, but 36 seconds is 36 seconds and even played twice, my little slideshow only consumed about 90 seconds of time that Saturday night, enough for a couple of sips of wine and a few nods of appreciation. Then we moved on to some striking analog prints of China and Egypt.

In part, the lack of applause was due to friendly one-upmanship, which was certainly the spirit of the night. More likely, since my wife and buddies aren't technical, they just didn't appreciate how difficult it was to pull the slideshow together. In contrast, when I show the slideshow to students in my seminars, and other digital-video-aware professionals, it almost always triggers a mini-epiphany, as in "wow, I can use digital still images in my videos."

Since then, digital cameras have become much more capable, and video editors more still-image aware. In many ways, slideshows are easier to produce than actual video and add a different feel that renews and engages the audience. I usually carry both a digital still and video camera to important events and try to integrate both types of media into my productions.

As you've probably guessed from the title and story, this is the digital still-image chapter. Here, you will learn how to edit your digital images and build a simple slideshow in several different programs. Then I'll look at tools for animating still images and creating your own Ken Burns–type effects. Finally, I'll conclude with a quick look at how to create and implement image overlays, where images like logos and watermarks display over the background video.

Producing Slideshows

The key issue facing most digital camera owners, when it comes to producing slideshows, is the proper way to crop their images for use in a video slideshow. For example, Figure 13-1 is a video of my girls in my wife's water garden. As you can see, I shot in landscape mode, turning the camera sideways to capture their full lengths.

Inserting the image into a project is usually fairly simple. Most editors have libraries of assets for audio, video, and still-image content. Find the library and the insert tool associated with the library to insert the image, which should be similar to the procedure used to load audio and video files. Then, drag it down to the timeline to include in your project.

Figure 13-2 shows the image inserted into Microsoft's Movie Maker 2 and Pinnacle Studio. As you can see, both programs display the entire image without smushing, squishing, or otherwise bending, folding, or mutilating the picture. In technical terms, this means that they preserve the aspect ratio or the relationship between horizontal and vertical pixels.

Cross-Reference

For more on aspect ratios, turn to Chapter 16.

Specifically, the original image was 1440x2160, or an aspect ratio of 1:1.5, which means that for every horizontal pixel there are 1.5 vertical pixels. As shown in the preview windows of Movie Maker and Studio in Figure 13-2, both programs adhere to this aspect ratio, Movie Maker at 254x381 and Studio at 140x210.

Figure 13-1: Girlies in the garden — the starting point for our cropping adventure.

Figure 13-2: Girlies in the garden inserted into Movie Maker 2 (on the left) and Pinnacle Studio (on the right). Looking good, neither program changed the aspect ratio, as you'll see in the next figure.

Compare this to the treatment of prosumer editors, as shown in Figure 13-3. Both Adobe Premiere 6.5 (not the newest version, Premiere Pro) and MediaStudio Pro (on the right) stretch the image to achieve an aspect ratio of 4:3, or four horizontal pixels for every three vertical pixels. That's because 4:3 is the aspect ratio of television, and in default mode, each editor thinks that every image should conform to this aspect ratio.

In MediaStudio Pro, if you know where to look, you can tell the editor to maintain the original aspect ratio. In Premiere 6.5, I never found this knob and had to preprocess all my images so they displayed at the proper aspect ratio. Thank goodness Adobe fixed this with the newer Premiere Pro.

Finally, in the middle of Figure 13-3, is Pinnacle Edition, which shows the whole image at the original aspect ratio. Edition includes a fairly rich image manipulation feature set that allows you to shrink the image to size with or without changing the aspect ratio.

What's the point? First, that if you're building a slideshow in a consumer video editor, life is pretty easy, since the editors are working in your favor. You typically must adjust the image in some way to make slideshows work in prosumer editors. Second, when cropping your images to better fit in the video window, you should trim to an aspect ratio of 4:3, since that's the aspect ratio of the video project itself.

428x321 (4:3)   340x255 (4:3)

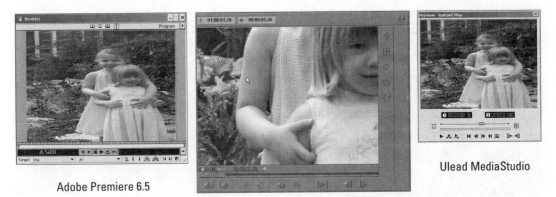

Adobe Premiere 6.5   Ulead MediaStudio

Pinnacle Edition

Figure 13-3: Prosumer editors aren't quite as image friendly and make it a bit harder to produce slideshows. Note that Premiere Pro displays the same image as Edition, keeping the aspect ratio correct, but it shows only a segment of the image.

Cropping Your Images

Let's look at an example. I've decided that I want to edit "Girlies in the Garden" to show primarily facial shots. There's an easy way and a hard way to do this.

The easy way is to use a tool like Ulead's PhotoImpact (see Figure 13-4) that allows you to crop to a constrained aspect ratio. Note the Shape drop-down box that lets you choose an aspect ratio like Computer/TV (4:3), which I've selected. Two icons to the left of the drop-down box is a Lock icon that lets you lock the aspect ratio so that your cropping is constrained to the selected aspect ratio, in our case, 4:3. Next to the lock you see that the image I've cropped out is 1,200 pixels wide and 900 high, or four pixels wide for every three pixels high.

The hard way is how I used to do it before PhotoImpact 8 came out: You sit with a calculator open on your desktop and check the 4:3 ratio yourself each time you crop. Choose your target width — say 1,600 pixels, divide your target width by four, which is 400 pixels, and multiply the result by three to get 1,200 pixels. The result, 1600x1200, is a perfect 4:3. Needless to say, it's much easier to use a tool like PhotoImpact.

Using PhotoImpact, I saved the file in 1,200x900 resolution and loaded it back into Movie Maker, Pinnacle Studio, Premiere, and Ulead MediaStudio. As you can see from Figure 13-5, all editors preserved the aspect ratio, and the image fits the screens perfectly. If I wanted to zoom in even further, I could crop the original image even more tightly, so long as the aspect ratio of the pixels was 4:3.

Where's Ulead's VideoStudio in all this? Actually, as shown in Figure 13-6, VideoStudio has the most flexible image import options of all, capable of keeping the proper aspect ratio, fitting the image to the project size, or maintaining the original size, basically all the options shown in Figures 13-2 and 13-3. You've also gotta love the ability to rotate images by 90 degrees either way, a great time-saver when you've shot a mixture of portrait and landscape shots.

Lock aspect

Choose aspect ratio

Figure 13-4: Ulead's PhotoImpact simplifies cropping for slideshows by allowing you to constrain your crops to a 4:3 aspect ratio.

Note

I'm not saying that you must crop your images to include them in a slideshow. Oftentimes it's preferable to include images like that shown in Figure 13-1 in their full glory, even if there is blank screen space on either side. As you'll see in the following slideshow example, many of the images were not cropped. It's just that if you do crop and want to maximize screen area, crop to an aspect ratio of 4:3.

The only other point is you should never change the aspect ratio of the image that you're editing during cropping or resizing. You can generally prevent this by finding the Keep aspect ratio control like that shown in the lower-left corner of Figure 13-7 (as well as in Figure 13-6), or the equivalent.

MediaStudio Pro

Premiere

Movie Maker 2

Studio

Figure 13-5: Looks like 4:3 is a hit with all the video editors!

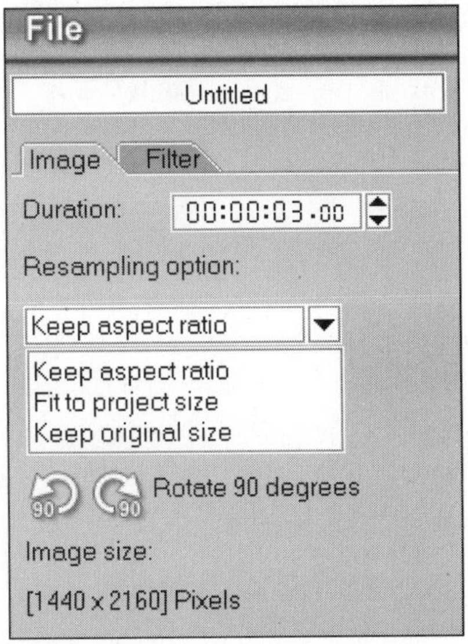

Figure 13-6: Ulead VideoStudio offers the best flexibility, with three modes of still-image support. For most slideshows, use Keep aspect ratio.

One More Time

Let's pull this all together with one more example. Figure 13-8 shows my daughters in front of the aforementioned garden. It's a large shot, full 2160x1440 resolution, an aspect ratio of 4:2.6, meaning that for every four pixels across, there are 2.6 vertical pixels.

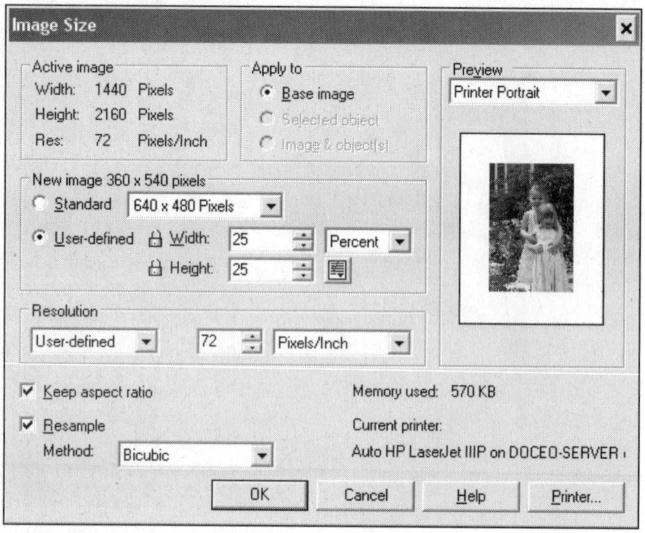

Figure 13-7: Don't ever change the aspect ratio of the image that you're editing; you can prevent this with controls like the "Keep aspect ratio" checkbox shown here.

In Screen 1 of Figure 13-8, I'm using PhotoImpact to zoom in to my daughters at a constrained 4:3 aspect ratio. I save the file, input it back into Studio, and voilà, instant zoom, no black lines.

Screen 2 in Figure 13-8 shows the image in Studio before cropping. Note the black lines above and below the image in the monitor. This tells you that Studio is preserving the image's original aspect ratio by adding black pixels above and below the image so that the entire image, black pixels and all, has a 4:3 aspect ratio.

Building the Slideshow

Now that I've got my images prepped, it's time to build the slideshow. I hope I haven't gotten your hopes up too much, because most of the consumer editors offer little by way of dedicated slideshow functionality, at least to this point.

This should change over the next few months, simply because consumer DVD editors like Pinnacle Expression and Ulead MovieFactory offer great slideshow tools. As soon as Pinnacle, Ulead, or even another vendor offers great slideshow functionality within their consumer video editors, all other vendors will have to follow.

Figure 13-8: One final time, this time zooming into the image. The black lines in Screen 2 show you the image doesn't have a 4:3 aspect ratio. Our zoomed image, constrained in PhotoImpact, does and fits perfectly as shown in Screen 3.

For now, however, building a slideshow is pretty much like building a bunch of little movies, with little of the automation assistance provided by the DVD-authoring programs. Using Movie Maker as an example, let's go through the process:

1. Step 1 is to locate the picture and transition duration options that all programs offer (see Figure 13-9). Movie Maker 2 uses a default of 5 seconds for images, and 1.25 seconds for transitions. The key here is to time both slide and transition durations to the background music you plan to use. If it's very fast, 5 seconds will seem like forever. For example, in my "Walk Like an Egyptian" slideshow, I had 29 images in 34 seconds, for an average duration of about 1.5 seconds. Transitions were about one quarter of a second. On other projects, I've gone much longer, say 3 to 4 seconds, but transitions are always 1 second or below. Note that you'll be able to modify the duration of each asset on the timeline once it's there, but changes made to the default duration typically don't impact those already included in the project.

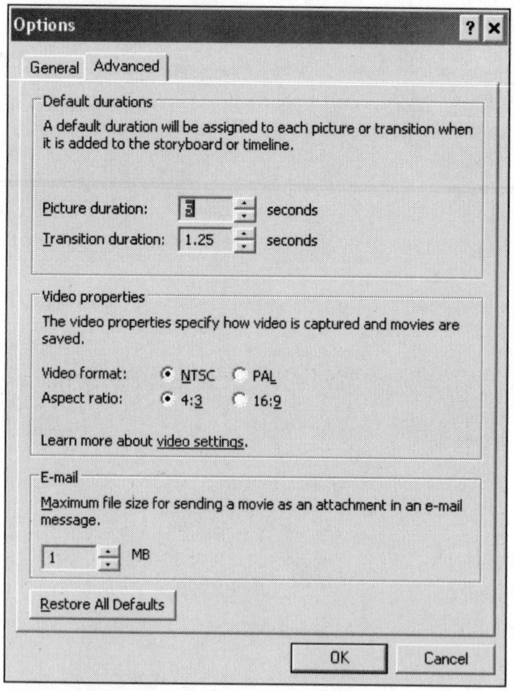

Figure 13-9: Here's where you can set the picture and transition duration options.

2. Import your still images into the program, preferably into a new folder. Unless your program can rotate images, like VideoStudio, you'll have to rotate all shots before importing them. In addition, perform any cropping beforehand.

3. Working in storyboard mode, if available, drag your images down into the project. Note that you typically can change the order at any time by dragging an image to a new location, or dragging a new image in front of another. With Movie Maker, you can only change image duration after you convert to timeline view by dragging the clip to a different length. Other editors allow you to change duration in a Properties or similar window. Note that with most editors, you can drag the still images to the storyboard en masse by selecting them all (either with your mouse or menu commands) and dragging them down to the movie window (see Figure 13-10).

Figure 13-10: Storyboard view.

4. After you've placed your images in the proper order, drag the desired transition effects between the still images. Use simple dissolves unless you have a compelling reason to the contrary. It may be easier to use right-click commands to copy the transition and then paste it into subsequent transition slots (refer to Figure 13-10) than to drag the transition down again and again.

5. Convert to timeline view to add audio. Audio can be narration or music, your choice (see Figure 13-11).

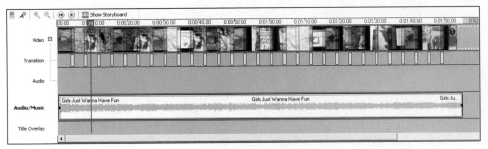

Figure 13-11: Adding audio in timeline view. Just a simple drag and drop into the Audio/Music track.

Now you're ready to preview, make any necessary tweaks, and move on to the next movie component.

Beyond this basic toolset, Pinnacle Studio adds two additional capabilities. First and most important, Studio can automate the insertion of transitions between your slides. Once you've dragged your first transition into the timeline between the first and second clips in the slideshow, select all images, right-click, and choose Ripple Transition (see Figure 13-12). Studio inserts the transition between all selected clips.

Figure 13-12: Studio's Ripple Transition automates the insertion of transitions into your slideshow.

The other advantage, which I discussed in the last chapter, is Studio's ability to access SmartSound audio tracks to build a custom-length background track for your slideshow. This is a killer feature that you may choose to access even if Studio isn't your main editing application.

For example, often I produce DVDs in Ulead's DVD Workshop or edit videos in Pinnacle Edition. Neither of these programs offers SmartSound. So, if I have a slideshow component, I have to create it in Studio, add the audio, export it as a DV file, and then import that file into the other program for further editing or rendering.

This highlights one lovely characteristic of the DV format — it's the Visa of digital video codecs — accepted nearly everywhere. This means that you can access the best features of certain programs, like Studio's SmartSound, Movie Maker 2's AutoMovie, or Canopus Imaginate, discussed in the next section, to produce very specific effects that you can then very simply import as an AVI file into your video project.

Cross-Reference

For more on Movie Maker 2's AutoMovie, turn to Chapter 15.

Animating Your Images

Slideshows are great, but high-resolution scanners and megapixel still-image cameras provide another opportunity: creating video from still images. This is known as the Ken Burns effect, after the movies produced by Burns about *Baseball* and the *Civil War* that primarily used still images with motion created by a camera zooming into and panning around the image.

Back in the day, videographers produced this effect with a camera sitting in a mechanical apparatus that physically moved the camera around the image, with the camera lens zooming into and out of the picture as required. How analog, eh? Keep that image in your mind, however, because the digital equivalent of this, called *image pan,* duplicates the same efforts.

For example, look at Figure 13-13, which is Adobe Premiere's Image Pan control. On the lower left is the starting point for the image. You can see the image in the background, with the black box isolating that portion of the slide I actually wanted in the video. Note from the width and height indicators above the image that my box has a resolution of 640x480, which is, of course, a 4:3 aspect ratio. On the right is the end of the clip, with a much smaller box around the sign in the man's hands, once again at 4:3 aspect ratio (120x90).

At a high level, what I'm doing is telling Premiere that for this clip, start at the 640x480 view and then zoom into the picture to highlight the Ozer name. This dramatic moment illustrates the exhilarating release from the severe angst of traveling into an exotic country with no real idea how you'll be getting from airport to hotel (at least that's what my drama coach told me). Essentially, Premiere duplicated the mechanical apparatus used with real video cameras, producing a killer feature for anyone working with still images.

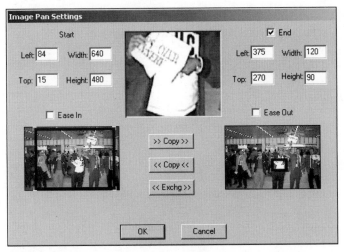

Figure 13-13: Image Pan controls in Adobe Premiere. They've changed with Premiere Pro, but this is how they looked when I actually produced the slideshow.

That's great, I hear you saying, but what if I want to do more than just move from point A to point B? Suppose I wanted to zoom into a portion of the picture, then another, then another, and finally zoom out to show the whole enchilada?

Well, in Premiere 6.5, you could do that, but you'd have to chop the image into multiple pieces and manage each camera move separately. And, you'd have to accomplish this within Premiere's somewhat cramped image pan interface. Or, you could use a program called Canopus Imaginate to design the entire image pan, export into DV, and import the resultant file into any video editor.

Using Your Imaginate-tion

Figure 13-14 shows the main interface window of Canopus Imaginate. The workspace window displays the image that I'll be exploring, my wife's water garden. In keeping with the whole French Provincial look, you'll notice that the lawn is relatively un-mowed (at least until I finish this chapter). It's a large, high-resolution image, and I'm going to scan around the image to create a video file so my wife can identify the various plants that she chose and describe why she chose them.

Figure 13-14: Touring around my wife's water garden in Imaginate.

Though it's faint, you should be able to see a small gray box around the statue of the little boy fishing in the pond, which represents the current project view, which is displayed in the preview window on the upper right. On the bottom is the timeline window, and on the right are the camera controls.

A critical concept for Imaginate and the special effects you'll study in the next chapter is a *key frame*. A key frame is a point on the timeline where any camera position, scale, 3D angles, and perspectives are all defined. Each of the squares and diamonds you see on the timeline are key frames. When you build a movie in Imaginate or customize a special effect in your editor, you move from key frame to key frame, customizing the available parameters for each location.

For example, I start the tour with a close-up of the bushes in the front left. First, I position the camera and scale it to the proper size and angle. Then I touch the timeline at point B creating another key frame, and so on. During rendering, Imaginate plays connect-the-key-frames, producing video frames for the key frames I defined and all frames in between, creating a 30-frame-per-second file in the desired format.

Imaginate enables four different camera controls. First is sizing the video, controlled via a simple slider or manual positioning controls. Enlarge the window and you see more of the image, in effect zooming away. Shrink the window, and you zoom into the image. Second is panning around the image, again controlled manually or via X and Y positioning sliders. If you want to move from right to left, simply grab the view port in the workspace, and position it where desired.

Third are the three-dimensional camera controls, which can spin the image in 2D space around any of its three axes, and finally, the ability to adjust perspective, or the focal distance of the camera. After you plot your course through your image, you can manually adjust the motion path, and with different interpolation techniques to smooth the motion between key frames.

All this technical jargon sounds confusing, but it's not. You just click a point on the timeline to create a key frame, adjust your camera size, position, and angle, and move to the next key frame. When you're done, Imaginate can output an AVI file to input into your video editor, or if you're working in Premiere, you can insert the project file directly into your video projects.

On the CD-ROM

You can check the results on the CD-ROM in the Chapter 13 subdirectory by playing Imaginate.mpg.

Edition's Version of Panning

At least one prosumer video editor, Pinnacle Edition, includes Imaginate-like functionality within its core feature set (see Figure 13-15). This bodes well for this feature showing up in other prosumer editors in the near future. In addition, since Apple included "Ken Burns" effects in iMovie 3, essentially the equivalent of Premiere's panning controls as shown earlier, I would expect panning capabilities to appear in Windows-based consumer programs very soon.

Figure 13-15: Pinnacle Edition provides similar functionality to Imaginate, a trend that should expand to other prosumer and consumer editors.

Overlaying Titles and Other Still Images

One very common still-image effect is to overlay an image like a logo over a background video. You see this all the time during prime time television when networks place their transparent logo on the bottom right corner of the screen. Many producers mimic this with corporate videos, and it adds a nice professional touch to all productions.

Overlay is a concept that sounds difficult, but it's really not. What you're attempting to do is combine two screens, one over the other. The only hard part is telling the video editor which part of the top movie you *don't* want to see.

Consider the Doceo Publishing logo shown on the left in Figure 13-16. You can't see it in this black-and-white book, but the frame is completely blue except for the logo. When you place this over another video on the timeline, you tell the editor (through program controls, of course) to eliminate the blue and just show the logo. This is called "keying" or "chromakeying." Then the editor displays the background video, plus the logo, as shown on the MediaStudio preview screen on the right in Figure 13-16.

The most common use of video chromakeying is the weatherperson, generally filmed in front of a green screen. Then, the video feed is "keyed" over the weather map so the weatherperson can show us (yet again) that it will rain over the weekend. Technically, when you create a title and place it over the video, you're using an overlay technique, though most editors do this automatically and shield you from the details.

Logo file   MediaStudio preview

Figure 13-16: Overlaying the Doceo logo (a simple BMP file with a completely blue background) over a video file in MediaStudio.

Not all consumer programs can overlay an image over the video, and those that can do it differently. For example, Movie Maker 2 has no overlay capabilities.

In addition, note that consumer-oriented programs usually have one, fixed technique for overlaying graphics, which makes it simple for users but limits flexibility. Operation is also generally "binary," as in it either works (if you've got the right file format in the proper parameters) or doesn't (if you don't).

In contrast, prosumer programs offer multiple "keying" options, like Bluescreen, Chroma Key, an "Alpha Channel," or a transparent channel built into many image formats precisely for the purpose of allowing seamless overlay. Each of these techniques has different controls, and most video editors limit overlay capabilities to certain tracks, which complicates operation.

For example, VideoStudio can both overlay images and videos, but they have to be 32-bit files with an Alpha Channel. This simplifies operation with Ulead's excellent logo and animation tool, Cool 3D Studio, but it makes things a bit more complicated with PhotoImpact, which I cover in the next section. Once you have the files produced in the proper format, you simply load them as either image or video files and drag them down to the overlay track. VideoStudio should do the rest automatically as shown in Figure 13-17.

With Pinnacle Studio, you have two options. It's easiest to double-click the title track, which opens the title editor, and then drag your logo into the editor and position and size it to your liking (see Figure 13-18), using the safe zone margins as guides. Once on the title track, you can fade into and out of the logo, a nice effect, and drag the still image file to any length.

Figure 13-17: We had to create a transparent PNG (Portable Network Graphics) file in PhotoImpact to work with VideoStudio.

The other alternative is to create a full-screen file, like that shown in Figure 13-16, and drag that directly to the title track. Studio assumes that the pixel color in the upper left-hand corner is the color to be eliminated and performs this automatically. That's the theory, anyway; in my tests, performance has been a bit spotty, and I've had better luck with the Title Editor.

Contrast this with operation in MediaStudio (see Figure 13-19). First, the logo has to be on the correct track (any track except Va, Fx, or Vb). Then, you have to find the overlay control (right-click), choose the proper overlay type (color key), and adjust the controls as necessary. Note that there are some advantages to this complexity, as you can do neat things like adjust the transparency values to create a see-through logo.

Typically, however, selecting the values for a properly prepared still image is simple. When I discuss overlaying video files in the next chapter, selecting and adjusting parameters get a bit more intense.

Figure 13-18: Pinnacle Studio is a bit more flexible. You can drag your logo into the Title Editor and shape and resize at will, or lay your full screen title directly on the title track, which worked less well.

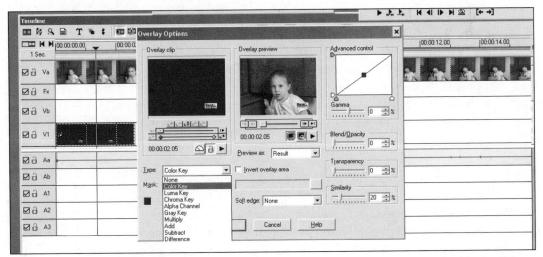

Figure 13-19: Ulead's MediaStudio has professional features that offer advanced functionality like the ability to create semi-transparent overlays. Here I choose the color key "Type" to overlay the logo over the video.

Creating a Logo in PhotoImpact

This exercise assumes that you already have a logo or similar file to overlay. Though some video editors work well with existing files, the easiest way to build a logo file that will overlay without muss or fuss is to build it full screen, or 640x480 in resolution. Note that I'll have to render the file two different ways to work in all video editors, but it's simpler than it sounds. Here are the steps:

1. In PhotoImpact, select File → New Image (see Figure 13-20).

   If creating an image for PhotoImpact, make the canvas transparent, and select 640x480. PhotoImpact will create the file.

   If creating an image for any other program, select Custom color for the canvas and select 640x480. Note that resolution may vary by image editor, since they all work slightly differently. This is the correct size for Pinnacle Studio; check your editor's documentation for details.

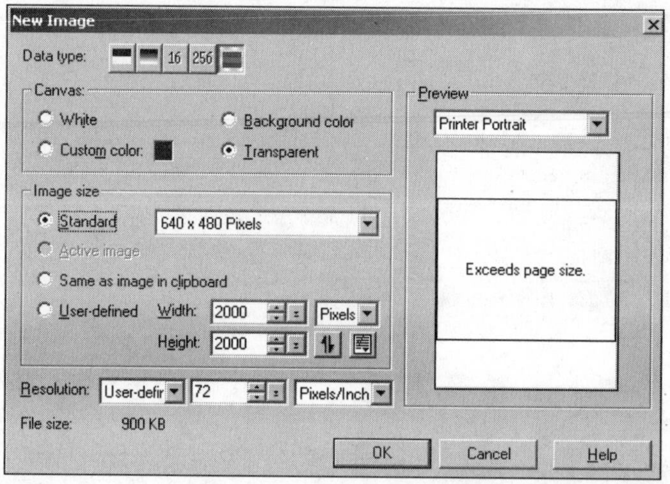

Figure 13-20: The New Image dialog box, where you create the new image file.

Note

If you need to use a color-key technique to apply your logo over the background video (as opposed to the transparent image I'm creating here), the color you select for your background canvas should provide a good contrast with your logo. For example, if your logo is black, choose white; if red, choose green. This makes it easier on the editor to discern what should be eliminated in the keying process.

2. Open your logo file, and copy and paste it into the new image.

3. When positioning the logo, remember the title safe zone for videos to be played on a television set, whether via optical format (DVD, Super VideoCD, or VideoCD) or by writing back to tape (see Chapter 11 for details). Basically, you should count on about 60 pixels on all four sides being cut off as overscan and not visible when played back (see Figure 13-21).

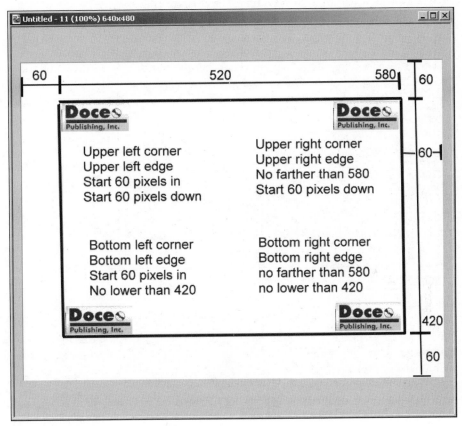

Figure 13-21: Positioning your logo in the new image.

4. If creating an image for VideoStudio or MediaStudio:

Choose File → Save As and scroll down in the Save as Type drop-down box for PNG (Portable Network Graphics). Input a filename and click Save.

The Ulead PNG Image Optimizer screen should open (see Figure 13-22). Check the transparency checkbox if not selected, and click OK. PhotoImpact will save the file. Note that this file now has an Alpha Channel and should work in any video editor that supports PNG (Premiere 6.5 and Studio do not, but MediaStudio does).

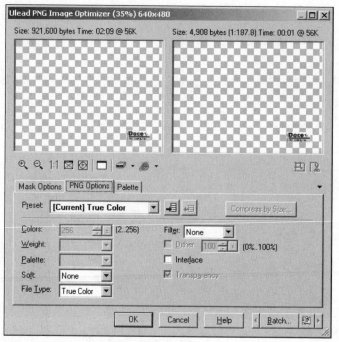

Figure 13-22: The PNG Image Optimizer.

5. If creating an image for Studio or any other editor, choose File → Save As and save the image as a BMP file. There should be no options screen. Note that this file should be usable in Studio, Premiere, or any other video editor that supports Blue Screen, Color Key, or Chroma Key overlays.

Figure 13-23 illustrates what happens if you don't mind the title safe zones when creating your logo file. The top two screens show the right way to do it; the bottom two show what happens if you don't pay attention to the safe zone. Remember, this is only important when displaying out to a television set; you can come much closer to the corners and sides when creating files solely for display on your computer.

Basically, this same approach should work similarly in any other image-editing program, assuming that it can create PNG files with an Alpha Channel. If you're familiar with PhotoShop and other high-end image editors, any 32-bit file with an Alpha Channel for the transparency should work.

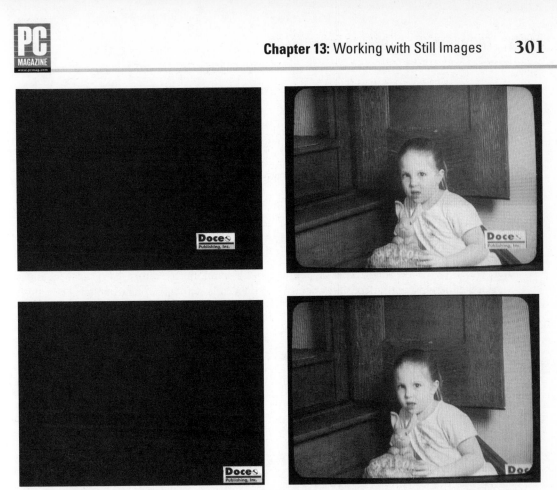

Figure 13-23: The case of the disappearing logo. If you don't mind the safe zone when designing your logo and position it in an absolute corner (on the bottom left), you'll lose part of it when displayed on a television set (bottom right).

Summary

Here is a summary of the key points made in this chapter:

1. When producing slideshows, consumer video editors generally preserve the image's aspect ratio (which is what you want), while most prosumer editors don't unless you find the proper controls.

2. When cropping a digital image for use in a video slideshow, crop your images to a 4:3 aspect ratio for the best on-screen fit, and never change the image's native aspect ratio.

3. Most video editors have separate libraries for images. To create a slideshow, first set slide and transition duration time to match your background music. Then drag the images

down into the storyboard, arrange them, and add transitions if desired. Then convert from storyboard to timeline to add your audio.

4. The "Ken Burns" effect allows you to pan around and zoom into and out of still images. This is generally possible in most prosumer editors, though Pinnacle Edition has the richest interface for accomplishing this. A standalone tool, Canopus Imaginate, offers a very visual and flexible environment for panning and zooming in and around a large image.

5. Not all consumer editors support still-image overlays, though VideoStudio and Pinnacle Studio both do. Techniques are very specific to each product but generally fairly easy once you know what you're doing. Prosumer products like MediaStudio and Edition offer a much more flexible interface with more features, but operation is more complex.

6. If you already have a logo, creating an overlay file in an image editor is fairly easy for most video editors except VideoStudio, which requires a file with an Alpha Channel. The steps are as follows:

   a. Create a 640x480 file in any solid color that contrasts well with your logo.

   b. Paste in your logo, mindful of the safe zones.

   c. Export as a BMP or other file format.

   d. You can key the resulting file with chroma- or color-key controls on your video editor, assuming they're available. If you know how to produce them, 32-bit Targa (TGA) files are almost universally supported.

Chapter 14

Producing Special Effects

Special effects are another tool in your endless quest to provide frequent visual changes to your viewers. There are two general categories of special effects: *curative effects*, which fix problems in your video, and *artistic special effects* that enable almost endless creativity.

Artistic special effects break down into two further classes: two-dimensional (2D) effects, which occur on the flat surface of the video — the width (X) and height (Y) space — and three-dimensional (3D) effects, which occur in the so-called Z space as well. Virtually all consumer programs offer 2D effects and one or two 3D effects, which are generally more fully exploited in prosumer programs.

Entire books have been written about special effects, and it's not my intention to delve deeply into the offerings of the respective products. Rather, I'll start by exploring where to find special effects in your programs and how to apply them. Then I'll explore the most important curative special effect, color correction.

After that, you'll get a quick tour of the artistic effects generally available on consumer programs, and I'll discuss when and how to use them. I'll conclude with a brief look at 2D and 3D effects generally available on prosumer programs, including picture-in-picture effects and video overlay.

The Basics First

Most special effects are more properly called *filters*, which change how the video appears when finally rendered. Like all edits, they are applied non-destructively and don't actually impact the captured footage on disk until you render the final project.

Special effects are usually contained in their own library and applied by dragging them down onto the target clip. In most instances, special effects have customizable parameters that let you set the level of effect. The most notable exception is Microsoft's Movie Maker 2, which has no levels for any special effects. Instead, to double the effect, you simply apply the filter to the clip twice.

Figure 14-1 shows Movie Maker's special effects library, with the effects previewed on the upper right. Notice the Effects control window, which shows the blur filter applied twice. A more common approach is shown in Figure 14-2, which contains two configuration screens for VideoStudio's blur filter. I'll explain why you need two in a minute.

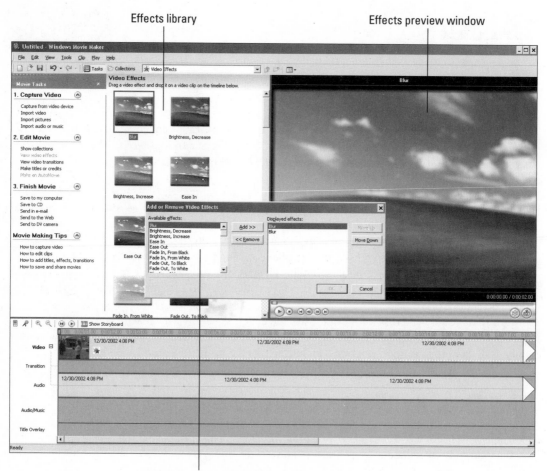

Figure 14-1: The basic special effects setup: the library of special effects, preview screen, and Effects control window.

Rather than dragging multiple filter effects to the timeline, VideoStudio lets you set a level, which is simpler, faster, and easier to control. In addition, note the little diamonds under the small preview screen on the left. These are key frames, or those points in the video where you define a precise setting for the effect being applied.

In the top filter setting in Figure 14-2, the slider bar under the video on the left is set to the first frame, and though you can't see it, the diamond is bright red, indicating that it's active and the settings can be edited. In this position, you set the level for the initial key frame, choosing 1, the minimum setting. On the bottom, with the slider set all the way to the right, you can set the level for the final key frame, choosing 5, the maximum setting.

Key frame (first)

Key frame (last)

Figure 14-2: VideoStudio provides levels for most filters and allows you to set key frames, which makes their special effects much more usable.

During rendering, VideoStudio implements your configuration choices, starting at a relatively low setting and increasing the blur level as it moves through the video. VideoStudio allows the user to set multiple key frames, providing a great level of customization unusual for consumer programs.

Unlike transitions, which can only be applied one at a time, you can apply multiple filters to a clip simultaneously. Most programs provide one window, which lists all the applied effects so you can delete or reconfigure them. This, of course, is Movie Maker's Effects control window shown in Figure 14-1 and VideoStudio's Filter panel as shown in Figure 14-3.

Pinnacle Studio offers few special effects but conveniently houses them in one screen, so it's easy to ascertain their respective status. Like Movie Maker, Studio provides no key frame control over filters. As you'll see, key frames are a standard feature on virtually all prosumer video editors.

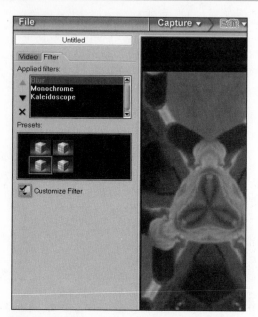

Figure 14-3: Keeping track of applied filters is easy in VideoStudio's Filter panel.

The Many Shades of Color Correction

Color correction is kind of like anti-virus software. You really don't think about it until you have some footage that's unusable without correction.

Last December, I got my hands on a hot new Panasonic three-CCD camera and took it to Zoo Atlanta with my kiddies and their former nanny. The camera was stunning, the weather glorious, and the kiddies and animals in extraordinarily good form.

There was only one problem. I forgot to white balance the camera after my previous use under fluorescent lights, and the camera wasn't in automatic mode. So the video was all tinted blue, and that made me feel mighty blue (I feel a song coming on, but I'll spare you) since I needed the video as sample footage for a book I was writing at the time.

Needless to say, in my next few high-end video editor reviews, I had a driving interest and some great test footage for each editor's color-correction capabilities. Since every shooter at one time or another ends up with video that's poorly color-balanced, too bright or too dark, it's a great area to explore. As you'll see, it's also one of several areas where the capabilities of prosumer video editors simply outstrip the consumer products.

Consumer Color-Correction Tools

To effectively correct poor color balancing in your video, configurability is absolutely essential. Since Movie Maker offers only the bluntest of configuration options, it's not particularly useful for this task.

In contrast, Pinnacle Studio's all-in-one-box approach works surprisingly well for color correction because four very relevant controls — hue, saturation, brightness, and contrast — are all available in one place (see Figure 14-4). Compare this with VideoStudio (see Figure 14-5), which offers color adjustment in one filter and brightness and contrast controls in another, forcing you to switch back and forth between them to fine-tune your adjustment.

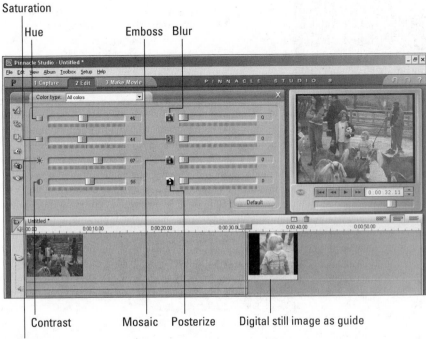

Figure 14-4: Pinnacle Studio provides all necessary controls in one window, simplifying color correction.

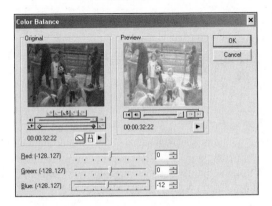

Figure 14-5: VideoStudio spreads the same controls over two or three filters (color correction, which they call Color Balance, is shown here), which complicates color correction.

In terms of technique, whenever you're correcting color or brightness, it helps to have a sample to guide your efforts. Fortunately, I also brought a digital camera to Zoo Atlanta, so I used the still image shown on the right of the Studio timeline as a guide (see Figure 14-4).

If you don't have an image available, sometimes it helps to retrieve an article of clothing worn during the shoot and use that as a guide. Otherwise, use images in the video with known color values, like jeans that look like blue jeans, or a sweatshirt that looks white. For example, when color correcting the Zoo Atlanta video, it helped that I knew that my daughter's hair was blonde and her sweater blue.

Beyond this, at least with consumer tools, color correction is more art than science. If one color is clearly too dominant and the editor provides color-specific tools (like VideoStudio), you might start by reducing that color. For my blue, blue Zoo Atlanta shots, I started by reducing the blue component. Beyond this, it's trial and error.

Be sure not to make a final decision based upon one frame. All video editors let you scan through the entire file before finalizing your settings, so you can check multiple frames before finalizing your values.

If you have multiple clips to color correct, be sure to jot down the final values you applied. That way, you can easily apply the same parameters to multiple clips. Prosumer tools generally offer the ability to "paste attributes," so you can easily copy and paste the filter settings from one clip to another, but consumer editors typically don't (see Figure 14-7 in the next section).

Prosumer Tools

Contrast the preceding consumer tools with those from Sonic Foundry's Vegas in Figure 14-6. Rather than simple color sliders, Vegas provides a color wheel for low, high, and mid-tone color correction with saturation, gain (brightness), and gamma controls available on the same screen. The kicker is the split display window, showing "before" and "after" in the same window, which you can display on-screen and/or on an external television set. This toolset accelerates adjustment time and increases accuracy.

Once you've finalized your values, Vegas' Paste Event Attributes function allows you to paste color correction and other filter settings (an *event* is a filter in Vegas-speak), speeding up multiple track color correction (see Figure 14-7).

The most promising color-correction-related news from 2003 are tools that attempt to automatically color balance your video, like Pinnacle Edition's Auto-Color Correct filter shown in Figure 14-8.

Briefly, you use the eyedropper shown in the color-spectrum table to select a white section of the video, essentially white balancing after the fact. This provides a great starting point for further customization efforts; using the Color Shift slider and Contrast Gamma helped seal the deal for me, producing the most realistic color correction I've seen to date.

This semi-automatic solution is both simpler and more effective than any of the methods currently used by consumer programs today. Whether it's from Pinnacle or another vendor, expect these types of solutions to show up on consumer programs by early 2004.

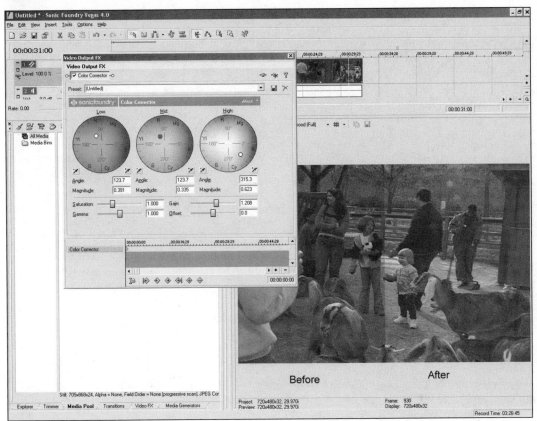

Figure 14-6: The outstanding selection and preview tools offered by Sonic Foundry's Vegas, especially the split screen preview window on the right.

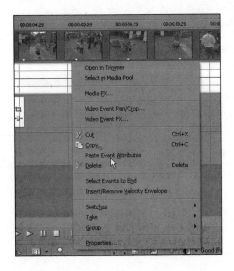

Figure 14-7: Most prosumer programs have a Paste Attributes function that lets you copy special effects and other settings and paste them onto others, kind of like the Format Painter in Microsoft Word.

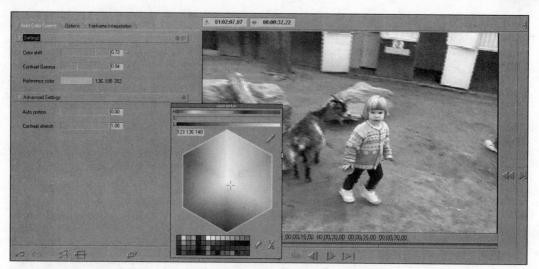

Figure 14-8: Pinnacle Edition's Auto-Color Correct filter Grab the little eyedropper, touch an area of the video that's supposed to be white, and it automatically white balances. Then you can finalize the settings with the other controls.

Consumer Special Effects

Though the specific collection varies from program to program, most consumer editors offer several different categories of effects, which generally include the following:

- **Speed-related effects.** These effects give you the ability to speed up or slow down your video. Note that while video quality can be quite good, adjusting playback speed typically renders your sound file useless. Some editors, like Pinnacle Studio, simply mute the sound file when you adjust speed; others (like VideoStudio) don't, so you'll have to mute or delete the audio file manually.

- **Color-related effects.** These effects convert your video to black and white or sepia. Some products, like Movie Maker 2, also use special effects to fade to and from black or white, rather than transition effects (Pinnacle Studio) or other dedicated controls (VideoStudio).

- **Faux film-related effects.** Used in combination with the black-and-white filter, these effects produce an interesting old-film look that's useful in a variety of situations. Two good examples are Movie Maker 2's Film Age or Film Grain, and VideoStudio's Old Film effect.

- **All the rest.** For example, VideoStudio offers 35 filters, including filters that add lighting and bubbles to your video (see Figure 14-9), that make your videos look like oil paintings or charcoal drawings, or that turn your video into a kaleidoscope.

In my personal productions, I've used effects in the first three classes, but I generally shy away from the more aggressive effects in the fourth category — but it's strictly a matter of taste. Remember, however, that from a compression perspective, most special effects add motion that makes it more difficult for codecs to produce high-quality results. While OK for DVD or CD-ROM-based productions, be careful when producing streaming video.

Figure 14-9: Bubbles, anyone? I'm all for special effects that have even a hint of association with the content of the video (that whole motivated thing).

Prosumer Effects

As you would expect, the effects offered by prosumer products are both more extensive and more configurable than consumer products. One effect that's widely available on prosumer tools is a panning or motion effect that allows you to pan across, into, or around an image or video.

Motion Effects

One great example is the Vegas motion control shown in Figure 14-10. On the left is the Pan/Crop control, with the video frame in the background and a square in a wheel that represents the viewport, or what's actually being shown in the video. Like most prosumer effects, this control is fully key-frameable, providing frame-by-frame control over height, width, and rotation angle of any given frame.

As you saw with Imaginate's image pan in the last chapter, you move through the video, creating a key frame, adjusting parameters, and then moving to the next key frame. As with most tools, Vegas allows you to set the parameters manually, by dragging the controls around, or with precision, using the size and positioning values on the left of Figure 14-10.

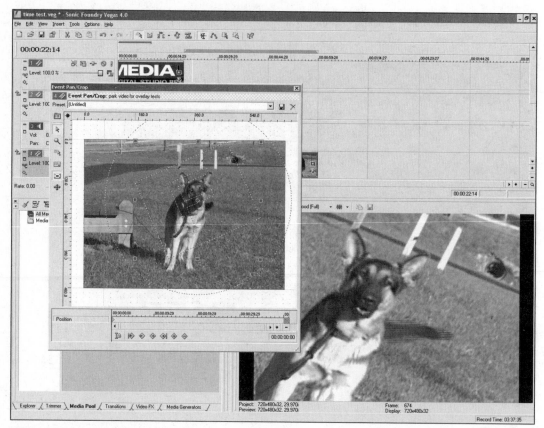

Figure 14-10: Vegas' lovely visual pan and crop control zooms in on Clifford, the Big Black Dog. You can drag the viewport manually, or use the numeric controls on the left.

Note that unlike consumer editors, prosumer tools treat motion or panning as a separate effect that can be applied to any form of content, whether title, still image, or video. This is slightly more complicated than the dedicated tools consumer editors use to add motion to titles, but overall it's simpler because motion controls are identical irrespective of the type of content. Motion tools are generally also much more robust on prosumer tools, with key frames providing almost unlimited flexibility.

For example, Figure 14-11 shows the motion controls for Pinnacle Edition, which apply equally to all clips. One interface directs position, size, rotation, transparency, border curve, shadow, and cropping, with full key-frame support. This unified approach works extremely well for a range of 2D and 3D effects. As you'll see a little later in this chapter, it also works well with picture-in-picture effects, both 2D and 3D.

Figure 14-11: You can apply Pinnacle Edition's motion controls to any media inserted into the project, with many highly configurable options.

Video Overlay (Keying)

Video overlay is a "don't try this at home" operation, not because the software controls are difficult to learn and use, but because shooting video that can be accurately "keyed" over other clips is extremely complicated. The theory is simple enough: Shoot video against a bright blue or green background, capture the video to disk, and then tell your video editor to eliminate that color and overlay everything else in the frame over the background video or still image.

The problem is that keying only works well when the color to be removed is very consistent. For example, in Chapter 13 I pasted a logo over a blue background to overlay the bit image over our video. Since the blue background was digitally created, every pixel in the background was the same exact color, making it easy to eliminate via keying.

In contrast, no real-world scenario can create similarly ideal conditions. Professional studios use special paints and uniform, shadow-free lighting to get as close as possible to a consistent color, but the actual colors in the background end up being a range, rather than one color. As you'll see shortly, video-overlay tools handle this by choosing one color and then allowing the user to expand the range of similar colors to eliminate via keying.

However, if the original video has a background that's not smooth or is unevenly lighted, you'll have to expand the range so far that it begins to encroach on colors in the foreground video, eating into clothing and other objects that aren't supposed to be eliminated. It's not rocket science by any means, but if you think you can hang a blue sheet on a wall and create your own keying, you'll definitely be disappointed.

Working within Ulead's MediaStudio, here are the steps for keying one video file over another:

1. Start by inserting the background video or image into the timeline, and then inserting the video to be overlayed *above* the background track. With MediaStudio, this actually means placing it beneath the background track, but if you follow the track labeling, you'll see that

the blue-screen video I'm using is on V1 (Video track 1) while the background is track Vb (see Figure 14-12).

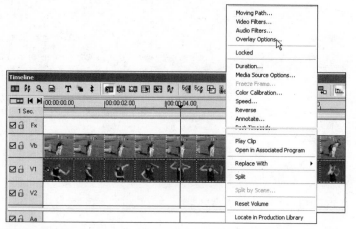

Figure 14-12: Overlaying video with Ulead MediaStudio Pro. Note that MediaStudio works from the top down, so the track with the blue screen is below the background track. Most editors work the other way, with the background on the bottom.

2. Open the overlay editor, usually via a right-mouse click command (see Figure 14-12).

3. Once the Overlay Options are exposed, define the type of keying you'll be using. Chroma key and Alpha Channel are almost always available. Since I shot against a blue-screen background, I'll use the blue screen.

4. Using an eyedropper or similar control, identify the background color by selecting the tool and clicking on the background (though some programs like Edition can identify the background color automatically).

5. Increase the range of colors eliminated with the Similarity control.

6. After eliminating the background, soften the edge between the background and foreground video with the Soft edge control. With some programs, this smoothes the transition between the background and foreground object; with others, it creates an unacceptable halo around the object. Experiment with your program and see what works best for you.

7. Finally, preview your keying efforts using the supplied options to ensure that settings are optimal (see Figure 14-13). Many tools also let you zoom into the image to further evaluate your results; rather than pursuing this route, MediaStudio lets you preview the result to the larger general preview window or an analog monitor.

When you're done, click OK, and the operation is complete. Once again, this sounds complex, but it's really a matter of dragging the video to the right track and experimenting with the controls to see what works best. Most editors offer a greater range of controls than MediaStudio, usually with very different names. The two most critical controls are always similarity and edge smoothness; find those or their analogues, and you can make it work.

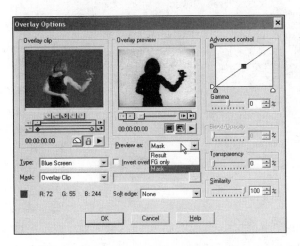

Figure 14-13: Previewing your keying efforts. Also note the Soft edge control, which is very common, and the Similarity control, which increases the range of colors eliminated during overlay.

3D Prosumer Effects

Let's take a quick look at the type of 3D effects offered by prosumer programs. Figure 14-13 shows the picture-in-picture controls (P-i-P) offered in Pinnacle Edition. Though P-i-P is generally a 2D effect, Edition makes it 3D by allowing you to manipulate the pictures in three dimensions, with effects like the tilting forward and sideways, and the background shadows seen in Figure 14-14.

You produce P-i-P effects much like overlay effects; you start by laying down the background track — in this case, a still-image picture of the gym — and then you insert track after track on top of the background. Rather than keying out the background, you use the size and position controls to the left of the preview screen to make the upper four tracks smaller and spread them around. The exposed shear controls in Figure 14-14 are those that provide the 3D appearance; otherwise the controls are virtually identical to the 3D controls shown in Figure 14-11.

Edition enables key-frame manipulation of all effects, so I could move, spin, or rotate these frames around, or make them slowly disappear and reappear a la Patrick Swayze in *Ghost*. I settled for the simple geometric pattern shown.

Other than P-i-P effects, most 3D effects fall in the category of "page curls" and similar effects, as shown in Figure 14-15. Rather than simply fading the logo off the screen, I'm using a page curl to remove it. What's great about Edition and most prosumer editors is that like 2D effects, these 3D effects can be used on any type of visual content, whether title, graphic, or video.

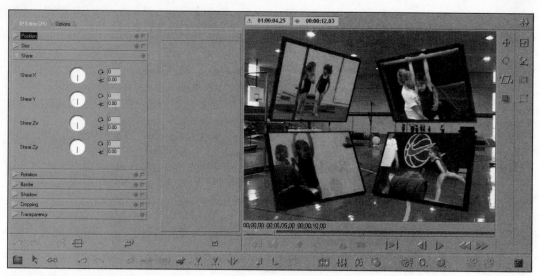

Figure 14-14: Pinnacle Edition's 3D picture-in-picture effects.

Figure 14-15: Edition's other 3D effects include page curls, but there's not much else.

Summary

Here's a summary of the key points in this chapter:

1. Special effects are another tool in your efforts to make your videos more dynamic.

2. Most video editors have folders for special effects, which you apply by dragging them from the library to the target clip. Most offer some degree of customization, but VideoStudio is the only consumer editor that offers key-frame control.

3. Color correction is an invaluable tool for correcting video that's off color or too dark or bright. Prosumer tools definitely offer more configuration options and better preview, which generally translates to better results. Whichever tool you use, it definitely helps to use some digital image or sample clothing to help correct the video color.

4. Video overlay is a standard feature on prosumer tools. Generally, all tools work fairly well; the difficult part is ensuring that the video is shot properly in the first place.

Chapter 15

Automatic Movie Generation

Not all video that you shoot can or should be edited into a cohesive, polished video. Perhaps you film your child ice skating on a frosty, wintry day. Lazily she skates up and down the ice, falling once or twice, but otherwise having a grand time. Maybe it's soccer or a Little League game, or maybe just some footage of your kids dancing at a wedding.

Worth saving and showing again? Most definitely. The problem is there is no plot; no beginning, middle, and end; no real story to tell. So how do you create a video worth watching?

Well, the best way is to let your computer do the heavy lifting for you. Specifically, there are several programs that can take your raw footage, isolate the most interesting scenes, and patch them together to meet the beat and duration of any background song you select. Basically, they turn your raw footage into a music video.

It might sound a bit far-fetched, but it actually works quite well. Here you'll get a look at three programs' approaches to the problem—two that you can try for free and one better solution that wasn't quite available when I completed the CD-ROM at the back of this book. (However, this chapter still gives you a sneak peak at this one, muvee's MegaProducer, which may now be available for trial download.) In this chapter, you'll learn how to use all three programs and understand some of their key strengths and weaknesses.

On the CD-ROM

The CD-ROM includes a demo copy of muvee's autoProducer, while you can download Microsoft's Movie Maker 2 for free.

Movie Generation Workflow

The workflow for all three products is similar. You choose one or more video segments, say 10 or 15 minutes long, then a background music track or tracks that are typically shorter in duration.

In the example I'll use in this chapter, the two dancing sequences I wanted to condense were about 6 minutes and 30 seconds long. My background music track was 3 minutes and 2 seconds long. So, I wanted each program to find the best 3 minutes and 2 seconds of video, cut them up into bite-sized pieces, add appropriate transitions and special effects, and produce the music video.

All three programs discussed in this chapter can capture video directly. However, what typically happens with these types of productions is that when you're finished, you watch it and say, "Wow, there was Uncle Billy asleep at his table. Sure wish we could cut that out." Alternatively, you watch the video and say, "Where was that cute scene where little Marjorie was dancing with grandma? Why isn't that in there?"

The best solution is found in muvee's megaProducer, which lets you exclude unwanted frames and designate desired frames. This makes it easy to capture within megaProducer, choose the frames to include and exclude, and move through the production steps.

With both Movie Maker 2 and muvee autoProducer, there's no way to designate frames to include or exclude. For this reason, you'll get the best results if you exclude unwanted frames before starting the process. You can do this directly in Movie Maker 2, of course, but you'll need a third-party editor to do the same within autoProducer. Essentially, this means don't use autoProducer's capture capabilities unless there are no scenes that you positively want to exclude.

Unfortunately, neither autoProducer nor Movie Maker 2 lets you designate frames to definitely include in the production. The best approach here is to trim as much unwanted video as possible before submitting the video into the automated process, which at least improves your chances.

Stylin'

As you'll see, once you import your videos and background audio files, you select a style, which dictates the pace of change, the range of effects applied, and several other factors. Then you'll select how to prioritize audio levels between the background music track and the audio captured with the original video.

In most instances, the best decision is simply to mute the video shot with the original video. That's because during production, all three programs are going to cut your video into very small segments, perhaps change their order, and often slow them down or speed them up.

If your original video includes music, as mine did, all the flow will be lost, and it will sound choppy and downright weird if the order changes and it's sped up or slowed down. Ditto for the spoken voice, where you might chop the wedding toast into four different components placed non-sequentially throughout the production, sometimes sped up, sometimes slowed down.

I can see leaving in the original audio in sporting events, like a hockey or soccer game, when the shouts and grunts add valuable context and won't get distorted if chopped up, but then only if you're using a style that doesn't change video speed. Otherwise, if there's lots of speech or music in the original video, you're probably better off muting the original audio.

Once you choose the style and audio prioritization, you press the proverbial button and the program analyzes your audio and video and produces the music video. Typically this takes a few minutes the first time around, but all three programs retain their analyses, so experimenting with different styles thereafter is nearly instantaneous.

Output

In terms of output, Movie Maker 2 produces the video and puts it on the timeline where you can tinker at will. While you could exclude undesired clips at this point, you'll obviously have to compensate and replace these scenes with other footage, which is why it's better to exclude them up front. If Movie Maker 2 is your primary editor, you can add other segments and produce as desired. Otherwise, you can output your video into DV or other format for importing into another editor.

Similarly, both muvee programs can produce a DV file you import into other video editors. Or, in the autoProducer product, you can output into a variety of other formats for otherwise distributing your video. Some versions of muvee can even write to a DVD, though authoring capabilities are limited.

You may recall that Chapter 12 concluded with a look at how to create you own music video. Working with the same basic footage (my daughters and some friends dancing at a wedding), let's see how these programs automate the same task. Let's start with a look at Movie Maker 2.

Microsoft's Movie Maker 2 — AutoMovie

Microsoft's AutoMovie features are less flexible than muvee, but it's free and provides a great introduction to the capabilities. I've already captured and imported the video footage. Note that AutoMovie is supposed to work with video in either the collections pane (library) or contents pane (timeline/storyboard). However, in my experience, it only works with videos in the collections pane.

For example, when I excluded segments on the timeline and then created an AutoMovie, Movie Maker 2 still used the videos in the collections pane (which included segments that I wanted to exclude) as the source of the AutoMovie. If I changed the collections pane from video to special effects or transitions, Movie Maker 2 grayed out the AutoMovie function.

Accordingly, it appears that the only way to exclude segments in Movie Maker 2 is to edit out the undesired segments, render the video, and then re-import it back into Movie Maker 2 as a separate collection. Once you've got your target scenes isolated in the collections pane, here's how to proceed (see Figures 15-1 through 15-3):

1. Select the videos in the collections pane to include in the project (see Figure 15-1).

Figure 15-1: Selecting videos in Movie Maker 2's collection pane.

2. In the Tools menu, select Make an AutoMovie.
3. Select a style from the five choices (see Figure 15-2). I'm choosing Music Video, though this turns out to be a fairly tame option, with simple cuts between clips and no special effects. Most other options are more aggressive.

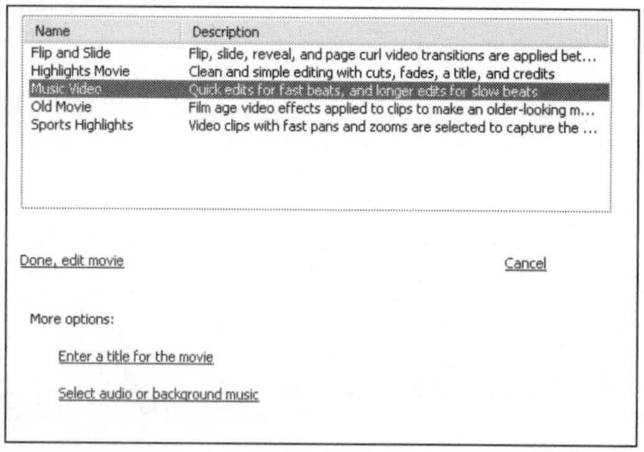

Name
Description
Flip and Slide
Flip, slide, reveal, and page curl video transitions are applied bet...
Highlights Movie
Clean and simple editing with cuts, fades, a title, and credits
Music Video
Quick edits for fast beats, and longer edits for slow beats
Old Movie
Film age video effects applied to clips to make an older-looking m...
Sports Highlights
Video clips with fast pans and zooms are selected to capture the ...
Done, edit movie
Cancel
More options:
Enter a title for the movie
Select audio or background music

Figure 15-2: Selecting a style from the available options. Note the controls on the bottom left for entering a title and adding an audio track.

4. Add a background audio track and choose how to prioritize your background and foreground audio. As previously discussed, I'm prioritizing the inserted audio at 100 percent.
5. Type text for the title. Note that you can't change the font or any other characteristics here, but you can later using normal program controls.
6. Click Done (as shown in Figure 15-3), and Movie Maker starts analyzing. As you can see from Figure 15-3, Movie Maker 2 carved up my 6:30 of video into over 40 separate clips ranging from three to eight seconds, with most under four seconds.

Show Storyboard
Video
latin beat
latin beat
Audio/Music
Title Overlay
Ready

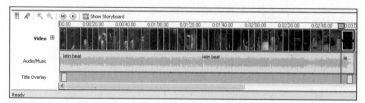

Figure 15-3: Viewing how Movie Maker 2 cuts your videos up for you.

Microsoft is pretty closemouthed about the technology underlying AutoMovie, but if you scan through the movie, you'll notice that Movie Maker 2 tends to emphasize the head and face shots and eliminate the rest. This works well for me; I get a highlight reel of pictures of my little girls that's short, sweet, and synchronized to the background music. The entire process, net of capture time, was about three or four minutes.

muvee autoProducer

Now let's have a look at muvee autoProducer. Figure 15-2 documents the steps in the production process.

On the CD-ROM

You can sing along by running the trial version of muvee autoProducer on the CD-ROM and grabbing a few audio and video files.

Here's how you create a movie with autoProducer:

1. Welcome to autoProducer (see Figure 15-4). The program nicely directs workflow with buttons that you access sequentially from top to bottom.

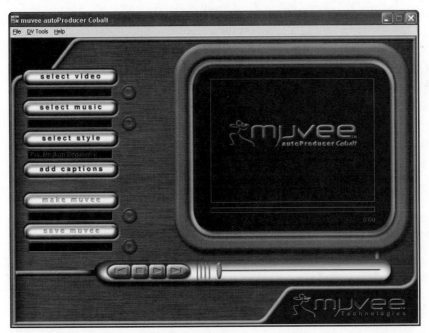

Figure 15-4: Creating a movie in muvee autoProducer. Note the controls on the left for selecting video, music, styles, and captions.

2. Click Select video to choose your video file(s). Once again, this is where I choose my audio allocation, and I elect to go 100 percent with the inserted music file.

3. Click Select video to choose your audio file(s).

4. Click Select style to select a style. Where Movie Maker 2 has five styles, autoProducer has 24. I'll go with the Simple Music Video.

5. Click Add captions to add captions. Note that I can either change fonts or leave the decision to autoProducer.

6. Click Make movie to move to the final production step (see Figure 15-5). Here I can lengthen the movie, which autoProducer will achieve by running the background audio track more than once. I can also elect to allow video segments to be repeated. If you allow repeats, you're increasing the odds that desired segments might not appear, so I'm choosing not to repeat.

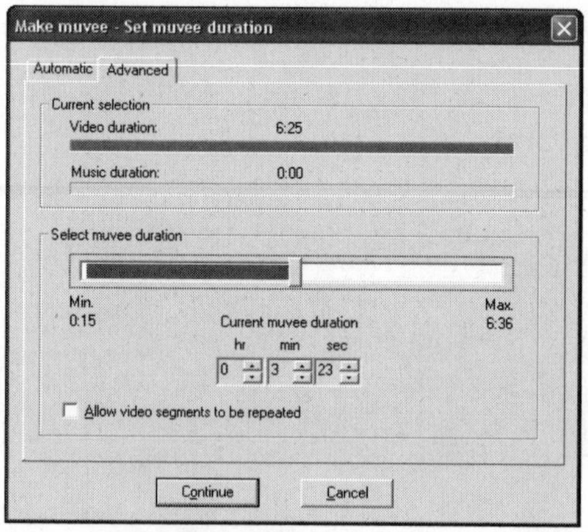

Figure 15-5: Setting duration, the final production step.

7. Click Continue, and autoProducer starts making the movie.

According to muvee, their technology first analyzes the video content in terms of color, texture, motion, and other characteristics. Then, the program analyzes the audio for tempo and rhythm. Finally, the program takes into account the selected style and builds the movie.

muvee megaProducer

Now let's look at the Cadillac of automatic movie creation, muvee megaProducer. The following figures document the steps in the production process.

1. megaProducer directs workflow via menu tabs, rather than buttons (see Figure 15-6). In the first tab, you choose visual assets, either video files (top button on the right of the inserted videos), still images (middle button), or by capturing the video directly (bottom button). On the right are muvee's new tools for including and excluding segments. Basically, you use the highlight tool to identify sections in the video, and then the Include and Exclude controls to retain or eliminate sections from the final production. These will save a lot of trimming time over the manual trimming methods necessary with Movie Maker 2 and the older muvee products.

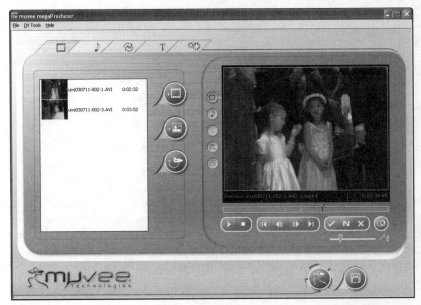

Figure 15-6: The ability to force the program to include some segments and exclude others is a key feature in megaProducer.

2. Next you choose your audio file or files.

3. Here's the real special sauce (see Figure 15-7). Where Movie Maker 2 has five styles and autoProducer has 24, megaProducer has 47, ranging from very sedate (simple Edit cuts) to content-specific (such as Sweet Kids, which is shown in Figure 15-9), to functional, like the Summarizer, that pulls excerpts from the clips and builds a quick highlight reel. Effects range from simple cuts to wild pans, flashes of colors, and other inserted shapes and objects.

4. Insert the desired title, then click the Credits tab and insert the closing credits. Note the ability to change fonts and insert a custom background.

5. Next select the audio balance between the original audio from the video and the background audio inserted into the clip. Note that you can select all sequential shots, or you can shuttle shots out of sequence, another option unavailable in Movie Maker 2.

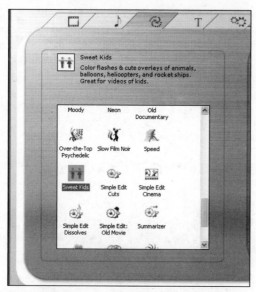

Figure 15-7: Plus you get a whole lot more style choices with more cool effects.

6. Click the running woman icon on the bottom right of Figure 15-6 to access your final options. Once again, you can extend the movie by allowing the music clip to repeat (see Figure 15-8) and choose project duration with the slider bar. If you elect to repeat audio files, you can also choose to have muvee repeat video clips. Click Continue to start the processing. Figure 15-9 shows how you can preview what you've done so far.

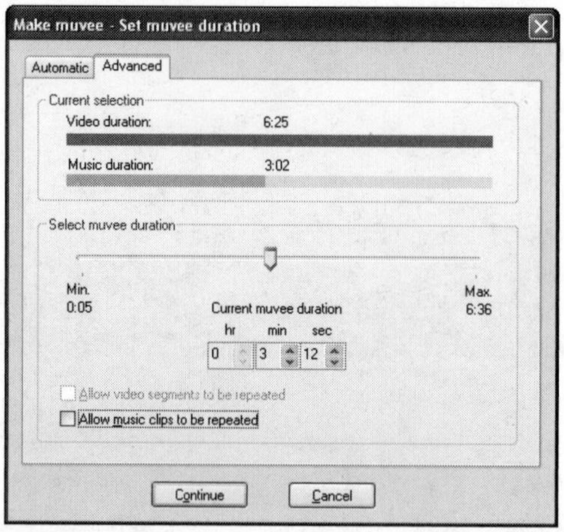

Figure 15-8: Again, choosing the duration of the video.

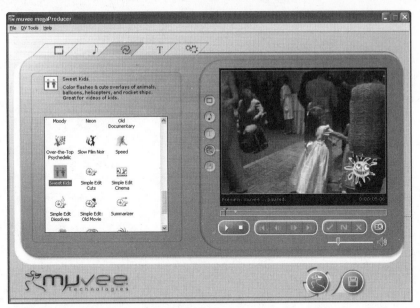

Figure 15-9: Note the fun icon in the lower right. This is one of the special effects inserted by muvee when the Sweet Kids template is selected.

On a Pentium 4 3.2 GHz system, all three products completed their analysis and produced the final file within two minutes. As mentioned earlier, after the initial analysis, all programs store the results, so you can test additional styles almost instantaneously.

Overall, these types of effects are a welcome tool in the arsenal of all consumer videographers, and I expect to see functions like these appearing more frequently in the consumer space.

Summary

Here's a summary of the key points in the chapter:

1. AutoMovie and similar functions work well when the original video doesn't have a clear story line or compelling dialogue.

2. Different products have different workflows. For most, you'll have to exclude unwanted segments before inputting the video files into the process.

3. Most of the time, you'll get the best results by boosting the inserted audio file to 100 percent, which mutes the original audio file.

4. The first time you create an automatic movie in Movie Maker 2 or any muvee product, the program may take a few minutes to analyze your video and audio before creating the final video. To aid your experimentation, all three programs retain their analyses, so additional movies created with different styles will be nearly instantaneous.

Chapter 16

Rendering Your Project

O K, you've cut, pasted, split, and trimmed; you've added titles, transitions, and (tasteful) special effects; and it's time to render your project and share it with the world. This chapter covers rendering your project back to tape and creating digital files for distribution on DVD, CD-ROM, e-mail, and the Internet as well as for playback on your hard drive.

If you're producing DVDs in an integrated product like Pinnacle Studio or Edition, or even VideoStudio, rendering and writing to disk is a one-step process that is covered in Chapter 19. If you're working with a separate DVD-authoring program like Ulead DVD Workshop or Adobe Encore, I'll describe how to render files from your video editor for input into those programs in this chapter as well.

Let's start with a quick refresher course on concepts like resolution, frame rate, and the like, and then jump right into rendering.

Preliminaries

Let's discuss at a high level what happens during rendering and the decisions that you'll be making. During capture and editing, you do your best to retain the highest quality possible. This means capturing and working in DV, MPEG-2, or a similar high-quality format, and then rendering to a distribution format for delivery to your viewers.

Rendering really involves two separate stages. First, the video editor produces all the lovely effects that you selected, creating the frames necessary to produce the transitions between frames, the titles, and overlays. Then, it compresses the video into the selected format.

If you're writing back to tape, whether DV or analog, you have very few decisions to make, in that your editor will know which format to use and how to send the video back to the camera or VHS deck.

If you're distributing on DVD, you also have very few decisions to make, since most programs include DVD presets you can set and forget. Ditto for VideoCD and Super VideoCD, two CD-recordable-based optical formats.

On the other hand, if you're producing for distribution on CD-ROM in non-VideoCD or non-Super VideoCD format, Web streaming, e-mail delivery, or even playback from your own hard drive, you have some pretty big decisions to make. I'll cover them in detail in the following sections, so no worries, but let's isolate and understand the parameters, which are similar to those discussed in Chapter 10:

- First, you'll be choosing a *compression technology*, or *codec*. Codecs you may have heard of include MPEG-1, MPEG-2, Cinepak, RealVideo, Windows Media, and others.

- Then you'll be choosing *output resolution*, or the height and width of the video expressed in pixels. Your starting point for capture and editing is usually DV, which has a resolution of 720x480 pixels. However, to make the video more compact, you'll probably want to scale the video to a smaller resolution, say 320x240 for CD-ROM or 240x180 for e-mail or streaming.

- You may also be asked to select *frame rate*, or the number of frames per second (fps) of video saved in the video file. Once again, the starting point for video when stored in DV format is 29.97 frames per second, or more accurately 60 fields per second (each field contains one half of the lines in the frame, the first field the odd lines and the second field the even lines). MPEG-2 is also field-based, but all other codecs are frame-based, so you'll generally be choosing a rate of 30 fps, appropriate for MPEG-1, or less, like 15 fps for streaming video.

- You'll almost always have to select a *video data rate*, or the amount of video data per second stored in the compressed file. This is also called *bit rate* when applied to streaming media. Just for reference, the original data rate of DV video is 3.6MB per second, which is much too large to distribute even on DVD. When streaming over the Internet, data rates get down as low as 20 to 30 kbps, which is why it tends to look so degraded.

- In some instances, you'll be asked to choose an audio format, either compressed, which is usually some variant of MPEG or AC-3 (Dolby Digital) technology, or a streaming format like RealAudio or Microsoft's Windows Media. Alternatively, audio may be uncompressed, usually in some variant of Pulse Code Modulation (PCM format).

- You may also have the ability to set the *audio data rate*. As with video, this is the amount of data stored per second with the audio file.

Regarding these choices, sometimes you'll have them, and sometimes you won't. This is primarily determined by the output medium that you've selected. Table 16-1 illustrates this point.

Table 16-1   Configuration Options by Output Medium

Output Medium	Codec	Constraints on Encoding Parameters
To tape	DV or MPEG-2	Complete. Use defaults.
VideoCD	MPEG-1	Complete. Use defaults.
DVD	MPEG-2	Some. You can select video data rate, audio compression technology, and audio data rate.

Output Medium	Codec	Constraints on Encoding Parameters
Hard disk	Any (MPEG-1/2 recommended)	None. You can adjust full range (but can also use program presets). Must have a special player to play MPEG-2 files.
Non-standard CD-ROM	Any (MPEG-1 recommended)	None. You can adjust full range (but can also use program presets). Disk space (700MB) is a factor.
Web e-mail	Any (streaming formats recommended)	The file produced must not be larger than file attachment rules for your or your target's ISP.
Web — post to Web site	Any (streaming formats recommended)	None. You can adjust full range (but can also use program presets).
Web streaming	Format supported by server	The files should be encoded at the connection speed most used by target video consumers.

If you're writing to tape, most video editors don't even let you see any encoding parameters, because the formats are so constrained. That's certainly the case when writing back to a DV camera. If you're working with an MPEG-2 capture device, you'll need to render to MPEG-2 format using presets supplied by the vendor, generally with few, if any, encoding options.

In addition, when writing to VideoCD, the MPEG-1-based CD-recordable format, the specifications for the included files are so precise that more programs provide no access to any encoding parameters. This situation loosens a bit with DVD, which is not quite so tightly defined, allowing you some additional configuration options.

In contrast, when writing video to play from your hard drive, you can choose any codec available on your system, whether MPEG-1, Windows Media, or RealVideo. In fact, if you use the preset for storing video for playback on your computer provided in Microsoft's Movie Maker 2, you'll be encoding into Windows Media format — no great surprise.

Here, it's important to note that MPEG-2 files offer a great blend of quality and compression, but you'll need a special player that *is not* included on all computers to play the file. If you have a software DVD player, that will probably do, but if you plan to send the file to someone else, you can't assume that they will be able to play it.

If you're delivering video to grandma on a CD-ROM that's *not* a VideoCD, you also have complete flexibility. Again, I recommend MPEG-1 as the best blend of compatibility, file size, and quality. The space available on a CD-ROM (700MB) used to feel like a lot, but if you put average quality MPEG-2 on a CD-ROM, you'll be limited to around 12 to 15 minutes.

When sending a file via e-mail, there are no format restrictions, but most ISPs limit attachment size coming and going. This means you'll need to produce very small files, which generally means a streaming format like RealVideo or Microsoft's Windows Media Technologies.

Similarly, when posting a video file to a Web site for download and playing — or even simple streaming — where there is no server, you can use any format you like. In fact, MPEG-1 was widely used on the Web for this purpose until streaming formats became prevalent, and at this point, they are better choices.

Finally, if you're posting video to a Web site supported by a streaming server, check with the Web master about which formats the server supports. The RealServer has almost universal flexibility of Windows Media, Real, and QuickTime formats, while Microsoft supports primarily Microsoft-related formats.

What's Missing?

Many readers will be surprised that I got this far without mentioning Video for Windows codecs, like Cinepak and Indeo, or any QuickTime codecs. Here's why I don't recommend using these technologies for video file delivery.

In the beginning there was QuickTime, which produced MOV files on the Mac for playback on Macs and Windows-based computers. Then came Video for Windows, which produced AVI files (Audio/Video Interleaved) on Windows, first for playback only on Windows, then for playback on the Mac, as well. What was lovely about QuickTime and Video for Windows was that they supplied architectures for developers to build tools around, from video editors to capture cards to codecs. So long as you could input and output an AVI file, MOV file, or both, you could work with any other product that could do the same, and everything was good.

Of course, those were the days of 80386 and 80486 computers that could barely recalculate a spreadsheet without stalling, much less play a video file. So Video for Windows and QuickTime codecs like Cinepak and Indeo concentrated on producing acceptable quality that didn't require too much processing power to play back.

Back then, MPEG-1 was a strange creature that really didn't fit in. It looked great in trade shows and product demos, but first you needed special hardware to play back MPEG-1 files, which never really worked, and then (gasp) a Pentium 90 computer. So CD-ROM producers kept using Cinepak and Indeo well into the late 1990s and even early 2000.

Today, even the slowest computer can play MPEG-1 files, which look better than Indeo and Cinepak at equivalent data rates, and many can play MPEG-2 as well, though, as mentioned previously, MPEG-2 doesn't enjoy MPEG-1's near universal playback compatibility.

Accordingly, it's time to lay Cinepak and Indeo to rest, because they no longer have any practical use. Use MPEG-1 instead, which delivers better quality in less space. In addition, though the QuickTime Sorenson codec has been used to great acclaim for Hollywood trailers, it competes poorly against RealVideo and Microsoft Windows Media formats in trials at similar data rates, and is very slow to encode.

That said, while Video for Windows and QuickTime have little applicability for video distribution, both architectures still live on as the cornerstone of video development tools on both platforms. I'll use them to compile my high-quality DV-formatted production files and just choose to distribute using another format.

With this as prolog, let's jump into writing back to tape.

Writing to Tape

In most instances, you write back to tape to distribute your video via VHS or some other analog format, or as a convenient way to store the production video. If you're editing in DV, for example, you can write the video back to the DV camera and then dub it over to a VHS deck to send to your low-tech relatives without DVD players. Of course, if you have a capture device that has analog input/output, like some of those discussed in Chapter 2, you can skip the DV camera and write directly back to the original analog camera or deck.

There is another option. Since a 60-minute DV tape that costs under $10 can store over 12GB of data, it's a convenient medium for storing your video, even if you are actually distributing it via DVD or other mechanism, just to clear hard disk space for your next project.

Note

You can send DV video back and forth between hard disk and camera without degrading quality, since you're simply copying and recopying a digital file.

On the other hand, quality definitely degrades if you store your analog video on analog tape, since you'll perform a digital-to-analog conversion when writing to tape, then an analog-to-digital conversion, and additional compression, when recapturing from the camera. DV tapes are an effective way to archive DV video, but unfortunately, analog tapes are not.

Writing to tape involves three steps. First you set up your hardware, then you render your video, then you write to tape. Let's have a closer look at all three steps.

Hardware Setup

Connecting your camera for writing back to tape is pretty much the same as connecting for capture, so look back in Chapter 10 for the details. If you're working with a DV camera on Windows XP, the operating system will let you know when the camera is connected, usually with a bell and a dialog box saying, in effect, "Hey, there's a camera connected, what do you want to do?"

On the other hand, if you're writing to an analog camera, you're pretty much flying blind since there's no feedback loop between the operating system and the camera. The only way you'll know it's working is if you see video in the camera LCD or on the attached analog device. That's why it's important to have a setup like that shown in Figure 16-1, with a TV or analog monitor attached to your camcorder — and essential if you're writing to VHS or some other type of analog deck.

If you're writing to a DV camera, make sure that it's in VCR or Play mode, and don't worry about needing to turn recording on and off; the computer software will almost always handle that. Just make sure you've got plenty of tape and that it's not write-protected.

Analog cameras and decks are all different. For example, with my old Hi8 camera, I would have to manually set the analog connectors to "Input," set the camera in VTR mode, and press Record before the video started coming. Figure this out beforehand, make sure you've got plenty of open and unprotected tape, and get ready to roll.

Rendering and Writing Your Video

Rendering and writing to tape are two stages, but most consumer programs lump them into one. That is, you select Record to tape, or some similar command, and the program checks to make sure the camera is connected, then renders the complete project and starts writing the finished video to tape.

For example, with Movie Maker 2 (refer to Figure 16-2), you click Send to DV camera, and follow the instructions, first to cue the tape, then to start the rendering process. Then, Movie Maker chugs along and automatically starts writing to the DV camera when complete. It's generally this simple for all video-editing programs; once you find the right control, you simply follow the prompts. You may have to click OK to start writing to disk (so you can't walk away), but it's a very simple process.

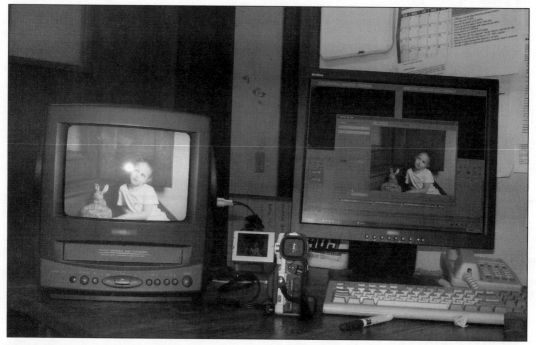

Figure 16-1: Here's my five-year-old looking like a teenager. The TV attached to the DV camera is a practical necessity for writing back to analog cameras and decks.

Tip

When rendering to print to tape, the video editor creates temporary files for each effect that you've used in the project, which is why you should expect to hear your disk whirring around like crazy. Most programs don't delete these temporary files after writing to disk, and they can quickly consume tons of disk space. For this reason, be sure to set the location for these files within the program so you can delete them later.

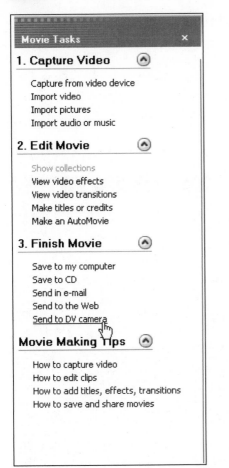

Figure 16-2: Writing back to tape in Movie Maker 2 is fairly simple.

Producing MPEG Files for DVD

When producing files for DVD, you have two main concerns. First, any file you create must be compatible with your chosen authoring program. Second, once you input the file into the authoring program, that program shouldn't recompress the file, taking additional rendering time and degrading image quality. I cover this topic extensively in Chapter 17.

Bottom line is that before encoding for DVD production, be sure to identify the file parameters required by the authoring program, which is usually provided in the help files. If you're not sure you can prevent the authoring program from recompressing, then output a DV Formatted AVI file, using the procedures described in the following sections, and input the DV file into the authoring program.

Producing DVD Compatible MPEG-2 Files

Once you've checked the specs, and made sure you won't double compress, it's time to produce the MPEG-2 file. Understand that all optical formats, including DVD, have very strict file-compatibility requirements, which are necessary so they can play on $80 consumer DVD players. The key rule here is no freelancing; use DVD presets whenever possible.

Fortunately, all software vendors make this pretty simple. As you can see in Figure 16-3, showing Ulead's VideoStudio, you select Share → Create Video File → NTSC DVD, then name your file, and you're done.

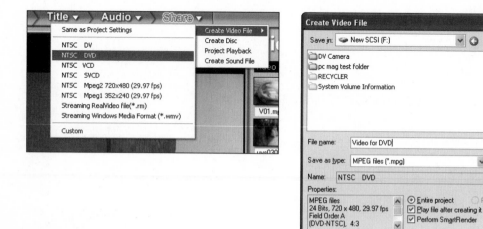

Figure 16-3: Creating a DVD-compatible file in Ulead VideoStudio.

Encoding in Adobe Premiere Pro

That was way too easy, so let's take a look at the encoding controls from Adobe Premiere Pro. You get there by selecting File → Export → Adobe Media Encoder (see Figure 16-4). Note that Premiere can now export directly to DVD, which basically creates the MPEG-2 file and burns the disk without menus. This is convenient for sending content to a reviewer or customer, but insufficient for true authoring.

Once you're in the Adobe Media Encoder, you must select a DVD-compatible MPEG-2 file. From this point on, Premiere's in charge of only showing you valid DVD-encoding parameters, so you can freelance a bit, but I still recommend staying within a fairly narrow range of parameters.

Premiere offers a range of DVD presets for both NSTC (United States) and PAL (Europe); let's briefly discuss some of the adjustable parameters. CBR stands for constant bitrate encoding, which encodes all scenes, complex and simple, to the same data rate. In contrast, VBR stands for variable bitrate encoding, which is a technique that intelligently spreads the encoded data rate around the video, allocating more bits to hard-to-compress regions and less bits to easier-to-encode sections, all the while ensuring that the stream in total complies with DVD requirements.

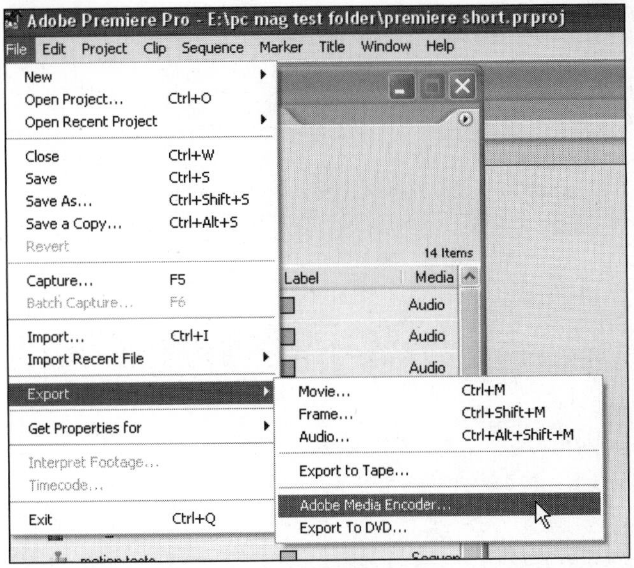

Figure 16-4: Producing DVD-compatible MPEG-2 files in Premiere Pro. Note the Export to DVD selection, which burns a simple menu-less disk.

Two Pass VBR technologies scan the entire project first to identify the easy- and hard-to-compress sequences and then encode. This takes longer than single-pass (or 1 pass) VBR but produces the best possible overall quality. Use 2 Pass VBR where available unless encoding speed is absolutely paramount.

Finally, the SurCode for Dolby Digital 5.1 is the third-party technology Adobe licensed to provide Dolby Digital encoding from within Premiere. Basically, you get three trial encodes, then you have to purchase the third-party software for $295. Note that Ulead's DVD Workshop and Adobe Encore offer AC-3 encoding, so unless you're producing in another authoring program or absolutely need surround-sound capabilities, you probably don't need the third-party software.

Figure 16-5 shows the video-encoding parameters. If you were rolling your own preset or starting from scratch, this is where you would select niceties like VBR, CBR, and the number of passes. The first six lines, through Field Order, should all automatically carry over from your video-editing project, so don't adjust these at all.

Then you select your bitrate-encoding method (VBR or CBR), and choose one or two passes if VBR. As the name suggests, the target bit rate is the average rate you want the encoder to produce. When using VBR techniques, you also tell the encoder the maximum (highest bit rate in the stream) and minimum values allowed.

In general, unless you're producing for a known number of very current DVD players, it's probably safest not to exceed an average of 7 to 8 mbps, which should produce very good quality and play on most DVD players, even older ones. If you stray beyond 9MB, quality goes up slightly, but you risk being incompatible with an increasing number of DVD players.

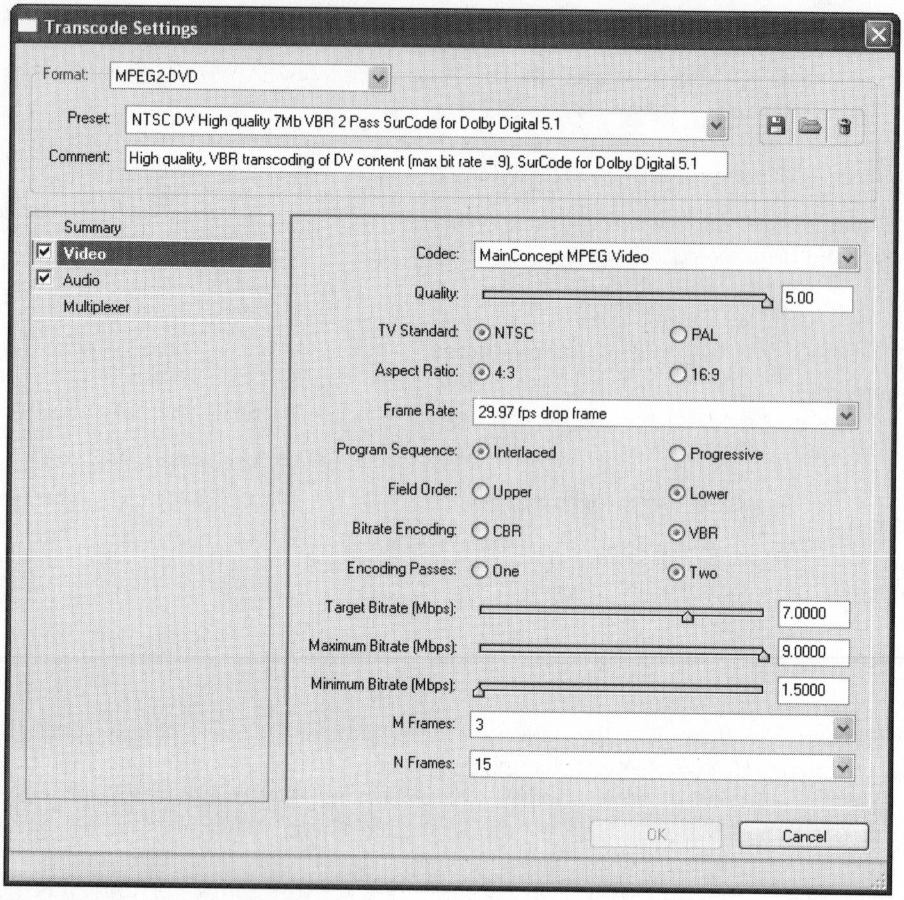

Figure 16-5: Video-encoding parameters.

M and N frames are parameters best left to compression pros (also known as compressionists). Definitely stick with the presets here; what you don't know *can* hurt you when it comes to DVD encoding.

Moving right along to the audio parameters controls dialog box (not shown), you have three choices: AC-3 and MPEG, both compressed formats, and PCM, which is an uncompressed format. As discussed in Chapter 3, as far as the two compressed formats go, AC-3 is compatible on *all* DVD players sold in the United States, while MPEG is only compatible on *most* players.

If you have to compress to get all the audio and video on disk, use AC-3, if available, for business and other disks that absolutely, positively have to play on your target. The risks of MPEG audio not playing are slight, but they're real. On the other hand, if disk space isn't an issue, PCM provides universal compatibility and, since it's uncompressed, slightly higher quality.

And finally there's one last encoding option, the Multiplexing Type. Briefly, a multiplexed file, also known as a program stream, contains audio and video interleaved together. In contrast, without multiplexing, the program outputs what are called elementary streams of separate audio and video.

The only reason to output elementary streams is if your authoring program requires it; otherwise, a multiplexed (or muxed) program stream produces one less file to worry about.

So to summarize the findings regarding encoding for DVD:

- Check the requirements of your DVD-authoring program before you start encoding to make sure the files you produce are compatible.

- If you're not sure that you can avoid double compression, output an AVI file in DV format as shown the following section.

- Use DVD presets where available.

- Variable bitrate encoding (VBR) usually produces a superior result to constant bit rate in either quality, disk efficiency, or both, with 2 Pass VBR preferable over one pass. The only reason not to use VBR is when encoding speed is your most important parameter.

- Keep your average bit rate around 8 mbps or less to maximum compatibility with older players.

- If you have to compress audio to get the content on disk, AC-3 is more compatible than MPEG compression. If disk space isn't an issue, PCM is fine.

Outputting DV Files

The DV file format has become the lingua franca of the digital video world. You can send it back to the camera, as well as input it into an authoring program to create a DVD or even input it into another video editor to access some unique capability. For example, I often use Pinnacle Studio to produce bits of productions, whether slideshows or homemade music videos, because of its SmartSound audio creation capabilities and automated slideshow transitions. I'll build this portion of my project, render out to DV, and import this file into another editor or authoring program.

Accordingly, no compression chapter would be complete without a visual explanation of how to accomplish said rendering.

Let's use Studio as our sample application for outputting an AVI file. Briefly, like DVD files, which are tightly regulated so they play on consumer DVD players, DV file-encoding parameters are tightly constrained so that inexpensive DV cameras can recognize them. This means creating a DV file is a writer's dream—one choice, one option, let's move on.

As with all Studio renders, you start by selecting Make Movie in the upper-left corner. You click AVI files and then the Settings button to open the encoding parameters dialog. Dial down to the DV Video Encoder (see Figure 16-6) taking the time to wave goodbye to Cinepak and Indeo—they really were lovely codecs in their day.

As you can see in Figure 16-7, the only option is Audio Sample rate, for which you want to match the rate set during filming and used in the project. Click the Same as Project button in Studio to make it so, and you're ready to name your file and start rendering.

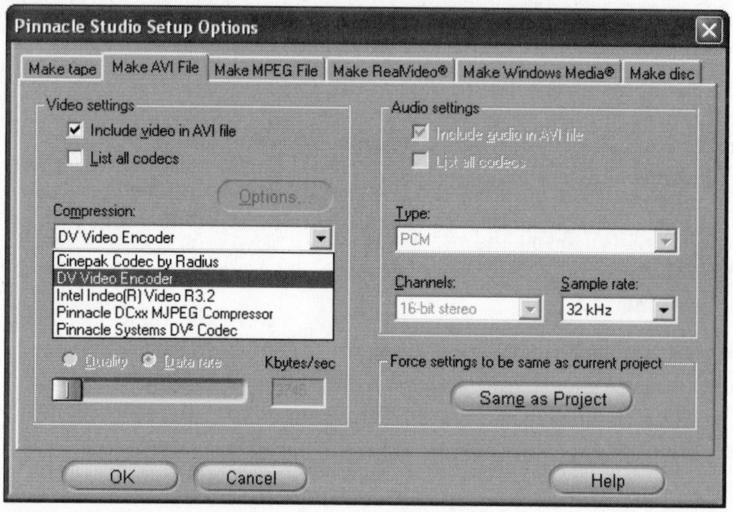

Figure 16-6: Producing a DV file in Pinnacle Studio.

By graying out virtually all DV-encoding parameters, Studio is providing a great service by preventing its users from creating incompatible files. However, many programs, including Premiere and VideoStudio, expose many of these same parameters for users to modify. The best course toward creating the most compatible file is to use the default settings. In short, even though they may not be grayed out, treat them as if they were.

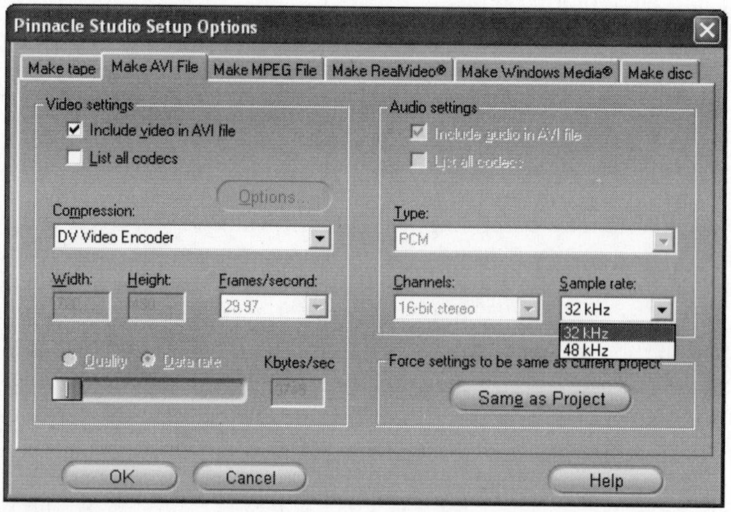

Figure 16-7: Use the Same as Project button in Studio to make the Audio Sample rate the same as you used in the project.

Type-1 versus Type-2 DV Files

I hope you never need to know the difference between Type-1 and Type-2 DV files, but you might, so here goes.

When a DV camera produces a DV file, it interleaves audio and video data together. When originally transferred to the computer, this interleaving stays intact and is referred to as a Type-1 DV AVI file.

On the computer, some video editors started to split the streams, because separating the audio and video made it easier to edit. DV files with separate audio and video streams are referred to as Type-2 DV AVI files.

As long as you work within one program, you probably don't need to know which type the editor produces or works with because this is all handled by the editor behind the scenes. However, as seen in Figure 16-8, when you're rendering a DV file for input to another program, some editors, like VideoStudio here, let you choose Type-1 or Type-2. And not all authoring or other programs can handle both types.

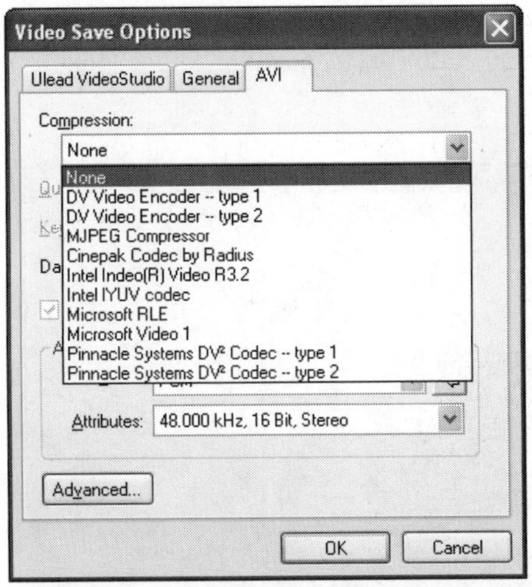

Figure 16-8: VideoStudio can output DV files in both Type-1 and Type-2 formats.

Unfortunately, there's no way to tell which type will import successfully. So here's a decidedly low-tech solution: If you're exporting for immediate import into another program, render as a Type-1 file and then try to import it. If it doesn't work, Type-2 should.

Producing MPEG-1 Files

MPEG-1 files are your best choice for high-quality playback on the broadest possible range of computers, from Windows and Mac to Unix and Linux. Virtually every video editor on the planet produces MPEG-1 files quickly and easily, making it a very accessible format.

Hip to Be Square

The term *aspect ratio* describes the relationship between the horizontal and vertical pixels in a video file. For example, a file with a resolution of 640x480 has an aspect ratio of 4:3. For every four horizontal pixels, there are three vertical pixels.

DV, the starting point for most digital video, has a resolution of 720x480 and an aspect ratio of 4:2.6. For every four pixels across, there are 2.6 pixels north and south. This aspect ratio is slightly wider than 4:3, which means that the image will look slightly stretched in comparison to the same image displayed at 4:3.

Virtually all images rendered for display on the computer are rendered at the 4:3 aspect ratio, be it 320x240, 240x180, or 160x120. The obvious technical question is if we're starting all of our video production with an image with an aspect ratio of 4:2.6, and immediately change it to 4:3, why doesn't it look funky on one playback medium or the other? The answer is that television sets squeeze the image slightly during display, using a rectangular pixel, while computers use a square pixel.

You can see the difference in Figure 16-9. On the left is the DV frame, captured at 720x480 resolution, while on the right is the same frame, shown on a television set and captured via a digital camera. My face looks decidedly wider on the left, because on the computer, the 4:2.6 resolution image looks stretched.

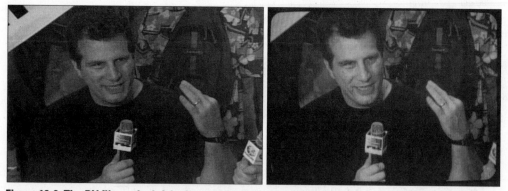

Figure 16-9: The DV file on the left looks stretched compared to how the frame actually looks on a television set (on the right). Here I am performing my first rap single at the NAB show in Las Vegas.

The dichotomy between how computers display video and how televisions display video produced the following rule: When producing video for display on computers, you use a 4:3 aspect ratio, whether for streaming or playing off a CD-ROM or hard drive.

In contrast, when producing video for display on television sets, whether writing back to tape, or optical formats like DVD or VideoCD, you should use a 4:2.6 aspect ratio. That's why DVD files are encoded at 720x480 and VideoCD files at 352x240.

Originally, since most MPEG-1 files were produced for VideoCD, the developers of video editors started using 352x240 for all MPEG-1 presets, which has the 4:26 aspect ratio that makes folks look about 10 percent wider than they actually are when played back on computer screens.

In addition, because much of the original work with streaming files was done by European standards bodies working off the PAL format, 176x144 became a popular video resolution for streaming media, though the aspect ratio was 4:3.27, which at the very least made you look 10 percent skinnier rather than 10 percent fatter.

In fact, when I tested for the first streaming roundup we did at *PC Magazine*, we used 176x144. Then I did the math, discovered that 176x132 was 4:3, not 176x144, and we corrected all test videos. Then I went on a rampage to stamp out non-square pixels in computer video. The problem reached ridiculous proportions, where companies like Microsoft and many others used different aspect ratios in different presets for their streaming media encoder. Some presets used 176x144 (4:3.27), while others used 320x240 (4:3). Surely, one or the other had to be correct.

This led to an article I wrote in *Extremetech* with my only published piece of poetry, obviously inspired by the great muse Dr. Seuss. Railing against Microsoft's use of the 176x144 preset, I wrote:

I do not like it on ABC,
I do not like it on MTV.
I would not, could not on CNN,
I would not, could not on ESPN.
It can't be 176x144, Bill G.
Because then it isn't 4:3!

Ah, the power of the pen. I'm happy to report that Microsoft banished non-4:3 aspect ratios from its streaming media tools forever. They discovered that it was hip to be square. Anyone interested in more details can find them at `www.extremetech.com/article2/0,3973,838509,00.asp`.

If you're producing MPEG-1 files to include on a VideoCD, find an encoder with a VideoCD preset, because the required parameters are very precise. Otherwise, if you're encoding for viewing on a computer, MPEG-1 is a very diverse, flexible format.

Table 16-2 contains the parameters appropriate for MPEG-1 files. While there is some wiggle room on data rate, most of the others should be strictly adhered to.

Table 16-2　Suggested MPEG-1 Encoding Parameters for Non-VideoCD Playback

	Video				Audio		
	Codec	Resolution	Frame Rate	Data Rate	Audio Format	Sample Rate	Data Rate
CD-ROM/ Hard disk	MPEG-1	320x240	29.97	1.5 to 3.0 mbps	MPEG Layer-2	48 kHz	224 kbps

Scanning through some of the presets used by the various video editors, you'll have your work cut out for you to stay within these guidelines. For example, Adobe Premiere and Sony Vegas use 720x480 as the default resolution for MPEG-1 files, while VideoStudio uses 352x240. I'll look at the Studio MPEG-encoding tool as the best starting point for seeing how it should be done.

Megabits? Megabytes?

Most compression for early codecs was represented in terms of bytes per second, whether kilobytes or megabytes of data. For example, back in the day, I encoded Cinepak and Indeo files at 125 kilobytes per second to play smoothly from 1X CD-ROM drives that could read only 150 kilobytes per second. I still refer to DV video in terms of 3.6 megabytes per second.

Since then, however, other technologies like modems, ISDN, and Ethernet were measured in bits per second. So Table 16-2 recommends encoding MPEG-1 files to no more than 3 megabits per second, and with DVD, it's 7 megabits per second.

How do the two relate? It's simple, 8 bits equals 1 byte. To get from bits to bytes, divide by 8. So, the 3-megabit-per-second MPEG-1 file is really 375 kilobytes per second, while our 8-megabit-per-second MPEG-2 file for DVD is 1 megabyte per second.

To get from bytes to bits, multiply by 8. So our 125-kilobyte-per-second file on CD-ROM is actually 1 megabit per second.

Interestingly, how fast is a T-1 line? Well, T-1 runs at 1.54 megabits per second, which if you do the math, is only 192 kilobytes per second, less than a 2X CD-ROM. No wonder it's so tough to make streaming video look good.

Click Make Movie to get started, then MPEG to produce the MPEG-encoding panel. Select Multimedia (see Figure 16-10) as the starting point. Though it's grayed out and faint, the resolution is set to 320x240, and all other configurable options match those suggested in Table 16-1.

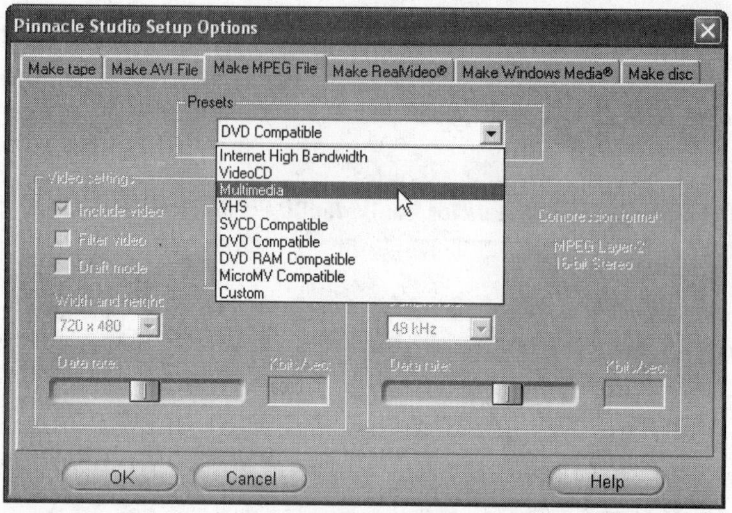

Figure 16-10: Pinnacle Studio's MPEG-1 production toolset.

In the Presets box atop the screen, click Custom to customize the encoding parameters. Here I'm boosting the data rate to 3,000 kbps, or 3 mbps, to boost quality. In my experience, MPEG-1 quality levels off after this, and you start wasting serious disk or CD space for only incremental benefits in quality. That's why as a general rule, I recommend not exceeding 3 mbps.

If you're producing MPEG-1 files on other tools, bring Table 16-2 with you to help you choose the proper encoding parameters.

Streaming Media

There are two primary streaming media technologies out there today, Microsoft's Windows Media technologies and RealNetworks RealVideo. Each operates differently, and I'll cover them both.

A few preliminary points: First, most streaming media encoding is performed with presets that relate to a connection rate. So, if your target audience is connecting to the Internet with a 56 kbps modem, this presupposes that you should encode your file using the 56-kbps preset. This works well if you're posting files on an Internet site, but if you're sending the file via e-mail, it's largely irrelevant.

Sure, the recipient may have to wait for a while to download the e-mail, but it's usually worth the wait. Video encoded at 56 kbps is going to look pretty degraded, no matter which technology you use.

Probably the biggest obstacle to sending files via e-mail is the attachment limits used by public and private ISPs. For example, Mindspring chokes on files larger than 5MB, while Hotmail limits files to 1MB.

Most video editors support both Windows Media and Real formats. In these instances, which do you use? In my view, though the differences have been dramatically reduced, RealVideo still looks better at equivalent data rates. On the other hand, there are some people who haven't yet down-loaded the RealOne Player, especially in the corporate environment. For this reason, I use RealOne for most personal videos; for most business-oriented videos, I use Windows Media.

Let's start with a look at how Microsoft's Movie Maker 2 encodes Windows Media files.

Microsoft's Windows Media Technologies

As you would expect, Movie Maker 2, Microsoft's own video editor, is a showcase for encoding Windows Media files. I like saving the file to my computer and then either uploading it or sending it via e-mail. So let's examine this route.

Start by clicking Save to My Computer, then name the file and choose a storage location. Click Show more choices in Figure 16-11 to bring up the screen shown in Figure 16-12, which provides a host of additional presets and the ability to create a file to a specific target size, a very helpful feature if you're e-mailing your file. Otherwise, if you're posting the file on a Web site, choose the preset that matches your target user. Click Next, and the encoding begins.

Congratulations, you've created your first streaming file. Note that Microsoft gave you absolutely no control over any encoding parameter, which is probably a good thing if you're a newbie.

Most other consumer tools provide limited and inconsistent access to Windows Media encoding parameters, which means every interface is different. Figures 16-13 through 16-15 show the relevant encoding options screens from both Pinnacle Studio and Ulead VideoStudio.

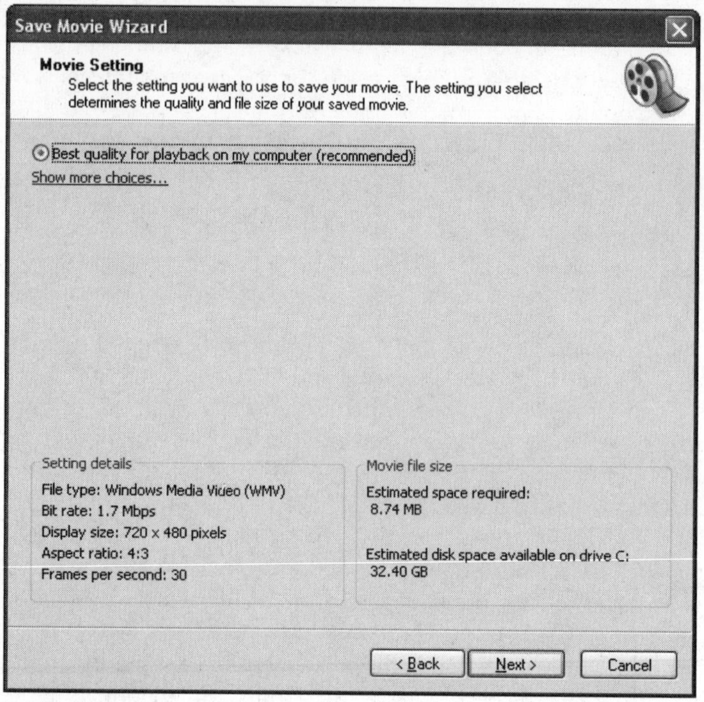

Save Movie Wizard ☒

Movie Setting
Select the setting you want to use to save your movie. The setting you select
determines the quality and file size of your saved movie.

◉ Best quality for playback on my computer (recommended)
Show more choices...

Setting details
File type: Windows Media Video (WMV)
Bit rate: 1.7 Mbps
Display size: 720 x 480 pixels
Aspect ratio: 4:3
Frames per second: 30

Movie file size
Estimated space required:
8.74 MB

Estimated disk space available on drive C:
32.40 GB

[< Back] [Next >] [Cancel]

Figure 16-11: Microsoft's Movie Maker 2 makes it simple to output
files in Windows Media format.

Studio (see Figure 16-13) provides three presets, Low (dial-up and single channel ISDN), Medium (dual channel ISDN), and High (broadband), or you can select Custom and choose from additional presets, with no further editing allowed. Studio does expose some non-square pixel presets like 176x144, so avoid these.

You may notice that some of the presets, like Video for LAN, cable modem, or xDLS (100 to 768 Kbps) appear to serve multiple data rates, which is correct. Files like these are called "scalable" because they can send low bitrate files to low bitrate connections, and more, higher-quality data to higher-speed connections.

Note that this only works when your video is distributed from a Web site using the Windows Media server. Otherwise, you should choose a preset that only serves one data rate.

Studio also gives you the ability to insert title, copyright, and other metadata; it will appear during playback, as shown in Figure 16-13. You can also create markers within the video to serve as jump points into the video file from Media Player.

As mentioned, VideoStudio's options are different and limited. If you select Streaming Windows Media format from the Share → Create Video File menu, VideoStudio won't provide any encoding options at all; it will simply encode using preselected parameters. Select Custom to avoid this, and then select Windows Media from the drop-down box to access the custom controls (see Figure 16-14).

From there, you can choose to encode the entire project or just the preview range, as well as whether to use SmartRendering, which, if you've already encoded the project once and made only minor changes, will only re-encode any scenes that have changed. Keep this checked—it's a great timesaving feature.

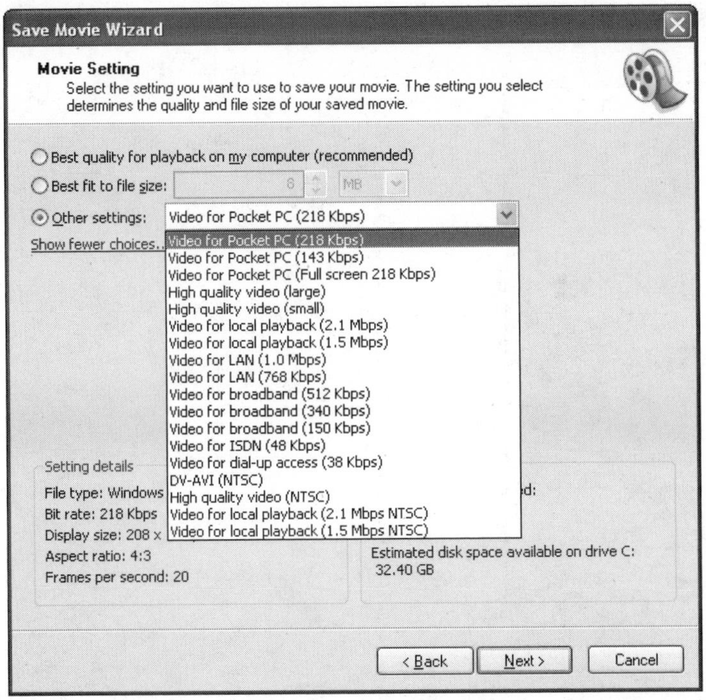

Figure 16-12: Additional presets.

Next you choose a preset (see Figure 16-15), which VideoStudio will not allow you to modify in any way. Finally, VideoStudio allows you to enter the same metadata as Studio, which appears in Media Player during playback.

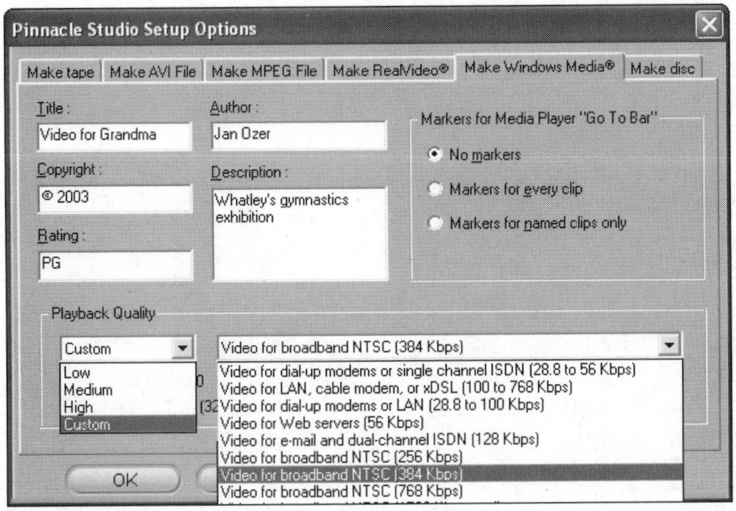

Figure 16-13: Producing Windows Media files in Pinnacle Studio.

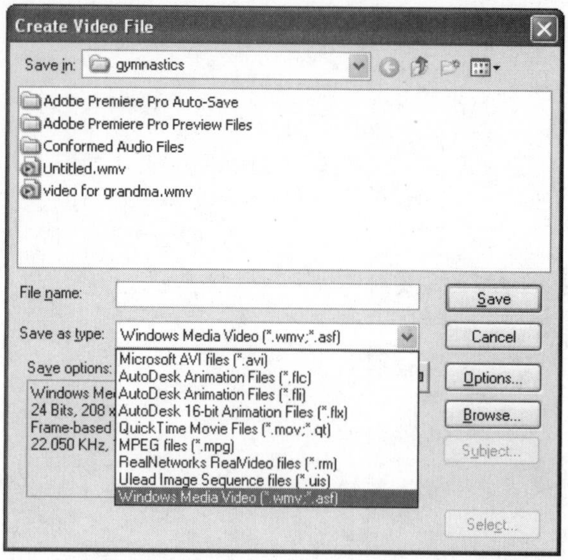

Figure 16-14: Starting the streaming media encoding process in VideoStudio.

While functional, none of these applications allow the developer full access to all encoding and preprocessing options. They're good for casual use, but those interested in greater control should use a prosumer product like Premiere, or download the Windows Media Encoder at `www.microsoft.com/windows/windowsmedia/default.aspx`.

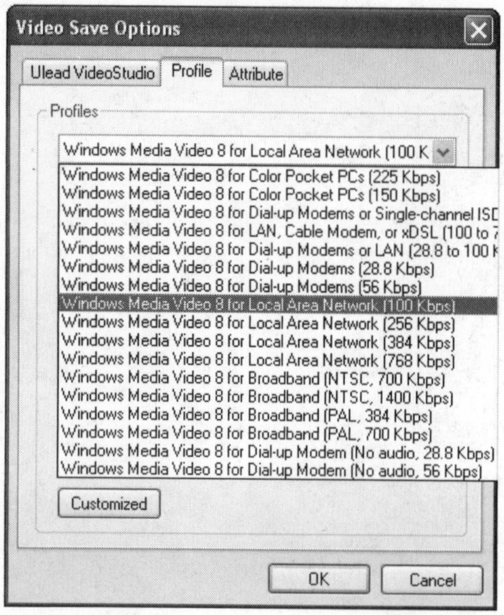

Figure 16-15: Choosing a preset in Ulead VideoStudio.

Creating RealVideo Files

As with Windows Media, support for Real Media is sketchy among consumer editors (and non-existent on Microsoft's Movie Maker 2, no surprise there). You can definitely get the job done, but configuration options are limited. Once again, Pinnacle Studio does the best job laying all this out, so let's use the Studio interface to encode to RealVideo format (see Figures 16-16 and 16-17).

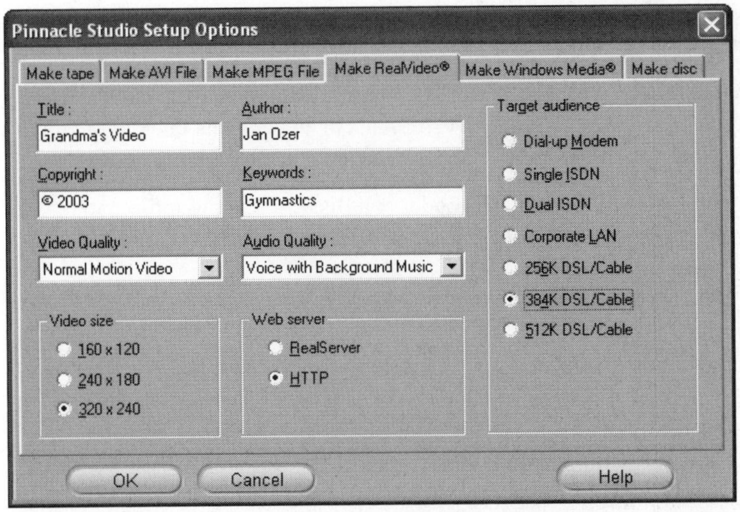

Figure 16-16: Creating a RealVideo file in Pinnacle Studio.

Figure 16-17: In the encoded file playing in Real Player.

Hierarchy of Streaming Encoding Tools

There are several levels of tools for encoding primarily streaming files:

- Consumer video editors perform the basics, but they don't provide access to all critical encoding parameters. These are good for casual use but definitely should not be used for serious production.

- Prosumer video editors generally provide access to all encoding parameters, but only within their own fixed interfaces, which can get confusing, and offer little by way of automation and advanced help. They typically also can't be used to stream live events.

- Vendor-based tools from Real Networks and Microsoft provide complete access to all encoding parameters, expert help, and the ability to produce live events in an interface customized for live streaming. Generally they lack batch capabilities and provide little editing functionality.

- Third-party batch rendering tools like Canopus ProCoder and Discreet Cleaner offer batch encoding to multiple formats, filtering, and access to other formats like MPEG-1 and -2, but no live event support.

To encode to RealVideo format, follow these steps:

1. To open the RealVideo encoding screen, click the Make Movie button, then Stream, then Settings (or on the menu select Setup → Make RealVideo File).

2. Complete the desired metadata in the four fields on the upper left-hand side of Figure 16-16.

3. In the Video Quality box, choose one of the following options:

   - **Normal motion.** RealVideo will produce a good balance of quality and frame rate.

   - **Smoothest motion.** RealVideo will produce a high frame rate, sacrificing frame sharpness.

   - **Sharpest image.** RealVideo will produce the sharpest image, but playback frame rate will be slow.

   - **Slideshow.** RealVideo will reduce frame rate to one or two frames per second.

4. In the Audio Quality box, choose the menu option that matches the audio in your project.

5. Use the following guide to choose Video size in Figure 16-16 (referring to the Target audience on the right hand side):

   - 160x120 for Dial-up modem.

   - 240x180 for Single ISDN.

   - 320x240 for all other target audiences.

6. Choose the type of Web server you'll be posting your video to. If you know you'll be streaming from a RealServer, you can select multiple target audiences. If not, you can select only one.

7. Select your target audience(s).

8. Click OK, name the file, and click Create Web file back on the main encoding screen.

Summary

Here is a summary of the key points from this chapter:

1. Writing to tape. Requires the same hardware setup as capturing. Most editors have very easy-to-follow prompts for writing back to tape.

2. To produce the best files for your DVD project, do the following:

   - Check the requirements of your DVD-authoring program before starting encoding to make sure the files you produce are compatible.

   - If you're not sure that you can avoid double compression, output an AVI file in DV format.

   - Use DVD presets where available.

   - Variable bitrate encoding (VBR) usually produces a superior result to constant bitrate encoding in either quality, disk efficiency, or both, with 2 Pass VBR being preferable over 1 Pass. The only reason not to use VBR is when encoding speed is your most important parameter.

   - Keep your average bit rate around 8 megabits per second or less for maximum compatibility with older players.

   - If you have to compress audio to get the content on disk, AC-3 is more compatible than MPEG compression. If disk space isn't an issue, PCM is fine.

3. Outputting DV files — DV files are a convenient, high-quality exchange medium between programs. A highly constrained format, the only configuration option will generally be the audio sample rate, and you should always use the rate selected during filming.

4. When outputting files for viewing on television, use the 4:2.6 or similar aspect ratio (720x480 or 352x240). When outputting files for viewing on computers, use 4:3 (640x480, 320x240, or 176x132).

5. MPEG-1 files offer the best balance of quality, file size, and compatibility of all formats and should be used for all general-purpose disk and CD-ROM-based distribution. MPEG-2 files need a special player that many potential viewers don't have while MPEG-1 enjoys near universal compatibility.

6. All consumer editors can output streaming media files, but for serious work, download an encoder directly from the Real Networks or Microsoft, and use a prosumer editor or a third-party encoding tool.

Part IV

DVD Production

Chapter 17

DVD Production Basics

Depending upon the type of DVD you're creating, by the time you get to this chapter, you're either just beginning or halfway home. That is, if you're simply converting a tape to DVD, video editing may not be necessary, so authoring is your starting point. Conversely, if you're creating a DVD with lots of edited video, you're probably arriving after editing and rendering your final output, and now you're ready to author a DVD. Whatever road brought you here, welcome!

First, I'll examine the workflow paradigms for various products and product combinations. That is, you approach DVD authoring differently depending upon which video editor and which DVD-authoring program you use. What's critical is the handoff between the programs, primarily the format of the files output by the editor for inputting into the authoring program.

Errors here could compress your video twice — once by the editor and once during authoring — which doubles compression time and unnecessarily degrades the quality of your video. So, I'll start by exploring how to avoid double compression. Then I'll review the components of the typical DVD and conclude with a list of issues to consider when planning your DVD project.

Editing to Authoring Workflow

Your primary concern when moving from editing to authoring is to avoid compressing your video files twice. As shown in Table 17-1, the nature and extent of this problem depends entirely upon your editing and authoring application.

Table 17-1   The Four DVD-Authoring Workflow Paradigms

Category	Workflow Paradigm	Example	Resolution
A	Integrated editing and authoring	Pinnacle Studio/Edition, Ulead MovieFactory 2, Pinnacle Expression, Sonic MyDVD	No problem — double compression not possible

Continued

Table 17-1   The Four DVD-Authoring Workflow Paradigms *(continued)*

Category	Workflow Paradigm	Example	Resolution
B	DVD authoring is a post-process after editing	Ulead VideoStudio and MediaStudio Pro	Should not be a problem; insert project rather than rendered asset
C	Editing and authoring program from same vendor	Vegas and DVD Architect	Handoff usually defined — check documentation
D	Editing and authoring from different vendor	Adobe Premiere and Ulead DVD Workshop or Sonic DVDit!	Experiment to ensure no double compression

If you're working with an integrated editing and authoring application like Pinnacle Studio or Edition, it's almost impossible to double compress, because you don't compress your video until it's time to write your DVD. This is one of the beauties of the integrated approach. Similarly when you're working with programs like Ulead MovieFactory, Pinnacle Expression, and Sonic MyDVD, which capture, perform minor editing, and then create your DVD, double compression is also not an issue.

In Category B, DVD production is a post-process that occurs after editing, but within the same program you used to edit. You finish editing, then start authoring, usually using a wizard-like interface. Ulead's VideoStudio is an example of this approach.

VideoStudio avoids double compression by importing your current video *project*, before rendering, into the wizard. You can also import files and other VideoStudio projects into the wizard. The ability to insert a project (as opposed to a file) again means you don't have to encode before inserting the video file, which avoids double compression.

VideoStudio also has the lovely checkbox shown in Figure 17-1, that forces the program not to re-compress MPEG-compliant files that you've imported into your project, another way to prevent — you guessed it — double compression. Hey, I'm obviously not the only one who thinks it's a problem.

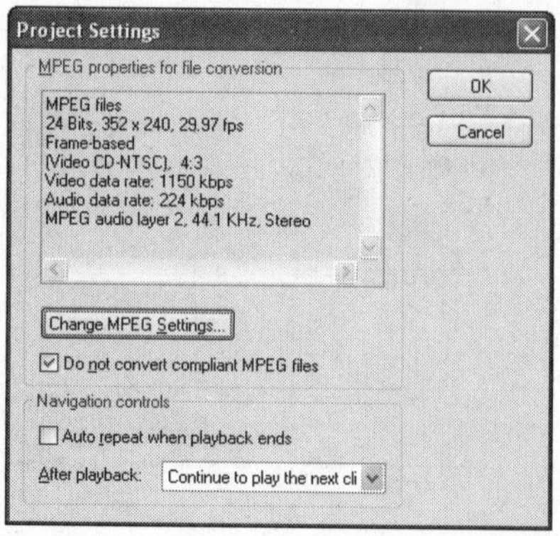

Project Settings

MPEG properties for file conversion

MPEG files
24 Bits, 352 x 240, 29.97 fps
Frame-based
[Video CD-NTSC], 4:3
Video data rate: 1150 kbps
Audio data rate: 224 kbps
MPEG audio layer 2, 44.1 KHz, Stereo

OK   Cancel

Change MPEG Settings...

☑ Do not convert compliant MPEG files

Navigation controls

☐ Auto repeat when playback ends

After playback: Continue to play the next cli

Figure 17-1: VideoStudio makes it easy to avoid double compression with the "Do not convert compliant MPEG files" option.

In Category C, you're working with separate editing and authoring files from the same vendor. In most instances, the vendor knows this is an issue and will provide some direction in the program help files, usually those of the DVD-authoring program. For example, the help file for Sonic Foundry's DVD Architect states (emphasis supplied):

"DVD Architect includes support for many file types and can convert your media to the formats required for DVD as needed. However, for best performance (decreased disc preparation time and recompression), use existing rendered files. *MPEG-2 video files rendered with the DVD NTSC or DVD PAL templates in Sonic Foundry Vegas will not need to be recompressed.*"

This is pretty clear direction that you should encode using the presets supplied with Vegas to avoid recompression. So, when using products from the same vendor, you should review the help files of both editor and authoring program to identify the best technique for handing files from editor to authoring program.

While you're perusing the help files, you should also check regarding using markers inserted into the video files as chapter points in the DVD. For example, markers set in Adobe Premiere are recognized as linkable chapter points in Adobe Encore.

The fourth category, D, is the most complicated. Here you need to submit files in the proper format *and* avoid double compression. I'll deal with each issue in turn.

Regarding the proper format, many early authoring programs could only accept "elementary" streams, where the audio and video were produced as separate files. This was a real problem, since most video editors could only output "program" streams, where the audio and video were interleaved. In addition, many authoring programs couldn't accept AVI files, only files already encoded into MPEG format.

Today, most consumer and prosumer DVD-authoring products can input program and elementary streams, and convert AVI files to MPEG. Still, when working with programs from different vendors, it's critical to first ascertain the types of files that the authoring program can accept, which is usually provided in the help files.

Avoiding double compression is another issue. Sometimes programs have a switch you can set like that shown in Figure 17-1 to "Do not convert compliant MPEG files." Other times you may find direction in the help files. Unfortunately, when all else fails, you may have to insert a compressed file and render a project (to hard disk, not to your recorder) to see if the authoring program double compresses.

Usually, if the program is chugging away for a while with "rendering" flashing on the screen, you know that it's recompressing the files. Of course, sometimes this occurs because the selected data rate used by the editor was higher than the data rate set on the authoring program.

Specifically, if you output your files from the video editor at 8 mbps and then build your DVD with a data rate of 6 mbps, the authoring program will always re-encode to achieve the target data rate. Sometimes if you bump the rate in the authoring program to 9 or 10 mbps, you can avoid recompression.

At the end of the day, unless you can figure out a way to avoid recompression, the best course is to render files from your editor in your capture format (usually DV) and let the authoring program encode into MPEG-2. Otherwise, if you know that the authoring program isn't recompressing, output from your editor in MPEG-2 format, which is more compact, saving disk space.

DVD Components

Chapter 4 discussed what comprises a DVD in detail, but let's quickly review. Then, at the end of this chapter, we'll consolidate this information into a planning checklist.

At a high level, DVDs have two components: menus and content, which can include video, audio, text, and images. Menus contain text and/or graphic links to other menus and content. Graphic links are generally called buttons. In terms of menu creation, different programs provide different options; however, most provide the following capabilities (see Figure 17-2):

- **Insert background** — You can insert an image as background or create a video background.

- **Include buttons** — You can use images supplied with the program as buttons or create and insert your own.

- **Change the "state" colors for buttons** — You can also change the colors the buttons turn to as the viewer clicks through the menu. The "active" or "focused" state is the color the button changes to as the viewer accesses that button. The "selected" state is the color the button turns to when the viewer clicks and selects that button.

- **Create text** — You can create text for menu and button titles and for linking.

- **Frames** — You can use small objects supplied with the program to surround thumbnail images of the video files to which they are linked.

- **Create audio menus** — You have the option of inserting an audio file to play while the viewer makes a menu selection.

- **Video buttons** — You can animate the frames, essentially playing the video the button image links to in the smaller window. The control for doing this is not shown on this screen; you access it from the button tab on the upper left.

You'll learn how to actually make these selections and modifications in Chapters 19 and 20. Here, you just want these options fresh in your mind as we discuss the planning issues related to DVD authoring.

DVD Content

Regarding content, recall that you can link to the beginning of any video, insert chapter points in the video, and link to any chapter point. In Figure 17-3, I'm manually creating chapter points in Ulead MovieFactory 2, providing extra points of entry into this long video file.

The ability to create chapter points means you don't have to cut your video into pieces to link to specific spots in the video, which is a good thing. In some programs, however, it also forces you to create the additional menus, buttons, and links necessary to jump to the chapter points, which can get time-consuming.

Menu timeout

Audio menu Change the button state

Motion menu Frames Text

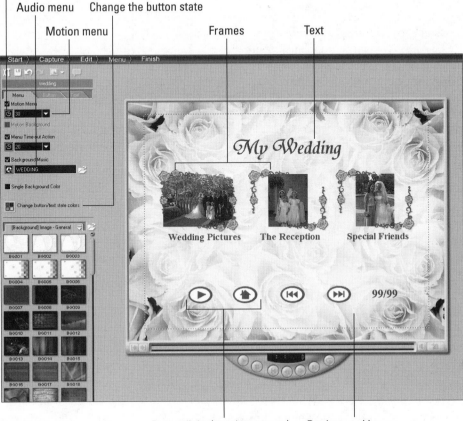

Button links (to other menus) Background image

Figure 17-2: Creating menus in DVD Workshop.

In addition to selecting chapter points, many authoring programs let you designate a "First Play" video, or the video that appears first before any menus when the DVD initializes in your player. If your authoring program supports this, it's another opportunity to customize your DVD.

DVD Navigation

Sitting above content and menus is the navigation issue, or how your viewers will move through the DVD content. Navigation has two general aspects.

First is how the viewers will flow from menu to menu. As discussed in Chapter 4, all consumer-oriented products except Pinnacle Studio enable only sequential inter-menu navigation, with limited branching possible in Sonic's MyDVD. Sequential menus are shown in Figure 17-4. One benefit of this approach, however, is production simplicity, since the authoring program usually builds all inter-menu and content links, including those to chapter points.

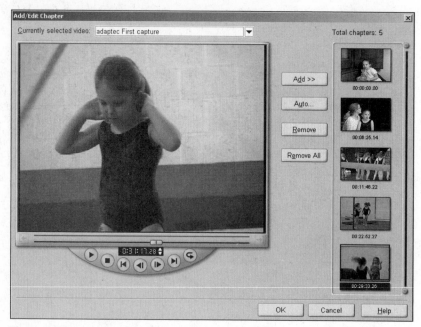

Figure 17-3: Inserting chapter points to link to different locations within a long video file. Move the video slider to the desired chapter point, and click Add. Chapter points are shown in the panel on the right.

In contrast, Studio and all prosumer products provide complete flexibility regarding menu navigational structure, as shown in Figure 17-5. For obvious reasons, these menus are often called "branched" or "nested" menus.

With this flexibility, however, comes additional responsibility. You're in charge of linking menus to menus and menu to content, which can get tricky with projects with lots of assets. This is one reason that programs like Studio and Ulead's DVD Workshop enable template-based, sequential menu production as well as template-based custom menus.

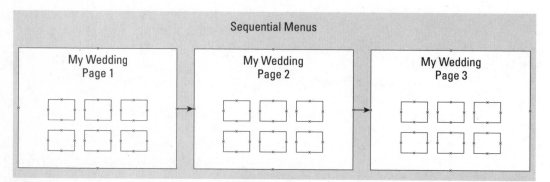

Figure 17-4: Most consumer products enable sequential menus like this, which limits design flexibility, and means a lot of clicks and waiting to get to the honeymoon pictures.

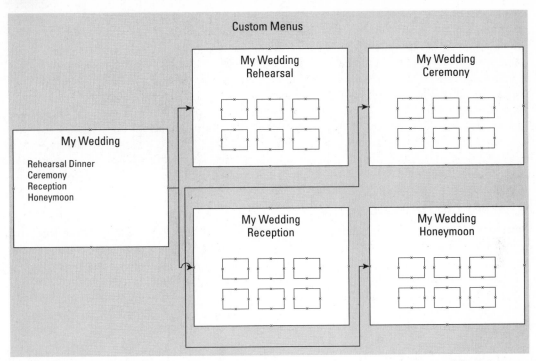

Figure 17-5: Programs that provide custom menu capabilities enable much more navigational flexibility.

PRE-PLAY AND POST-PLAY OPTIONS

Pre-play options define what happens after the DVD first appears on-screen and before the viewer clicks a button. You have two basic options: hold the menu on-screen with any media repeating until the viewer clicks, or launch into the first video on the menu after a designated duration. Note that not all authoring programs allow access to either or both of these options.

Post-play options define what happens when the video or slideshow finishes playing. Most programs allow you to send the viewer back to the originating menu or to continue on to the next video. Prosumer programs may also allow you to loop the video and send the viewer to a menu other than the originating menu.

Planning Your DVD

With these options in mind, let's start planning.

Historically, DVD production was a group enterprise, and the authoring program accepted only finished assets. Under the direction of a producer or project manager, your videographer shot and edited the videos; your audio person produced the audio; your compressionist encoded audio and video; your menu designer created the menus; and your authoring geek pulled all the asset types together and meticulously programmed in the desired interactivity. Planning was obviously a huge necessity.

Today, for most consumer and small business projects, you may play all those roles, and so does the authoring program, making it very simple to pull together entire projects with one $49 program. Planning is much less important.

In most instances, if I'm creating a DVD by myself, I just wing it, creating menu background files, ripping audio files for the audio menus, and making design decisions on the fly. It's the digital content creation equivalent to John Daly's "grip it and rip it" approach to a golf swing.

On the other hand, if I'm working with others, especially a client, more planning is necessary. In addition, when first starting out, it probably doesn't hurt to think a bit about the project in advance.

Here's a list of questions I would answer before starting serious production. My assumption is you're planning simple consumer and small business projects starting with DV video, as opposed to film or high-definition video, which raises a bunch of other questions beyond the scope of this book.

How Much Time Do I Have?

Sometimes it's best to set a limit on overall creation time associated with a particular project. This means editing and authoring, with editing getting the bulk of the time. Remember, people show up to watch the video, not the motion menus or custom backgrounds.

Goal number one should be to get the project finished with great-looking video and a reasonably navigable DVD. Cut back on the creative side of authoring if necessary, since baubles like video menus and motion buttons can significantly boost creative and rendering time. Either way, figure out a time goal before you sit down, and modify your creative expectations accordingly.

How Much Content?

The issue here is disk space and compression ratio. MPEG-2 is a scalable format, and you can dial down the rate to any number you like. With most encoders, however, quality starts to suffer below 6 mbps.

Assuming there's no other content on the disk, this translates to about 104 minutes of video, less if you trick out your DVD with motion menus, audio menus, and similar high bandwidth effects. Generally, if you're under one hour of video, you're leaving disk space on the table and quality won't be an issue. Between 60 and 80 minutes, quality should still be quite good, but if you go much beyond 80 minutes, quality may suffer.

Note that all authoring programs track disk space more or less continuously (see Figure 17-6), so you'll know long before it becomes a problem. If you like to plan ahead, check out Jim Taylor's excellent calculator at `www.dvddemystified.com/files/DVDcalc.xls`.

How Do I Want My Content to Flow?

This question addresses how you build your underlying video file. Specifically, if you create one long video file that viewers access via chapter points, it will play smoothly through these chapter points on disk. However, if you insert multiple smaller files, there will be slight breaks as the DVD player moves from movie to movie. Not a huge deal, but a factor to consider when assembling your project.

Where Will I Create and Hand Off My Video?

With simple conversion projects like those discussed in the next chapter, you can produce the entire project in one program. On the other hand, if your source video needs substantial trimming or effects like transitions and titles, you may need a video editor. Before encoding or rendering, be sure to understand how you'll hand off your video from editor to authoring program without double compression.

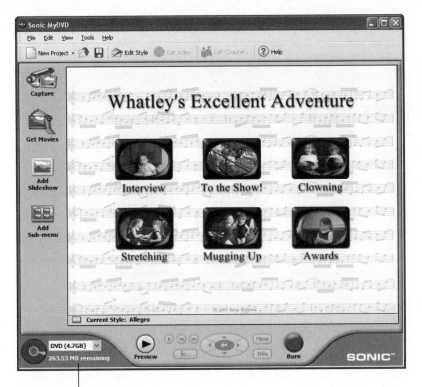

Space remaining on disk

Figure 17-6: MyDVD letting you know that you have 263MB of data left on the disk (lower left).

WHERE WILL I CREATE MY SLIDESHOWS?

Slideshows are a big deal to me and are included on most DVDs that I produce. Though most authoring programs enable slideshow production, sometimes you get better features like transitions and background audio if you create the slideshow in a video editor.

For example, often I'll use Pinnacle Studio to create my slideshows simply because it can insert transitions between the slides, maintains the proper aspect ratio, and can create background music via SmartSound. In these instances, I'll almost always export in DV format and let the authoring program perform the final encoding.

CAN I USE A FIRST PLAY VIDEO?

First Play isn't widely supported by consumer programs, so the first question really is whether or not you can select one. If so, the First Play video is a fun way to dazzle your audience from the start (just don't use the FBI copyright notice — it's been done before). Be sure to make it short and introductory, a teaser for the main content.

WHERE WILL I ASSEMBLE MY ASSETS?

Generally, it's easiest if you create a project directory off the root directory of your capture drive and store all bitmapped images and audio and video files there. I generally use the same folder I created for the video project for capture and temporary files.

Note that when you actually render your DVDs, the authoring program creates gobs of temporary files on disk, generally placing them somewhere deep in the My Documents folder where they can't be found and deleted. To avoid this bloat, I always set my temporary file locations for both authoring and editing to my project folder.

How Will I Create My Menus?

Depending upon the program, you may have up to three options:

- Use a completely canned menu, background images, links, and all. It's easy and fast, but it has a cookie-cutter look to it.

- Customize a canned menu with your own background image. This is probably the easiest way to avoid the cookie-cutter look, while retaining all the benefits of the template.

- Create a menu from scratch. If you add up menu creation and debugging time, this option probably takes five or six times longer than the first and has a much greater risk of failure, primarily in the form of video content or menus that never got linked.

You can generally choose your template during authoring and even quickly grab a screen and customize the background without investing too much time. But if you're truly the artistic type and plan on creating a custom menu from scratch in PhotoShop, you better build that time into your production schedule.

Screen Capture Alternatives

When I'm customizing a menu, changing backgrounds is a must. Probably the easiest approach is to grab a frame of your video and lighten it up a bit in your image editor to create contrast for the text and buttons.

The problem with video is that it doesn't capture like most screen objects. Press Alt+Print Screen with Media Player running, and you'll capture a big, black box. The technical reason is that the video isn't playing in main system memory, like the dialog boxes and other screen elements; it's actually being played in the video card courtesy of a Microsoft Windows standard called DirectX. It's a good thing, for the most part, because graphics cards are better at playing video than your computer's main processor, but it can be a pain when it comes to capturing a background screen for your DVD.

There are three good alternatives to the problem. First, virtually all video editors have the ability to grab a single frame of video and convert it to a bitmapped file. Usually, with consumer editors it's a dedicated screen capture facility, while with prosumer programs you generally "export" a single frame.

Second, most software DVD players have screen grab functions, so if your video is already encoded, you can play the video and capture the frame (see Figure 17-7).

Figure 17-7: Grabbing screens in Sonic Cineplayer.

Finally, there are several screen capture utilities available that can capture video screens. My favorite is HyperSnap-DX from Hyperionics (www.hyperionics.com). It's one of two programs running on virtually all of my test and production computers.

Once I grab my frame, I pull it into the other program running on all my computers, Ulead's PhotoImpact (www.ulead.com) still-image editor, to lighten it a bit to create contrast with the foreground buttons, text, and other objects.

WILL I USE CHAPTER POINTS?

Once again, chapter points are designated points inside a longer video that a menu can link to. If you've got one or more long videos in your project, chapter points make them much more accessible to the viewer.

As shown in Figure 17-3, most authoring programs allow you to manually designate chapter points or automatically create them based upon duration (for example, every five minutes) or by detecting scene changes in the video (time-code- or content-based). Most template-driven programs can also automatically create links to chapter points. However, if you're designing your menus manually, you'll have to create the button and link it to the chapter point.

How Dressy Will I Make My Menus?

Do I plan to create audio menus, video menus (video underneath the menu elements), or video buttons (I vote no, but hey, it's your project)? For audio menus, what music will I use and how will I digitize it if necessary? For video menus, is it video I'll produce myself or canned motion menus supplied by the project?

What's My Navigational Structure?

Part of this depends upon your authoring program, but assuming you have the flexibility to create any desired structure, what would it be? Sketching out a design on a piece of paper (or Visio, like in Figures 17-3 and 17-4) is never a bad idea.

If you have separate menus for each major section (rehearsal dinner, wedding, reception, and honeymoon), will they use different backgrounds and/or music? For example, one DVD I created for a trip to Zoo Atlanta had custom menus for each major section (Savannah, Reptile Hall, Big Cats, and so on as shown in Chapter 20 in Figure 20-1), each with a different background image. Will your menus link to each other (mine didn't, but perhaps they should have), or just back to the main page?

PRE- AND POST-PLAY OPTIONS

If the menu comes up and no one clicks a button, what do I want my DVD to do? Keep repeating the background audio/video or jump into my first video?

How do I want the videos to flow both within my major menus (flow sequentially or return to menu) and between major menus (jump to videos in the next menu or return to menu)?

HOW WIDELY WILL I DISTRIBUTE THIS DVD?

This is only a problem if you're bumping disk capacity, because if you have the space, you can always supply audio in LPCM format, which is big but compatible. If you're at 60 minutes or more, however, and need to compress your audio, AC-3 audio is necessary in commercial settings where the disk absolutely, positively has to play. On the other hand, if it's just friends and family, the broad (but not absolute) compatibility of MPEG audio may be enough.

Remember, not all programs can encode or even handle AC-3 audio files. For example, at the low end, only MyDVD can produce AC-3 audio (with version 5), while Ulead VideoStudio and Pinnacle Studio can't. Among prosumer packages, Pinnacle Edition can't, while Adobe Encore, Sonic Foundry DVD Architect, and Ulead's DVD Workshop (AC-3 Edition) all can.

DO I NEED MULTIPLE AUDIO TRACKS, SUBTITLES, AND/OR ENCRYPTION?

Adobe Encore enables all these functions, as should an upcoming version of Ulead's DVD Workshop. At this level, however, you probably need a better resource; check out Ralph LaBarge's book, *DVD Authoring and Production*, for more details.

Summary

Here is a summary of the key points from this chapter.

1. When handing off files from editor to authoring program, it's critical to avoid double compression. When using integrated editing/authoring programs, which encode just prior to writing to disk, this isn't a problem. For other programs, check the authoring program's help files to determine the best format for inserting your videos. If you're sure

double compression won't occur, output from your video editor in MPEG-2 format. If double compression will occur or you're not sure, output in DV format.

2. Questions to ask when planning your DVD:

- How much time do I have?

- How much content?

- How do I want my content to flow?

- Where will I create my video and how will I hand off?

- Where will I create my slideshows?

- Can I and will I use a First Play video?

- Where will I assemble my assets?

- How will I create my menus?

- Will I use chapter points? If so, how will I create and link them?

- How dressy will I make my menus?

- What's my navigational structure?

- What are my pre- and post-play options?

- How widely will I distribute this DVD, and do I care if it doesn't play?

- Do I need multiple audio tracks, subtitles, and/or encryption?

Chapter 18

Converting Tapes to DVD

One of my favorite movie lines is from *It's a Wonderful Life*, the great, great movie with Jimmy Stewart and Donna Reed. George Bailey (Stewart) walks into a bar with Clarence, his guardian angel, sent to teach him his critical life lesson. The bar is a cacophonous joint filled with raucous men and bawdy women, and Clarence starts asking about fruity drinks sans alcohol. Nick, the bartender, leans over and says aggressively "Look, mister, we serve hard drinks in here for men who want to get drunk fast, and we don't need any characters around to give the joint atmosphere."

I've always thought this was a brilliantly focused marketing statement, identifying target audience and a unique selling proposition in one clear sentence. If only all marketing communications were this crisp and precise.

If you're reading this chapter, I'll assume you want to convert analog or DV tapes to DVD fast. You want to set up the computer, press a few buttons, walk away, and return to the finished DVD. No slideshows, no animated buttons, no fruity drinks.

In short, you're going to convert the tape to DVD with minimum fuss or fanfare. If you're looking to learn how to create fancy menus and slideshows, jump ahead to Chapter 20.

Recall that in Chapter 4, I discussed factors to consider when purchasing a product to convert tape to DVD, so if you haven't purchased a product yet, you should start there. Here, I'll discuss the required hardware and software, and then detail how to convert tapes to DVD with two products: Ulead's MovieFactory 2 and Sonic's MyDVD. You'll get in, get out, get it done, and go have a beer at the local pub.

Cheers.

Note

Any DVD-authoring program can capture and write to disc, but most require your presence during the process. This chapter focuses solely on those products that automate the process.

What You'll Need

In the computer software business, there are lies, darn lies, and minimum system requirements. Ulead says that MovieFactory should run on a Pentium III 450 MHz with 64MB of RAM, but I don't believe it for an instant. In a recent *PC Magazine* review, I tested USB-based hardware encoders on a Pentium III 1 GHz with 128MB of RAM, and not one product reliably produced a DVD; in fact, most failed miserably. So, if you want to convert tapes to DVD quickly and easily, you'll need at least a Pentium 4 computer with 256MB of RAM.

If you're capturing video from an analog source like VHS, you'll need a capture product, internal or external, that can accept analog inputs. If your primary goal is conversion to DVD, your best bet is a USB Analog Capture Device like those described in Chapter 2. Products include Adaptec's VideOh!, which ships with Sonic's MyDVD, and ADS Technologies Instant DVD, which ships with MovieFactory. You might also check out Hewlett Packard's excellent dvd movie writer dc3000, a unique capture card, DVD writer combo.

On the CD-ROM

Trial versions of MovieFactory and MyDVD are on the CD-ROM that comes with this book.

If you're capturing video from DV sources, you can probably work without an external MPEG-2 encoder if your computer is a Pentium 4, 2 GHz or faster. Anything slower than this and the computer won't be able to encode the incoming video to MPEG-2 in real time. Accordingly, you should consider an external USB-based solution.

Note that MovieFactory can only write to DVD in real time if you're using a DVD+RW drive and +RW media. If you have any other type of drive or are using +R medium in your DVD+RW recorder, it will first write to your hard drive, then to the DVD recorder.

Cross-Reference

Recall that in Chapter 4, I discussed factors to consider when purchasing a product to convert tape to DVD, so if you haven't purchased a product yet, you should start there.

Writing to Disc in MovieFactory 2

Just for the record, I'm converting a DV tape from Whatley's gymnastics presentation into a DVD for grandma. I'm working on an HP xw4100 3.2 GHz Pentium 4 computer that should be plenty fast to convert the DV video to MPEG-2 in real time, and writing to an HP DVD Writer 300n, which is DVD+RW-compatible with a DVD+RW disc loaded.

Since I'm converting a DV tape, I'm connecting via the FireWire port. If you were converting an analog tape, you'd first have to make sure that the analog device is properly installed and that MovieFactory recognizes the device.

Then proceed through the following steps shown in Figures 18-1 through 18-4. I'm going through them one by one, so the list looks intimidating, but as you'll see, it's actually a bunch of simple administrative steps.

1. Run MovieFactory, and click Direct to Disc (see Figure 18-1).

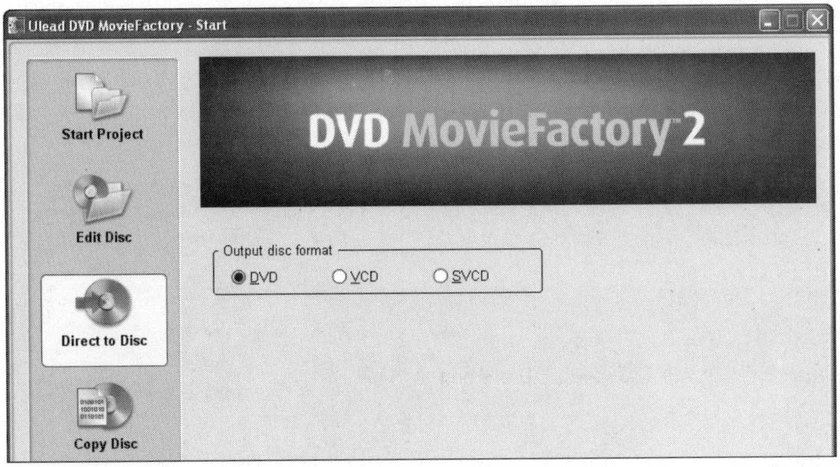

Figure 18-1: Selecting DVD format in MovieFactory 2.

2. Select the DVD format; note that you can also write directly to VideoCD and Super VideoCD.

3. Click On-the-fly (see Figure 18-2). Note that if this option isn't available, you either don't have a DVD+RW drive, or you don't have DVD+RW media loaded. In these instances, you can proceed through the following steps, but MovieFactory will first write the data to hard disk, then to DVD.

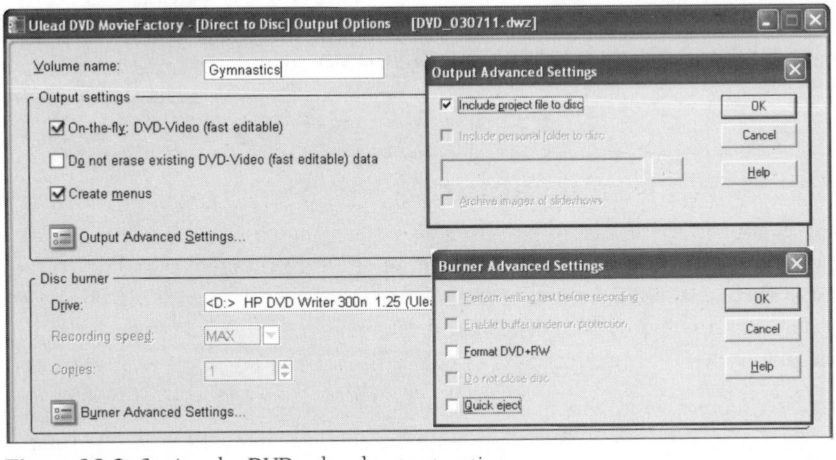

Figure 18-2: Setting the DVD-related output options.

4. Click Create menus, which you'll work on in Step 7.

5. Click Output Advanced Settings and check Include project file to disc. This will enhance your flexibility down the road if you attempt to edit the disc.

6. Click Burner Advanced Settings and uncheck Format DVD+RW (there's no need for this; the burner can just overwrite any content). Also uncheck Quick eject (which makes the recorded DVD+RW disc less compatible on some older DVD players). Close both windows and click Next at the bottom of the dialog.

7. You're now in the menu creation window (see Figure 18-3). Click the title on top of the menu to open a small window allowing you to change the text, font, and font color.

Figure 18-3: Creating your menu and background audio file.

8. If desired, insert another background image, or choose a different template on the right. Note that there is a 30MB limit for menus recorded in real time with MovieFactory. If you select a background audio file (which I didn't), make sure it's short or you may bump up against that limit.

9. Click Add chapter menu, which adds menus for the chapters you're going to create in the next screen. If desired, click Show thumbnail number, which will show the thumbnail number along the chapter frame.

10. Select Capture by total duration and insert the duration of the tape you're converting (see Figure 18-4). This is *very important*, because it's the control that lets you walk away. If you don't select this, MovieFactory will continue recording until you tell it to stop or simply run out of disc space.

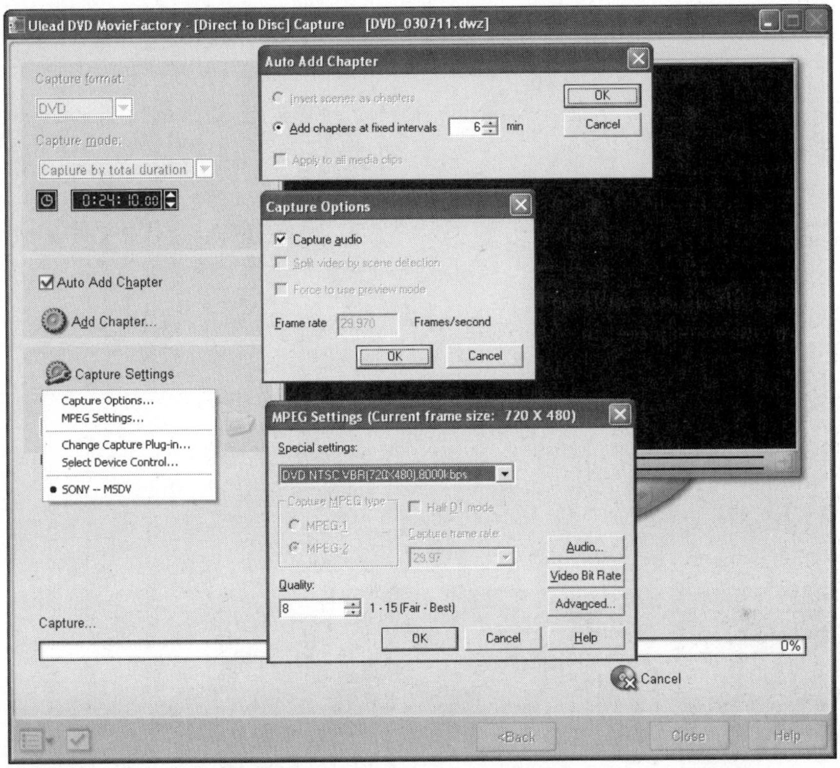

Figure 18-4: The Capture dialog box where you control the capture settings.

11. Click Auto Add Chapter to add chapters to your video.

12. Click the Add Chapter button to open the Auto Add Chapter menu; enter the desired interval (I used six minutes).

13. Click the Capture Settings button and select Capture Options. Make sure Capture audio is checked and close the dialog.

14. Click the Capture Settings button and select MPEG Settings. Here you need to select the highest data rate that will capture and store your video on disc. Table 18-1 shows the approximate number of minutes available for each data rate. Choosing variable bitrate encoding (VBR) as opposed to constant bitrate encoding (CBR) will probably deliver more minutes per disc, but you can't count on it (though I would choose VBR nonetheless). Close the dialog after making your selection.

Table 18-1:   Minutes of Stored Video for Each Encoding Setting

2,000 kbps (MyDVD only)	311 minutes
4,000 kbps	155 minutes
6,000 kbps	104 minutes
8,000 kbps	78 minutes

15. Turn on your analog source, press play, and you should see video in the preview window. If you don't, either you don't have the capture device properly installed and selected or your cables aren't connected. Make sure you see video in the window before clicking Capture & Burn.

At this point, MovieFactory takes over, and the recording light on your DVD recorder should show frequent action. You can cancel at any time, but you lose what's been captured. One irritating feature of MovieFactory is that it doesn't save your project settings, so if you cancel and start over, you have to go through every step again.

After the video reaches the timed ending point, VideoStudio takes a moment to create the final menus and then finalizes the disc. Figure 18-5 shows the final result. It's time to lick the envelope and send the disc to grandma (wonder if she'll notice the title was missing).

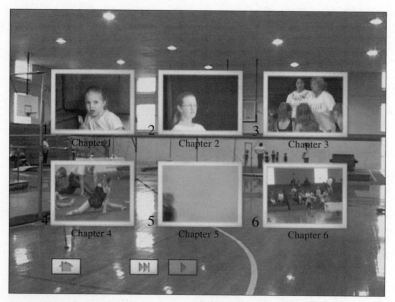

Figure 18-5: Here's our final video, converted and stored in real time. Oops, no title!

A Quick Note on Converting VHS Movies

Legalities aside, note that Hollywood VHS tapes that can't be copied from VHS deck to VHS deck can be captured by your computer and converted to DVD. That's because the copy protection scheme used by Hollywood subtly affects VHS deck writing heads in a way that doesn't impact video capture on the computer.

As with all video captures, however, you'll get substantially better results if you capture via S-Video, an output most consumer VHS decks don't support. It will work with composite inputs, but you may be disappointed with the quality.

One-Step Conversion in MyDVD

Unlike MovieFactory 2, MyDVD doesn't write to the disc in real time; it stores the captured video into a temporary file, then encodes, creates the menus, and finally writes to the recordable disc. You can start things running and walk away, but the process takes slightly longer than MovieFactory 2.

For the record, I'm working with a Pentium 4 3.06 GHz computer, writing to a Pioneer A05 DVD-R/RW drive. Once again, I'm capturing from a DV camcorder via a FireWire port.

By now you're familiar with my pathological dislike for placing temporary and captured files in the Windows My Documents folder where they can't be easily found and deleted. This wasn't an issue with MovieFactory since all files were written directly to the DVD. Here, however, MyDVD will be storing a boatload of captured and temporary files, and you need to place them in a separate folder.

So run MyDVD, choose File → Preferences from the top menu bar to open the screen shown in Figure 18-6. Change the location, if desired.

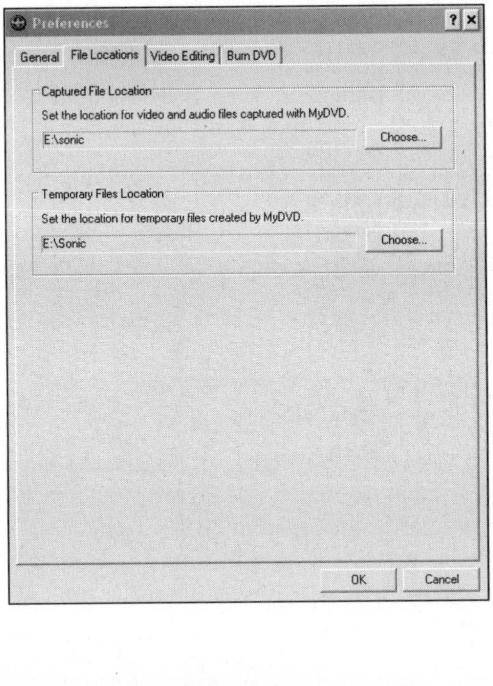

Figure 18-6: You gotta put those captured and temporary files where you can find them.

Now that that's squared away, let's begin the process, which not surprisingly is similar to MovieFactory 2. Follow the bouncing ball in Figures 18-7 through 18-12.

1. Run MyDVD and select Transfer Video Direct-to-DVD (see Figure 18-7).

Figure 18-7: Converting tapes to DVD in MyDVD begins here.

2. Check Record to DVD (see Figure 18-8).

3. Type the desired project name, which becomes your title (Whatley's Gymnastics 2003 in this case).

4. Either check No menus. Just play movie., or click Edit Style to customize your menus.

5. Customize your menu as you desire (see Figure 18-9). In this case, since there is no limit on the menu-related data stored to disc, I chose a background audio track. When complete, close this window and click Next to move to the next screen.

6. Set the capture duration by entering the total length in the field below the Set capture length option (see Figure 18-10). Once again, if you don't set this control, MyDVD won't automatically stop, and you'll have to be there to stop it manually.

7. Click Settings to open the Record Settings screen (see Figure 18-11). Here you select the desired encoding rate, and whether to encode audio and video. See Table 18-1 for estimated durations, and note that MyDVD also tells you the "Record time available" in the Details screen shown in Figure 18-10. Click OK to close the dialog.

8. This is a tough call. MyDVD offers both content-based and time-code-based scene change detection. The problem is that in many instances, either technique (see Figure 18-12) will produce too many scenes. For example, in the gymnastics video, I had 38 scene changes, which is probably too many for comfortable DVD navigation. Since I had to hang around and write this chapter anyway, I chose to select chapter points by hitting the space bar, but if you select this option, you obviously can't walk away.

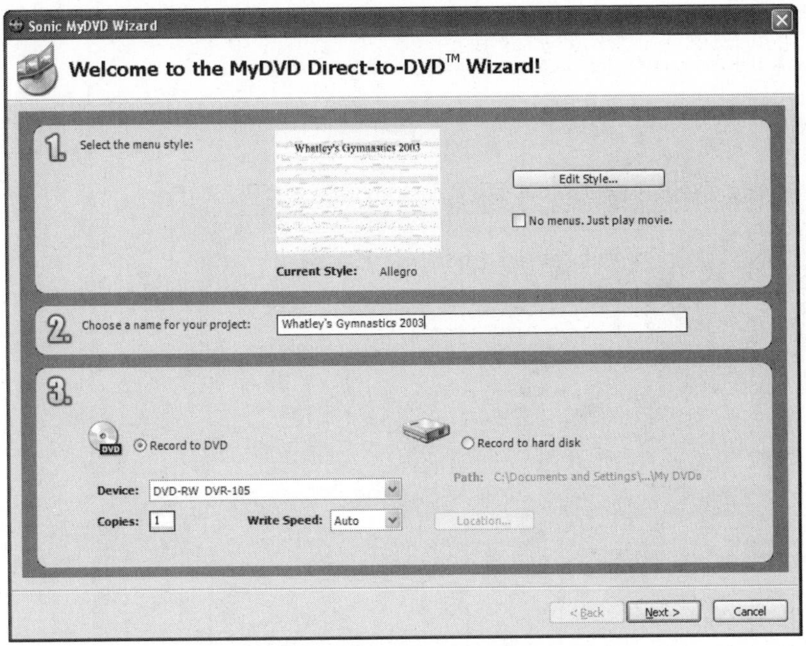

Figure 18-8: The first MyDVD Direct-to-DVD wizard box.

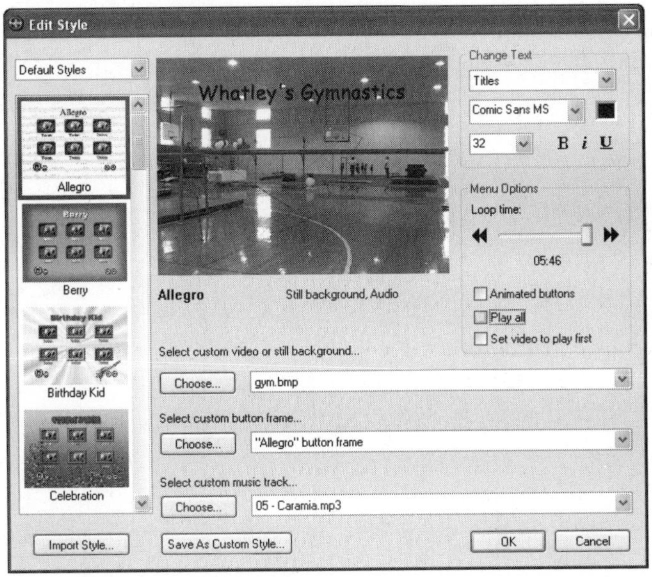

Figure 18-9: The Edit Style dialog where you can customize
your menus as you like.

9. If you roll tape, you should see video in the window. Click Start Capturing, and you're on
   your way.

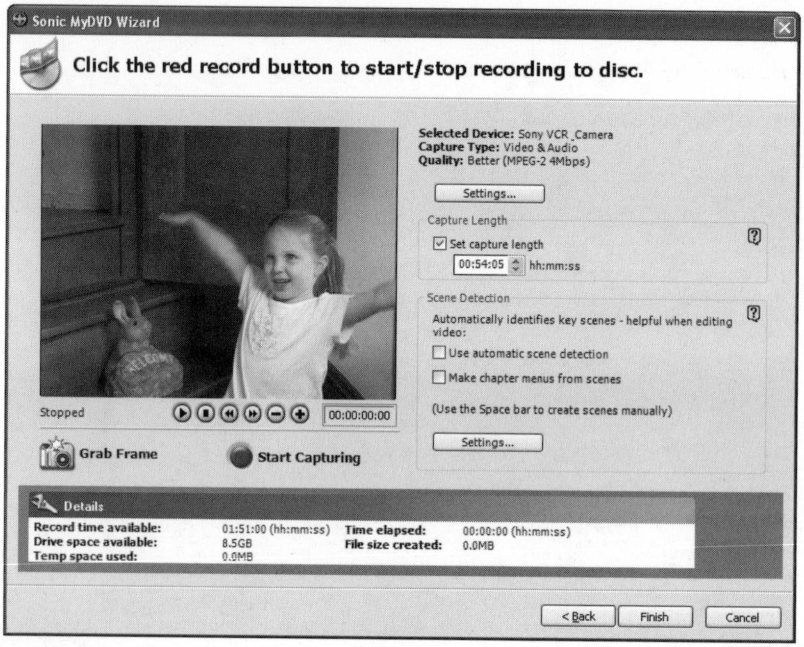

Figure 18-10: Last stop before burning to DVD.

After capturing the designated duration or stopping capture by clicking Stop Capturing, MyDVD starts assembling the project. While this took only a few moments with MovieFactory, MyDVD took 30 minutes after capturing the 54 minutes of video to finalize the disc. (See Figure 18-13 for the finished result.)

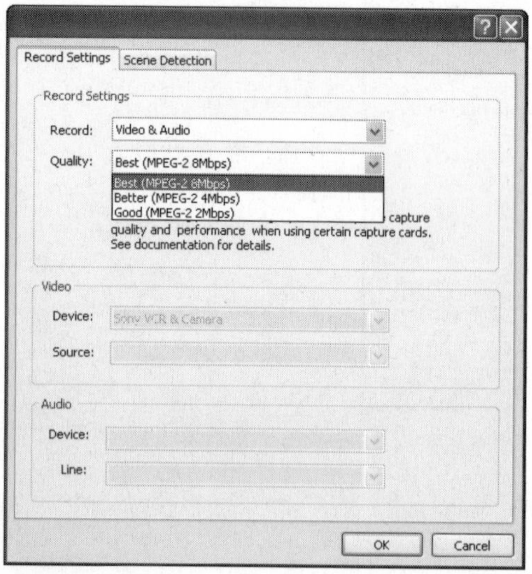

Figure 18-11: Setting the encoding rate in the Record Settings dialog box.

Figure 18-12: The Scene Detection dialog box.

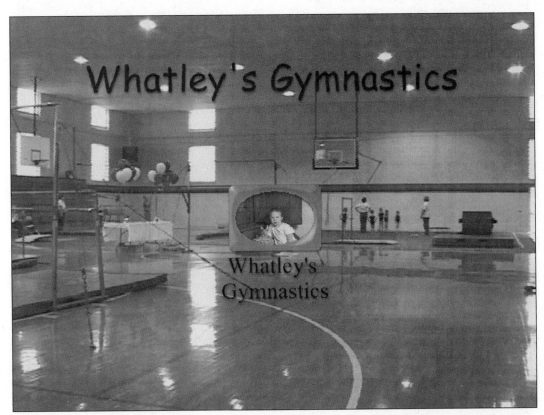

Figure 18-13: The completed DVD produced by MyDVD (title and all). Clicking the icon on the screen will take the viewer to the first menu with chapter points.

The primary difference, of course, is that MovieFactory was encoding and writing to the disc all along, while MyDVD didn't start writing to disc until after capturing and creating all necessary files. Still, you can set it up and walk away, which is a nice luxury.

Summary

This is a summary of the key points from this chapter:

1. To convert VHS or other tapes to DVD, you'll need:

   - The appropriate capture device (analog or FireWire).

   - A software program that automates this function.

   - A fast computer.

   - The appropriate recordable drive and media. For example, MovieFactory 2 can only operate in real time when writing to a DVD+RW recorder with +RW media.

2. Note that direct-to-disc doesn't always mean direct-to-disc. For example, MyDVD first stores the video to hard disk, then writes to DVD. The advantage of this is that you have complete flexibility regarding options like audio menus, which may be limited in true direct to DVD schemes, or even video menus and buttons. The obvious disadvantage is time.

3. Setting capture duration is the critical parameter that lets you get up and walk away from the computer. Forget this at your own risk.

4. Remember to choose encoding parameters that match the duration of the tape you intend to convert to DVD.

5. Time-code- or content-based scene detection is a great feature while capturing for editing purposes but may create too many menu points if used as the basis of selecting chapters on your DVD.

Chapter 19

Basic DVD-Authoring Techniques

M ost readers approach DVD production from one of three directions. The first is that you've shot your video and want to capture and convert it to DVD in a program like Pinnacle Expression, Sonic MyDVD, or Ulead MovieFactory. You may also have captured and edited in Movie Maker 2 and decided to use one of these programs to create your DVD.

The second is that you've been editing in Pinnacle Studio or VideoStudio, and you're ready to start the authoring component. You'll be using the same program; you're just done editing and ready to start authoring and burning.

The third direction is that you're using a video editor to produce your video and then a stand-alone prosumer editor, like DVD Workshop or Adobe Encore, to produce your DVD, probably because you need more authoring functionality than consumer programs provide.

This chapter covers the first two cases, describing how to capture, create menus, and burn DVDs in prosumer programs. Chapter 20 deals with the type of advanced DVD production capabilities that can only be handled in an advanced DVD-authoring environment.

Our Sample Content

Let's take a moment and examine the footage that I'm starting with. It's from a wedding weekend on Saint Simon's Island off the coast of Georgia where my eldest daughter was one of two flower girls. I wasn't shooting the event as much as trying to show a flower girl's view of the wedding, and I was in recording mode most of the weekend, shooting what walked in front of my camera and not trying to build a story.

There are four video scenes I want viewers to access directly from the DVD menu. These are:

- Pool — Our visit to the pool with grandmommy and granddaddy Johnson.

- Pre-wedding practice — Some practice sessions with the flower girls prior to the wedding and a brief pre-wedding moment with the bride.

- Wedding ceremony.

- Wedding reception.

In addition, a cousin provided two groups of digital photographs I want to include in the project, one from the rehearsal dinner, which I attended sans video camera, and the other from the reception/ceremony. What I'm building is a DVD with (hopefully) links to the major scenes, along with links to the two slideshow packages.

The programs vary significantly in their capability in this regard, so there will be significant application-specific instruction throughout the chapter.

One-Stop DV to DVD

Here you're going to look at the operation of Pinnacle Expression, Sonic MyDVD, and Ulead MovieFactory, working through the stages of moving from DV to DVD. There's a lot of similarity between the programs, so I'll work through the process once with all three, investing time at critical stages, like menu and chapter creation, to isolate the key capabilities of each of the three programs.

I'll assume in my discussion that you have your capture card or external unit installed and up and running and that you're ready to go.

Step 1: Plan Project

Though you can make decisions on menus, background music, scenes, and the like in real time, there's one decision that you need to make up front, at least with these one-stop DV-to-DVD products, and that's navigation. You need to plan this up front because it affects the way you capture your video.

The big question here is what level of navigational flexibility does the program provide? There are four basic levels:

- **No flexibility.** Menus are sequential. This applies to Pinnacle Expression (see Figure 19-1).

- **One-level branching.** You can link from one menu to a submenu containing chapter points. This is the case with Ulead MovieFactory (see Figure 19-2).

- **Multiple-level branching.** You can link from one menu to another that can contain videos or additional menu links, but all navigation is sequential, from submenu to sub-submenu, and so on, so you can't link menus to menus free form. This pertains to Sonic Solutions MyDVD. Though you can do more with MyDVD, our project requires only simple branching and will end up looking like Figure 19-2.

■ **Free-form navigation.** You can link any menu to any other menu or content without restriction. This is Pinnacle Studio, Ulead DVD Workshop, and Adobe Encore.

Figure 19-1: Sequential menus only, a flat DVD with no navigational flexibility.

When capturing for Pinnacle Expression, you might as well capture the entire video at once, because capturing scene by scene provides no added navigational flexibility. In contrast, with both MovieFactory and MyDVD, you want to capture each major scene separately, because it makes it easier to access each program's branching capabilities. I'll discuss how to capture for Pinnacle Studio and Ulead VideoStudio in the following sections.

After you identify the navigational flexibility provided, draw a little schematic identifying the major segments of your project and how you hope to structure your DVD. For your purposes, Figure 19-1 will serve as the diagram for Expression while Figure 19-2 will serve for both MovieFactory and MyDVD.

My time budget for this project is about an hour, exclusive of capture and burn time. I assume that the bulk of this time will be spent isolating the video that I want to retain in the project. I will create a very simple custom background for the project and add an audio menu, but I don't have time for heavy menu customization.

Step 2: Set Project Type

Now we're ready to fire up the program and start moving. All three programs can burn DVDs and VideoCDs, Super VideoCDs, or both. So it's generally a good plan to identify the type of project you'll be creating early on.

With Expression, you have to click the Project Settings icon on the bottom right, then choose the output format in the Settings window (see Figure 19-3). Check the appropriate output format on the upper left. While you're here, click the advanced toolbar and direct Expression to encode at 8,000 kbps, saving a step when you're ready to encode. I'll explain why shortly.

With MyDVD and MovieFactory (see Figure 19-4), you can't get by the first screen without setting the project type.

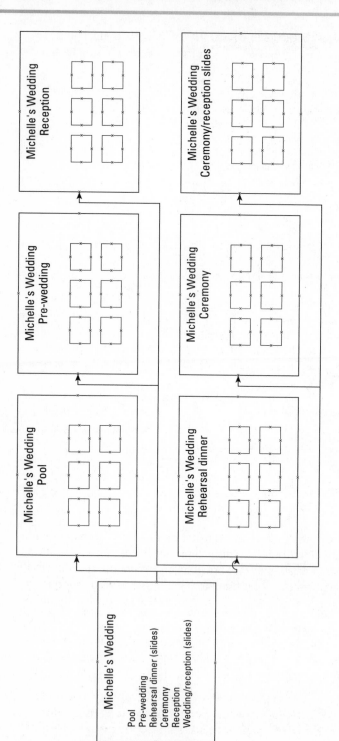

Figure 19-2: One-level branching gives you the ability to link to your major scenes — a nice option.

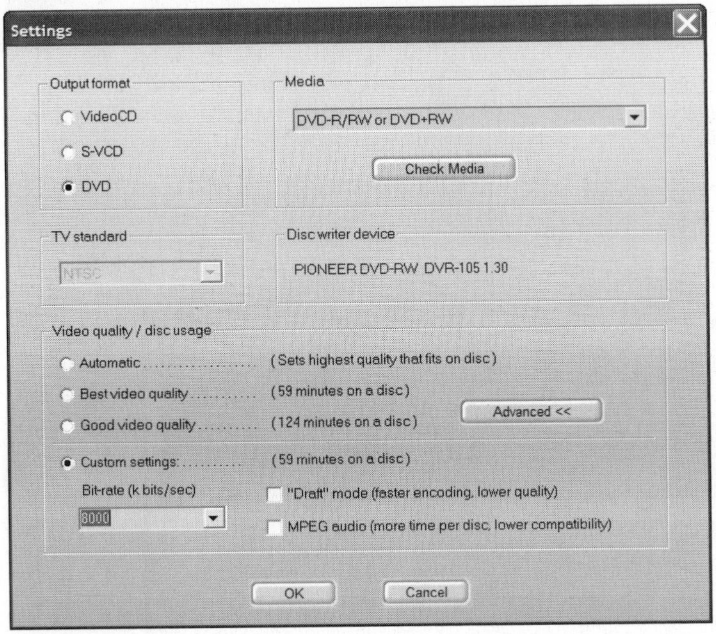

Figure 19-3: Choosing your output format in Expression's Settings window.

Step 3: Set Capture Parameters

You must set several options prior to capture, including file location, capture file format, scene detection options, and capture duration if available. Here are my recommendations:

- **Choose file location.** I always create a separate folder off the root of my capture drive for each project and then point the video editor or authoring program toward that drive for all capture, preview, temporary, and DVD component files.

- **Set capture format.** If you're capturing from a DV camera, capture in DV format, even if the program can capture directly into MPEG-2. This will maximize your scene detection options and produce overall better quality video. Though many programs can capture DV to MPEG-2 in real time, the algorithms are optimized for compression speed, not quality. Though it takes longer to capture in DV and later encode into MPEG-2, quality should be higher.

  If you're capturing video from an analog source, use the standard capture format recommended for the hardware device, usually Motion JPEG for internal devices, and MPEG-2 for external.

- **Set scene detection options.** Scene detection refers to the program's ability to identify scene breaks in the captured video. The most accurate way to do this is by using time codes in the source video that identify when you start and stop shooting, but this is only available with DV video. The other technique uses changes in the content itself, which is much less accurate.

All programs will give you the chance to manually break the video into scenes after capture, so if there are several clearly defined segments (rehearsal dinner, wedding, and reception), you can disable scene detection and insert these chapter points manually later. On the other hand, if you have lots of scenes to try and include and exclude, scene detection may assist the process.

■ **Set capture duration.** This is a convenience feature that lets you walk away from the capture after starting the capture.

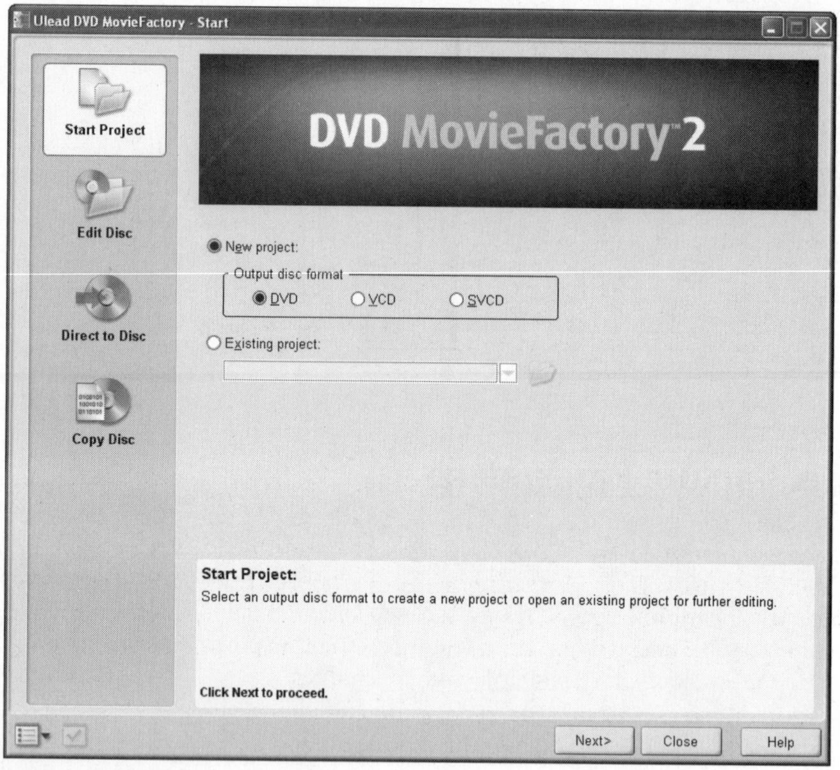

Figure 19-4: MovieFactory doesn't let you past the first screen without selecting your project type (neither does MyDVD, which isn't shown).

PINNACLE EXPRESSION

With Pinnacle Expression, you click the camera icon on the upper left of the main screen to access the capture program (see Figure 19-5). From there, you click the filmstrip setting beside the Captured and imported files box to access the Scene Detection Options dialog, and then you click the camcorder atop the box to access Expression's capture controls. That's where you direct Expression to save video to your capture folder.

Figure 19-5: Pinnacle Expression's consumer-friendly interface.

MYDVD

Your first task with MyDVD is to identify your capture folder, since the program won't let you do this after you enter the capture module. From the MyDVD menu, select File → Preferences → File Locations to see the dialog where you set the location for capture files and temporary files.

MyDVD's ability to select chapter menus from scenes is a great feature when you don't have that many scene changes. On the other hand, if you have 149, like I did on the wedding tape used for this chapter, it's very ungainly. I definitely need to consolidate some videos before selecting chapter menu points.

Click Capture in the main program window to access the capture controls (see Figure 19-6). Here you set the screen detection options and also the capture duration. Before clicking Start Capturing, click the Settings button to access the screens where you select you capture format and fine-tune your scene detection techniques.

MOVIEFACTORY

In MovieFactory, you enter the capture interface by clicking on the Capture icon in the main screen. From the top down, the capture screen (see Figure 19-7) has controls for setting capture format, capture duration, and capture folder. Click the Capture Settings icon to access the scene detection options.

Step 4: Capture Video

To capture in Expression, click Start Capture in the capture video from DV camcorder screen, which will take you to the window that displays scenes as the program detects them, and a stop button for terminating the capture process. With Expression, you probably should capture the entire tape at once, since capturing separate segments provides no additional navigational flexibility, and capture with scene detection, to assist the lengthy editing process.

To capture with MyDVD and MovieFactory, press the Play button to start video playback, and then click Capture. The button will convert to a Stop capture you can use if you didn't set the capture duration.

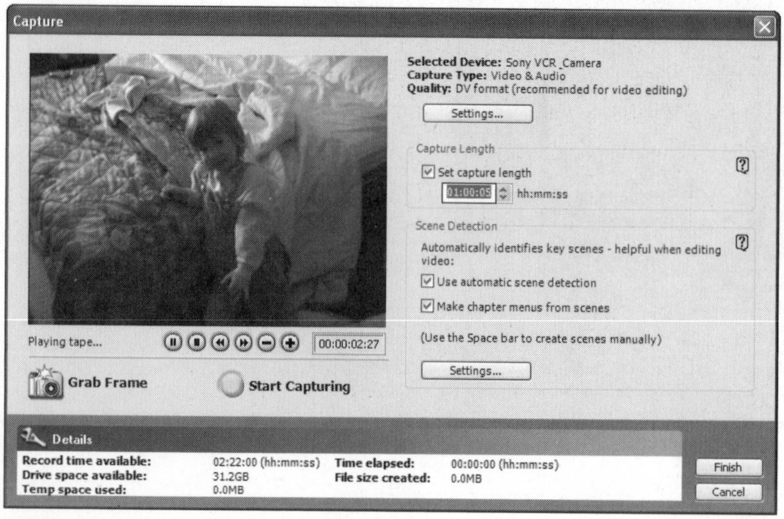

Figure 19-6: Setting capture duration and scene detection options in MyDVD.

With MyDVD, it's better to capture individual scenes separately, since this is the easiest way to create the desired navigational structure. As you'll see, scene detection assists the editing process, so I would capture with scene detection enabled.

Though MovieFactory can split clips, I still found it easier to capture and input separate clips for each major segment. As you'll see, however, since MovieFactory's editing tools are so easy to use, scene detection provides little benefit, so I would capture each major scene separately with this feature disabled.

Step 5: Create Final Videos and Chapter Points

This is the critical stage where you combine, delete, trim, split, edit, and otherwise reduce the amount of scenes to a manageable number. In the wedding video that I'm editing here, for example, there are 149 discrete scenes, representing 149 times that I started and stopped the camera over the course of the weekend. I could choose a template and let the authoring program create enough menus for all scenes, but navigation would be pretty ugly and the disc would contain a lot of videos just not worth watching.

Figure 19-7: Choosing capture duration, settings, and capture folder in MovieFactory.

Instead, the goals during this stage are to

- Delete undesired videos.
- Create a manageable number of chapter points or scenes.
- Change the video title and thumbnail image.

Now let's see how this works with each of the three programs.

PINNACLE EXPRESSION

With Pinnacle Expression, I start with 149 scenes that desperately need to be weeded down to a much more manageable number. In fact, because there are no submenus, I would probably take it down to six items that fit on one screen. Fortunately, while the toolset is a bit clumsy, it can definitely get the job done.

After capture, click button number 2, the TV icon, to access the main editing screen. Your video should be sitting in the menu, probably with lots of other thumbnails, each representing a scene. Then click the scissors on the bottom right of the preview window to bring up the screen shown in Figure 19-8.

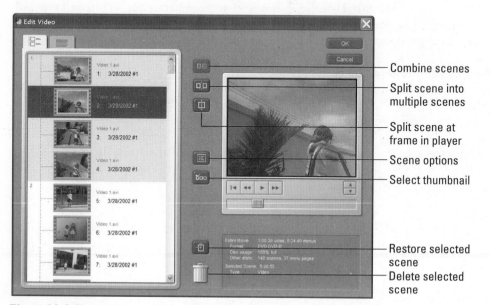

Figure 19-8: Expression is a touch clumsy when it comes to trimming up your videos, but it can get the job done.

Deleting Scenes

To delete unwanted scenes, simply touch them and click the Delete icon (see Figure 19-8). If you only want to delete a segment of a scene, you have to first split the scene into two parts, one to keep, one to delete. To split the scene, touch it to highlight it in the player, move either to the first frame you want to delete (if the desired segment is at the start of the video) or the first frame you want to keep (if the desired segment is at the rear), and then click the Split scene icon. Delete the unwanted scene, and repeat this process until all you have left are keeper scenes.

Note

If you didn't capture with scene detection, you can click the Split scenes into multiple scenes button and select one of the options.

Creating a Manageable Number of Scenes

Expression allows you to move scenes around at will, simply by dragging and dropping them into the desired position. Once accomplished, you can combine scenes by holding down the Shift key and touching the scenes to combine. Note that the scenes must be contiguous in the edit window to combine them and also that you have to touch the scene *anywhere but on the thumbnail*; otherwise the program will select just that scene. Once you have the group selected, click the Combine scenes icon.

Note the Scene options button, which opens the Scene options window (not shown). Here, you can insert transitions into the scenes, display the scene title over the video when playing, and return to the menu after playback is finished. Within scenes, I usually go without transitions, so I haven't checked these, and I can live without the title displayed over the video. I'm also opting to have the video play back sequentially through the scenes rather than return to the menu at the conclusion of each.

Changing the Title and Thumbnail Image

Now it's time to change the title and thumbnail image. Changing the title is simple; just touch the text description to make it active and then type in the new title. Press Enter after completing the title, as opposed to clicking elsewhere with your mouse; otherwise, Expression will revert back to the previous title.

To change the thumbnail, touch the scene to display it in the player, move to the desired frame, and then click the Select thumbnail button. Click OK to return to the main screen, and now you have a much more manageable production.

SONIC MYDVD

I captured four separate videos for MyDVD, so first I'll insert them by clicking Get Movies on the left panel and using the standard file open screen (see Figure 19-9). From there, Sonic simplifies all steps with its new editing tools.

Deleting/Combining Scenes

Working clip by clip, I touch the clip, right-click, and select Edit video. If you haven't yet selected your scenes, follow the prompts through the scene menu first, which will create the scenes visible on the storyboard beneath the preview window in Figure 19-10. From there, you can touch and delete any clip, or touch the clip and use the trim handles beneath the video window to eliminate unwanted frames. Note the new ability to insert transitions, effects, and titles in the same window. Click OK to return to the main window.

Creating Chapter Points

After editing, you may want to create chapter points that viewers can quickly jump to from the DVD menu. To add chapter points, touch the clip, right-click, and select Add/Edit Chapters (see Figure 19-11). Use the slider bar to move to the desired starting point of each new chapter and select Add Chapter. When you click OK, MyDVD will change the clip icon to a chapter icon that will take the viewer to a submenu page to select the chapter videos. Click OK when completed to return to the main window.

Changing the Title and Thumbnail Image

Now for the final steps. To change the title, simply touch it with the cursor, which activates the text, and type in the new text. You'll learn how to change fonts and font sizes in a later section in this chapter. To change the thumbnail, touch the target video, right-click, and select Set button image. This brings up the Set Button Image window where you drag the slider to the desired image and click OK.

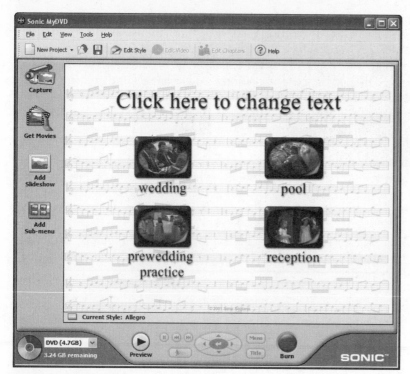

Figure 19-9: MyDVD's new video-editing tools highlight a streamlined mechanism for excluding unwanted video scenes. Note the counter in the bottom-left corner telling me that I've got 3.24GB of space left.

Note that when you create chapters, the icon on the main screen changes to chapters. It looks ugly, but I'll fix it later. Double-click the wedding chapters icon to see the submenu where viewers will be sent when they click this button. Update these titles and thumbnails to your liking.

ULEAD MOVIEFACTORY

Ulead has excellent tools for trimming clips, so let's get to it. As with MyDVD, I captured four separate clips which I'll insert using the Add Video button on the upper left (see Figure 19-12).

Deleting/Combining Scenes

Click the clip to edit and select the Extract Video button to activate the namesake control shown in Figure 19-13. Move the slider bar to the first desired frame to include, and type F3 or click the In button. Then move to the first frame to exclude, and type F4 or click Out. Follow this process through to the end of the video, and then the end of the click to identify and delete unwanted scenes. Click OK to return to the main window.

Creating Chapter Points

Touch the target clip, and then click Add/Edit Chapter. Move the slider to the desired chapter points, and click Add to add a chapter. You can also add a chapter using the Auto button. Click OK to return to the main window.

Figure 19-10: New in MyDVD 5.0 are basic editing tools for creating scenes and adding titles and dissolves.

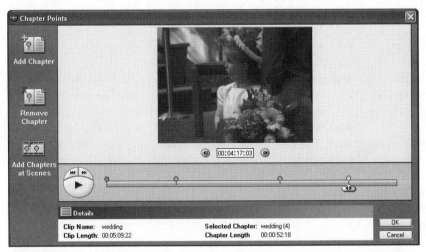

Figure 19-11: Choosing chapter points in MyDVD. The "Add Chapters at Scenes" control automatically adds chapter points at scene changes as determined by DV time code.

Figure 19-12: Adding our videos into the MovieFactory interface. Love that huge preview window.

Note that while you can create a chapter point in MovieFactory, you can't create labels for the videos, as you can with MyDVD. When the viewer clicks, he'll see a page with icons and transport controls leading to the next page or back to the main menu. This makes it especially critical that you take a moment and reset the thumbnail for each chapter to a meaningful, recognizable image.

To do this, highlight the chapter point with the cursor. Then move the player control to the desired image, right-click, and choose Change Thumbnail.

Changing the Title and Thumbnail Image

To change the title, touch any title to make it active and type in the replacement text. To change the thumbnail image, touch the clip to make it active, move the slider in the preview window to the desired thumbnail frame, and then right-click and choose Change Thumbnail (see Figure 19-14).

Step 6: Create Slideshow

Now it's time to create the slideshows. The dedicated slideshow functions all these products offer provide a real benefit, because digital pictures — done well — can be such a powerful medium. As you'll see, however, the features vary fairly widely between the programs.

Figure 19-13: MovieFactory's excellent Extract video control makes short work of scrapping the unwanted frames from each sequence. The thumbnails at the bottom represent scenes retained in the video.

These are the basics steps in slideshow production:

- Inserting images
- Arranging the images and inserting transitions and background audio
- Arranging menus to the desired order

When creating a slideshow, I've found that the optimal per-slide duration is around three to five seconds. The examples that follow took seven seconds per slide because it's a family event, and my mother-in-law, the primary target viewer, will enjoy poring over the slides. Most audiences, however, start to chafe above the five-second mark, so faster is definitely better.

PINNACLE EXPRESSION

The ability to create slideshows from digital pictures is one of Expression's strongest capabilities. Let's see why.

Figure 19-14: Changing the thumbnail image in MovieFactory.

Inserting Images

To load slides in Pinnacle Expression, you go back to the capture screen by clicking the Camcorder icon atop the video, and then click the Import a digital photo icon to open a file dialog and load the images. Unlike the other two programs, you can't load the two slideshows separately; you have to load them into one slideshow and then split them into two using the Split scene controls.

Arranging Images and Inserting Transitions and Background Audio

To access the images, close the Capture window to return to the main screen. The slideshow is the first image shown on the upper left. Click the Scissors button to edit the slideshow, which takes you back to the Edit video screen (see Figure 19-15).

To split the slideshow into two, click the + icon to reveal all the underlying slides, scroll down to the first slide of the second group, and click the Split scene icon, just as if you were splitting a video. This creates two slideshows. One image in this screen was taken in portrait mode and needs to be rotated 90 degrees to the left. Fortunately, Expression has a full complement of tools for this and other image editing, including color correction and cropping. Since it's my father-in-law, caught in a rare silly mood, I'll use the crop tool to zoom in so it will look fantastic on our big-screen TV.

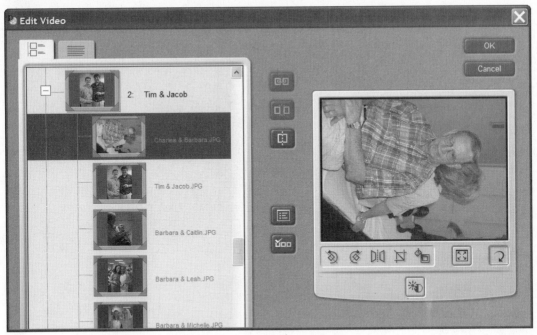

Figure 19-15: Pinnacle Expression's slideshow tools include the ability to rotate and crop images, which can save a trip to your still-image editor and shave production time.

Of course, I can drag the slides to any order and click the Scene options icon to insert transitions between my slides, insert a background audio track, and fit the slideshow to the background audio track. I can also save the digital images to a data portion of the DVD in case grandma wants to edit them further, all in all a very comprehensive feature set (see Figure 19-16). As a last step, I'll click the Select Thumbnail button while it's on my father-in-law to make this the thumbnail for the slideshow.

Arranging Menus to Target Order

To get the slides in proper order in the DVD menu, I click the minus sign next to the image to condense all slides into one icon, then drag them to the desired location, here the second video down because the rehearsal dinner occurred chronologically after the pool and before the pre-wedding (see Figure 19-17). Then I change the titles to the desired text.

SONIC MYDVD

Sonic's slide-creation toolset is very competent and lets me build slideshows individually, a nice change from how Expression groups all images.

Inserting Images

Click the Add Slideshow icon on the left to open the Create Slideshow menu (see Figure 19-18). Click the Get Pictures icon to load the pictures into the work area.

Figure 19-16: Other great features in Expression are the ability to match slide duration to the background audio, insert transitions between the slides, and archive files on the disc so they can be later accessed from a computer.

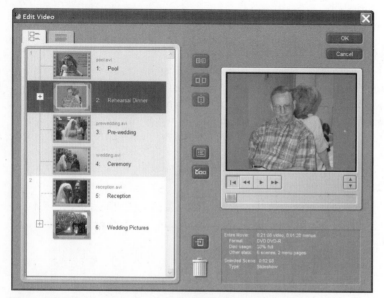

Figure 19-17: Arranging the slideshow into the proper sequence.

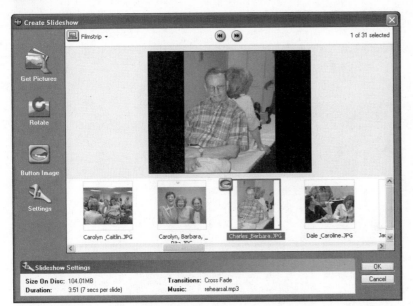

Figure 19-18: Creating slideshows in MyDVD. The little button on the upper-left corner of the third slide from the left means this is the "Button Image," which represents the slideshow on the menu.

Arranging Images and Inserting Transitions and Background Audio

I click the Rotate button on the left toolbar to restore my father-in-law to vertical, wishing that I could zoom in again, but MyDVD doesn't offer this feature, or the ability to adjust image brightness and contrast. I console myself by once again making my father-in-law the icon for this slideshow by clicking Button Image.

I click the Settings icon to reveal the Slideshow settings, where I choose the audio track, the slides I'm going to synch up with music, and the cross-fade transition. MyDVD also allows me to save the original files on DVD.

Arranging Menus to Target Order

To arrange the icon order in MyDVD, I simply drag and drop the icons to the desired location. As before, clicking the text makes it live so I can enter the desired title.

Then I do it all over again for the wedding pics, and I'm ready for the next step. Starting to shape up into a right attractive DVD, now, isn't it?

Ulead MovieFactory

Let's try the same three tasks with MovieFactory. As you'll see, while competent, MovieFactory left us wishing for more, especially the ability to synchronize slide duration with the background music and insert transitions between the slides.

Inserting Images

Like MyDVD, MovieFactory deals with slideshows individually. Click the Add Slideshow icon on the left to open the Add/Edit slideshow dialog (see Figure 19-19). From there, use the Explorer-like controls to click over to the folder containing the images and then add them individually or en masse.

Figure 19-19: Creating slideshows in MovieFactory. Here I'm inserting the slides, and using the controls above the timeline to rotate images when necessary.

Arranging Images and Inserting Transitions and Background Audio

MovieFactory's image window has a very restricted palette for rearranging the images, but if you click the 1,2,3 icon on the lower right, you get a stretchable window that can go as large as you need to display all images (see Figure 19-20). Once in the proper order, shut the window, and you can use the basic controls to rotate or delete images.

While you can insert a background audio track, you can't automatically synchronize the slideshow to the music, so you'll have to do the math yourself. The obvious formula for duration is the number of seconds of music divided by the number of slides. In our example, the song is three minutes and 51 seconds long (231 seconds), and there are 31 slides, so the duration would be 7 seconds each, which will end the slideshow about 14 seconds before the song ends. Seven seconds per image is going to feel especially long given that MovieFactory doesn't offer inter-slide transitions.

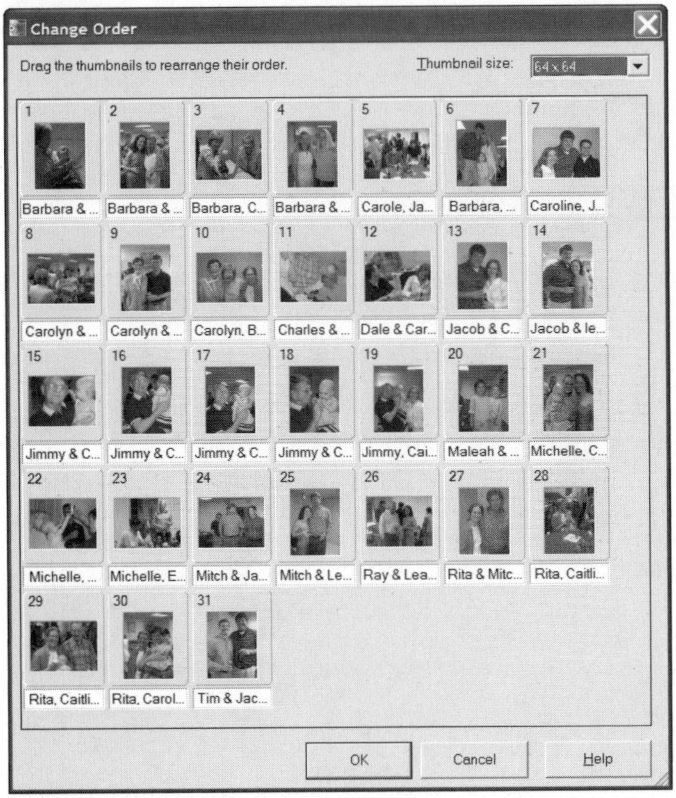

Figure 19-20: MovieFactory has a lovely palette you can open up to reorder your images.

Arranging Menus to Target Order

Click the Slideshow icon to open the Edit slideshow text description dialog. It would be easier and cleaner if we could simply touch the text to make it active and edit directly like the other programs; perhaps next version.

Once back in the main program, I can drag and drop the content to the desired order, including slideshows. As with the videos, I change the thumbnail by using the player controls to move the desired slide into the preview window, then I right-click and select Change Thumbnail.

Step 7: Create Menus

Now that I've isolated my content, let's take the next step: building my menus. This can be as easy as using a template, or (in most cases) you can also customize to a great degree. Characteristics that I'll look at changing or adding include the following:

■ **Background.** I've created an image to use as the background for the DVD menus and sub-menus. I won't use a motion background for this project because it adds complexity and increases the chances of crashing.

- **Buttons.** I'll surf around for a template that has frames that I like and simply use those, including the standard "state" colors.

- **Text.** I need to choose the font and size of my text.

- **Video buttons.** Most of the programs can create these, but they're just time-consuming eye candy that dramatically increases the potential for something going wrong. No thanks.

- **Create audio menus.** I will complement each menu with the same audio track, which is simple, fast, and really sets the tone for the video.

Note

My background audio track is about four minutes long, which keeps it from getting too repetitive. Tracks shorter than a minute or so get repetitive, then boring, then irritating.

- **Pre-play and post-play options.** If available, I will launch the first video after the background audio track finishes playing and have all videos continue on to the next rather than returning to the menu.

Not all of the programs provide equal access to these features, which will become obvious in the following sections.

PINNACLE EXPRESSION

My goal is to get all six menu items on the same screen, and the easiest way is to find a template with six frames. I click the bottom of the menu selection control on the left, scroll down until I find a template with six frames, and double-click it to select it (see Figure 19-21).

On the bottom of the menu selection screen is the Create custom menu icon, which I click to open the Create Custom Menu screen (see Figure 19-22). On the bottom are buttons for changing the five key characteristics of the menu: background image, frame, layout, text style, and background music.

Using the Import button on the lower right, I import my background image, then adjust frames and text, and add my background audio. Since I couldn't find a layout that didn't obscure the bride's and groom's faces, I caved on having only one menu. This is one of the limitations of the consumer products, but it's definitely outweighed by the ease of use the structure brings.

Pre-play options are limited; basically, the background audio track will continue to play until someone clicks a menu option. As you may recall, I selected post-play options back when I arranged the scenes, electing to have each scene play forward to the next scene.

SONIC MYDVD

Let's see how I do with my one-menu goal in MyDVD. I click Edit Style above the monitor window to open the Edit Style window (see Figure 19-23). Scrolling through the available templates, there are no good templates that don't obscure my bride and groom, so I stay with what I've got and insert my background frame anyway.

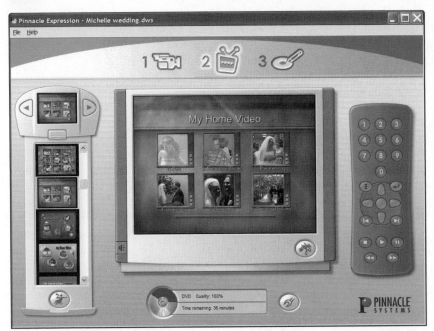

Figure 19-21: Building menus in Pinnacle Expression. Note the diskometer on the bottom, which displays how much space remains on the DVD.

Frame choices are limited, and I can't find one less obtrusive than the original, so I go with baby blue. I find myself wishing for the text style options that Expression provides, but I choose a formal but highly readable font. Below the text controls are the menu options. I elect to let my song loop completely and then start over. I also opt not to torture my audience with animated buttons, and I don't select a First Play video; they're all a bit too long to serve well in that role.

ULEAD MOVIEFACTORY

You access MovieFactory's Setup Menu by clicking Next from the Add/Edit screen. Menu templates on the upper right reveal some lovely templates (see Figure 19-24) that I can customize further with a layout that allows me to place three frames on each side of the video (see Figure 19-25), which is ideal for my background image.

I can also customize the frame, which I do, but you'll find changing text painful, since you have to change each text object manually, one by one, rather than globally. There are no styles or effects like outlines or shadows, which would help against this white background. I add my background audio track by clicking the music icon beneath the preview window in Figure 19-24 and end up with a pretty good-looking menu, if I do say so myself (it will look better with the thumbnail images instead of the frames you see in Figure 19-25). MovieFactory's post-play options will be covered just before burning the disc a little later in the chapter.

Figure 19-22: The Create Custom Menu dialog.

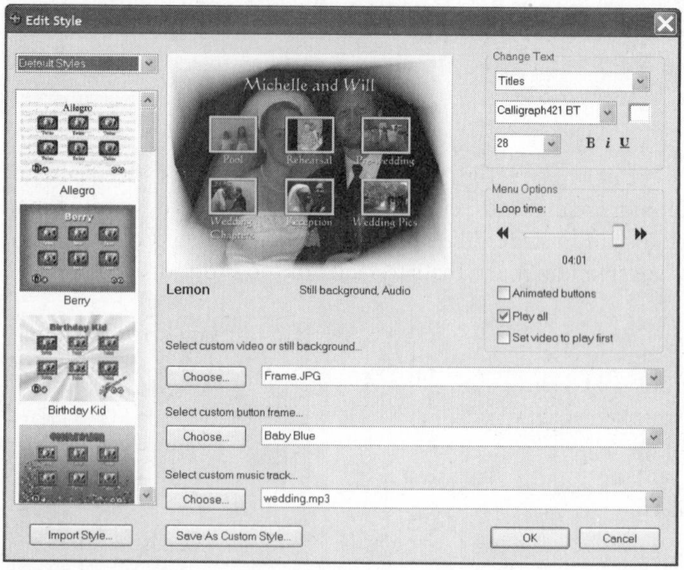

Figure 19-23: MyDVD's menu customization options.

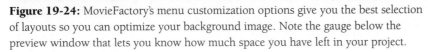

Figure 19-24: MovieFactory's menu customization options give you the best selection of layouts so you can optimize your background image. Note the gauge below the preview window that lets you know how much space you have left in your project.

Step 8: Preview

Each program has a separate preview component that mimics how playback will look after you burn the disc. Since menu creation and linking are all fixed here, it's pretty difficult to make a mistake in this regard. However, it's a great time to find mistakes like misspelled words and incorrectly labeled scenes, and to catch aesthetic issues like an audio menu that's too loud or too short, or a video menu that obscures the scene titles.

While blank recordable discs only cost a few dollars, the true cost of a burning error is the rendering and burning time, which could be several hours. That said, it takes at least an hour to preview an hour-long DVD, which is probably more than most of us will invest, especially for a title destined for grandma, as opposed to a client or paying audience.

Step 9: Burn, Baby, Burn

Now it's time to physically burn the disc. At a high level, there are only one or two issues involved, and most are fairly obvious. The first issue is *video data rate*. As you'll see shortly, you'll achieve maximum compatibility at around 8 mbps or below. So even if you have more than enough space on the disc for a higher data rate, I wouldn't go above this rate.

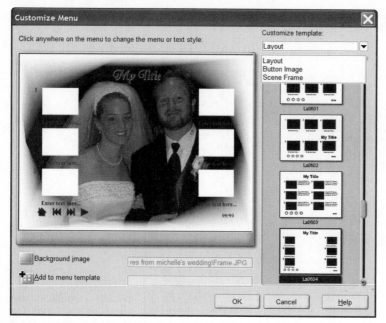

Figure 19-25: MovieFactory allows me to select where the thumbnail images are displayed on the page, which really helps here.

The second issue is *audio format*: uncompressed PCM, compressed AC-3, or MPEG. If you've got the space, as I do with my project, PCM is the best answer. If space is running short, and AC-3 is an option, you can choose AC-3 without worrying about the slight potential for compatibility issues that MPEG audio brings. If MPEG is your only choice, and the disc has to play at the target — say, in a business setting — either choose an authoring program with AC-3 or increase video compression to allow the use of uncompressed audio.

To burn with Expression, click the DVD icon atop the program. The only options are the number of discs to burn, burn speed, and the location of your temporary files. That's because way back in Figure 19-3, I told Expression to encode at 8 mbps. This same screen allowed me to encode using MPEG audio and to use a special draft mode to speed encoding at the cost of some quality, both of which I declined.

Access Sonic's Burn DVD options by clicking File → Preferences and selecting the Burn DVD options tab. As you can see in Figure 19-26, I can optimize encoding algorithm for speed or quality, and opt for either PCM or AC-3 audio. However, I can't choose the target data rate, which is a bit unsettling.

Ulead provides the most controls, which is generally good, though you have to like the other two programs' ability to simply automatically select the optimum encoding parameters for the available content (see Figure 19-27). Creating DVD folders and/or an image file is a convenient way to produce another copy fast, though they do gobble hard disk space quickly.

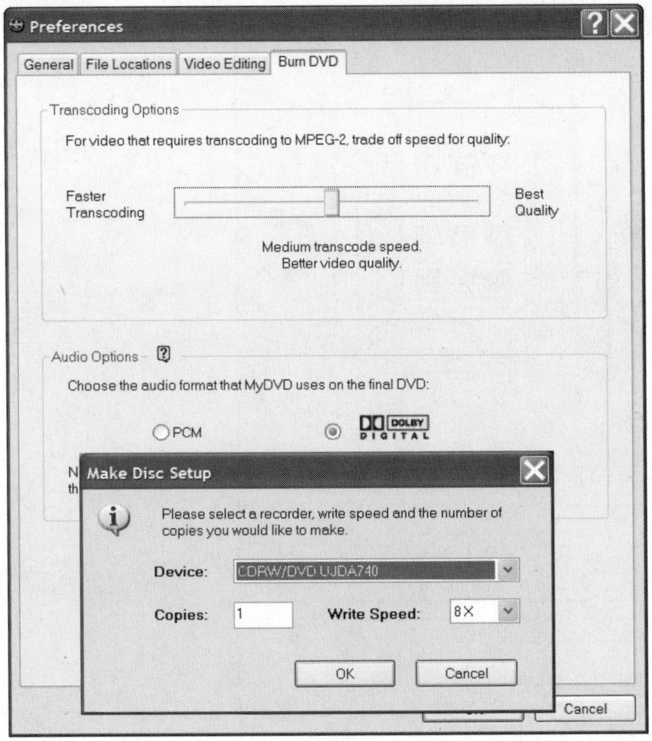

Figure 19-26: Burn controls for MyDVD — we like simple!

The Output Advanced Settings provide the ability to include the Ulead project files to disc, which allows you to re-create the project down the road and modify the content. Here you can also elect to store any random folder and the slideshow images on the disc. The Burner Advanced Settings window provides the ability to enable buffer underrun protection, and several other more arcane options.

The Project Settings screen (see Figure 19-28) provides the highly useful option to avoid reconverting compliant MPEG files, avoiding double compression for any files imported into the project. Here you'll also find post-play options for all videos, either play on or return to menu. Consistent with other programs, I choose the former.

You can also see that MovieFactory is encoding at 8000 kbps, which is my target, and the Change MPEG Settings dialog, which is my path toward accessing parameters like choosing my audio encoding method.

Depending upon the length and complexity of your project, and the speed of your burner and computer, anywhere from an hour to several hours from now, you'll have a DVD to send to Grandma. The obvious question is, will it play?

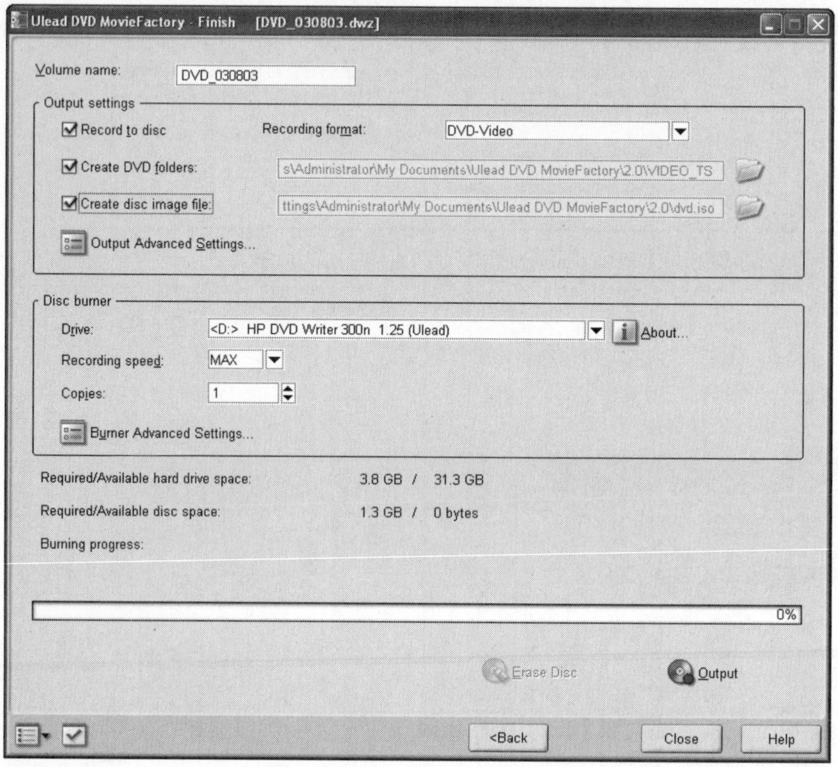

Figure 19-27 screenshot of Ulead DVD MovieFactory - Finish [DVD_030803.dwz]:

- Volume name: DVD_030803
- Output settings
  - ☑ Record to disc | Recording format: DVD-Video
  - ☑ Create DVD folders: s:\Administrator\My Documents\Ulead DVD MovieFactory\2.0\VIDEO_TS
  - ☑ Create disc image file: ttings\Administrator\My Documents\Ulead DVD MovieFactory\2.0\dvd.iso
  - Output Advanced Settings...
- Disc burner
  - Drive: <D:> HP DVD Writer 300n 1.25 (Ulead)   About...
  - Recording speed: MAX
  - Copies: 1
  - Burner Advanced Settings...
- Required/Available hard drive space: 3.8 GB / 31.3 GB
- Required/Available disc space: 1.3 GB / 0 bytes
- Burning progress:
- 0%
- Erase Disc   Output
- <Back   Close   Help

Figure 19-27: MovieFactory provides more advanced burning controls that are slightly more intimidating.

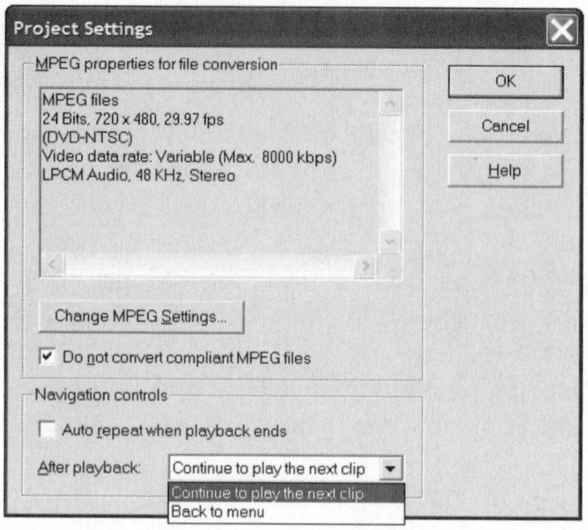

Project Settings screenshot:
- MPEG properties for file conversion
- MPEG files
  24 Bits, 720 x 480, 29.97 fps
  (DVD-NTSC)
  Video data rate: Variable (Max. 8000 kbps)
  LPCM Audio, 48 KHz, Stereo
- OK
- Cancel
- Help
- Change MPEG Settings...
- ☑ Do not convert compliant MPEG files
- Navigation controls
  - ☐ Auto repeat when playback ends
  - After playback: Continue to play the next clip
    - Continue to play the next clip
    - Back to menu

Figure 19-28: MovieFactory has a simple checkbox that prevents the recompression of compliant MPEG-2 files, and also lets you choose to jump back to the menu after a video finishes or play the next clip. These are commonly referred to as "post-play" options.

Rolling the Dice with DVD Recordable

In Chapter 5, I mentioned that not all recorded discs play on all target players. Results vary by format, and Table 19-1 shows the latest statistics from Ralph LaBarge, from an article that had not been published yet when I wrote this. Check Ralph's site at www.alphadvd.com for details.

Table 19-1   Playback Compatibility by Disc Format

	DVD-R	DVD-RW	DVD+R	DVD+RW
Played in this percentage of target players	86.2%	80.3%	89.5%	84.7%

As you can see, best case is with DVD+R, with close to 90% compatibility, with worst case around 80 percent (DVD-RW). Taking these statistics into account, as well as advice from Ralph's article "DVD Compatibility Test" (*DV Magazine,* July 2002), here are some tips to produce the most compatible discs:

■ Don't distribute rewriteable discs of any format. Not only are they more expensive, they are significantly less compatible.

■ Buy brand-name burners and media, since they perform the quality control and compatibility testing necessary to achieve extensive playback compatibility. Off brands most decidedly do not.

■ Burn your DVD-R projects at no more than 7–8 mbps. I typically use 8, which has worked well for me, but if one of your targets reports playback problems, try re-encoding at 7. Anything higher delivers only minimal additional quality and increases the incompatibility risk dramatically.

■ When using off-brand media, burn at 1X.

Authoring with Video Editors

When you're authoring within a video editor like Pinnacle Studio and Ulead MediaStudio, you should assemble all content within the editor, including movies and slideshows. Basically, when you switch to authoring mode in both programs, you're at "Step 7: Create Menus," and need to accomplish this, preview and burn.

Ulead VideoStudio essentially uses sister product MovieFactory as its DVD-compiling-and-burning engine. When you've completed your edit in VideoStudio, click Share→Create Disc on the upper right, which opens the Authoring screen (see Figure 19-29). Though not as well featured as MovieFactory — for example having no dedicated slideshow controls — you can use the direction provided earlier to work through the various screens.

Figure 19-29: From editing to authoring with VideoStudio — if you speak MovieFactory, you're in like Flint.

Pinnacle Studio

Though I'm sure that Studio and Expression share many under-the-hood components, the interfaces are entirely different, and for good reason — Studio is a much more flexible tool. Let's start by being un-ambitious, however, and merely re-create the project that I completed earlier using all three products. Next chapter, I'll freelance a bit and study Studio's flexible menu options.

ADDING MENUS

As with VideoStudio, I'll start with all content created and ready on the timeline, shown in Figure 19-30. With Studio, the easiest way to convert a video project into a DVD project is to drag a menu down to the first timeline. I've got the menu templates screen open and have selected a template with six video windows, perfect for our projects.

I drag this to the start of the video project, and Studio asks if I'd like to insert chapter points at the start of every scene. I have too many scenes in the project, so I'll have to decline and create chapter points and link them manually.

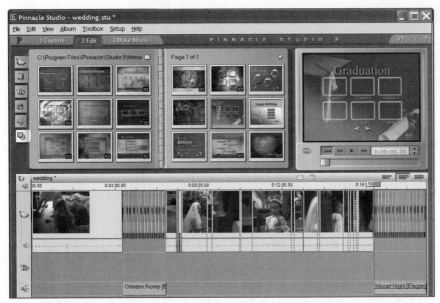

Figure 19-30: Inserting and linking menus into Studio is as simple as drag and drop.

Before starting this, however, I want to create my audio menu, which I accomplish by dragging my background music to the background audio track, and manually dragging the new menu so that it's the same duration. I could create a video menu the same way, but I won't for this project.

To create a chapter link, I move the timeline scrubber to the desired starting point and click the Set chapter control in the Edit menu window (see Figure 19-31). You should see a little flag with C1, which stands for chapter 1. If your production has more than one menu, which this doesn't, the flag colors would change with each menu.

I could select to return to menu by moving to the end of the scene and clicking the Return to menu button, but I want this project to play through. Add additional chapter points by clicking the next open frame in the menu, then moving the timeline scrubber and clicking the Set chapter control.

Note

If you don't change to the next frame after setting a chapter point, Studio will simply keep updating the same frame to the new chapter point.

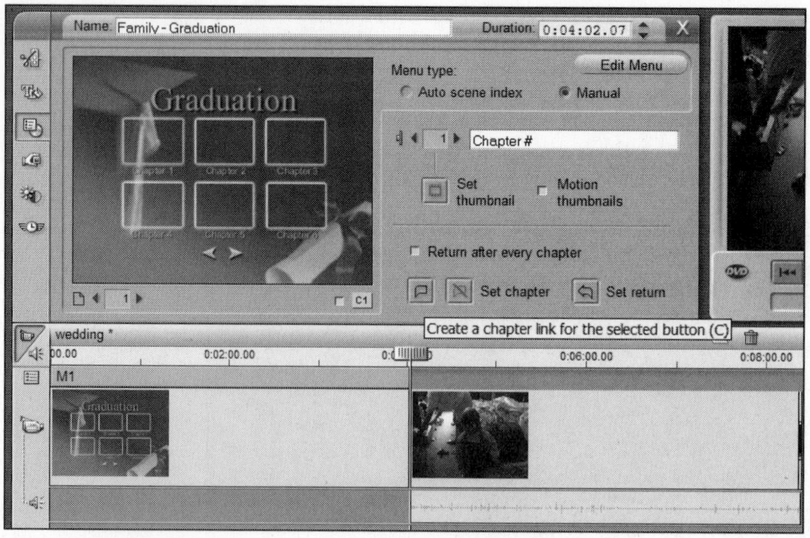

Figure 19-31: Setting a chapter point in Pinnacle Studio's timeline. Love that integrated video editing/DVD authoring.

Once you've got all your chapters linked, Studio should look like Figure 19-32. Note that all six frames have unique images, and that there are six menu links above the timeline. You can easily change the thumbnail, of course, by touching the frame, moving the cursor to the desired frame, and clicking the Set thumbnail button.

Figure 19-32: All chapters linked, ready to start working on the menu.

EDITING MENUS

Now it's time to update the menu background and text. Click the Edit Menu button in Figure 19-32 to enter the menu editor shown in Figure 19-33. Unlike all the prosumer products that you've seen, this editor allows you to make significant changes, like moving and resizing frames. I'll start by inserting the background image, which will dictate all other changes. No excuse for blocking the bride's face in Studio.

Figure 19-33: Studio's menu editor provides full control over frame location and size, allowing almost complete customization. Note the font presets on the right, which are very helpful.

On the upper right toolbar in Figure 19-33, just below the *A*s, is a little cactus, which you click to expose the background menu images library. Click the folder to open the directory containing your background image, and click the image to select it (see Figure 19-34).

I'm still blocking their faces, so I definitely have to resize the frames, which Studio allows me to do manually, with simple PowerPoint-like controls for alignment sizing. The result is a good-looking menu that maximizes the background image of the handsome couple (see Figure 19-35).

PREVIEW AND BURN

You access Studio's preview control by clicking the DVD icon on the bottom left of the preview window. As earlier, since all navigation is automatic, you're watching primarily for misspellings in the menus.

Then it's time to burn the DVD. Click Make Movie to access the rendering controls (see Figure 19-36), including the diskometer that lets us know we have plenty of room to spare. Mindful of the compatibility issues discussed earlier, I'm still going to dial down compression to 8,000 kbps, and decline MPEG audio since space isn't an issue.

I'll also eschew filtering, which blurs high-quality video, and draft mode, which uses a faster algorithm that delivers slightly degraded quality. Click OK here, and then Create disc in Figure 19-36 to start the encoding and burning process.

Call grandma, tell her that DVD you promised is on its way.

Figure 19-34: Editing the menus. I've inserted the new background, now I have to adjust the frames so we can see the faces of the bride and groom.

Figure 19-35: There they are! Much better.

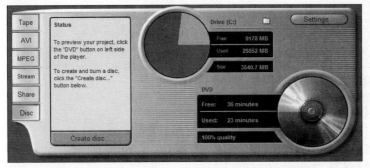

Figure 19-36: Pinnacle Studio's main compression interface. Note the diskometer telling us that we have plenty of space on the disc.

Summary

Here is a summary of the key points made in this chapter:

1. When planning your project, sketch out the menu structure you'd like to achieve and set a target time (exclusive of capture, rendering, and burning) that you'd like to spend.

2. These are the options to consider when capturing video:

   ▪ **File location** — It's best if you use a separate folder off the root.

   ▪ **Capture format** — You should use DV if available; otherwise go with the recommended format for your capture device.

   ▪ **Set scene detection options** — This depends upon the footage and authoring program. It's not always helpful, but seldom harmful.

   ▪ **Set capture duration** — I highly recommend that you do this so you can walk away after starting the capture process.

3. When capturing for MyDVD and VideoStudio, it's easier if you capture each major scene as a separate file. For Expression, VideoStudio, and Studio, one long capture works just as well.

4. When editing your captured videos, your primary goals are to delete the undesired video and create a manageable number of scenes for the project.

5. Common slideshow features include simple image-editing capabilities, like rotation, intra-image transitions, and the ability to input background music and synchronize slide duration with the music.

6. When creating your menus, you generally can customize background image, font, font sizes, thumbnail layout, and thumbnail frame. If you decide to use an audio or video background for your menus, make it at least one minute long; otherwise, it will be irritatingly repetitive.

7. Since all navigational choices were implemented by the programs, preview is more for checking for misspellings and similar errors on all menus and submenus.

8. When burning your disc, limit the data rate to around 8 mbps to maximize compatibility with older players. If space isn't an issue, use uncompressed PCM audio. Otherwise, AC-3 is slightly more compatible with older players than MPEG audio.

Chapter 20

Advanced DVD Production

In the last chapter you worked within the constraints of template-based authoring programs. In this chapter, you'll start with a blank slate, creating a free-form menu system that fits your content, rather than fitting your content to a template-based system. As a teaser, we'll also look at two advanced capabilities from Adobe Encore: creating multiple text and multiple audio tracks.

Planning Your DVD Production

As always, the first step for any DVD production is to create a schematic drawing to guide your menu creation and linking efforts. Figure 20-1 is my schematic, a palette for videos shot at Zoo Atlanta. Navigationally, I could get almost to the same place with either MovieFactory or MyDVD, but I couldn't easily use text menus with either programs or achieve the precise positioning I can with Pinnacle Studio.

As you'll see, the price I'll pay is time and effort. I'll create each menu from scratch, which means I'll have to link all the menus to videos and those menus to menus manually, and really pay attention during preview to ensure that I haven't dropped any links. Total time budget for this production, exclusive of capture and rendering time, would be in the three-hour range.

I want this video to play from start to finish smoothly, so I'll insert transitions between all major sections and have the video play through, rather than returning to the menu, after completing the scenes from each menu.

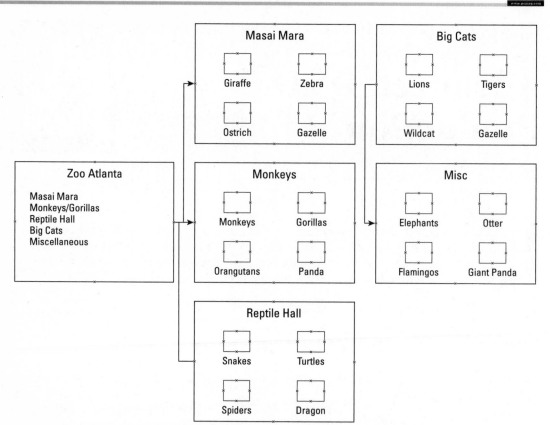

Figure 20-1: Here's my project schematic, showing six total menus, one main and five submenus.

Capturing and Creating Final Videos

I've already created my project folder off the root of my video drive and captured about 33 minutes of video to disk with scene detection, which will really help me isolate the desired clips. My starting point is shown in Figure 20-2. There are 109 clips that I need to isolate down to about 20 clips.

My primary tool will be the combine function in Studio's library, which I'll use to combine clips with similar content and identify content that I won't use. Since I can't delete clips in the album, I'll group them together and label them "not used."

After this, I'll drag each scene into the movie window in the same order as the menu structure. Since Studio's album can't combine discontinuous clips, I'll do this on the timeline, for example, combining two disparate shots of the gorillas into one video. Figure 20-3 shows the keeper clips in storyboard view; 21 sequences add up to a total of 18 minutes, including my 20 target clips plus one extra gorilla clip to combine on the timeline.

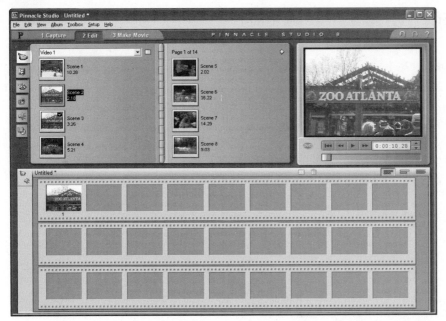

Figure 20-2: Here's my starting point with 109 clips to condense down to around 20.

Figure 20-3: These are the keeper clips in Studio's storyboard view.

Creating Menus

Once all the required videos are on the timeline, I'm ready to convert my video to a DVD project by adding a menu. I move the timeline scrubber to the start of the project, select Toolbox → Create Title (see Figure 20-4), and then I click Full Screen Title (see Figure 20-5) to get to the Title Editor.

Figure 20-4: Creating the custom main menu. As you'll see, Studio includes lots of tools for the design and artistically challenged.

Background images for all screens will be frames grabbed from the video, which I've already done. So I click the cactus shown on the upper-right toolbar below the As and use the standard File Open commands accessed by clicking the tiny folder in the upper right to navigate to where I've stored my images. One of Studio's best features is the library of text styles on the right (Figure 20-6), so I grab the most handsome one for the title and text that I'll use to hyperlink to the submenus. I could use objects, images, text, or frames to link to the submenus, but I'll keep it simple and go with the text. Once entered, I align and size the text using Studio's excellent tools, producing the title shown in Figure 20-6.

Figure 20-5: Here's where you create your title. Nice big palette to work on with the ability to create objects like circles and boxes on the bottom, and background images on the right.

Figure 20-6: Note Studio's excellent font presets on the right, which are fully customizable. Wonderful for the font challenged.

Here's the critical step. Until this moment, Studio thinks that this menu is a full-screen title. To convert it to a menu and the current project to a DVD-authoring project, I have to click the button icon on the upper right, click one of the text links, and select Normal button (see Figure 20-7), which converts the text to a normal button.

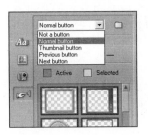

Figure 20-7: Converting the text to buttons, which also converts the static title to a DVD menu.

After converting all the text items to Normal buttons, I click OK and return to the menu-editing screen. Studio is now in DVD-authoring mode, ready and fully able to start linking. First things, first, however; I still have to create my submenus.

Note

Though not necessary for this production, there are several other buttons you will probably use at some point in creating menus in Studio. The Thumbnail button is a button frame that a video plays within, and Previous and Next buttons are used when building templates to move the viewer to the previous or next menu. On submenus, you also need to place the home button so viewers can return to the main menu.

Creating and Linking Submenus

My first submenu will be adjacent to the main menu. I position the timeline scrubber next to the main menu, then open the title editor as before, dragging in my background image and setting the title.

Then I convert the title into a menu by dragging in and aligning four frames from the library, plus the small arrow icon on the bottom left to use to link the submenu back to the main menu (see Figure 20-8). Then I save the menu as a template that I can use to build my other submenus (by selecting File → Save Menu As). Figure 20-9 shows the zoo template in the menu template library. This makes quick work of producing the other submenus, since I can just drag in the template, change the background image and title, and move on.

Figure 20-8: Creating and linking custom submenus in Pinnacle Studio.

Once I've finished creating all the submenus, it's time to start linking. To successfully link all menus and content within this project, I have to do the following:

1. Link all submenus to the main menu. Click the main menu on the timeline to open it in the linking window. Then select the submenu on the timeline, hold down the left mouse

key, and drag it over to the desired text link (see Figure 20-10). To check my work, I click the C1 checkbox on the bottom right of the menu window to reveal the active links in the menu page.

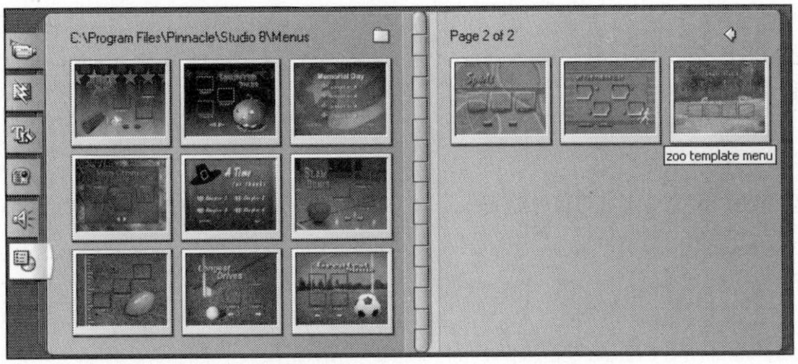

Figure 20-9: My project template in the template library.

2. Link the "home" button on all submenus to the main menu. Same procedure; click the submenu to load it into the linking window, then click and drag the main menu into the return link on the bottom left.

Figure 20-10: Linking submenus to my menu.

3. Link the video content into the frames on all submenus. Similar procedure; click the submenu to load it in the linking window, then click and drag the videos into the frames.

Again, you can check your work by checking the C1 checkbox to reveal the links. Note that you can create and link to a chapter point on the fly simply by selecting the target frame with the timeline scrubber and clicking Set thumbnail in the linking window.

Previewing the Project

As I did in the last chapter, preview by clicking the DVD icon next to the Player window in Figure 20-11. Since I went custom, Studio is no longer in charge of linking, so you have to check all links that you've created. This includes

- Links from the main menus to the submenus.

- Links from submenus back to the main menu.

- All links to content from the submenus.

Figure 20-11: You can preview the project by clicking the DVD icon on the bottom left of the video Preview window.

Once you've completed previewing, it's time to burn your project, following the same procedures as outlined for Studio in the last chapter.

Ulead DVD Workshop

The Achilles heel of Pinnacle Studio, and Expression for that matter, is the inability to produce or even import AC-3 audio. For titles crowding the 4.7GB barrier that can't use uncompressed audio, Ulead's DVD Workshop is the next logical choice, since it's very capable and the least expensive product with AC-3 Audio ($475 download).

After looking at Ulead MovieFactory and VideoStudio, DVD Workshop will look very familiar (see Figure 20-12), with a large capture/edit/preview window and tabs on top that direct you through the DVD production stages of DVD creation. Immediately below the preview window is a filmstrip containing finished menus and titles, which can be either videos or slideshows, with activity-specific menus on the top left, and libraries of assets and styles on the bottom left. On the right are chapter points.

Figure 20-12: Working with Ulead DVD Workshop.

You can capture or import video and then set chapter points and thumbnail frames. To create a slide show, you drag the images from the library to the filmstrip, which is easy enough, but Workshop can't produce transitions or synchronize slide duration to the background music.

Menu creation is very flexible; you can start with a completely blank slate, and build your own menus, which is the approach I took in Figure 20-12, use a canned or previously created template, or use a wizard to create all menus for you.

Ulead assists your design efforts with alignment controls and the ability to copy and paste attributes. This makes it simple to ensure that your text and other objects are properly spaced and the edges align, and if you ever decide to change fonts, you don't have to tweak each text line by hand. Ulead also added controls to make buttons equal height and width, extraordinarily useful when resizing multiple objects that ultimately need to be the same size.

You perform all linking via drag and drop. Then, you burn your disc using controls reminiscent of VideoStudio and MovieFactory, except on the newest version of DVD Workshop you have the option of encoding audio into AC-3 format.

Adobe Encore — The Next Big Thang

Without question, Adobe made this year's most significant splash in the DVD-authoring market when it introduced Encore, its $549 DVD-authoring program (see Figure 20-13). Encore has two key strengths, which are critical to some, but not all producers.

First, if you design your menus in PhotoShop, or want to, you can seamlessly transfer the file from Encore to PhotoShop at any point in the production, preserving the layered file architecture so popular among PhotoShop artists. For many producers, this alone makes Encore the only choice.

In addition, Encore offers many features not found in programs like Studio or DVD Workshop, like the ability to use multiple audio tracks and multiple subtitle tracks, or to create dual-layer discs with copy protection and region coding required for mass-reproduced DVDs (region coding prevents the disc from being played outside of certain regions).

On the other hand, Encore (and PhotoShop for that matter) lacks many basic menu-design capabilities, like the ability to center a menu heading or copy and paste attributes, which are typically found on much less expensive programs, and really speed menu creation. There are no wizards to be found, complicating use by beginners, templates are scanty, and integration with Premiere isn't as seamless as with PhotoShop.

Specifically, Encore can only accept a completely rendered file, not a project file, so each time you edit your video, you have to completely re-render. Adobe makes this easy for you with good hand-off controls between the programs, but you still have to re-render the file, which is time-consuming.

Contrast that with Pinnacle Studio or Edition, where editing and authoring are integrated. Since no video file is rendered until the final DVD is produced, you can edit your video files at any time, and you don't have to re-render. This suits my production style, where I create the videos and author the DVD simultaneously, and frequently make changes to the video late in the production. Edition is also around $600, while PhotoShop, Encore, and Premiere together will cost over $1,000.

On the other hand, Encore is much better suited for the decentralized workflow used by most production shops and corporations, where graphics artists create the menus, video folks the videos, and a third party does the authoring. In addition, if you need multiple languages and text tracks, or the other unique features identified earlier, you have no other alternatives in the price range.

Figure 20-13: Designing in Adobe Encore.

Summary

Here is a summary of the key points from this chapter:

1. When creating DVDs with custom menus, it's critically important to sketch out your intended navigation before you start designing menus.

2. When creating custom menus, there are three key links you have to create and test during the preview stage. These are

   - Links from the main menu to all submenus.
   - Links back from all submenus to the main menu.
   - Link the video content into the frames on all submenus.

3. Obviously, if your projects has any links between submenus, you also have to create and test these links.

4. Ulead's DVD Workshop is an easy-to-use and highly competent DVD-authoring tool and the cheapest mechanism for producing AC-3 files. Unlike Adobe Encore, it's a very self-contained product that can perform all required capture, editing, menu creation, and other activities.

5. Adobe Encore is very well featured but utilizes PhotoShop as its main menu creation engine, a negative for non-PhotoShop users.

Appendix

What's on the CD-ROM

This appendix provides you with information on the contents of the CD that accompanies this book. For the latest and greatest information, please refer to the ReadMe file located at the root of the CD. Here is what you will find:

- System requirements
- Using the CD with Windows
- What's on the CD
- Troubleshooting

System Requirements

Be advised that all programs on the CD have minimum system requirements for operation. Please consult the program-specific list later in this appendix before installing the program.

Using the CD with Windows

To install the items from the CD to your hard drive, follow these steps:

1. Insert the CD into your computer's CD-ROM drive.

2. A window appears with the following options:

    Install: Gives you the option to install the supplied software and the author-created samples on the CD-ROM.

    Explore: Enables you to view the contents of the CD-ROM in its directory structure.

    Exit: Closes the autorun window.

If you do not have autorun enabled, or if the autorun window does not appear, follow these steps to access the CD:

1. Click Start → Run.

2. In the dialog box that appears, type *d*:\setup.exe, where *d* is the letter of your CD-ROM drive. This brings up the autorun window described in the preceding set of steps.

3. Choose the desired option from the menu. (See Step 2 in the preceding list for a description of these options.)

What's on the CD

The following sections provide a summary of the software and other materials you'll find on the CD.

Author-Created Materials

All author-created material from the book, including samples, are on the CD in the folder named Author.

Applications

The following applications are on the CD:

DVD Workshop, Ulead Systems, www.ulead.com. The CD includes a 60-day trial version of Ulead's prosumer DVD-authoring program. **Requirements:** Microsoft® Windows® 98, 98SE, ME, 2000, XP, Intel® Pentium® III 450 MHz or higher, 64MB of RAM, 150MB of available hard-disk space for program installation, 4GB+ hard-disk space for video capture and converting. **NOTE:** One hour of DV video requires 13GB of hard-disk space, Windows®-compatible display with at least 800x600 resolution, a Windows®-compatible mouse or pointing device, and a Windows®-compatible soundcard.

Imaginate, Canopus Corporation, www.canopus.com. This is a 60-day trial version of Canopus' still-image animation program. **Requirements:** Windows ME, Windows 2000, Windows XP Home, Windows XP Professional, CPU with MMX Support, 64MB System Memory, and 20MB free hard-disk space.

MovieFactory, Ulead Systems, www.ulead.com. This is a 60-day trial version of Ulead's consumer DVD-authoring program. **Requirements:** Microsoft® Windows® 98SE, ME, 2000, XP, Intel® Pentium® III 450 MHz (700 MHz or higher recommended), 64MB of RAM (128MB or more recommended), 150MB of available hard-disk space for program installation, 4GB+ hard-disk space for video capture and converting, Windows-compatible display with at least 800x600 resolution, Windows-compatible soundcard, and a Windows-compatible CD-R/RW or DVD burner.

muvee autoProducer, www.muvee.com. This trial version automatically creates theme-based music-video-like productions from your source videos and music selections. The trial version places a DEMO watermark over the final video. **Requirements:** Windows 98 SE, Windows ME, Windows 2000, Windows XP, 550 MHz Pentium III, AMD K-6, or equivalent processor with MMX support, 128MB RAM, 16MB Video RAM, and 7,200 rpm or faster hard drive.

MyDVD 5.0, Sonic Solutions, www.sonic.com. This is a 60-day trial version of Sonic's best-selling consumer DVD-authoring program. **Requirements:** 550 MHz Pentium III Compatible, Windows 98SE, ME, 2000, XP Home, and XP Pro, 128MB RAM, 18GB hard-disk space, 24-bit color-graphics display, Microsoft DirectShow 8.0 or later, and a FireWire/i.Link/IEEE 1394 Card.

PhotoImpact, Ulead Systems, www.ulead.com. This is a 60-day trial of Ulead's excellent still-image editor. **Requirements:** Microsoft® Windows® 98, 98 SE, NT 4.0 SP6 and above, 2000, ME or XP, Intel® Pentium® Processor or compatibles, 64MB RAM (128MB recommended), 500MB available hard-drive space (for full program and content files), a CD-ROM drive, a Windows-compatible pointing device, and a True Color or HiColor display adapter and monitor.

RealOne, RealNetworks, www.realone.com. The CD contains a full version of Real's player for RealVideo and RealAudio files. **Requirements:** 233 MHz Intel Pentium II processor, 64MB of RAM, 28.8-kbs modem, 6-bit soundcard and speakers, 65,000-color video display card set to display at 800x600 (video), Windows 98SE, Windows 2000, Windows ME, Windows NT 4.0 with Service Pack 4 or later, Windows XP, and Internet Explorer 5.0 or later.

Studio, Pinnacle Systems, www.pinnaclesys.com. This is a 60-day reduced-feature trial of Pinnacle's award-winning consumer video-editing program with integrated DVD authoring. **Requirements:** Intel Pentium or AMD Athlon 500 MHz or higher, 128MB RAM (256MB RAM recommended), Windows 98SE, ME, 2000, XP, DirectX-compatible sound and graphics card, mouse, CD-ROM drive, 300MB of disk space to install software, 4GB of disk space for every 20 minutes of video captured at best quality. Hard disk must be capable of sustained throughput of at least 4MB per second. All SCSI and most UDMA drives are fast enough (dedicated hard drive recommended).

VideoStudio, Ulead Systems, www.ulead.com. This is a 60-day trial of Ulead's consumer video editor with DVD authoring. **Requirements:** Intel® Pentium® III 800 MHz or higher, Microsoft® Windows® 98SE, 2000, ME or XP, Microsoft® DirectX® 9 required, 128MB of RAM, 500MB of available hard-drive space for program installation, 4GB+ hard-drive space for video capture and editing (**NOTE:** 1 hour of DV video requires 13GB of hard-disk space), Windows-compatible display with at least 1024x768 resolution, a Windows-compatible mouse or pointing device, and a Windows-compatible soundcard. Real-time features perform best with at least Pentium 4, 1.4 GHz CPU, 512MB RAM, 7,200 rpm IDE Hard Drive. Also optimized for Intel® Hyper-Threading Technology and Dual-CPU systems.

Shareware programs are fully functional, trial versions of copyrighted programs. If you like particular programs, register with their authors for a nominal fee and receive licenses, enhanced versions, and technical support. *Freeware programs* are copyrighted games, applications, and utilities that are free for personal use. Unlike shareware, these programs do not require a fee or provide technical support. *GNU software* is governed by its own license, which is included inside the folder of the GNU product. See the GNU license for more details.

Trial, demo, or evaluation versions are usually limited either by time or functionality (such as being unable to save projects). Some trial versions are very sensitive to system date changes. If you alter your computer's date, the programs will "time out" and will no longer be functional.

Troubleshooting

If you have difficulty installing or using any of the materials on the companion CD, try the following solutions:

- **Turn off any anti-virus software that you may have running.** Installers sometimes mimic virus activity and can make your computer incorrectly believe that it is being infected by a virus. (Be sure to turn the anti-virus software back on later.)

- **Close all running programs.** The more programs you're running, the less memory is available to other programs. Installers also typically update files and programs; if you keep other programs running, installation may not work properly.

- **Check the recommendations** in Chapter 6 under the heading "8. Steps Before Installing."

If you still have trouble with the CD-ROM, please call the Wiley Product Technical Support phone number: (800) 762-2974. Outside the United States, call 1(317) 572-3994. You can also contact Wiley Product Technical Support at www.wiley.com/techsupport. Wiley Publishing will provide technical support only for installation and other general quality control items; for technical support on the applications themselves, consult the program's vendor or author.

To place additional orders or to request information about other Wiley products, please call (800) 225-5945.

Index

Numerics

A

continued

continued

continued

continued

Wiley Publishing, Inc.
End-User License Agreement

READ THIS. You should carefully read these terms and conditions before opening the software packet(s) included with this book "Book". This is a license agreement "Agreement" between you and Wiley Publishing, Inc. "WPI". By opening the accompanying software packet(s), you acknowledge that you have read and accept the following terms and conditions. If you do not agree and do not want to be bound by such terms and conditions, promptly return the Book and the unopened software packet(s) to the place you obtained them for a full refund.

1. **License Grant.** WPI grants to you (either an individual or entity) a nonexclusive license to use one copy of the enclosed software program(s) (collectively, the "Software," solely for your own personal or business purposes on a single computer (whether a standard computer or a workstation component of a multi-user network). The Software is in use on a computer when it is loaded into temporary memory (RAM) or installed into permanent memory (hard disk, CD-ROM, or other storage device). WPI reserves all rights not expressly granted herein.

2. **Ownership.** WPI is the owner of all right, title, and interest, including copyright, in and to the compilation of the Software recorded on the disk(s) or CD-ROM "Software Media". Copyright to the individual programs recorded on the Software Media is owned by the author or other authorized copyright owner of each program. Ownership of the Software and all proprietary rights relating thereto remain with WPI and its licensers.

3. **Restrictions On Use and Transfer.**

   (a) You may only (i) make one copy of the Software for backup or archival purposes, or (ii) transfer the Software to a single hard disk, provided that you keep the original for backup or archival purposes. You may not (i) rent or lease the Software, (ii) copy or reproduce the Software through a LAN or other network system or through any computer subscriber system or bulletin-board system, or (iii) modify, adapt, or create derivative works based on the Software.

   (b) You may not reverse engineer, decompile, or disassemble the Software. You may transfer the Software and user documentation on a permanent basis, provided that the transferee agrees to accept the terms and conditions of this Agreement and you retain no copies. If the Software is an update or has been updated, any transfer must include the most recent update and all prior versions.

4. **Restrictions on Use of Individual Programs.** You must follow the individual requirements and restrictions detailed for each individual program in the About the CD-ROM appendix of this Book. These limitations are also contained in the individual license agreements recorded on the Software Media. These limitations may include a requirement that after using the program for a specified period of time, the user must pay a registration fee or discontinue use. By opening the Software packet(s), you will be agreeing to abide by the licenses and restrictions for these individual programs that are detailed in the About the CD-ROM appendix and on the Software Media. None of the material on this Software Media or listed in this Book may ever be redistributed, in original or modified form, for commercial purposes.

5. **Limited Warranty.**

   (a) WPI warrants that the Software and Software Media are free from defects in materials and workmanship under normal use for a period of sixty (60) days from the date of purchase of this Book. If WPI receives notification within the warranty period of defects in materials or workmanship, WPI will replace the defective Software Media.

(b) WPI AND THE AUTHOR(S) OF THE BOOK DISCLAIM ALL OTHER WARRANTIES, EXPRESS OR IMPLIED, INCLUDING WITHOUT LIMITATION IMPLIED WARRANTIES OF MERCHANTABILITY AND FITNESS FOR A PARTICULAR PURPOSE, WITH RESPECT TO THE SOFTWARE, THE PROGRAMS, THE SOURCE CODE CONTAINED THEREIN, AND/OR THE TECHNIQUES DESCRIBED IN THIS BOOK. WPI DOES NOT WARRANT THAT THE FUNCTIONS CONTAINED IN THE SOFTWARE WILL MEET YOUR REQUIREMENTS OR THAT THE OPERATION OF THE SOFTWARE WILL BE ERROR FREE.

(c) This limited warranty gives you specific legal rights, and you may have other rights that vary from jurisdiction to jurisdiction.

6. **Remedies.**

(a) WPI's entire liability and your exclusive remedy for defects in materials and workmanship shall be limited to replacement of the Software Media, which may be returned to WPI with a copy of your receipt at the following address: Software Media Fulfillment Department, Attn.: *PC Magazine Guide to Digital Video*, Wiley Publishing, Inc., 10475 Crosspoint Blvd., Indianapolis, IN 46256, or call 1-800-762-2974. Please allow four to six weeks for delivery. This Limited Warranty is void if failure of the Software Media has resulted from accident, abuse, or misapplication. Any replacement Software Media will be warranted for the remainder of the original warranty period or thirty (30) days, whichever is longer.

(b) In no event shall WPI or the author be liable for any damages whatsoever (including without limitation damages for loss of business profits, business interruption, loss of business information, or any other pecuniary loss) arising from the use of or inability to use the Book or the Software, even if WPI has been advised of the possibility of such damages.

(c) Because some jurisdictions do not allow the exclusion or limitation of liability for consequential or incidental damages, the above limitation or exclusion may not apply to you.

7. **U.S. Government Restricted Rights.** Use, duplication, or disclosure of the Software for or on behalf of the United States of America, its agencies and/or instrumentalities "U.S. Government" is subject to restrictions as stated in paragraph (c)(1)(ii) of the Rights in Technical Data and Computer Software clause of DFARS 252.227-7013, or subparagraphs (c) (1) and (2) of the Commercial Computer Software - Restricted Rights clause at FAR 52.227-19, and in similar clauses in the NASA FAR supplement, as applicable.

8. **General.** This Agreement constitutes the entire understanding of the parties and revokes and supersedes all prior agreements, oral or written, between them and may not be modified or amended except in a writing signed by both parties hereto that specifically refers to this Agreement. This Agreement shall take precedence over any other documents that may be in conflict herewith. If any one or more provisions contained in this Agreement are held by any court or tribunal to be invalid, illegal, or otherwise unenforceable, each and every other provision shall remain in full force and effect.

What could make 2004 your best year, technically?

How about a daily dose of *PC Magazine's* best technology trivia, dynamite downloads, product reviews, and insightful commentary from editors Bill Machrone, Michael J. Miller, John C. Dvorak, and Bill Howard? Weekly topics cover everything from PowerPoint® pointers to game controllers to solar PDAs, with tech tips, historical milestones, wild Webs, and some of your favorite columns from recent issues. Like the magazine? You'll love the book.

Available wherever books are sold.

PC MAGAZINE
www.pcmag.com

Æ
Product reviews | Tips from the top

Tech Topic of the Week

Editor's Choice recommendations ...and much more!

With comments and insights from Michael J. Miller and the PC Magazine editorial team

TECHNOLOGY ALMANAC 2004

▶ 366 days of tech tips, cool downloads, great moments in tech history, and more!

WILEY
Now you know.
wiley.com